NATIONS OF THE MODERN WORLD

AUSTRALIA

O. H. K. Spate
*Director, Research School of Pacific Studies,
Australian National University, Canberra*

CEYLON

S. A. Pakeman
*Formerly Professor of Modern History, Ceylon
University College; Appointed Member, House of
Representatives, Ceylon, 1947–52*

CYPRUS

H. D. Purcell
*Lecturer in English Literature, The Queen's University,
Belfast*

MODERN EGYPT

Tom Little
*Managing Director and General Manager of
Regional News Services (Middle East), Ltd, London*

ENGLAND

John Bowle
Professor of Political Theory, Collège d'Europe, Bruges

FINLAND

W. R. Mead
*Professor of Geography, University College, London;
Formerly Chairman, Anglo-Finnish Society*

MODERN GREECE

John Campbell
Fellow of St Antony's College, Oxford
and
Philip Sherrard
*Assistant Director, British School of
Archaeology, Athens, 1958-62*

MODERN INDIA

Sir Percival Griffiths
*President of the India, Pakistan and Burma
Association*

MODERN IRAN

Peter Avery
*Lecturer in Persian and Fellow of King's College,
Cambridge*

ITALY

Muriel Grindrod
Formerly Editor of International Affairs *and*
The World Today
Assistant Editor of The Annual Register

JAPAN

Sir Esler Dening
H.M. Ambassador to Japan, 1952–57

KENYA — A. Marshall MacPhee
Formerly Managing Editor of The East African Standard Group; *producer with British Broadcasting Corporation*

MALAYA — J. M. Gullick
Formerly of the Malayan Civil Service

MOROCCO — Mark I. Cohen
and
Lorna Hahn

NEW ZEALAND — James W. Rowe
Director of New Zealand Institute of Economic Research, Inc.
Margaret A. Rowe
Tutor in English, Victoria University, Wellington

NIGERIA — Sir Rex Niven
Colonial Service, Nigeria, 1921–54; Member of Northern House of Assembly, 1947–59

PAKISTAN — Ian Stephens
Formerly Editor of The Statesman *Calcutta and Delhi, 1942–51; Fellow of King's College, Cambridge, 1952–58*

SOUTH AFRICA — John Cope
Formerly Editor-in-Chief of The Forum; *South African Correspondent of* The Guardian

SUDAN REPUBLIC — K. D. D. Henderson
Formerly of the Sudan Political Service; Governor of Darfur Province, 1949–53

TURKEY — Geoffrey Lewis
Senior Lecturer in Islamic Studies, Oxford

THE UNITED STATES OF AMERICA — H. C. Allen
Commonwealth Fund Professor of American History, University College, London

WEST GERMANY — Michael Balfour
Reader in European History, University of East Anglia

YUGOSLAVIA — Muriel Heppell
and
F. B. Singleton

NATIONS OF THE MODERN WORLD

CYPRUS

CYPRUS

By
H. D. PURCELL

FREDERICK A. PRAEGER, *Publisher*

New York · Washington

BOOKS THAT MATTER

Published in the United States of America in 1969
by Frederick A. Praeger, Inc., Publishers
111 Fourth Avenue, New York, N.Y. 10003

Library of Congress Catalog Card Number: 68-9731

PRINTED IN GREAT BRITAIN

Preface

I AM FULLY AWARE that some of those to whom I am indebted for information do not recognise one another's official titles, and may not even be pleased to appear together on the same page. Nevertheless, I ought to express my gratitude to the following persons, each of whom has granted me one or two interviews : among the Cypriote Greeks, His Beatitude Archbishop Makarios III, Mr Glafcos Clerides, Mr Spyros Kyprianou, Mr Tassos Papadopoulos, Mr Renos Solomides, Dr Constantinos Spyridakis, Mr Zenon Vryonides, Mr Costas Montis, Mr Patroclos Stavrou, Mr Georghios Seraphim, Mr Andreas J. Jacovides, Mr A. Nicolaides, and Dr Harris Menelao; among the Cypriote Turks, His Excellency Dr Fazil Küçük, Mr Osman Örek, Dr Orhan Müderrisoğlu, Mr Kemal Pars, Mr Aziz Altay, and Dr İhsan Ali. Archbishop Makarios was kind enough to let me go through all the records of his interviews with the press over the past five years, and Dr Küçük kindly gave me bound volumes of the news bulletin which has expressed Turkish-Cypriote policy since 1963. The Greek-Cypriote, Turkish-Cypriote, and United Nations information officers in Nicosia were very helpful, providing me with pamphlet material and, in the first two cases, arranging visits and interviews. Among these, I am particularly indebted to Mr Peter Stylianakis, the Greek-Cypriote Government Publications and Public Relations Officer, and to Mr Necati Sağer, the Turkish-Cypriote P.I.O. I also obtained information from British information officers at the High Commission and at Episkopi. Mr Miltiades Christodoulou, Director of the Greek-Cypriote Information Office, extended hospitality to me and so did Mr Sağer. Greek-Cypriote forestry officers took me on an enjoyable trip in the Paphos forest area, and Cypriote Turks went to a lot of trouble in showing me the enclave north of Nicosia. For the most part, however, I travelled alone, sometimes on foot, and sought the opinions of a large number of persons, including Cypriotes, Britons, and United Nations personnel. The Queen's University of Belfast kindly made me a grant to cover my air fare and some of my expenses in Cyprus.

In writing the historical chapters, I am indebted to Dr V. Karageorghis, who allowed me to see the typescript of his forthcoming work on excavations in Cyprus, to Sir Frank Adcock, Professor G. L. Huxley, Dr James Mellaart, Mr A. Papageorghiou, Mr Vergi Bedevi, Mr E. D. Phillips, Mr J. W. Gray, and Brigadier R. J. C. Broadhurst.

The views here expressed are my own, and no error that may occur is to be attributed to any of the persons above-listed.

In dealing with recent events as described by Greeks or Turks, I have tried to apply the principle of evidence against interest. That is to say, when one side admits a misdeed or concedes a virtue to the other I accept the statement as evidence, but where one side ascribes a virtue to itself or a misdeed to the other I have not accepted the statement as evidence unless I have reason to believe it accurate.

No attempt has been made at consistency in the transcription of Greek names because the results would sometimes look odd in English. I have simply used the forms which I consider most acceptable in the context. The form 'Cypriote' (influenced by the French) has been preferred to the commoner 'Cypriot' (influenced by the Italian -otto ending), mainly because the -ote ending is found in most other similar cases : Candiote, Corfiote, Epirote, Cibyrrhaeote. It is also the normal form among classicists and was used by Sir George Hill in his monumental *History of Cyprus*.

6 June 1968   H. D. PURCELL

Contents

List of Illustrations

Maps

13

Acknowledgements

ACKNOWLEDGEMENT for kind permission to reproduce illustrations is made to the following, to whom the copyright of the illustrations belongs.

Camera Press Ltd, London : 15, 21, 22, 23, 24

Cyprus Tourism Public Relations Office, London : 2, 6, 7, 27

Keystone Press Agency, London : 9, 11, 16, 19, 20, 25

Paul Popper Ltd : 10, 12, 13, 14

Republic of Cyprus Information Office, Nicosia : 1, 3, 4, 5, 8, 26, 28, 29

United Press International, Ltd : 17

Chapter 1

An Introduction to Modern Cyprus

I N WRITING this short history the author has come to see Cyprus
from two main points of view : as an island with strong pecu-
liarities and as a microcosm of ethnic conflict.

The very concept of Cyprus has long exerted its fascination upon
us. When Edward Gibbon refers to 'the island of Cyprus, whose
name excites the ideas of elegance and pleasure', he is echoing the
tradition of the ancients, a tradition in which Aphrodite Cytherea
was overshadowed by Aphrodite Pandemos! But the aetherial and
hedonistic manifestations of the goddess are evenly balanced.
Shakespeare speaks of her 'cutting the clouds towards Paphos'[1] and,
approaching in the prosaic aeroplane, one experiences a similar
apprehension of beauty on sighting the clear-cut peaks of the Pentadactylos range. Such dramatic views are by no means rare in
Cyprus. Flecker exactly describes a common sunset effect when he
writes of 'Old Ships' :

> With leaden age o'ercargoed, dipping deep
> For Famagusta and the hidden sun
> That rings black Cyprus with a lake of fire.

Yet, pleasure and beauty notwithstanding, Lawrence Durrell has
rightly described it as 'an island of bitter lemons'.

The present stalemate between Cypriote Greeks and Turks is not
a problem like the party division of a single people, which can safely
be left to the healing hand of time. It is a problem which will remain
as long as each group retains its corporate identity. Mere withdrawal
of United Nations troops, whether now or in twenty years' time,
will mean gradual reversion to the previous unstable situation,
except that the opponents will be much better armed. Any lasting
solution must necessarily involve large-scale separation of the
peoples, and acceptance of this fact in the case of Cyprus must
logically lead us to reconsider the ethnic struggles of the world at
large. In the following pages the author intends to make clear how
he came to adopt this position.

[1] *The Tempest*, IV.i.

The Land

Cyprus is situated in the eastern Mediterranean, south of Turkey
and west of Syria, between latitudes 34° 33′ and 35° 43′ north and
longitudes 32° 16′ and 34° 37′ east. It is the third largest island
in that sea (after Sicily and Sardinia), its greatest length being
138 miles, its greatest breadth 59 miles, and its area 3,572 square
miles (slightly larger than the combined areas of Norfolk and
Suffolk). The coastline measures some 486 miles, and the shape of
the island has been likened to a flayed deer's hide, though to the
author it looks more like a heavy helicopter travelling west. The
nearest point on the mainland is Cape Anamur in Turkey, 44 geographical miles north of Cape Kormakiti. The tip of the Carpass
'pan-handle', Cape Andreas, is 64 miles from the coast of Syria and
Cape Gata in the south is 211 miles from the coast of Egypt. To
the west, the islands of Rhodes, Carpathos, and Crete are over 240
miles away, but influence from the Aegean has always been greater
than the position of Cyprus seems to warrant, largely owing to the
Etesian breezes, which blow from the north-west for some forty
days in the height of summer, and are conveniently offset by a
northerly current up the Syrian coast which facilitates a return for
sailing-ships under the lee of Asia Minor. Other factors contributing
to influence from the Aegean are the physical conformation of mainland Greece, the ranges and valleys of which tend south-eastwards,
and the lack of a good natural harbour on the nearby coast of Asia
Minor.

The naturally fertile plain of Cyprus is called the Mesaoria, owing
to its position between the two mountain systems: the Troödos
massif, occupying about a third of the island and rising to 6,401 feet
above sea level at Mount Chionistra, and the Kyrenia coastal chain
in the north, the highest peak of which is Mount Kyparissovouno,
otherwise known as Akromandra (3,360 ft. a.s.l.). As a result of age-
long deforestation, the undulating, alluvial Mesaoria suffers in places
from sheet erosion, and there is a certain amount of gully erosion
also. However, mainly as a result of the afforestation policy of the
British administration, 670 square miles, mostly in the hilly areas,
are now covered with trees. The rivers, of which the biggest is the
Pedias (Pediaios), do not reach the sea in summer.

The island lies within the earthquake belt, and suffers periodic
tremors, the most recent being in 1953. As one would therefore
expect, it is of fairly recent geological origin. The Kyrenia range
was formed under pressure from the north and (since scientific information in Cyprus has inevitable political implications) exponents
of the Turkish case have made the most of it. It is also true that

from the end of the Miocene period to the latter half of the Pliocene the two Cypriote ranges were continuous mountains to the north and south of the Orontes valley, an area now largely Turkish, though it belongs both geographically and historically to Syria. The Mesaoria is mostly of pleistocene origin. Good sandstone for building purposes abounds in Cyprus, and there is plenty of limestone on the Kyrenia (Pentadactylos) range, whereas the limestone cap of the Troödos has been eroded, leaving the plutonic rocks exposed. Minerals will be dealt with in the section concerning the Cyprus economy.

The Climate

The weather in Cyprus is generally sunny and dry, with greater humidity on the coasts. The wet season is from October to March, and annual rainfall can vary from as low as ten inches in the Mesaoria, where summer drought is common, to over forty inches in the mountains. In Nicosia it is about twelve inches. Of recent years the rainfall has tended to increase. During the winter, troughs of low pressure from the Atlantic and Adriatic frequently linger over the island, making for changeable weather. Snow often lies for several months in the high Troödos, gleaming pinkly in the sunshine, and there are cold winds both from the Troödos and the Taurus.

The average annual range of temperature is about 35–45° Fahrenheit, but these figures come nowhere near the extremes. The mean average winter temperature is some 50–55° F in the Mesaoria, but the enclosed situation of that plain makes for high summer temperatures, averaging 85–95°F, and occasionally rising to over 105°. At Cairo, by comparison, the average is some 81°F in July, the hottest month, but Egypt does not experience the sharp drop in temperature which makes the evenings in Cyprus so comfortable. The dryness and the big changes in temperature make the island a healthy place to live, especially now that so much marshland has been drained. For those who wish to avoid the heat of the plain in summer there are cool villages in the mountains, and the fact that Cyprus has the warmest sea-climate in the Mediterranean is being discovered by growing numbers of northern tourists.

Flora and Fauna

Parts of the island are rich in trees, and there were also extensive forests in ancient times. At Curium, for instance, Apollo was worshipped as Hylates, god of the woodland. Forests now technically occupy 18.74 per cent of the total land area, but agriculture and

2—C

grazing have encroached to some extent on the minor state forests.
The tree most favoured by the forestry authorities is the pine :
the Aleppo variety, *Pinus brutia,* up to 5,000 feet above sea level,
and the *Pinus nigra* from that altitude upwards. The stone-pine
Pinus pinea, with its edible seeds was successfully used for binding
the sands at Ayia Irini, and the wattle (*Acacia cyanophylla*) at
Salamis. Common small tree species are the golden oak, *Quercus
alnifolia,* which exists naturally nowhere but in Cyprus, and *Arbutus
andrachne,* with its light green leaves and pink bark and berries.
The Mediterranean cypress is especially frequent in the northern
range, and the excellent native variety of cedar, *Cedrus brevifolia,*
is being encouraged by the forestry authorities in the Paphos region.
Hardwood species, such as the maple (*Acer obstusifolia*) and the
alder and oriental plane, grow beside mountain-stream beds. Down
in the lowlands are found the eucalyptus (introduced by the British
from Australia) of which fine examples are to be seen on the out-
skirts of Nicosia, the silver-stemmed poplar, and several other
varieties of tree. The climate is suited to the growth of aromatic
shrubs, though these are now little utilised for commercial purposes. Two kinds of juniper occur, *Juniperus foetidissima* in the high
Troödos and *Juniperus phoenicia* on the northern peninsulas.
Among the useful herbs is *Salvia cypria,* which is infused in hot
water when tea is unavailable. There are carpets of cyclamen and
anemones on the Kyrenia range, and many exotic flowers grow
remarkably well. *Tulipa cypria* is peculiar to Cyprus, and grows only
on clayey soil near Myrtou. It may disappear altogether, as it is not
protected from over-picking. *Arabis cypria* grows only in the Kyrenia
range, while *Arabis purpurea* is the Troödos variety. Scent is distilled
from wild roses, and common flowers like the corn poppy brighten
the fields of the Mesaoria. Indeed, the island would be one large
garden, were it not for the lack of water in lowland areas.

  The fauna shows a connexion with the Asiatic mainland. Perhaps
the most interesting of the native animals is the moufflon (*Ovis
ophion,* Blyth), a timid but palatable variety of wild sheep, which
is now confined to the forest area west of Kykko Monastery. It is a
close relative of the Sardinian, Corsican, and Taurus varieties. A
few have been shut within a high fence near the forestry station
at Stavros tis Psokas, and others are to be seen in the public gardens
of Limassol and Larnaca. About two hundred still exist in the wild
state, and one has seen some of them on the forested slopes of Mt.
Tripylos, but their numbers are dropping year by year owing to the
inadequacy of the penalties for poaching. Also, as in so many other
newly-independent countries, the poaching laws are insufficiently
enforced, and animal life is suffering dramatically.

Other animals include the fox, the Cyprus hare, and the hedgehog. Among the snakes the viper (*Vipera lebetina*, Linn.) is especially dangerous. Three hundred and thirty-three species of bird have been classified, there being local variants of the hooded crow, the jackdaw, the jay, and eleven others. In both mountain ranges one may see eagles, often circling below the observer. Cyprus is on one of the great migratory routes of the world, and through it pass twice yearly most of the species of birds to be found in Europe, including many rare species which winter in the island. Unfortunately, there are 25,000 registered shot-guns in Cyprus (perhaps the highest proportion relative to population in the entire world), and Air Commodore C. D. North-Lewis has estimated that about a million birds are shot each year, while a further two million are caught on limed twigs for pickling. In a letter to the *Cyprus Mail* of 4 June 1968, Mr A. J. Stagg estimated that ten to twelve million birds are killed in Cyprus each year. Since the island is on one of the main migration routes, this helps to account for the decline in the bird population of Europe. Now that such indiscriminate slaughter is being checked even in Italy, it is to be hoped that some more legal measures may be forthcoming, and those in existence more often enforced. The British have set a good example at the Akrotiri salt lake, where their sanctuary is attracting more and more migrants. December 1967 saw a big increase in the number of flamingoes on Larnaca salt lake, though latterly they have been leaving earlier each year. Elsewhere in the island the rarer species are dying out. By contrast, game birds technically enjoy a close season, and even pigeons are protected to some extent. There are several species of bat, including fruit-bats, and the insects include sixty-three species of butterfly (out of the 1,300 so far identified in the world).

Cyprus is rather poor in fish, owing to the lack of rain and rivers, but small varieties of red and grey mullet are caught round the coasts, where sponges are also found.

The Peoples of Cyprus

At the latest census, in 1960, the population of the island was 577,615, of whom 442,521 were Greeks, 104,350 Turks, 3,628 Armenians, and 2,708 Maronites, while 24,408 were designated as 'British and Others', including 3,351 Britons in the two Sovereign Base areas of Akrotiri-Episkopi and Dhekelia, and 2,796 Latins, descendants mostly of Italian traders. Since that time the number of Britons has declined very considerably. The Armenians, Maronites, and Latins were each given a seat in the House of Representatives, the Latins not because they were the only Roman Catholics in

Cyprus (there were 4,505 in all), but because they constituted an ethnic group long associated with the island. In 1960, the representatives of these three Christian peoples elected to throw in their lot with the Greek Orthodox majority; so the Turkish community, numbering less than a fifth of the whole, was effectively isolated. This is what President Makarios has meant by saying that 81.14 per cent of the population of the Republic is 'Greek', as against 18·86 per cent Turkish. Since 1960 there is good reason to believe that the overall population has gone up to about 620,000, though there is no evidence to show that the proportions of the native groups have substantially altered. Any new island-wide census is quite impossible while the present impasse persists.

Quite apart from the fact that most Cypriote Greeks consider themselves as belonging to the Greek nation, and are so considered by most other Greeks, they have the moral and economic support of the Greek-Cypriote emigrants. The exact numbers of these emigrants are in dispute, owing to disagreement as to whether their offspring should be included. At any rate, there are sizeable Cypriote communities in North America which, together with other Greek-Americans, have been able to exert considerable political pressure over Cyprus. In Australia there are 15–20,000 Cypriotes, while by far the biggest expatriate community of all is in Great Britain. It numbers some 120,000, or roughly one-fifth of all Cypriotes in the world, and most of them are Greeks. Half of them are residents in the borough of Camden. The Greek-Cypriote authorities take the reasonable view that the children of these emigrants to Britain should also be considered as Cypriotes, and are taking steps to ensure that their Greek education is not neglected. The Cypriotes in Britain have nearly all entered since the war and, in common with hundreds of thousands from elsewhere, were given special inducements, including cash-hand-outs, to encourage them to enter an island already much more overcrowded than Cyprus. By contrast, there are now, according to the British information service in Nicosia, only 690 residents of British origin in Cyprus outside the two Sovereign Base areas. They have no automatic right to vote like the Cypriotes in Great Britain, and they may not take up any position which Cypriotes are available to fill. It is quite understandable that the Cypriote authorities should treat them as foreigners : 'Caelum non animum mutant qui trans mare currunt'. But there is no good reason why their numbers should not be encouraged to rise to the same proportion of the population as the Cypriotes constitute in Great Britain, and even less reason why they should not enjoy reciprocal rights. Elsewhere in the world the Cypriote communities are much smaller, but there are several in Africa, and they include perhaps the best-known Cypriote businessman overseas, Mr John Maltas, former chairman of the Rhodesian National Export Council.

The Armenians have been associated with Cyprus since the sixth century A.D. Most of them (3,378 out of 3,628) are Gregorians, for the Uniates are more at home with the Maronite Uniates in the nearby Lebanon. The Armenian community is proportionately by far the most prosperous in the island, and the Cypriote Greeks are fond of referring to the fact that in the unitary state before 1963 the Armenians paid more in direct taxes than all the Turks put together. However, as an alien minority wielding economic power out of proportion to its numbers, the Armenians are little more popular with the Greek masses than with the Turks. For example, one is inclined to believe the Turkish allegation that they were made to pay unofficial taxes commensurate with their wealth to EOKA and other irregular forces. The wealth mostly derives from factories, such as a tannery in Larnaca, a pottery-firm in Kyrenia, and factories for processing paper and wool in Nicosia. They are also prominent in the import-export business. In politics they are like Armenians elsewhere. A few Communist-oriented ones look to the Armenian Republic as part of the Soviet Union, while the great majority hark back to the short-lived independence of that republic from 1918 to 1920, and hope for the establishment of a greatly enlarged Armenian state.

The association of the Maronites with Cyprus is of even longer standing than that of the Armenians. Only 8–10 per cent of them are in trade, and the others are villagers, chiefly in the Kormakiti area. They are not easily distinguished from the Greeks, but they naturally have connexions with the dominant Maronite community in the Lebanon. The Latin community is well represented in the professions. There were also 502 Gypsies, according to the last census.

In 1960, the Cypriote Turks, besides concentrations of from 12 to 23 per cent in the major towns, lived in villages scattered throughout the island. Out of 619 villages, 393 were wholly or predominantly Greek, 120 were Turkish, and 106 were classed as mixed, although in these last the two communities tended to occupy separate quarters, remaining completely separate in religion, and to a large extent in language and culture also. Thus, just over 19 per cent of Cypriote villages were entirely Turkish, while under 18 per cent had 'mixed' populations. It is in the latter that most communal clashes have taken place. The Turks (according to their own reckoning) were forced to abandon some seventeen mixed villages during the Emergency, to which they still could not return after independence. The map which appears as Figure 1 will make clearer the position in 1960. During the upheavals of December 1963 and early 1964 they wholly or partly abandoned 102 villages,[1] and gathered for self-protection and the facilitation of partition in their more defensible areas. The directions of their flight are shown in Figure 2. According to the Report of the Secretary-General of the United Nations dated 10 September 1964, there were then some 25,000 Turkish refugees, and his Report of 13 June 1967 estimates that there are still some 20,000 unwilling to take the risk of returning to their homes. The historical tendency for a larger proportion of Turks than Greeks to live in the towns has now been greatly enhanced, though of course the Greeks are a majority in the towns, also. However, peasants make up the largest single grouping among the Turks, just as they do, to a lesser extent, among the Greeks. In addition, the Turks are much less well represented in commerce and the professions, and the proportion of poor persons among them is greater.[2] They have been confined within small areas, mostly without sufficient resources, their trade disrupted and much of their most profitable land lost, so the economic gap between the two peoples has steadily widened. Only aid from Turkey enables the Cypriote Turks to survive as a separate entity.

There can be no doubt that the Cypriote Turks constitute a separate entity. To step into a Turkish quarter is to step into another world, and the same was true before independence. U Thant, in the former of the Reports to the Security Council mentioned above, estimates that the scattered Turkish areas and pockets contain 'probably between one third and one half' of the Turkish-Cypriote community, but even the Greek-Cypriote Minister of Labour, Mr Tassos Papadopoulos, does not claim that more than 40 per cent of Turkish Cypriotes live in areas under the control of the Greek authorities. In fact, a short but extensive tour of the island in the spring of 1967 has convinced the author that only a handful of Turks are integrated with the Greek community. The areas surrounded with road blocks and check-points were obviously separate, and continued to be so when the visible obstacles to freedom of movement were withdrawn. The Turkish leaders do not permit any Greeks into their main areas, except to travel through the Limnitis enclave or along the Kyrenia road twice a day with a U.N.

---

[1] See the *Special News Bulletin* for 9 September 1967. A few uneasy mixed villages (e.g. Dhali) remain.

[2] The Greeks have made great play with the fact that the Turkish contribution to the public revenue before the troubles was only 10 per cent of the total, but the Turks claim that, in 1962 for example, 25 per cent of that total came from non-residents (mainly British) and a further 2 per cent from the sale of national resources. It is difficult to see why the Turks take so much trouble to refute the Greek allegations. Cyprus must be the only modern case in which the relative poverty of a minority is used as an argument against it.

escort, and they do not allow their people to leave the enclaves without permission. The first of these restrictions is for the maintenance of security; the second is partly to ensure that *de facto* separation is not eroded from the economic point of view, partly to protect Turks from maltreatment by the Greeks. The average Turkish village is not fortified, and is technically under control of the Greek-Cypriote authorities, but the foreigner who can speak Turkish soon discovers that the villagers look to the Turkish-Cypriote leaders, save in case of necessity, as when they have to apply to the local Greek District Commissioner for a passport or a permit for building materials. The true situation is revealed by U Thant (or rather by UNFICYP, for U Thant has no personal experience of the matter) when he says in his Report of 13 June 1967 that the Greeks are denied access 'to most Turkish villages at all times'. In these circumstances, it is little wonder that even the Greek Public Information Office admits that 'the bulk of the Turkish Cypriots' are under the control of Ankara. The claim of the Greek-Cypriote authorities to control over more than 98 per cent of the island is exaggerated (in reality it is some 92 per cent), and is motivated by the consideration that governments with *de facto* control have always been accepted as *de jure* in the long run. The Greek Cypriotes do not stress the fact that this argument is also applicable to Rhodesia, the government of which can lay claim to more widespread control. Again, despite the fact that they have the backing of the majority, the Greek-Cypriote authorities need to impress the world with their brotherly concern for their Turkish compatriots, and therefore make full use of such Turks as come over to them. Of these, the foremost is Dr İhsan Ali, whose views will be set forth at length in a later chapter. Another is Dr Ali's cousin, Özdemir Özgür, whose presence on the Permanent Mission of Cyprus at the United Nations lends verisimilitude to the claim of the Cyprus government to represent the Cypriote Turks. Then there is Ahmet Cemal[1] of Limassol, described in the *Cyprus Bulletin* for 3 April 1967 as 'a moderate voice' appealing for 'help to rid the Turkish community from the throngs of the phanatic [sic] Turkish Cypriots'. Tevfik Süleyman, the broadcaster, is another who faithfully serves the Makarios government. Such men, we must assume, give their services freely, and genuinely disapprove of the policies of the Turkish leadership. However, pictures of the President chatting with Turkish villagers (sometimes with a Turkish flag in the back-

---

[1] I have transcribed modern Turkish names according to the system introduced by Atatürk. The reader should remember that Turkish 'c' is pronounced like English 'j', and 'ç' and 'ş' like English 'ch' and 'sh' respectively. 'ı' as a more central vowel than 'i', and 'ğ' merely lengthens the preceding vowel, though it is sometimes uvular in the dialects.

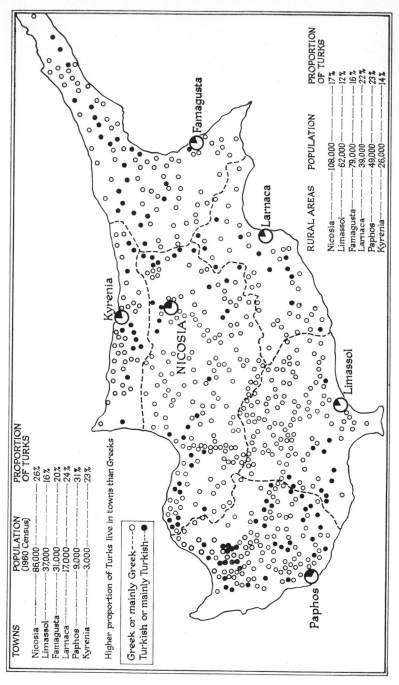

TOWNS

	POPULATION (1960 Census)	PROPORTION OF TURKS
Nicosia	86,000	26%
Limassol	37,000	16%
Famagusta	31,000	20%
Larnaca	17,000	24%
Paphos	9,000	31%
Kyrenia	3,000	23%

Higher proportion of Turks live in towns than Greeks

Greek or mainly Greek---◯
Turkish or mainly Turkish---●

RURAL AREAS

	POPULATION	PROPORTION OF TURKS
Nicosia	108,000	17%
Limassol	62,000	12%
Famagusta	79,000	16%
Larnaca	39,000	22%
Paphos	49,000	23%
Kyrenia	26,000	14%

1. The distribution of Cypriote Turks at the last Census, of 1960

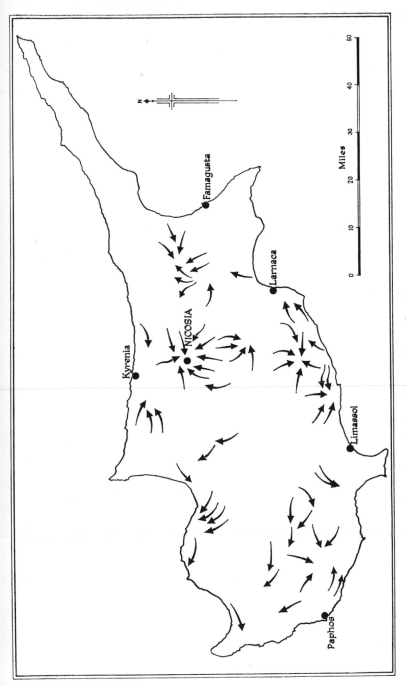

2. How the Cypriote Turks took refuge during the troubles of 1963-4

ground !) have no more validity than the articles written by Armenians for the Turkish *Special News Bulletin* which testify to the loving concern of the Turks. The evidence of those who are in the power of the propagandist is quite worthless. This holds true in spite of the kindly behaviour of Makarios, or the fact that Armenian buildings in the Turkish quarter of Nicosia have nearly always been left intact.

Despite recent normalisation measures, the situation in Cyprus remains a deadlock. The Greeks proclaim the independence of Cyprus without, in most cases, wishing to retain it, and the Turks cling to their rights under the constitution of 1960, with no intention at all of returning to the situation created by it. To put it another way : 'The Government treats the Turkish Cypriots as rebels and the Turkish Cypriots regard the Government as unconstitutional and devoid of legal standing' (U Thant, Report of 13 June 1967). President Makarios has not been willing to recognise the Turkish Vice-President, Dr Küçük, or hold any talks with him unless he gives up his cantonal policy, which is against the constitution; and Dr Küçük has not been willing to recognise Makarios unless he observes all the provisions of the constitution which have been unilaterally altered by the Greek majority. Nor is this situation to be blamed upon the leaders. The genuine dislike, amounting in many cases to hatred, of the ordinary people is a much more lasting factor. As the President himself has put it : 'The Greeks of Cyprus will continue to feel as Greeks, and likewise the Turks will feel as Turks'.

Over this situation flies, in theory, the Cyprus flag, though in fact it is only to be seen on a few government buildings. It is a map, with the mystique of a map. Naturally, the Greeks prefer the flag which reflects the blue of the Mediterranean around them, and the Turks one which is red, the colour preferred by the inhabitants of the Eurasian plains, and which incorporates the Byzantine crescent moon and star as a symbol of Turkish victories in the West.

Religion

For reasons which it is hoped to make clear in subsequent chapters, the Christian sects of Cyprus are strongly attached to their religion. In England and the United States a believing Christian is by no means necessarily a practising one (and *vice versa*), whereas in Cyprus the two are usually synonymous; and those Cypriotes who neither practise nor believe in any religion nevertheless identify themselves politically with the aspirations of the religious community into which they were born. Anyone who doubts the fervour of Cypriote religious feeling should attend a service at, say, the Phaneromeni Church in Nicosia, or visit one of the monasteries, say Machaeras, when some national occasion is being celebrated. It is no accident that the Archbishop is now President of the Republic. By virtue of being elected Archbishop he is also the Ethnarch, or leader of the Greek-Cypriote people.

The Orthodox Church is the biggest landholder in the island. Makarios, who shows no wish to acquire riches, has set up a public commission to control the archiepiscopal lands, but the bishops and abbots would not follow suit. However, his desire to distribute Church lands is qualified by a determination that the Church should not have to 'beg' to provide for its needs.

The number of monks has dropped considerably in recent years, though several of the monasteries are well financed and will probably continue to attract enough novices to survive. In the past the Church has often come into conflict with the Left, but the Left in Cyprus, as in Italy, is not hostile to religion as such. However, the *coup* of April 1967 in Greece has inhibited the gradual *rapprochement* of the Church with the Left in Cyprus.

The Armenians and Maronites are ethnic sects, rather as the Jews are, and so do not proselytise. On the other hand, the Latins have made attempts to proselytise in the past, and the Greek Church still does so to some extent. Individual Moslems have been converted, usually voluntarily through marriage, but sometimes through influence on those Moslem children who attend Greek schools. The environmental influence of the Orthodox Church on the Moslem community can be seen in little details, as when a Turk crosses himself (albeit ironically) to stress a point.

Although the appellation 'Moslem' is practically synonymous with 'Turk' in Cyprus, the Turks are far more secular-minded than the Greeks. This is because they revere the memory of Atatürk, one of whose achievements was the establishment of a lay state in Turkey. On the whole, it is older men who pray five times daily according to the precept of the Prophet. The average Cypriote Turk is far more inclined to appeal to his ethnic connexion with Turkey than any vague notion of Moslem unity, though Turkish policy is becoming more sympathetic to the problems of other Moslems. The pronouncements of the Mufti of Cyprus are now being published in the *Special News Bulletin* as a counter to the well-known political activities of Orthodox bishops. A certain amount of Moslem ritual is observed by the mass of Cypriote Turks, especially on Fridays, and all celebrate the big feasts, such as the *Kurban Bayram,* when sheep are slaughtered and the meat is shared with the poor. The *Evkaf,* or religious trust organisation, is still a growing concern, and is the biggest of Turkish landholders. Like the Orthodox institutions, it has the advantage over the private landlord of greater permanence. A few Greeks are occasionally converted to Islam, usually through marriage.

There remains the importance of religion in underlining cultural differences. The Turks are well aware that the voice of the *muezzin* over a loud-speaker has the same effect on the Greek quarters as the enthusiastic ringing of church-bells has on the Turkish quarters. In almost every Cypriote town a Greek may see every day a minaret surmounted by the Turkish flag, and the Greeks have raised their flag on high buildings overlooking the Turkish quarter of Nicosia, creating a similar psychological effect. The symbolic differences between the religions point to fundamental differences in outlook : on the one hand, the colour and liveliness of the Mediterranean world, the gorgeous garments, the icons encrusted with silver, the complex ritual, and the impassioned sermons of the Orthodox Church; on the other, the white silence of the mosque, broken only by the repetition of simple and dignified prayers. The Christians express the very unity of their God in trinitarian terms, while for the Moslems there is only the One.

The United Nations Force in Cyprus and the Military Situation

The precarious situation in Cyprus is chiefly maintained by United Nations troops. The United Nations Force in Cyprus (UNFICYP) was established by a Security Council resolution of 4 March 1964. The Force arrived in the island within the same month, and took over peace-keeping duties from the British, who also provided the largest contingent of UNFICYP. Its mandate has been continuously extended up to the present time, to begin with, and recently, at three-monthly intervals, but in between, and in the second half of 1968, for six-monthly periods. The terms of the resolution, which has frequently been reaffirmed since, require the Force 'to use its best efforts to prevent a recurrence of fighting' and also 'as necessary, to contribute to the maintenance and restoration of law and order and a return to normal conditions'. The meaning of this last injunction has been much in dispute, the Cypriote Greeks maintaining that the Force should help to enforce the dictates of the government representing the majority, and the Cypriote Turks insisting that it means that the Force should help to re-establish the *status quo ante* December 1963, when they were deprived of powers guaranteed under the constitution. The Force, as such, has wisely refrained from interfering in this legal dispute, and since August

1964 has been largely successful in containing the isolated outbreaks of fighting. It has done this by physically interposing itself between opposing forces in times of lull (a tactically justifiable manoeuvre in these days of all-round defence), and has nearly always applied the principle of minimum force when attacked. There have been none of the mistakes of the campaign in the Congo, where United Nations troops were engaged in killing secessionist tribespeople and four hundred million dollars were spent to no very obvious advantage. In Cyprus their aims have been limited and their conduct remarkable for its moderation and restraint. Sometimes the restraint has been overdone, and they have observed a good deal of destruction of property without protesting. Still, UNFICYP is meant to assist the Cypriotes, not to govern them. To this end, the Secretary-General's special representatives have operated through liaison committees, and have achieved some remarkable results. Foremost among these must be rated the agreement of September 1966 concerning the transfer of Greek land records from the Turkish sector of Nicosia and the restricted use by the Greeks of the Kyrenia and Limnitis roads.[1] In return, postal services (as regards letters, not parcels or newspapers)[2] were restored to the Turks of Lefka and the Nicosia enclave for the first time in nearly three years. That was in the following month, and UNFICYP has since made efforts to have postal services restored to Turks in other enclaves also. The 'normalisation' measures, involving the removal of road-blocks and restrictions, which the Greek-Cypriote government initiated in the Paphos and Limassol areas on 2 September 1967 were also undertaken through the initiative of UNFICYP. At the same time, the Moslems gained access to the Tekke of Hala Sultan and a Moslem caretaker was permitted to reside there.

The United Nations Civil Police (UNCIVPOL) has likewise played its part, especially in tracing missing persons and supervising the government checkpoints, abolished on 8 March 1968 after the exertion of pressure by Turkey. It was at these that tension most often rose. U Thant reported that 'in view of the volume of traffic passing through the check points, the number of substantial complaints outside periods of unusual tension and strictness' was 're-latively small', and this was meant to offset the many Turkish

[1] However, the road through the Kokkina enclave, the one between Kythrea and Lefkonico, and the one from Trypimeni which passes through Knodhara remained closed to the Greeks.

[2] In the spring of 1968 correspondence addressed by the author to Dr Küçük as Vice-President of the Republic was being returned undelivered, bearing the statement that 'there is no Vice-President in the Republic'; and many copies of the Turkish news bulletin sent from Cyprus did not reach the author in the United Kingdom.

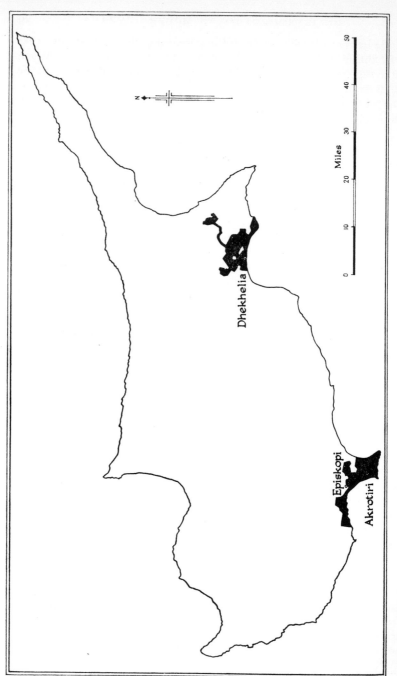

3. The British Sovereign Base Areas

allegations of maltreatment. However, it was rightly said that the Greek police tended to treat the U.N. supervisors with contempt, and closer observation on the part of the latter substantiated Turkish claims to some extent. This kind of work requires a remarkable degree of self-control, and it is no accident that all the UNFICYP contingents are of European ethnic origin. The Cypriotes made it clear that Afro-Asian contingents would not be acceptable, and Western insistence that each participating nation should pay the costs of its own contingent also helped to determine the composition of the Force. Nevertheless, two competent Indian generals, educated in the British tradition, have contributed greatly to UNFICYP's achievement. The present Commander of the Force is Lieutenant-General A. E. Martola of Finland, and the present special representative is Señor Bibiano F. Osorio-Tafall, a Mexican of Spanish origin. The former took up his appointment on 17 May 1966, and the latter on 20 February 1967.

It has been suggested that it would be desirable for UNFICYP to remain in Cyprus indefinitely, but the suggestion ignores both the cost and limited effectiveness of the Force. In March 1968 its strength stood at 4,570 military personnel and 175 civilian police. These totals were made up of an Austrian field hospital with 54 men, and Canadian, Danish, Finnish, Irish, Swedish, and British contingents of 885, 649, 607, 522, 608, and 1,245 men respectively, together with police units from Australia, Austria, Denmark, and Sweden, numbering 50, 45, 40, and 40 men respectively. In June 1967 New Zealand withdrew her police unit of 20 men, and the numbers were made up with ten additional men from Australia and ten from Austria. It was a minor withdrawal, but a straw in the wind. If Canada were to pull out, as she has threatened to do, it is doubtful whether the Force could survive. The total cost since its inception to 26 March 1968 was estimated at $84,435,000. It has been estimated that the costs of repatriation and liquidation would total another $610,000. But these estimates are exclusive of the costs absorbed by the countries providing the contingents. Thus, in the event of a six-month extension from 26 March 1968, Austria would have to foot a bill of $110,337, Australia $186,150, Canada $888,532, Denmark $240,000, Eire $521,000, and the United Kingdom $650,000. Finland and Sweden were also absorbing certain costs. Granted that the money spent goes mainly to nationals of the countries concerned, it is not spent in those countries, and it is most unlikely that their governments will be prepared to continue indefinitely to disburse sums disproportionate to their size and resources. There was a deficit of $7,685,000 on 26 March 1968,[1] and

[1] By 12 April the deficit had risen to c. $10 million.

costs for a six-month extension were estimated at $10,755,000, so the Secretary-General stood in need of $18,440,000 in pledges. Some countries were simply defaulting on their promised contributions.

During the period from 8 March to 7 June 1968 there have been no military clashes between Greeks and Turks, although unrelaxed Turkish vigilance has led to the Greeks reoccupying some of their vacated positions. However, suggestions that UNFICYP should be reduced in numbers have met strong opposition from the Turks, who have most to lose from weakening of the U.N. buffer.

UNFICYP could probably give an account of itself out of proportion to its numbers, supposing that the countries concerned permitted it to do so, but it is inferior in fire-power to the Greek-Cypriote forces, and probably to those of the Cypriote Turks as well. Besides, events in Sinai of May 1967 have demonstrated that United Nations forces remain only at the invitation of the government of the country. Thus UNFICYP cannot solve the military problem; it can only maintain, and to some extent civilise, the *status quo*.

In December 1967, the Cypriote Greeks had some 40,000 men in their National Guard, over 10,000 of the men and all of the officers being from mainland Greece.[1] Turkey has forced the withdrawal of most of the mainland troops, though a number of officers and soldiers remain. There is also a Greek mainland contingent of 950 men stationed in Nicosia under the 1960 Treaty of Guarantee. The Greek-Cypriote 'police' force is some 2,200-strong, and is equipped with tanks and 25-pounder guns. A 'police' tactical reserve battalion is also being trained. The police are clearly meant to act as a counterweight to the National Guard, which until December 1967 was under the supreme command of General Grivas and which is still Athens-dominated. Most of the arms for the police came from Czechoslovakia, as *Der Spiegel* revealed in its issue of 3 April 1967. Auxiliary to them are forty-one policewomen, who take part in searches. The Cypriote Greeks have about forty tanks in all, mostly medium or heavy and of Second World War vintage, some armoured cars, heavy machine-guns, heavy mobile mortars, and a wide variety of small arms.

The Cypriote Turks, by contrast, have no big weapons, but their estimated force of 6,000 fighters, with 6,000 in reserve, is well provided with small arms, mainly smuggled, though some are manufactured in the Nicosia enclave. Their heavy mortars (the most destructive weapon they have) could do a great deal of damage to the richer, Greek quarters of the towns. A further 3,000 men could probably be mustered at a time of crisis. Until December 1967 there

[1] The Turks put the number of mainland Greeks at 15,000.

were also 600–1,150 extra soldiers from the Turkish mainland. Most have now been withdrawn, though some remain.

In the towns the Turks are heavily concentrated. Their vulnerability to light artillery has been offset to some extent by the construction of emplacements inside houses, together with underground shelters (which the Greeks also have). Even so, some of their positions are weak and exposed. The smaller enclaves would certainly all be overrun by the Greeks, given enough time, and even the biggest Turkish area, stretching from Nicosia to the north and north-west, seems vulnerable to armoured attack across the plain, unless it is heavily mined and provided with many tank traps in areas which the author did not see. However, the 650-man Turkish army contingent is encamped on either side of the Nicosia–Kyrenia road, and Turkish-Cypriote fighters control the highly strategic Boghaz Pass through the northern range. Here again, they could be attacked, by mountain troops from further along the range on either side. Accordingly, the pass has now been heavily fortified, and many emplacements are to be seen overlooking the road and around St Hilarion Castle, which the Turks also hold. From the ridge villages of Mari and Kophinou in the south of the island they can fire on the main roads which join Limassol with Nicosia and Larnaca, and they have similar points of vantage overlooking other roads too. Apart from the beachheads at Kokkina and Limnitis, they have a short stretch of shallow water under their control to the south of Larnaca where arms might be run in or a landing made. The Cypriote Turks do not rely upon themselves alone, and plausibly maintain that in the event of any large-scale hostilities jets would arrive from Anatolia within a few minutes, and bomb the Greeks as they did in August 1964. If the jets were not enough to stop the Greek forces (as they probably would not be now) the Turks are probably right in thinking that the Turkish army would follow, as has frequently been threatened. In that event the army of Greece would inevitably also be involved. It is hoped to make clear why such a conflict will be avoided if possible by the governments of both Greece and Turkey.

The British Sovereign Base Areas

The two British Sovereign Base areas of Akrotiri and Dhekelia occupy an area of 99 square miles in all. They became sovereign under the Treaty Concerning the Establishment of the Republic of Cyprus in 1960, and their areas are demarcated in maps appended to that treaty. Under the same agreement, Great Britain obtained the right to make use of training areas outside the S.B.A.s and

3—C

retained control over Nicosia airfield, but few of the training areas are now used, and the British pulled out of Nicosia airfield in 1966.

The Akrotiri base is excellently sited, and is the biggest British air base outside the United Kingdom. As such, it contains the biggest overseas striking force of the R.A.F., composed hitherto of Javelins and Lightnings as well as some Canberras. By the end of 1968, the Canberras will be replaced by two squadrons of Vulcans, and the nuclear capacity of these has stimulated a protest from the left-wing Cyprus Peace Committee, despite the fact that the Canberras can also carry nuclear bombs. There may also be rocket weapons at Akrotiri. Dhekelia has a transit airfield for British forces in the Persian Gulf. It contains three enclaves: the villages of Ormidhia and Xylotymbou and the Dhekelia power station. As a whole, it is not easily defensible, especially as regards the outlying region around Ayios Nikolaos, and its garrison has been run down drastically. Cypriote villages in both base areas are an advantage rather than not because they make it unlikely that water and electricity will be entirely cut off. The laws are separate, but are kept in step with those of the Nicosia government, provided these do not conflict with the constitution.

In view of the fact that both Makarios and Küçük went out of their way to whittle down the areas to be agreed before independence, it is ironic that the S.B.A.s should have proved a mainstay of the Cyprus economy. In 1960, British expenditure on them exceeded the Cypriote government's revenue, and they still bring into the island more than £14 million yearly, acting as the linchpin of the economy. Makarios has made statements strongly implying that he disapproves of the very existence of the bases, and has also said that they should be leasehold, but he has explicitly objected to a reduction in their area, and has asked for a run-down period before any British withdrawal. The British government has announced its intention of reducing its garrison at the bases over the next few years, but has stated that a range of defence installations will remain. Galo Plaza, the U.N. Mediator, said in 1965 that the British 'would not stand in the way of any solution' to the Cyprus problem 'agreed upon by the other parties', but did not contemplate that such a solution would affect the S.B.A.s.

In view of the Suez adventure and tacit British governmental support for Israel, the Arabs have reason to fear that the S.B.A.s may be used against them. Indeed, except in the unlikely event of a direct Russian attack, that is their only politically possible use. Makarios has repeatedly stated that he will 'react in many ways' if they are so used, though since the June War of 1967 he has shown some signs of willingness to deal with Israel.

Meanwhile, the S.B.A.s provide excellent training areas, and British troops with their thousands of dependants enjoy themselves in Limassol, except on EOKA day, when they are confined to camp and blaring loudspeakers describe them in Greek as 'the barbarians of England'.

Government

Since December 1963 most of Cyprus has been effectively governed by the President, Archbishop Makarios, and a Council of Ministers nominated (in some cases by Makarios only) from the thirty-five Christian members of the House of Representatives;[1] while the fifteen Turkish representatives, led by Dr Küçük, have administered their residual areas. The executive authority rests with the President and the legislative with the House though, according to the constitution of 1960, much of the law-making is invalid without the consent of the Vice-President, and the Vice-President was given executive powers in many respects equal with those of the President himself. Archbishop Makarios himself appoints a cabinet to preside over the eleven Ministries, and in practice certain Ministers hold more than one portfolio.

The most striking thing about the Cypriote leaders is their quality. Several of them give the impression of being far more intelligent and wide-awake than some of their opposite numbers in countries which number their populations in tens or hundreds of millions, rather than hundreds of thousands. Above all, they usually lack that inferiority complex which so often makes social intercourse with intellectuals from ex-colonial territories exceedingly trying. President Makarios in particular is a very remarkable person, and impresses those with whom he comes in contact far beyond their expectations. The author remembers a British Intelligence officer remarking that Cypriote entry into a united Europe would present problems, because it was hard to imagine Makarios as anything but President of the entire union. Cypriotes, who tend to have a very inflated idea of the importance of their country, and are capable of imagining that Khrushchev was overthrown owing to his meddling in the Cyprus dispute (on the *post hoc propter hoc* principle),[2] will not perhaps see the joke; but it is nevertheless a tribute to the

---

[1] Legally, Ministers need not be members of the House, but in practice they nearly always are. According to the constitution of 1960, ministerial appointments should be made jointly by the President and Vice-President. However, Ministers may be designated, or their appointments terminated by the President or Vice-President, according as to whether they are Greeks or Turks.

[2] Gargarin has admitted that when he said that he had distinctly seen Cyprus during his Sputnik flight, it was in order to flatter the Cypriotes.

Archbishop's personality. A measure of his own level-headedness is that he has never made exaggerated claims regarding the political importance of his country.

In two lengthy interviews with the President I received the impression that I might ask him whatever questions I wished, and the answers were remarkably consistent. When I went through the records of his interviews I came to understand one of the reasons for this consistency. He has never neglected an opportunity to present the Greek-Cypriote case to the world at large, and for years journalists and broadcasters wishing to interview him have submitted lists of questions in advance, often essentially the same ones, but sometimes touching on the most abstruse details of the Cyprus problem. Little wonder that he is now able to answer so well without the benefit of either notes or notice of questions. But Makarios is far more than a mere verbal tactician. He gives an impression of complete sincerity even when his words leave several options open or evade a trap in the question. There are not many who can give such an impression while saying things like 'What is desirable is not always attainable' or 'I would not like to make any comment which might be misunderstood as interference with the internal affairs of other countries'. And this impression is enhanced by his very slight but perceptible impatience with silly questions such as 'Why do you, a priest, take part in politics?', a question which is silly because it shows complete ignorance of the history of the Greek Orthodox Church, especially in Cyprus, and because it ignores the political activities of Western prelates like the Archbishop of Canterbury and the late Cardinal Spellman. In this connexion, an illuminating quotation may be made from the account of Margaret Le Geyt, who taught the Cypriote Archbishop English during the thirteen months that her husband was Controller of the Archbishop's household on the Seychelles: 'Makarios has the most remarkable eyes. They suddenly begin to glow as if a lamp were lit, when he is amused, interested or enthusiastic. But when he is puzzled over something, or does not approve an idea, the lamp goes out, and a look of in-scrutability, of almost complete withdrawal, takes its place'[1] Incidentally, his English is clear, though not always accurate. For instance, like many Cypriotes, he insists on pronouncing his country as [saipru's], but he selects his words carefully and is quite fluent. Above all, he is affable, however unimportant his interlocutor may be. It is as though he wished it to be understood that deference is due to the offices he holds, rather than to him personally. He also shows an occasional flash of dry wit, as in March 1965, when there had been repeated threats of Turkish invasion, and he remarked:

[1] *Makarios in Exile* (Nicosia: Anagennisis Press, 1961), p. 102.

'The threats are intensified, but I personally believe that the risk has diminished'. Perhaps the most marked characteristic of his conversational style is his love of the symmetrical phrase, such as : 'If peace is endangered in one part of the world it is in danger everywhere, because peace is indivisible'. Less often, he shows a penchant for the striking phrase, such as 'the luminous way of virtue'.

St Paul rejoiced in being all things to all men, and the Archbishop follows in his footsteps. He is certainly aware of the ease with which representatives of other nations may be flattered and made to feel at home. Thus, in speaking to the Japanese he says : 'Although our countries are so far from each other, their devotion to the same ideals of justice and freedom brings them very close together'; to the Egyptians he uses a very Arabic turn of phrase when he refers to 'the splendour and brilliancy of President Nasser'; to the Latin Americans he says : 'It has always been my desire to visit and get acquainted with Latin America'. And, truly, he enjoys travelling and meeting people. Sometimes he combines goodwill with an obvious reference to the Cyprus problem, as when he tells the West Germans that he objects to the Berlin Wall because he is against partition on principle, when he tells the Finns that their policy of co-existence with their Swedish minority is a pattern for Cyprus, or when he appeals to the Irish by saying that 'there are many things in common in the history of the Irish people and the people of Cyprus'.

The author would not judge that the Archbishop is a very deeply-read man, though he is familiar with the Bible, the Fathers of the Church, and certain authors of Greek antiquity—rather more than most Presidents can lay claim to. Where he is superior to the men who surround him—men whose education is much more in keeping with the age than his own—is in his ability to select from what he reads those essentials which will help him to develop his world-view. At first sight, it might seem strange that he should admire four such different historical figures as Frederick the Great, George Washington, Abraham Lincoln, and the Mahatma Gandhi, but they each devised techniques which brought about the success of their respective causes. Also, they each had a sense of mission which Makarios also has. Some have said that this sense of mission (often misconstrued as pride) makes him pay mere lip-service to *Enosis* so that he should not have to give up his important post. Certainly, there are those around him, like his doctor-cum-dentist Vassos Lyssarides, who are working against *Enosis,* but one feels sure that to call Makarios an anti-Enotist is to slander him. He is just unwilling to pay the price which those who demand *Enosis* immediately must be willing to pay.

Makarios represents an ancient religious tradition, and his 'inexhaustible supply of patience' (to quote his own words) is largely attributable to his trust that, whether or not he is eliminated from the contest, that tradition will continue. The grave charge has been made against him that his policies have led to bloodshed, and it is a true one; but Makarios has as much right as any other archbishop to argue that Christian morality is not based upon what is, but upon what ought to be, and that misguided men on the other side must bear the responsibility for any damage done. When the matter is viewed in this light, there is no reason to doubt Makarios when he says : 'The moral principles in which I believe as a church leader I apply also as President'.

Mr Glafcos Clerides, President of the House of Representatives since 1960, was an R.A.F. pilot during the war, and legally represented members of EOKA during the Emergency. He has deputised as acting President during the absences of Makarios, was head of the Greek-Cypriote delegation to the London Conference of January 1964, and negotiated the secret purchase of Czech arms in 1966. A London-trained barrister and the son of another eminent barrister, he has a sound mind for argument, and is also able to make powerful patriotic speeches which warm the hearts of the Greeks. Altogether, he gives an impression of great toughness and strength of character, and in private conversation he does not find it necessary to make a mystery of what is already public knowledge. He has been attacked by those close to Grivas for mismanaging the campaign of December 1963, but failure to overrun the Turkish positions at that time can better be ascribed to unexpectedly strong Turkish resistance and the shortcomings of Polycarpos Georghadjis, Minister of the Interior, whose qualities are more those of an individual EOKA member than of an organiser. At the time of writing, Clerides is one of the strongest opponents of any deal with the Turks involving territorial concessions. The consideration that he would be considerably less important in a unified Greece may well weigh with him, as it certainly does with more obviously 'internationalist' Cypriotes in positions of importance. But in the case of Clerides one would judge that, given time, he expects *Enosis* to be won without territorial concessions. As a delegate to the Consultative Assembly of the Council of Europe and a member of its Political and Standing Committees, he gives the impression of being especially favourable towards the idea of association with the Common Market.

Mr Spyros Kyprianou, the Foreign Minister, has proclaimed himself an Enotist on the usual large number of occasions, but gives the very definite impression of being more of an internationalist than anything else. He has represented the Greek Cypriotes at the United Nations since 1956, and the successes of the Greek-Cypriote cause in the General Assembly can be ascribed in large measure to his political skill and ideological orientation. His loyalties to Europe are less obvious, and as President of the Council of Europe he has tended to run the Council rather as a sub-department of the U.N. Also, it has been argued with cogency that he has identified his country's interests altogether too much with those of the Afro-Asian bloc. Friendship with the Arabs is obviously good policy in the long run, but the rift between Arab and Negro Africa, already observable at many points along the line of ethnic contact, may well grow in the future, and this circumstance, combined with the fact that bigger oil tankers for Europe will have increasingly to be rerouted round the Cape, make it extremely unwise for Mr Kyprianou to take such a prominent part in the agitation for intervention in the internal affairs of South Africa. European and Arab unity are very much on the cards, but the unity of the third world is fragile because there is no traditional binding force.

Mr Tassos Papadopoulos has been Minister of Labour since 1960, when he was only twenty-six, and since April 1966 he has been Minister of Health also. Like his colleagues Clerides and Kyprianou, he began his career as a British-trained lawyer. He combines a pride in his Ministry with a very attractive and forthright manner, and the pride is justified for he is one of those primarily responsible for the extraordinary development of the economy since independence, without which diplomatic success would have been of no avail whatsoever. There have been hardly any serious strikes, wages have been realistically related to production costs, and the temptation to reduce unemployment by unnecessarily enlarging the bureaucracy has been resisted. Turkish workers, however, regard his achievement more sourly than the Greek because since 1963 they have not received a tithe of the benefits to which they were entitled. Papadopoulos is definitely one of those who believe in wearing down the recalcitrant Turks through a gradual policy of attrition, while rewarding those who do not behave as 'rebels'.

Mr Renos Solomides, Minister of Finance since July 1962, is a highly-regarded French-trained economist, and shares responsibility for sustained economic development. He is indeed its major theoretician in Cyprus. Before taking up his present post he was general manager of the Keo company, the biggest manufacturer of alcoholic drinks in the island, and before that he had been concerned with the textile and mining industries, so his previous practical experience has also stood him in good stead. Foreign aid to Cyprus has not been relatively very great, but Cypriote use of it has evoked the praise of the international organisations concerned. On 8 June 1968, it was announced that Mr Solomides would leave his post on the 20th.[1]

The late Mr Andreas Araouzos, as Minister for Commerce and Industry, showed considerable skill as a negotiator, and played an important part in the development of the economy.[2] Mr George Tombazos, Minister of Agriculture and Natural Resources, and Mr Titos Phanos, Minister of Communications and Works, have held their posts since April 1966.

Dr Constantinos Spyridakis has been Minister of Education since March 1965, and was Director of Greek Education in Cyprus from 1954 to 1959. He is a scholar, and obtained his doctorate of philosophy at the University of Berlin in 1934. In character, he is regarded as not forceful, though kindly, yet more than any other person he is responsible for modelling Cypriote education on that of mainland Greece. The organisation of the educational system and the disagreement over its future will be discussed in the appropriate section. The remaining Minister, Mrs Stella Soulioti, is Minister of Justice, and is an ex-barrister like several of her colleagues. She is the sister of Michael Cacoyannis, the film director.

For purposes of administration, the island is divided into six districts, each headed, as in the British period, by a Commissioner. The administrative centres are greatly disparate in population, the figures in 1960 being as follows : Nicosia (104,000 including suburbs), Limassol (47,000), Famagusta (38,000), Larnaca (20,000), Paphos (10,000), and Kyrenia (3,500). The District Commissioners in three cases at least (Vryonides, Benjamin, and Zachariades) appear to be men of a much harder type than most of the Ministers, and have been actively engaged in furthering the policy of containing the Turkish population. It should be remembered that for most practical purposes even outlying Turkish villages are separately administered, although the Turks have to apply to the Greek-Cypriote authorities for permits.

Since December 1967, when the Turks set up their 'provisional administration' pending implementation of the 1960 constitution, the Turkish-Cypriote leaders have been confined to the Nicosia enclave. The head of the Turkish administration is Dr Fazil Küçük. He became Vice-President[3] of the Republic in 1960, and retains that title, his reasonable argument being that if the Greeks lay claim to

---

[1] Mr Andreas Patsalides, of Larnaca, succeeded Mr Solomides as Minister of Finance on 24 June 1968.

[2] He died in office on 10 March 1968, and on 15 June Mr Nicos Demetriou was announced as his successor.

[3] Dr Küçük is so described in U.N. Security Council documents and in reports by representatives of the major powers.

titles valid until the troubles, the Turks also have a right to do so. Less logical is his retention of the title despite his refusal to recognise the validity of those held by the Greeks. Like most of the other Turkish leaders, Dr Küçük belongs to the professional classes. Personally, he is very dignified, and it is significant that Makarios himself expresses a liking for him, apart from his policies. As a moderate, Küçük is vulnerable to the overbidding of his military leaders, and explosions and broadsheets directed against members of his administration have underlined this vulnerability. However, with the departure of the secret organiser of Turkish resistance, Kemal Çoşkun, in early 1967, he seems to have regained complete control of the Nicosia enclave. In other parts of the island the Turkish leaders would not necessarily be prepared to accept any deal he might make.

Recently, the Ankara government has been shaking off the albatross of unconditional support for Israel, and Dr Küçük's diplomatic hand has been strengthened as a result. Representatives of the Arab countries, formerly reciprocally hostile to Turkish policies, have come to visit him. He has not the stature of Makarios in the world at large, and until recently could not travel to become better known, but he has considerable popularity among his own people, and has been especially active in helping the Turkish refugees.

Mr Rauf Denktaş, President of the Turkish Communal Chamber, is a very different type altogether. Like several of the Greek leaders, he is a British-educated lawyer. Some of his political actions in the past have been as doubtful as those of Georghadjis. He has had disagreements with Dr Küçük, and one may suspect that the latter was not entirely displeased when the Greek authorities refused to allow Denktaş back into the island in 1964. During his absence, Dr Şemsi Kâzim acted as President of the Communal Chamber and controlled education as well, his allegiance being entirely to Dr Küçük. Denktaş's pronouncements from Ankara were consistently extremist, but since his return in 1968 they have been more moderate.

Mr Osman Örek, Minister of Defence in the 1960 government, now performs his duties for the Turks alone, his Ministry having been taken over by Georghadjis. Mr Örek gives an impression of considerable intelligence, and the same, one understands, is true of Mr Fazil Plümer, Minister of Agriculture and Natural Resources in the 1960 government, and Dr Niyazi Manyera, Minister of Health. Together with Mr Cemal Müftizade, Under-Secretary and adviser to Dr Küçük, they represent a good deal of brainpower on the Turkish side. Nor should we forget the secret editor of the

Special News Bulletin and his staff. In the author's view, a major reason for the relative success of the Turks in putting over their case to the world at large is that the most able men among the Cypriote Greeks have their time largely taken up in activities other than propaganda, while on the Turkish side the most able men are confined in small areas with much less to do, and so have plenty of time to think about the deprivations they have suffered at the hands of the Greeks.

Other leaders in the eleven-man Turkish provisional administration are Mr Hakkı Süleyman, who deals with social service, Mr Ümit Süleyman (judicial matters), Mr Rüstem Tatar (finance), Mr Erol Kâzim (Communications and Works), and Mr Oğuz Ramadan (economics).

The Turkish leaders outside the main enclave impress one with being as different from those inside it as the District Commissioners are from the Greek-Cypriote Ministers. They are fighters rather than propagandists or diplomats and, though hospitable and welcoming, give a very definite impression of toughness. Three that the author has talked with at some length are Mr Aziz Altay, a barrister of Ktima, Mr Kemal Pars, formerly Assistant District Commissioner of Limassol, and Dr Orhan Müderrisoğlu, technically vice-president of the Cyprus House of Representatives, who controls the Turkish quarter of Scala in the town of Larnaca. All three are men of perception, but the third is in a class by himself. To meet Orhan Bey is a memorable experience. He is a man of middle age, with the frame of a wrestler, striking light eyes, and great reserves of energy. He will be delighted to hear himself described as the most outspokenly anti-Greek leader in Cyprus, and his favourite response to any encroachment by the National Guard has been not to waste time talking, but to hit back hard. Nor does he necessarily wait for the Greeks to make the first move. No wonder the UNFICYP reports have been full of complaints about the uncooperativeness of the Turkish leadership in the Larnaca area. Orhan Bey summed up the Cyprus situation as a matter of simple survival, quoting from a Turkish version of *Hamlet* the phrase 'Ölmek yoksa yaşamaktır' (literally, 'It is a question of living or dying'). One deplores his over-reaction, but his attitude is at least free of hypocrisy, and one confesses to a certain sympathy with a man who feels himself cornered and is determined to fight.

The principal efforts of the local Turkish leaders are directed towards ensuring that their enclaves are not gradually eroded, or quickly overrun in the case of a Greek attack. To this end they receive help from Ankara. Aziz Altay, for instance, has had a Turkish army adviser to train his fighters. The position of Kemal

Pars is more precarious, for the Turkish quarter of Limassol is not demarcated by natural features as is the one in Ktima, which dominates the plain on three sides. Isolated Turkish villages are much more insecure, and those interested in Cyprus who value their health are advised not to visit such villages and ask questions about arms and defensive positions. The author's own experience in one case was unfortunate but, in view of the vulnerability of the village in question, understandable. Besides, even in this case, the ordinary people were friendly. Only the village leader was hostile.

The Economy

In 1966, the Cypriote Gross National Product was £157.1 million, an increase of 6.6 per cent over the previous year. According to the figures given by Mr Andreas Araouzos at the annual meeting of the Cyprus Chamber of Commerce on 24 May 1967, the value of external trade in 1966 amounted to £84,606,000, an increase of about 9 per cent over the previous year. The value of Cypriote exports stood at £29,238,000, an increase of 15.6 per cent, though this was helped by an improvement of 13.9 per cent in the price of Cypriote exports and a decrease in the price of imports by 1.8 per cent. Also, the value of imports stood at £55,368,000, an increase of 7.7 per cent. However, the figure for the adverse balance of trade remained about the same—£26,130,000 in 1966, as compared with £26,119,000 in 1965. In 1967, imports totalled £58.7 million, exports £29.7 million.

In addition to the trade gap, there are said to be hidden debts of many millions, chiefly for arms purchases, but they are offset by nearly a year's foreign exchange reserves (£54.3 million). Fortunately too, there are other sources of revenue, so the balance of payments shows an actual surplus. This is owing principally to the expenses of the British bases, amounting to well over £14 million per annum, and to those of UNFICYP, together with the mainland Greek and Turkish military contingents and the mainland Greek component of the National Guard, amounting to nearly £7 million per annum. About £4 million is also remitted annually by Cypriotes living abroad. The rest is the balance of revenue (£27,054,928) over expenditure (£19,926,893). Fortunately, this balance can be used to help offset imports because the Cyprus pound (made up of a thousand mils) is equivalent to the pound sterling, and transferable at par. Sterling area membership is just one of the advantages enjoyed by Cyprus as a member of the Commonwealth. Another is the agreement whereby Cypriote agricultural products enter Great Britain duty free, and Cyprus wines pay a very small import tariff.

But these, like the military expenditure, must be accounted uncertainty factors. If Britain were to enter the Common Market, the tariffs would have to go up, and in that case Cyprus would apply for associate membership only (so as not to destroy her budding light industries). The point is important because in 1966 32.4 per cent of all Cypriote exports went to the United Kingdom. Then again, the run-down at the Dhekelia S.B.A. in 1967 has meant the loss of 2,000 jobs in the Larnaca area, a foretaste of worse to come. Clearly, the Cyprus government has to plan for the time when such invisible earnings are no longer viable.

Those who run the Cyprus economy are fully aware of the need to stimulate its more stable sections. Foremost among these is agriculture which, together with forestry and fishing, accounts for about a quarter of the Gross Domestic Product. In 1966, agriculture alone contributed only 20.8 per cent of the Gross National Product (£29.2 million) yet 38.8 per cent of the work force was wholly dependent on the land and another 25 per cent partially. It is reckoned that the percentage of the G.N.P. contributed by agriculture could be raised to 25 or 30 per cent. Cypriote wine, olive-oil, and wheat have been exported since ancient times and for climatic reasons, fruit and vegetables mature several weeks earlier in Cyprus than in Greece, Italy, or Spain. The eventual development of more competition on the southern and eastern seaboards of the Mediterranean is likely for the foreseeable future to be offset by tariff barriers, Commonwealth or European. Viticulture, in particular, is important to the Cypriotes, and in 1964 it was estimated that 30,000 of the 70,000 or so farming families were to some extent dependent on it. Unfortunately, there are too many low-yield mountain vineyards which would be more productive if planted with trees. Also, with the exception of *commandaria*,[1] Cyprus wines are not yet high enough in quality to compete very successfully on the continental market. Some three million gallons were exported to England in 1967, more than from Australia, South Africa, or Italy. In particular, the British drink large quantities of the cheap, sweet Cyprus sherry, but it is doubtful whether they could continue to do so if Spanish sherry were sold at the same price. Other Cypriote agricultural products are second to none. In the past, 65 per cent of agricultural exports have gone to the United Kingdom (including 90 per cent of the potatoes, carrots, and grapes), but the continental share of these is rising. An important factor in the promotion of Cyprus products has been the good packing of fruit and vegetables. The hospitable treatment of visiting importers has also played its part.

---

[1] Made at 3,000 ft. a.s.l. in a few villages north of Limassol. It is a strong, sweet red wine made from blended red and white grapes.

A big difference could be made through the introduction of better farming methods in Cyprus, and the Agricultural Research Institute, set up with the help of F.A.O., is experimenting with mixed farming and crop rotation. Marketing boards exist for potatoes and carrots, and carobs (for cattle feed and sweetmeats) are another important crop.

It is reckoned that 66 per cent of the island is potentially cultivable, though less than a quarter of that is cultivated now. Grants are made for the levelling of land for irrigation, but this in itself is not enough. The main problem is lack of the water to irrigate such land, and it is being tackled energetically by the administration. Snow water from the Troödos, as also rain-water, collects underground, but excessive pumping has a deleterious effect on the water-table. Hence the governmental limitation on the extent of citrus orchards. The obvious course is to construct dams, and during the first five-year plan £3 million was spent on them, as compared with only £1 million over the previous eighty years of colonial administration. Allowing for the fact that aid from Great Britain made such expenditure possible, the increase is remarkable. During the period of the plan (1962–66) twenty-three dams were constructed, increasing total water capacity in the dams 6½ times over what it had been before 1960. An equally large number are under construction or have since been completed. The dams are mostly of the earth-fill type, though three are rock-fill, and one is of concrete. Foreign companies are brought in for specific projects, and a study is being made of the underground water resources. Already a new deep aquifer has been discovered in the west-central Mesaoria. Progress is being made in the cementation of irrigation channels, which offsets seepage, but not evaporation. Clearly, a greater use of pipes is indicated. Government agencies do a great deal to prevent over-pumping and the 50 per cent wastage of water which still occurs, while at the same time encouraging more intensive cultivation. The forestry authorities play their part by planting trees in those eroded areas which disfigure the face of the island when seen from an aeroplane. However, until the conversion of sea-water into fresh becomes very much cheaper, and rainfall can be precipitated more easily than is now the case, the problem of water conservation will remain acute.

Animal husbandry improved in 1967, but insufficient effort has been put into improving the quality of the breeding stock. But the authorities are happily not wedded to dogmatic environmentalism, and have every intention of ameliorating the situation. The varieties of fruit are already being improved, and tinning factories set up for fruit out of season.

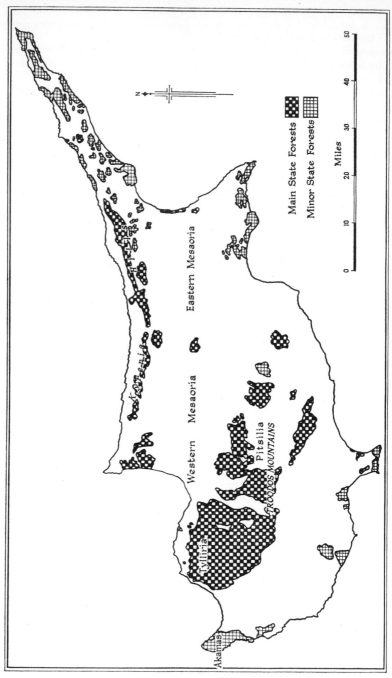

4. Cyprus Forests

The excellent system of state forests, for which Dr A. H. Unwin more than any other man was responsible, has been well maintained under the Cypriote administration. The two main forest areas are in the Paphos district (230 sq. m.) and along the Kyrenia range (118 sq. m.). The Forestry College, set up at Prodhromos in 1951, continues to attract students from several countries, in particular Libya. The two-year courses are presided over by Dr W. Finlayson, the Scotch Principal of the College, who thinks very well of the Forestry Department, though he considers much more should be done in the field of tree-genetics. However, a forest nursery has been set up near Morphou. At the moment only one-fifth of the state forests (c. 100 sq. m.) produces industrial timber, and the quality of the Cyprus soft-woods is not high, their main function being to protect the catchment areas. All the same, they are fetching excellent prices as material for the crates in which perishables are exported. Inclusive of manufactured products, the revenue from timber is now some £100,000 a year. There is no reason why this revenue should not rise considerably because, of $2\frac{1}{2}$ million cubic feet of wood which grow each year, only 1 million are cut (owing to the temporary insufficiency of saw-mills). There is less spoiled timber, now the custom of resin-tapping has ceased, and farmers are turning against the destructive goat because of the damage it does in their valuable orchards. Goats must officially be tethered in the forests, and even then are only legally permitted in certain areas. The two biggest disasters to the forests since independence are associated in the forestry officials' minds with the Turks. The first occurred during the Tylliria area bombing of 1964, and the second in September 1966, when fires were maliciously started in many places at the same time.[1] In each of these two cases about four square miles of good timber were burnt down. Reafforestation by the terracing method is taking place in these and other burnt areas. In future the emphasis will be on improving the quality of the timber. Cyprus hard-woods are valuable as furniture material, and the mechanised clearing of the riverine sites will enable the Cypriotes to grow more of them. Attempts are also made to educate the public to respect the forests, notably Arbor Week in December of each year, when the children plant trees.

High hopes are entertained for the expansion of the fishing industry, though it is difficult to see how this can be effected without providing the fishermen with equipment to go very much further afield.[2]

[1] Dr Küçük's staff deny this charge.
[2] Since this was written the Cyprus government has decided to subsidise the Cypriote fishing fleet.

Agriculture with its associated industries is one of the three pillars on which it is intended to build the Cyprus economy of the future. The second is manufacturing and construction. Manufacturing contributed £16.8 million to the G.D.P. in 1966 (12.2 per cent of the total), by comparison with £13 million in 1961, and contributed £4·7 million, or 17·3 per cent, to the total of exports. By 1971 it is expected to contribute 15 per cent to the G.D.P. Between 1960 and 1966, some ninety new factories were constructed. Light industry is being encouraged to replace imported goods with locally-produced items, and so has need of protective tariffs. Nevertheless, Cyprus does have manufactured exports. For instance, in 1964 she exported to Europe £100,000 worth of shoes, and in September 1967 an agreement was signed for export to the United Kingdom of £30–35,000-worth of matches. Eighty-four new light industrial units were established in the island in 1966, so that over £3 million in foreign exchange was saved from the decrease in imports, and employment was created for an additional 2,000 persons. Nor was the cost of living index affected, because the substitutes were found to be adequate. In particular the Vasiliko Cement Works, which began production in 1967, is reducing the need to import large quantities of cement. An industrial estate near Nicosia is nearing completion and another is being built at Limassol, but heavy industry is out of the question because of the smallness of the market.

Land speculation around Nicosia is attaining dangerous proportions and, as in Great Britain, too much agricultural land is being built on. The constructional work is not always carried out in the right areas either. Larnaca, for example, which has been hit hard by the British run-down at Dhekelia, stands in need of long-promised harbour works, though an oil refinery and a chemical fertiliser factory are at last being built. At Nea Paphos dredging is being undertaken, so that ships of up to 12,000 tons may be accommodated.

The third pillar on which the Cypriote economy stands is tourism, which is so important as to rate a section to itself. But we have by no means exhausted the other means whereby Cyprus is striving to close her trade gap. Most important among these is mining. The value of the minerals exported in 1966 was £12,225,000, an increase of £3 million over 1965 and £5.1 million over 1964, so that the percentage increase between 1964 and 1966 was 71.8 per cent. Unfortunately, prices fell in 1967, and the value of mineral exports for that year was only £9,111,048. The largest profits are derived from the sale of cupreous concentrates and of iron and copper pyrites from the pillow-shaped lavas (formed from molten rock bursting up through the sea). Asbestos from the plutonic rocks, notably the serpentinite, is found in particular at Amiandos, and fetches sums averaging £800,000 a year. Lesser sums are derived from the sale of cement-copper, chrome ore, umber, gypsum, and yellow ochre. Only Japan and Spain produce more pyrites than Cyprus, but Cyprus is unfortunately unique in exporting all its mineral products. Of course, it is hoped that some of these products will be exploited locally, if that can be done before the known deposits are exhausted, which will be within fifteen years at the present rate. Reports that the Skouriotissa open-cast pyrites mine is 'inexhaustible' should be treated with reserve. Electromagnetic surveys from the air have already been made.

Encouragement to ship-owners who wish to register under the Cyprus flag has raised the nominal size of the merchant fleet from two ships and 96 gross tons in 1963 to seventy-nine ships and 400,401 gross tons in 1967. The revenue has been small. In 1966 tonnage tax, registration fees, certificate fees, and stamp duties brought in only £33,267. However, one of the conditions of registration is that not less than 15 per cent of the crew should be Cypriotes, and Mr Titos Phanos has stated that this percentage is subject to increase at any time up to 50 per cent of the total crew. In 1966, Cypriote crew members made £10,000, and it seems likely that more will obtain similar employment in the future. The main drag on development has been the closure of the Suez Canal after the Arab-Israeli war of 1967.

A minor success has been the frequent issue of new postage stamps. For example, there have been at least thirty commemorative issues since independence. There had already been attractive stamps before that time, so it was more a case of maintaining and building on a tradition. As before, the stamps depict Cypriote products and antiquities, but they also celebrate events of local and national importance, and disseminate propaganda for the Greek-Cypriote cause. The Turks become especially incensed about the way in which words in Turkish are omitted or relegated to obscurity, or Greek emblems, such as the two-headed Byzantine eagle, are introduced into the pictures. The coinage, for which a good example had also been set in the British period, also brings in a modest revenue apart from its face value. Turks have not failed to notice that the pound note is now blue, the Greek colour.[1] But the encouragement of philately and numismatics is not seriously expected to

---

[1] Dr Küçük has publicly taken exception to Greek disuse of the Turkish language for official purposes. The Greeks plead their lack of translators, but that would hardly explain the omission of the Turkish name of the Republic from the cover of passports or from a stamp issued in November 1967.

solve the island's economic problems. The industry on which most hopes are pinned is tourism.

Tourism

Tourism is really the only way in which Cyprus can fill the gap resulting from the eventual withdrawal of foreign troops. Fortunately, the island possesses basic touristic advantages, in particular a combination of sun, sea, and antiquities. It is advertised as having 340 days of sunshine yearly (though in 1967 there were certainly fewer), more than any western European country. Its high altitudes make possible at least two months skiing each winter (more in 1967) and also cool summer resorts, to which the richer inhabitants of hot Middle Eastern countries may escape. Amateur skiers like the gradual slopes, although the few sharp ones are too short to compete with those of Austria or Switzerland; and it takes only three-quarters of an hour to drive from the coast to the summit of Mt Chionistra, where the white dome of the British signals station dominates the landscape. Except perhaps in the south-west, Cyprus has higher sea temperatures than any of its sister islands in the Mediterranean, and a number of good beaches, especially Golden Sands, south of Varosha, which was developed by the British army as a leave camp during the war. Unfortunately, the yearly blessing of the waters at Epiphany has not been enough to offset the danger of pollution from Famagusta harbour.

The motorable roads along the Kyrenia range and in the Paphos forest are a special attraction, and tourists may stay in the forestry station at Stavros tis Psokas. The archaeological sites are being exploited for what they represent rather than as mere centres for commercial ventures, but foreign companies are encouraged to perform at the ancient theatres of Salamis and Curium. Treasures are always turning up in Cyprus, such as the Greco-Roman mosaics discovered accidentally at Nea Paphos in 1962. Unfortunately, the Cypriote Greeks do not always show the same respect for non-Greek antiquities as they do for their own. For instance, the famous 'Othello' tower at Famagusta (the one which appears in the travel brochures) has been largely destroyed in the recent widening of the harbour. The Turks, for their part, have been accused of selling Greek antiquities. But such an attitude is not peculiar to Cyprus.[1]

There are, besides, many other factors which draw the tourist to

[1] In Ireland, for instance, some extreme nationalists resent the preservation of Georgian architecture, and certainly do not see why it should stand in the way of new and hideous office-blocks. Like Ireland, Cyprus is an island with a long history and beautiful landscapes, which are in themselves powerful romantic attractions.

Cyprus, among which hospitality must take first place. Despite the underlying tension, foreigners are made welcome, and the British are not excepted. Whatever the reason (and a Briton may be pardoned for thinking that a contributory factor was the relatively moderate British response to the extreme provocations of the Emergency), one is welcomed not only by those whose interests are directly involved, government officials and hoteliers, but also by ordinary people throughout the island. There cannot conceivably be any ulterior motive for the friendliness of villagers in remote areas and their almost embarrassingly lavish presents of food and drink. It is the hospitable tradition of a pre-industrial age, a tradition, incidentally, which still obtains in country districts of Greece and Turkey. However, the visitor is liable to be treated with some suspicion by the Greek police near the Turkish quarters in Cyprus.[1]

Language problems are non-existent, since most Cypriotes speak some English, and there are French and German speakers among the educated. It is inevitable that Cypriotes should feel strongly about the community question, but they very seldom show any resentment towards tourists on that account. In fact, the few truly anti-British Cypriotes, as a psychologist would expect, are mostly (in one's own experience) domiciled in Britain. Another fly in the ointment where conversations between Britons and ex-emigrant Cypriote Greeks are concerned is a regrettable tendency of the latter to boast of their amorous exploits in England. However, we ought not to stigmatise the Greeks for what is equally common among others. It is a minor drawback in a land where every prospect pleases.

The Cypriote authorities are doing everything in their power to lure the tourist. They advertise the orange-festival at Famagusta and the wine-festival at Limassol. The latter town is particularly suitable as a tourist centre owing to the nearness of the British base. The British provide pipe-bands and cooperate in making the carnival a success, besides taking part in the Shakespeare productions at Curium. A Limassol folk-dance and music festival has just been instituted. The first international power-boat competition, held in 1967, also went off well. The harbour at Kyrenia, enlarged since independence, provides good shelter for yachts. The festival of Kataklysmos, which is said to be inspired by the ancient homage to Aphrodite and Adonis, is a good time to witness sea-sports. There are various archaeological museums and a museum of Folk Art, set

---

[1] I was arrested, for instance, when I unwittingly left the Turkish quarter of Nicosia by a street other than the one permitted, but released when one of the plainclothesmen recognised me as having been at the monastery of Machaeras on a Greek-Cypriote national occasion a few days before.

up on the ground floor of the Archiepiscopal Palace in 1950 at the cost of £300,000. However, this last is not really comparable in standard to the archaeological ones. From 15 July to 15 August 1967, entrance to all public places of interest was declared free, which shows that the authorities do not have the penny-pinching mentality.

Food in Cyprus is plentiful, cheap, and good. One should mention in particular the *mezze*, or Cypriote hors d'oeuvres, which are provided in quantity with drinks. The best local food is to be had in the Turkish quarter of Nicosia. The Turks have heavily influenced the Greeks in the arts of everyday life, cooking, folk-dancing, and singing, just as the Greeks have influenced the Turks in matters of architecture and the plastic arts. Even rice, that staple of the Near Eastern kitchen, was introduced by the Turks. Both restaurants and patisseries in Cyprus are generally clean and service is quick and willing. The roadside *kapheneion* provides insights into local life.

The same applies in general to drink as to food. The visitor enjoys the excellent local fruit squashes, as well as Cypriote specialities such as *zivania*, or grape spirit, of which the best, a pink variety, is made by the monks of Kykko. Perhaps the most popular drink among tourists is the brandy sour (mild local brandy, lemon squash, soda-water, sugar, a slice of lemon, and Angostura bitters). Its introduction into Cyprus is claimed by Mr Alex Horsley, the English proprietor of a public house in Nicosia. As regards the wines, the whites (and to a lesser extent the reds) tend, like most southern ones, to be short of acidity, while the reds tend to an excess of tannin. However, apart from the rich *commandaria*, a few, like the Kokkineli rosé and the chilled white Aphrodite, are very drinkable.

Popular souvenirs include the famous lace of Lefkara, embroidery from the outlying regions of Paphos and the Carpass, pottery from Varosha and Lapithos, and silverware from Nicosia and the Larnaca district. The prices of these goods are fairly high but, as in Greece and Turkey, every official effort is made to ensure that prices in hotels and restaurants are the same for all, and even in souvenir shops the exploitation of tourists is uncommon.

For those who stand in need of them, there are bus tours to places of interest, and efficient guides. Taxis too are surprisingly cheap, partly because of the sensible Middle Eastern custom of sharing them, and they go to most parts of the island. For those who prefer not to risk being driven fast by a chauffeur eating a bun, with one nonchalant hand on the wheel (both hands off to brush the crumbs away), there is a car-hire system, and petrol is another relatively cheap commodity. Safety precautions on the roads are not all that they might be, but Cypriote drivers are less fatalistic than the Arabs or the mainland Turks and Greeks. Over 5,000 miles of uncongested roads, 2,135 asphalted by 1967, are an added bonus. In 1966 there were only 60,000 licensed vehicles in the country, 30,000 of them in private hands, so there was only one vehicle to every ten persons. However, that is a rather high figure for the Near East. There are only 80,000 private cars in the whole of Turkey, for example.

Cyprus did not share in the Europe-wide expansion of tourism in the 1950s because of the Emergency, and the tourist figures for the past nine years closely reflect changing political circumstances:

Year	No. of Tourists	No. of One-Day Visitors
1959	21,076	45,833
1960	25,703	60,951
1961	40,140	65,225
1962	50,236	85,931
1963	74,619	81,396
1964	16,084 (incl. journalists)	64,484
1965	33,246	84,713
1966	54,114	88,452
1967	68,397	72,099

Earnings from tourism in 1959 were only £1,445,000. In 1966 they were £3,590,000, and in 1967 £4.5 million.

Hopes for the continued expansion of Cyprus tourism rest on the following considerations. Some 75 million tourists visit the Mediterranean area each year, but of these only three million reach Greece. Given stability, one might expect a future 20 million tourists in the eastern Mediterranean, and Cyprus, at the crossroads of Europe and the Middle East, is in a good position to receive a fair proportion of them. Seen from this point of view, a target of 160,000 tourists annually, and 130,000 one-day callers, by 1971 is realistic. Eventually, expenditure by tourists in Cyprus could well rise to some £30 million, thus effectively closing the trade gap and providing for the employment of the increasing population. According to Mr Costas Montis, poet and Director of Tourism, the United Kingdom travel agents were fully booked in 1967, and 100,000 tourists could have been received if there had been enough space in the hotels. Admittedly, there is a school of thought which holds that conditions in country places are not good enough for the reception of visitors, and that social customs do not allow for the problems raised by an influx of young people into private houses; but such problems have been solved in other Mediterranean countries by the rent-a-villa system (not always honestly run) and the deliberate raising of living standards where families show a willingness to receive tourists. Provision is being made in the second five-year plan for a great increase in the number of hotel-beds. In 1967, there were 128 licensed hotels in Cyprus, with 6,100 beds, of which 300 were to be found in the new Hilton. The Ledra Palace Hotel, which represents an older and less obtrusive culture than the Hilton, has long been a favourite haunt of journalists and those who prefer to discuss politics in a bar. Like many other Cypriote hotels, it has a swimming-pool and tennis-courts.

As educational leisure becomes more common in most Western countries, more visitors can be expected to reject the big hotels and cellophane-packaged tours in favour of closer contact with the local people. An overwhelming advantage of the *pension* system is that the rent goes directly to the people instead of passing through the hands of the hoteliers, so that resentment is not felt against tourists who enrich the few while stimulating prices. It is true that hotels provide employment: 110 scholarships have been given to Cypriotes so that they can study in the hotel schools of Greece, Switzerland, and Scotland, while others are being trained in Cyprus. However, the money passes through relatively few hands, and a disproportionate amount sticks to them. The *pension* system will be considerably helped by the fact that Cypriote domestic architecture does not usually have the appearance of deliberate ugliness which renders certain regions elsewhere unattractive to the tourist. One glaring exception is to be found in the corrugated iron, reminiscent of some Australian country townships, with which some of the poorest houses are roofed.

It is the British who come to Cyprus in the largest numbers, and that is why a Cypriote tourist centre has been established in London. Of course, this British yearning to see Cyprus is partly the result of the financial limitation of £50 per person imposed on Britons holidaying outside the sterling area, but the Cypriotes have reason to hope that happy experiences will create new holiday patterns. At the same time, the authorities are aware that it is unwise to have all their eggs in the British basket at a period when interests other than British can determine British policies to the detriment of the British economy. The airways companies, of which there are seven, are cooperating by lowering fares for groups from all over northern Europe. A new airways terminal costing £1 million was completed in the spring of 1967, but this costly improvement tends to be offset by the lack of speed and efficiency shown by Cyprus Airways officials in dealing with a relatively minor matter, such as a suitcase broken in transit.[1] Steamship services from different parts of Europe and the Near East also serve Cyprus. In these

---

[1] I obtained a good replacement in the end, but only after three weeks of waiting and officials passing the buck from one to the other.

days of more rapid and convenient travel, the distance of Cyprus from the tourist-producing countries is less of a disadvantage, and the fact of its being an island protects it from road tourism. Mainland Greece has seen enough of begging by beatniks from people much poorer than themselves. On the other hand, people of small means who pay their way are more and more sought after by countries like Cyprus, and the package tours and mushroom resorts are the first stage in helping them to adopt the tourist habit. Unfortunately, Cyprus is not yet a country where the footloose person can wander everywhere without danger or suspicion, though an area like the Acamas peninsula is ideal for such a holiday, and so is the Paphos forest. Counting those in the state forests, there are 695 miles of unmetalled forest roads, together with numberless paths suitable for walking.

The principal uncertainty factor in the rosy future of Cyprus tourism is the attitude of the Cypriote Turks. At present they benefit proportionately very little from tourism, and pressures are sometimes brought to bear on foreigners who use their hotels or become too friendly with them.[1] Such restrictions are unwise, for if the Turks are allowed little part in the prosperity, they have it in their power to scare away large numbers of tourists with every bomb they feel like exploding.

The Success and Weakness of the Cyprus Economy

In 1960, *per capita* income in Cyprus was £184·8, in 1966 (for Christians) it was £260.5. World Bank statistics published in the latter year show Cyprus as thirty-fifth in terms of *per capita* income in a list of 126 countries, though it stood 125th in population. Only Israel, with its enormous volume of aid from world Jewry, has a higher *per capita* income in the Middle East, and even so it has more labour problems than Cyprus. Since 1965 there has been full employment (that is, an unemployment rate of under 2 per cent), though one must allow for the fact that this does not apply to the Turkish enclaves, and in the fact that military service has been introduced.

During the first five-year plan (1962–66) the average annual rate of growth was 5.7 per cent, and since 1960 it has been as high as 6.8 per cent. The G.N.P. rose by over 40 per cent between 1960 and 1965, and it continues to rise. Foreign exchange in 1960 stood at £17 million, whereas in 1967 it stood at £64 million. As Mr Solomides rightly remarked in his 1967 budget address, 'no other newly independent state has achieved a similar record and maintained it

---

[1] Turkish hotels are included in the official guide, but tourists who actually stay in them are regarded by the Greeks with some suspicion.

over so many years . . .' It will be of interest to examine the reasons for this unique achievement.

The success of the Cyprus economy is a tribute above all to the prudent and intelligent management of its finances, which has been highly praised by the Director-General of the International Labour Organisation and by the representative in Cyprus of the United Nations Development Programme. Foreign exchange has not been borrowed for mere consumption expenditure or for repayment of interest on former loans. All expenditure of an opportunist nature has been avoided, and surplus on the balance of payments is spent on development. Thus, Parkinson's Second Law (that expenditure rises to meet income) is only allowed to apply to real income. Of what other ex-colonial country can the same be said?

The Cypriote economy is capitalist, but not doctrinairely so. There is a sympathetic approach on the part of the authorities to the problems of the 861 cooperatives,[1] with their 176,000 members, and the 152 trades unions, with their membership of over 60,000. There are, besides, eighteen employers' associations (counting branches), with 600 members. Adequate machinery for considering grievances and complaints was set up in November 1962, the Federation of Turkish Trades Unions being a participant in the agreement. A year later the productivity centre was established, with $1.3 million in aid from the U.N., though it did not become operational until 1965. A social security scheme had already been in operation during the British period, covering marriage, maternity, old age, orphanhood, death, and industrial accidents, but compensation was insufficient, and has been extended. In 1960, a long-overdue scheme was introduced for the compensation of miners suffering from pneumoconiosis, and a social insurance scheme has since come into operation which technically covers all workers. Good statisticians are at work all the time, watching progress, and the number of man-days lost has steadily diminished, from 27,005 in 1960 to 2,708 in 1966. Cyprus has a better record in this respect than most of the 'developed' countries, though not so good as that of Greece. The 44-hour week (40 hours for underground miners) is now universal in the island, and a dedicated nucleus works longer hours than that. For instance, one was told by the Minister of Labour that employees in his Ministry often work up to 7 or 8 p.m., and on two subsequent occasions when passing the Ministry noticed that people were indeed at work in their offices until a late hour. Such willingness is encouraged by the practice, unusual in the Near

[1] Some of these are for consumers, particularly in the countryside. Even schoolchildren have their own (unofficial) co-operatives for plant-growing, bee-keeping, poultry rearing, etc.

East, of delegating authority. The rate of crime is among the lowest in the world,[1] though the cynical might be inclined to point to the outlets provided by communal friction.

It cannot be argued that independence came to Cyprus under particularly auspicious economic circumstances. British military expenditure during the Emergency (1955–59) provided great stimulation at first, but from 1957 the economy was seriously distorted owing to the disproportionate size of the services sector. Between 1958 and 1960 there was a serious flight of capital (c. £8 million) owing to fear of devaluation. The G.D.P. dropped 10 per cent, imports came to twice as much as exports, and the overall balance of payments was in deficit. Population was moving from the countryside into the towns, and emigration was running at 5–6,000 a year. In 1960, the emigration figure rose to 14,589. The foreign exchange reserves stood at £17 million, equivalent to only about five months' imports. Nevertheless, the upswing of the economy soon began, and there has been a balanced budget ever since. Only 3,000 emigrated in 1965, and 3,408 in 1966. And the emigrants themselves are showing their faith in the economy. Deposits in Cyprus banks by Cypriotes living abroad rose to £5.6 million in 1966, as compared with £3.8 million in 1965. In all, bank deposits in 1967 rose to £85.4 million.

The first five-year plan was essentially a public investment programme, based on guidance rather than compulsion. Sixty-five million pounds was allocated to it, but only £39 million spent, owing to the laudable determination of the authorities to permit expenditure only where it was justified. The results were good. Agricultural production, for instance, increased by 38.4 per cent over the period of the plan, and the infrastructure benefited enormously. Production of electricity expanded from 260 million K.W.H. in 1961 to 370 million K.W.H. in 1966. With the completion of the central power station at Moni and other improvements, electrical capacity increased from 84.3 thousand K.W. in 1961 to 159 thousand K.W. by the end of 1966. Two hundred and twenty-one villages were supplied with electricity, in addition to the ninety-six on supply before 1961. In 1967, the number of villages on supply was brought up to 358, and the lights across the Mesaoria twinkle more thickly than they used to. By 1971, it is estimated that 517 villages will have electricity and 97 per cent of the population will be on supply. There has been a similar big expansion of telephone communications, 11,000 new subscribers being added. Whereas in

---

[1] This happy state of affairs is unfortunately not paralleled among a minority of Cypriotes living a rootless, if profitable, existence in Great Britain.

1960 there were ninety-seven villages without a piped water supply, there are now only four in that position, out of all the 628 villages existing in 1966. Of course, a few contracts have been dishonestly fulfilled. The road system, already adequate before independence, has been greatly improved, but the asphalting of additional miles has not always been done well. The disintegrating road running from Klirou to Nicosia, over which the author passed in 1967, is an example.

The second five-year plan, which began in 1967, looks like being as big a success as the first. By the end of 1971 it is estimated that the G.D.P. will rise to £208 million as compared with £102 million in 1960. This presupposes a maintained growth rate of 6.5 per cent and the success of such schemes as the projected free trade zone. A master town and country plan, with British assistance, is already under way, and the success of the thirteenth Cyprus international Trade Fair in 1967 augurs well for the future. In addition, the Cypriotes are enthusiastic participants in trade fairs abroad.

The very important question next arises as to why the Cyprus economy has been uniquely successful among those of ex-colonial countries. Reasons advanced have included the tradition of efficiency and honesty left behind by the colonial administration, the legacy of good communications, the creation by the colonial power of a small but highly-educated élite, the drawing-off of surplus population into the home territory of that power, the large sums spent by that power during the struggle for independence, the enthusiasm generated by that struggle, and the aid granted to the newly-independent state, either directly or in the self-interested form of military expenditure. The same conditions have been fulfilled in other ex-colonial countries, with much greater natural resources than Cyprus, but without the same result. Nor is it an answer to point to the relatively high educational standards of the Cypriotes. Apart from primary education, which was officially controlled by the colonial government, Cypriote education was largely the creation of the Cypriotes themselves, and to admit it as the explanation of Cypriote success is to beg the question as to why the education created by other peoples was so much less effective. The most convincing explanation rests on the fact that individuals differ in their innate capacities, and that Cyprus possesses a larger proportion of persons innately capable of bettering themselves economically than most other countries with a similar background. The closest analogy to Cyprus is probably the Lebanon.

The weaknesses of the Cyprus economy are, however, not concealed by the authorities. Thus it is recognised that the collection of income tax will have to become more efficient. Indeed, the yield from this tax was less in 1967 than it was in 1960, partly owing to the loss of £60,000 then paid by Cypriote Turks and the abolition of the surtax on bachelors, which brought in approximately £80,000. But at least those whose profits come from productive enterprise are not being tempted to abandon it in favour of quick, untaxed returns on manipulation of the fruits of other people's enterprise. In 1963, the overall level of taxation in Cyprus was 16 per cent, as compared with 33 per cent in the United Kingdom, but it should be kept in mind that the British level of income tax, combined with creeping inflation, offers little encouragement to save. The tendency in Cyprus is to rely more and more upon indirect taxes, as in the Common Market countries. Indeed, Mr Solomides is in favour of adopting the Brussels tariff system. Indirect taxation makes tax collection much easier because it can be done by the customs and excise authorities before most consumers have a chance of evading the tax. In 1967, it is estimated that £11 million will have been collected in this way. Such a method of taxation has the beneficial effect of cutting down the number of bureaucrats, and it does not penalise the poor, because higher duties are imposed on imported luxury articles, while raw materials and primary necessities are largely exempt from duty. Also, tourists are not frightened off by a rise in the price of food and drink.

The Minister of Labour has not concealed the fact that, despite the reduction of wasted man-hours, low productivity and 'institutional obstacles' (i.e. bureaucratic lethargy?) are still a problem. The rate of economic dependency is increasing, as in so many other countries, and measures of improvement, such as the consolidation of land and the mechanisation of light industry, are likely to create problems in the redeployment of labour. The economy should be able to absorb the growing population for the time being, and Cyprus is most unlikely to be among those states which will have to take the lead in introducing selective birth-control. In the long term, however, the big trade gap presents considerable problems. Great Britain is cutting down her forces, those nations with costly contingents in UNFICYP are growing restive, and tourism, on which the expansion of the economy otherwise depends, is notoriously unstable. The calculations of the Cypriote economists have been based on the supposition that world trade will continue to prosper, but there are many danger signs. Countries with big, expanding industries are competing for limited markets. Since a favourable balance of payments depends upon exporting more than one imports, it is obvious that every country cannot do it at the same time. Equally obviously, if the cold wind of recession begins to blow, countries like Great Britain, let alone Cyprus, are going to be in a worse position than those which can fall back on greater resources. This fact alone should give pause to those Cypriotes (and Britons) who imagine that their country can remain forever independent of the larger economic blocs. Cyprus, like Britain, is not by any means wholly independent now, and she is likely to be less so in the future unless, paradoxically, she becomes part of a larger union.

Cypriote labour relations would not have been so happy, were it not for the political stalemate, which has induced greater cooperation within the communal groups. Since devaluation of the Cyprus pound, in line with the British pound, in the autumn of 1967, prices have risen and the price control law has not been efficiently applied. With the relaxation of communal tensions, economic considerations have come to the fore, and dissatisfaction has led to strikes in the summer of 1968. There exists a strong Communist Party, AKEL, which is not satisfied with the direction the economy is taking and the Pan-Cyprian Federation of Labour (which embraces over half the trades unions) is affiliated to the Communist-controlled World Federation of Trades Unions. Should the community question be solved, such organisations are ready to create new problems. However, the community question has not been solved.

The Economic Situation of the Cypriote Turks

The contention of many Cypriote Greeks that the withdrawal (or rather expulsion) of the Cypriote Turks from public life has permitted the economy to prosper is not borne out by the figures. Thus, only in the last year of the five-year plan did the growth rate (7 per cent) approach what it was in the year before the plan began, when Turkish officials were participating in the government. They helped to prepare the plan, and saw it through its first two years. It is true that they blocked income tax legislation (for reasons other than economic) but, as we have seen, income tax has played a small part in Cypriote prosperity. The Turks do not lay claim to the same type of commercial acumen as the Greeks, nor do many of them wish to emulate it.[1] Some of the Turks are merchants, and Turkish merchants were formerly much more prominent in the island's trade, but the average Turk would rather enter some branch of the public service. In Turkey they may not have created a very prosperous society as yet, but they are more than capable of feeding themselves, developing the institutions of a modern state, and dispensing a reasonable measure of social justice.

---

[1] According to a survey made in Turkey in 1959, only 2.4 per cent of lycée pupils chose business and commerce as the vocation for which they had the greatest respect.

The circumstances under which the Turkish enclaves came into being will be described in a later chapter. Suffice it to begin by saying that the Turks would have been quite capable of raising their parlous living standards were it not for the four-year Greek ban on the importation of road-mending and building materials. Recently, the Greeks have permitted the importation by the Turks of materials to be used under UNFICYP supervision for mending stretches of road which the Greeks also use, have cooperated in mending the slip-way of the Kanlıköy dam,[1] which was on the point of flooding a large area, and allowed modernisation of the slaughter-house at Orta Köy, which was a menace to health. All this was done through the mediation of UNFICYP. For the rest, electrical equipment, tape-recorders, nails, and shoe-laces were forbidden to the Turks, and in some cases even straw, which the Turks used in biblical fashion for making bricks. Indeed, the reason why tents have been used for so long in the Kokkina enclave is that there is little clay in it to make such bricks, and no sticks to support them.

However, the restrictions did not stop there. There was only one entrance, the Famagusta Gate, through which Turks might come into the main enclave, and they were searched by Greek police before they could go in. An especially frequent Turkish complaint was that the police forced them to lay out perishable goods on the dirty road, and a great deal of ill-feeling was created by the searching of women. The searching was done by female police, though the Turks allege that male police sometimes 'supervised' the proceedings. The difficulty here is that, once the principle of search is accepted, it is not reasonable to exclude the searching of women. The Greeks have employed them too often for carrying arms (used in EOKA killings) not to suspect that the Turks may be doing the same. Two kinds of fertiliser are also forbidden to the Turks, on the reasonable grounds that they might use them to manufacture bombs in EOKA fashion. Sulphur, necessary for dusting vines, has been forbidden on occasion for the same reason. Turks from outlying areas who come to Nicosia for medical treatment had to report to Greek doctors before they could be treated by their own, so that it could be ascertained whether or not they had injuries incurred in fighting with the Greek forces. Other restrictions were imposed on equally plausible grounds. The Turks of Nicosia were not permitted to bring in more than two gallons of petrol at a time, in case they should add it to their military stores. They might not have electric fittings because they had not paid for their electricity for four years, and would not allow officials of the Ministry of Communications and Works to inspect the numerous new connexions they had

[1] The work was finished in February 1968.

installed.[1] Water is also unpaid for in the Nicosia enclave, and on 6 March 1967 the *Cyprus Bulletin* reported that the Turks now owed at least £379,105 for electricity and water together. Dr Küçük admitted only to £280,000 being unpaid, but even the Greek figure is less than one year's (unpaid) subsidy to the Turkish Communal Chamber, not to mention the unpaid salaries of Turkish officials and the unpaid education grant, which has been hypothetically assessed at £2 million a year.

A great deal of resentment is felt when the water supply is cut off, especially by the Turks of Larnaca. It was the benevolent eighteenth-century Turkish governor, Bekir Pasha, who was responsible for providing Larnaca with its water-supply. Again, vehicles have to be licensed in order to pass through the check-points, but many in the enclaves have been unlicensed since January 1964. No spare parts have been allowed for either motor-cars or tractors unless ministry officials were allowed to inspect them, and no new vehicles either. The accumulation of such restrictions was clearly intended to render the Turkish enclaves unviable. As U Thant wrote in the Report of 13 June 1967 : 'The restrictions on the movement of persons and goods make it practically impossible for the Turkish Cypriots to share in the general prosperity prevailing outside their areas'.

In their enclaves, the Turks have done what they could with the materials available to them. For instance, a new Göçmen Köyü (Refugee Village) has been built north of Nicosia, and in Ktima particularly, where the Turks have a quarry, the author was struck with how much effort they were making to house their people. The results are scarcely palatial, but the new accommodation is a lot better than the tents which had to be used before. In one way at least the troubles were a blessing, for the Turkish professional class has been brought into much closer contact with the poorer members of the community, and is doing much more for them than previously. However, the families in fly-infested, waterless Hamit Köy (Hajji Mandres) live up to ten in a single room, looking across at good houses in the suburb of Omorphita from which they were driven to the number of 5,000 in December 1963. The same conditions, or worse, are to be found around the Alfa shoe factory at the Paphos Gate, and in the other major enclaves. Many of the refugees manage to keep up reasonable standards of cleanliness under the most adverse conditions, but their numbers are increasing and, with as many as three generations in a single room, their problems are as urgent as ever. The trouble is that publicising the conditions of refugees can make it appear that such conditions are natural to

[1] Inspection has now been permitted.

them.[1] In the spring of 1967 morale in most of the Turkish enclaves struck one as fairly good. An exception was Famagusta, but even there the Turkish population lines the walls of the old city to cheer the arrival of replacements for the military contingent from Turkey.

It is not only the refugees who are in a bad case. Some Turks have jobs in the enclaves, others, especially in Limassol, at the British bases. A few more are employed in the Greek public utilities, in the banks, or by the foreign missions. However, there has been little diminution in the number (56,000) of those who were dependent upon Red Crescent relief in September 1964. The number included 7,500 relations of persons who had been killed or 'disappeared' and 23,500 out of work, together with the refugees, who overlapped with the two former groups. No compensation has been paid to the Cypriote Turkish refugees, although Law no. 2 of 1968 specifically provides for the compensation of Christians who suffered losses during the troubles. At Skylloura, Turkish houses damaged by the Greeks have been repaired by the Greeks as a gesture, but the refugees have not thought it safe to return. Further, Turkish farmers have received no aid under the agricultural and conservation laws. Four thousand Turks in the public services have received no government salaries since the troubles began. The loss to them (including unpaid pension money) is estimated by U Thant at about £2 million a year. Old-age and widows' pensions are paid by the Ministry of Labour, provided they became due before December 1963, but of 28,000 Turks eligible for pensions of all kinds only 6,000 receive them, because Greek-Cypriote government and postal officials insist on being allowed to visit their places of residence before releasing the money, and the enclaves are closed to them. Even those who receive their pensions now are allowed no arrears. *Evkaf* monies are not paid over, nor is the £480,000 annual grant for the Turkish Communal Chamber. Turkish-Cypriote officials now receive salaries from Turkey, but these are by no means as high as previously. Here again there is a psychological difficulty. The officials cannot complain too openly of their present salaries without seeming ungrateful to Turkey. At the same time, they are well aware that Greeks in their jobs are drawing increased salaries. For some the strain has been too great, the most notable being the representative Halit Ali Riza, who is now in Canada. In the last months of 1967, some hundreds of young men left overcrowded Kokkina,[2] not to return for the foreseeable future.

[1] One thinks of the way in which interested parties have made the most progressive of the Arab peoples, rotting in refugee camps, appear as lepers parading self-inflicted sores.
[2] In 1968, there were still 1,200 refugees in Kokkina, which originally supported only 300 people.

The Turks have their own *ad hoc* courts and an economic system as separate as they can make it. The leaders have often been accused by the Greeks of imposing taxes on Greek goods imported into the enclaves, and of pocketing the proceeds. The first half of the charge is true, and the Turks can reply that they get no part of the customs dues at the ports. The second half is at least offset by the fact that prices of food in the Turkish sectors are little different, if at all, from what they are in the Greek. However, the Greeks have lent colour to their allegations by stating that the fighter leader, Kemal Çoşkun, was arrested for gross embezzlement on his return to Turkey from Cyprus.[1] Certainly, there was in 1967 a flourishing black market for restricted goods in the Nicosia enclave. No taxes are paid by the Turks to the Greek-Cypriote government for roads or anything else, but they are dependent upon it to some extent for permits, which the Greeks are slow to grant. For instance, UNFICYP have complained of the procrastination of the Ministry of Communications and Works in dealing with permits for the payment of rent to the Turks for property taken over by UNFICYP. The certainty that they will be compensated tardily, if at all, for such occupation of their property is a factor in occasional Turkish resistance to UNFICYP. One of the biggest obstacles to the Cypriote Turks ever accepting Greek terms is the thought that they will then be at the mercy of Greek bureaucrats. Not that Greek-Cypriote bureaucrats are inefficient. In fact, they compare rather well with those in Turkey. It is just that the very worst British experience can hardly have prepared the reader to appreciate how many 'difficulties' can be created by an unsympathetic Near Eastern official in dealing with the simplest form.

U.N. officials in Cyprus do their best to integrate the Turkish-Cypriote economy with the Greek, but they are up against considerable obstacles. Some Turkish factories are cut off in Greek areas, while the products of those which are not, such as macaroni and cigarettes, are not readily accepted for sale by Greek shop-keepers. Until March 1968 the Turks could not bring in spare parts or raw materials for their factories, and their lime-kiln at Ambelikou was too dangerous to approach. At the same time, it is not generally realised how much Armenian and Greek property there is in the main Turkish enclave. It includes a lime-kiln, a quarry, a flour mill, and a textile plant, besides 231 Armenian and 169 Greek houses in Nicosia alone, together with 100 shops and businesses owned outright, and sixty-nine rented. The loss to the owners in merchandise

---

[1] The Turks deny this. The truth about the matter will no doubt emerge in time.

and rents is now reckoned at over £1 million. Again, while there is a great deal of Turkish land in Greek-controlled areas, there is also some Greek land controlled by the Turks. Despite token attempts by the Greek authorities to resettle Turkish villagers, and the fact that Turks are sometimes allowed to collect their fruit and harvest their crops, it is very unlikely that the Greeks now farming most of the vacated land will ever be willing to give it up. Attempts have been made by UNFICYP to have property in 'sensitive areas' valued, but the Greek-Cypriotes will not send officials to do the valuation on the grounds that it is too dangerous, nor will they do it under the supervision of UNFICYP or allow it to be done by UNFICYP alone. In areas where economic integration officially exists, petty frictions continue. A representative example was Limassol in March 1967. A dispute over payment for public services led to confiscation of a Turkish refuse lorry and the Turks dumping their rubbish on the streets before they got it back, under terms.

The economic situation of the Turks remained basically un-changed for four years after the troubles, and foreign aid and loans for Cyprus still benefit them hardly at all. They rely upon aid from Turkey[1] and the relatively unlucrative tourism of the sympathetic and curious. Now that the restrictions have been eased, they can become more prosperous, but the gap in living standards between the Greek majority and the Turkish minority shows few signs of narrowing. If Cyprus alone is considered, the independent economic position of the Cypriote Turks must slowly be eroded.

Health and Education

The crude death rate in Cyprus is only 5.8 per thousand, as against a crude birth rate of 24.4 per thousand, while infantile mortality stands at 26.7 per thousand. There is reason to believe that the birth rate has gone up since these figures were compiled in 1965, owing to the drop in emigration. A Cypriote man's ex-pectation of life is sixty-four years, and a Cypriote woman's sixty-eight. These figures do not just reflect the influence of a good climate and medical service. The most important single health mea-sure in the history of Cyprus was the wiping out of malaria during the British period. One hundred and ten full-time doctors are em-ployed by the Government Health Service, and there are over three hundred in private practice; so that there is one doctor for every 1,300 people. Nicosia boasts a modern General Hospital (scene of an evocative semi-autobiographical novel set in the Emergency

---

[1] According to Tom Driberg (in *The Times*, 27 February 1968), Ankara's subsidy now amounts to £6.2 million a year.

period),[1] and there are hospitals in all the principal towns, twenty-one rural hospitals and health centres, a mental hospital, a leper farm, and a sanatorium in the Troödos Mountains.

The Turkish villages rely on Turkish doctors who volunteer to serve in them. There are hospital facilities in the Turkish quarters of the principal towns, including the Red Crescent hospital in Nicosia, which has been operating since 1964.

The illiteracy rate in Cyprus stands at 18 per cent, being largely confined to old people, women in particular. Most infant schools are private, fee-paying concerns, and lack of qualified teachers makes it impossible to set up a governmental system as yet. However, elementary education is free, co-educational, and compulsory for children between the ages of six and twelve, fourteen being the age limit if the course has not been completed. Secondary and technical education is intended for the thirteen to eighteen age-group. It is not free, but fees are low, and 70 per cent of the pupils leaving elementary school are able to take advantage of it, as compared with some 30 per cent before independence. On the one hand, there are the gymnasia, which arrange their education in two stages, the second being more specialised; on the other, there are the technical and vocational schools, the first course in which is cultural. There is an agricultural gymnasium at Morphou for those whose families own land, and attached to it is a vocational agricultural school. In the academic year 1966/7, there were 555 Christian elementary schools, with 2,200 teachers and 72,750 pupils, and also sixty-four secondary schools and ten technical ones (including the agricultural gymnasium), with 1,420 teachers and 33,660 students. The secondary schools include eleven foreign-run missionary schools with 3,390 pupils of both sexes. Education has never been inter-communal, largely because of religious, linguistic, and cultural differences, but before the troubles a reform school, a school for the blind, and another for the deaf were run on an inter-communal basis. Eighteen 'intercommunal' schools are listed by the Greeks, but the Turkish pupils at Greek schools are very few and far between. The Roman Catholics of the Latin rite run five of the missionary schools, and the Maronites, who are distinguished from them for statistical purposes, have a kindergarten, and five elementary schools aided by the government. The Armenians have a kindergarten, four elementary schools, and an educational institute founded by the Melkonian brothers in 1915 for children orphaned in the massacres of that year. These also are aided by the government.

The emphasis of Greek-Cypriote education is very much on the

---

[1] Peter Paris, *The Impartial Knife: a doctor in Cyprus* (London: Jenners, 1961).

Greek past, and it is deliberately tied in with that of mainland Greece. This gives it much greater literary and spiritual resources than if it were solely concerned with Cypriote culture (and the same holds true of the Turkish-Cypriote emphasis on the Turkish connexion). In 1966 the government of Greece decided to contribute £110,000 to cover half the expenses of pupils at secondary schools up to the age of fifteen. Both the Greek and Turkish educational systems lay admirable stress on corporate values, and the expression of these values inevitably entails a demand by the community concerned for control over its destiny. Where such demands conflict fundamentally, domination of one by the other or (preferably) separation is the only logical outcome.

About 13 per cent of the Cyprus budget is spent on education, and the proportion will probably rise when the planned higher technical institute is established. Also, schoolteachers are becoming increasingly restive over low pay, and in the autumn of 1967 they staged a sixteen-day strike. As in certain other countries, low pay tends to make teaching into a dead-end job, attracting a high proportion of failures. Teachers are trained in two colleges, one Greek, the other Turkish. Included among the institutions offering post-secondary education are the Forestry College, the Agricultural Research Institute, the School of Nursing, the Seminary, a private centre for higher studies, and six government institutes for the teaching of foreign languages. These last are especially popular, and were attended in 1964–5 by over 4,000 students. To some extent they fulfil the function of polytechnics, for their fees are low and they also offer technical evening classes and courses in commerce and banking. English and French are taught as part of hotel-training courses.

At present there is no university, though the island could certainly support one, and other islands with small populations (e.g. Malta, Tasmania, Newfoundland) already have them. Meanwhile, Cypriote students are sent abroad for higher education. Figures released in March 1967 show that there were 2,500 in Greece, 1,000 in Great Britain (excluding those with British passports),[1] thirty in France, eighteen in Italy, fourteen in Israel, eleven in the Lebanon, eight in Yugoslavia, eight in Bulgaria, six in the U.S.A., and a few more in countries like Romania and Czechoslovakia. At about the same time it was announced by Mr Solomides that 1,005 further students had been selected for higher studies or specialised training abroad. Dr Spyridakis regards a university as necessary in Cyprus, and thinks that it should begin with a school of agriculture. Part of

[1] On 24 May 1968, Mr C. Ashiotis, the Cyprus High Commissioner in London, estimated the total number of Cypriote students in Great Britain at nearly 2,000.

the deficiency may be supplied as part of the plan of President Makarios for setting up a 'World Peace Centre', including a 'World Academy of Art and Science', on two hundred acres of land he has bought for the purpose near the appropriately-named abbey of Bellapaïs. The centre would be used for international congresses of scientists, artists, and scholars, and would be operated under international trusteeship. The existence in Cyprus of such a centre would contribute towards the raising of educational standards, and there is no doubt that the President is seriously intent on the project. He is ready to contribute $200,000 towards the estimated $1 million which the building would cost, and has persuaded Professor Buckminster Fuller, the American specialist in the design of geodesic 'super-domes', to design the building. However, logic demands that the project should wait until peace is established in Cyprus itself.

In March 1967, an impassioned debate was taking place in Cyprus over future plans in the educational field. At a public meeting the Minister of Labour, Mr Tassos Papadopoulos, expressed concern because, of the 2,500 or so that graduate yearly from the gymnasia, about a thousand fail to find employment. (Of the remaining 1,500, about a thousand go abroad for further education, and some four hundred find clerical jobs at home.) On the other hand, the 500 graduates turned out yearly by the technical schools are readily absorbed into the economy. The solution, as he saw it, was to provide more technical education in the gymnasia. In reply, the Minister of Education, Dr Spyridakis, denied that more than 600 gymnasium graduates were unemployed. Accuracy is probably more on the side of Mr Papadopoulos, whose subordinates carry out an efficient manpower survey every three months. There is no doubt that Cyprus is facing a problem which is facing many other countries, whether developing or not, and it is to the credit of the régime that the problem can be aired between Ministers in front of an audience. Such a public confrontation illustrates also the familiarity and approachableness of politicians in a country with a small population. Dr Spyridakis stresses the cultural side of education, and is concerned lest Cypriote schools should get out of step with those in mainland Greece; whereas Mr Papadopoulos sees no reason why students should not be rounded culturally and also technically competent. The truth is that many students who seem to gain very little from arts courses are capable of becoming adequate technicians, whereas the author's experience in other countries of courses for the cultural education of technical students is that they are better than nothing, but not much. Still, workers with some general education are required in many occupations. On balance, it seemed in early 1967 that the apologists for technical training were winning the argument, for the influential Mr Solomides publicly stated that the rate of Cypriote economic progress might be dangerously retarded unless the educational system were oriented towards it. The strong emphasis of the new military régime in Greece on the cultural aspects of education has given pause to those who might otherwise have made all Cypriote education much more technically-oriented, but a Higher Institute of Technology is to be established in September 1968, financed by the Cyprus government, the U.N. Special Fund, and UNESCO. It will be run by the Ministry of Labour, not the Ministry of Education.

We should not forget the traditional and growing part played by athletics in the education of Cypriote children and in the furtherance of *de facto Enosis*. Cyprus takes part in contests on an equal footing with Crete and the provinces of mainland Greece.

On the Turkish side, a good deal is done to educate the children, in view of the inadequate resources of the Turkish-Cypriote community; and school-books are sent over from Turkey. According to figures supplied by Dr Küçük's advisers in May 1968, there are 154 Turkish-Cypriote elementary schools, with 598 teachers and 17,814 pupils, and twenty-one secondary schools, with 357 teachers and 6,582 pupils. The two secondary schools which the author has seen seemed well-run, though with fewer facilities than the Greek ones. One thousand two hundred of the secondary-school graduates are external students of the Turkish universities, and Dr Küçük takes a personal interest in the standards attained. However, in January 1967 the Greeks charged that sixty Turkish-Cypriote students who applied for full-time places in Turkish universities had been refused admittance on Dr Küçük's advice. His anxiety not to lose available talent would be understandable, but the Greeks also charge (and the Turks deny) that fifty other students, the sons of influential Cypriote Turks, were nevertheless allowed to go abroad for their studies when the Turkish army contingent was next rotated.

For the better-educated adults in the Turkish quarter of Nicosia lectures and discussion groups are quite frequently arranged, and certain technical courses (e.g. for waiters) as well. Foreigners are taking courses in Turkish as a second language, thus providing an oblique comment on the Greek refusal to regard Turkish as the official second language, as provided under the constitution. Football and the traditional Turkish sport of wrestling are popular in the Turkish community as a whole. Still it is a pity that the opportunity has not been seized to make use of enforced leisure by starting an island-wide programme of adult education at all levels. At the time of writing, the Turks were particularly incensed over the fact

that the projected Higher Institute of Technology will not benefit
their community.

The Mass Media

Cyprus has six Greek-language daily newspapers : *Phileleftheros*
(The Liberal) and *Eleftheria* (Freedom),[1] which are sympathetic to
the government, *Patris* (Fatherland), which expresses the idea of
those close to General Grivas, *Haravghi* (Dawn), the organ of
AKEL, *Agon* (Struggle) and *Makhi* (Combat), the editor of which,
Nicos Sampson, appears to be chiefly motivated by a poisonous
hatred of the British. (Sometimes, this hatred overbalances rather
amusingly into wish-fulfilment, as when *Makhi* reports that there
are twenty-one beautiful British spies frequenting the cafés of
Limassol.) In addition, there are two Greek-language evening papers,
Niki (Victory) and the left-wing *Teleftea Ora* (Final Hour). There
are seventeen Greek weeklies, of which the most noteworthy are
Alithia (Sincerity) and *Kypros* (Cyprus), which express government
views, and Dr Dervis's *Ethniki* (National), which is fiercely Enotist
at all costs, and sympathetic to Grivas. Besides these, there are two
Greek fortnightlies, fourteen monthlies, four bi-monthlies, two
quarterlies, and four annuals, including *Stasinos*, published by the
Paedagogical Academy, and *Kypriakai Spoudai*, published by the
Society of Cypriote Studies. Of course, most of these are specialist
magazines.

The two Turkish-language dailies are *Halkın Sesi* (Voice of the
People), which is owned by Dr Küçük, and *Bozkurt* (Grey Wolf),
which represents the less moderate Turks. There are, besides, a
Turkish evening paper, *Akın* (Foray), and a weekly, *Zafer* (Success),
together with a few specialist and local publications, like *Tuncer*
(Man of Bronze), for schoolchildren, and *Bucak* (Corner), published
in Ktima.

A report on 'World Press Freedom' in 1966 placed the Cyprus
press in the second of seven categories, 'Free with Moderate
Controls', along with the British! In early 1967 a law was passed
punishing with three years imprisonment any editor found guilty
of defaming the President. However, the English-language newspaper, the *Cyprus Mail*, bears abundant testimony to the indulgence
shown to the press in Cyprus, for it opposes *Enosis* and consistently
pumps out Zionist propaganda, in implied opposition to the official
policy of President Makarios and the government of Greece. The
contents of the *Cyprus Mail* are to a large extent syndicated, and

---

[1] Before 1932, when daily papers were permanently introduced, this one
was a bi-weekly, the others being weeklies. A short-lived daily had appeared
in 1923–24.

it is published every day of the week, including Monday, when all but nine of the Greek-Cypriote weeklies replace the dailies.

There is another English-language daily, published by the Cypriote Turks and called the *Special News Bulletin*. It began publication as a broadsheet at the very beginning of the troubles, on 21 December 1963 (a fact which indicates contingency planning) and, after appearing intermittently until 11 January 1964, it became a regular daily. It has been far more successful in influencing foreign opinion than its counterpart, the *Cyprus Bulletin,* which is put out by the Greek-Cypriote Public Information Office. To begin with, the *Special News Bulletin* comes out every day (sometimes twice a day during the troubles of 1964), whereas the *Cyprus Bulletin* comes out weekly, with gaps of up to three weeks for holidays, etc. The Turkish publication has shown a thorough grasp of the essentials of propaganda, winning the battle of specifics by repeating chapter and verse (including, above all, times and dates) for Greek misdeeds and belligerent statements. The *Cyprus Bulletin* provides too much information which has to be taken on trust because not enough detail is given for the observer to check it, and when it *does* give dates it is sometimes careless. For instance, it refers to a statement by Gladstone as made in 1919, when he died in 1898! The repetition of Third-World incantation in the *Cyprus Bulletin* is no substitute for the biting and sarcastic articles of the *Special News Bulletin,* written in racy, idiomatic English, and well calculated to get under the skins of the Greeks and appeal to their detractors. While the Greeks ignore the Turkish-language publications as beneath their notice, the Turks destructively analyse the Greek press for the benefit of their readers. The advantage is not all one way. Both publications would benefit a great deal from more frequent reference to the Oxford Dictionary for improvement of their spelling (and the same is true of the *Cyprus Mail*). Turkish over-use of words like 'genocide' and 'cannibalistic' in describing Greek actions has been counter-productive in that it has struck foreign readers as too intemperate to carry conviction. Also, the economic information provided by the *Cyprus Bulletin* is far superior. However, a case cannot depend upon economic information alone. It demands the human element. Credit for the Turkish success in this field should go to the secret editor and perhaps in part to Mr Necati Sağer, the Cypriote-Turkish Information Officer, who was acting-Director of the Cyprus Public Information Office at the time when the troubles began. However, the Greek-Cypriote Public Information Office makes up for much of the lost ground by its efficient use of greater resources in providing V.I.P. treatment for visiting foreigners.

Where the Greeks score fairly heavily is in the publication of their

English-language bi-monthly, *Cyprus Today*. This is produced at the Paedagogical Academy, and has articles of varying merit, many of them excellent, on various aspects of culture, economics, and politics in Cyprus. Here again the political articles are the weakest, and some of the devices are transparent, like one picture intended to convey the impression of widespread reaction in English-language newspapers to the Turkish bombing attacks of August 1964. The picture consisted entirely of cuttings from the *Cyprus Bulletin*, arranged in an artistic pattern. The translations in *Cyprus Today* of Greek articles on Cypriote history and archaeology are much more valuable, and there is no doubt that the magazine appeals to a small but influential readership.

Mention should also be made of the weekly *Blue Beret*, published, as its name implies, for U.N. troops.

The Cyprus Broadcasting Corporation provides unremarkable television and wireless programmes, the most interesting being those in which the Cypriote people themselves take part. The standard of the Turkish spoken by its announcers in that language is notoriously poor, and the Turks have more than made up for the deficiency by setting up no fewer than four wireless stations of their own : *Bayrak* (Flag), *Canbolat* (the name of a Turkish leader at the Conquest of Cyprus), *Doğan* (Falcon), and the Voice of Cyprus. These not only broadcast in Turkish, English, and Greek, but even transmit Greek songs. They are a constant thorn in the flesh of the Greek-Cypriote government.

By 1965 there were 135 winter cinemas in Cyprus, with 80,000 seats, and 145 open-air cinemas, with 90,000 seats, but now that television has come to the island, the popularity of the cinema is no longer growing. There is a big new theatre of classical type in Nicosia, which cost £220,000 and was opened in March 1967 by the President, who takes a special interest in the drama.

The Significance of the History of Cyprus

Political history is the record of the struggles of human groups for control of the available resources. In these struggles, ethnic differences, however defined, play a fundamental part. Scientists are perhaps readier than historians to recognise this truth.

Now, and throughout most of its history, Cyprus has been the scene of friction or outright conflict between ethnic groups. Of course, the struggle is not always clear-cut. Some individuals and organisations, either mistakenly or for their own advantage, betray the interests of their own people, while others, who appear to do so, may be striving for reconciliation with temporarily inimical but similar peoples, or seeking a settlement which involves separation with the minimum of bloodshed from more dissimilar peoples. In addition, there is the factor of interbreeding, but the offspring of such interbreeding, faced with the prospect of a rootless, proletarianised existence, tend to identify themselves with one or other of the parental groups. Since ethnic differences express themselves culturally, such intermarriage on a large scale will, for better or worse, modify the group which accepts such offspring. However, ethnic mixture does not lead to a cessation of conflict—rather the reverse, because the majority on either side resent the breakdown of their culture.

In a broader perspective, Cyprus is a scene of that continual conflict between East and West, which is always to be reinterpreted, but never to be ignored. Periods of relative peace, imposed by the strongest sea-power in the area, alternate with periods of relative independence, when diverse ethnic groups struggle for control. But the very smallness of Cyprus, which makes it impossible for the island to stand alone, has been a factor making for continuity. Since possession of Cyprus follows inevitably from wider power in the area, few invaders have expended a disproportionate amount of energy in establishing colonies or extirpating the natives. The island has seldom been a goal, but rather a base or a stepping-stone. Just as the frequent introduction of foreigners has never been on such a scale as fundamentally to alter the Cypriote physique of the Early Bronze Age, so the language and culture of the native majority have remained Greek since the end of the second millennium B.C.

Cyprus is an island of survivals. Sometimes they are survivals of what is generally eastern Mediterranean. Thus, two ox-drawn ploughs of the Early Bronze Age, discovered at Vounous, show a type of cultivation still in use; Byzantine representations of the Harrowing of Hell are reminiscent of a descent of Heracles into Hades; and the blue glimmer of a light wick in a coloured glass of olive-oil powerfully evokes the ancient world. Other survivals are more specifically Cypriote. Utensils such as coarsely-serrate sickles, and the big red pots, sometimes with rope-like strip decoration, are quite possibly a legacy from neolithic times. Votive clay figures, made with the 'mud-pie' technique of the Bronze Age, are still produced in Cyprus, and the tradition stretches back far beyond the extraordinary terra-cottas of Ayia Irini. The thin, tile-shaped mud bricks of classical Vouni are almost the same as the modern ones, and differ from those of Greece and the Aegean. Many other examples of cultural continuity will be adduced in the following pages. In matters of culture, as in matters of genetics, isolation is an important factor.

Chapter 2

Early History to the Time of Alexander

The New Stone Age

ARCHAEOLOGY IS AN EXTENSION of history and, as such, has many aspects which are relevant to modern politics. These aspects it is intended to emphasise; but it is found equally necessary to provide information which gives an idea of what life was like for those who lived at the relevant period. Concern only with political implications is apt to distort one's view of history.

No palaeolithic or mesolithic remains have as yet been discovered in Cyprus, and the island is largely lacking in flint. However, Carbon 14 tests carried out in 1955 have indicated that settlements such as those found by the Swedish archaeologist Gjerstad at Petra tou Limniti and by the Cypriote archaeologist Dikaios at Khirokitia were in existence by 5800 B.C. Petra tou Limniti is a little island off the north-west coast, while the bigger settlement of Khirokitia is situated on a small hill within a bend of the Maroni river, nearly five miles from the south coast. The inhabitants dwelt in large, round huts (*tholoi*), with domes of mud-brick or pisé on lower parts of rubble masonry set in mud. The dead were buried inside the dwellings, no doubt to placate them, while heavy stones were placed over them, no doubt to prevent them from haunting the living. Somewhat similar dwellings have been found for the preceding millennium at Jericho and at Jarmo on the Upper Tigris, but the neolithic culture of Cyprus is very much *sui generis,* as non-Greeks hostile to *Enosis* are especially quick to point out.

The neolithic inhabitants of Cyprus were extremely brachycephalic, in contrast to the dolichocephalic populations of the eastern Mediterranean littoral, but account must be taken of inbreeding, owing to isolation, as a standardising factor, and there is the possibility of deliberate cranial deformation in childhood. In stature they were short, and their average life-span, on the skeletal evidence, was some thirty-five years for males, thirty-four for females. It has recently been claimed that these people came from the Balkans, where there is another centre of brachycephaly, and arrived in Cyprus via coastal Anatolia—in other words that they

74

were forerunners of the Greeks—but the evidence is not conclusive as yet.

At first the settlers had only stone and bone tools, but the spread of those techniques which characterise the neolithic period made it possible to grind and polish the igneous rocks which are washed down the water-courses of the Troödos. Better tools, sometimes involving the use of imported Anatolian or north Syrian obsidian, facilitated the working of wood for simple agricultural implements. The provenance of the obsidian has not escaped the attention of Turkish commentators, for although the Turks did not establish themselves in Anatolia until the eleventh century A.D., they regard themselves as heirs to the preceding cultures in that peninsula—and with some justice, at least where the plateau is concerned.

Neolithic needles and spindle-whorls for weaving have been found in Cyprus, and corn, wild or otherwise, was ground in querns. It is even thought that the olive dates from this period. There were flint arrow and axe-heads in abundance, and some excellent stone bowls, smoothly finished and with lips for pouring, may be seen in the Nicosia Museum. Wood and leather containers must also have existed. Sheep, goats, and pigs were domesticated, as also the cat, and for hunting there were the boar, fallow deer, and moufflon, which last still survives in the island.

A continuation of the first neolithic stage has been discovered at Troulli near Kyrenia, and has been dated about 5250 to 4950 B.C., but it does little to fill the yawning gap between the end of the sixth millennium and the second stage of the Cypriote neolithic (3500–3000 B.C.), represented by finds on the lowest level at Kalavassos, near Khirokitia, and at Sotira, north of Episkopi. The gap is so large that Dr Vassos Karageorghis, Director of the Cyprus Department of Antiquities, is of opinion that further Carbon 14 tests should be carried out to test the accuracy of the method. It is difficult to believe that the island lay uninhabited for nearly a millennium and a half.

At Kalavassos the earliest dwellings are partly sunken into the ground, with upper parts of wattle and daub, unlike the later ones, which are free-standing, as at Sotira. The dead are buried outside, and the red pottery often has wavy parallel lines made as if with a comb. Such features are reminiscent of the Beersheba culture in Palestine. However, it seems there was little outside influence during the three and a half millennia assigned to the neolithic in Cyprus.

The neolithic settlements have their largest concentration on the sea-plain to the south and south-east of the Troödos. Very few are to be found in the Mesaoria, and those only near the water-supplies. It is almost certain that the Mesaoria was at that time choked with undergrowth, for the geographer Strabo, writing in Roman times, quotes Eratosthenes (276-194 B.C.) as stating that this was once so.

The Copper and Bronze Ages

For the next stage in human development Cyprus was exceedingly well placed, since she possessed the largest copper deposits in the Levant, and indeed either gave her name to that metal or was named after it.[1] The main copper mining areas were in the north-east foothills of the Troödos and near Morphou bay. The island also had plentiful supplies of timber for ship-building and export. By the end of the fourth millennium occasional copper tools make their appearance, but it is not until about 2300 B.C. that Cyprus can be said to have entered the Bronze Age. The intermediate period, from about 300 B.C., is best described as chalcolithic, for at that time the copper contained no more than 2 or 3 per cent of tin. The island now enters the history of the Near East, and its geographical position becomes of the greatest importance.

The early Cypriote chalcolithic is represented in the second level at Kalavassos and at Erimi, on the low peninsula in the far south a highly strategic area which was later to contain the ancient city of Curium, the medieval stronghold at Kolossi, and a modern British sovereign base. Erimi, incidentally, has been assigned to the chalcolithic on the strength of a single copper chisel. The red pottery, combed or plain, of the preceding period is gradually displaced by a painted red-on-white type, which is clearly under Anatolian influence. Female fertility figurines also make their appearance, somewhat similar to those found in Cilicia. Erimi was abandoned about 2500 B.C., but some of its traditions were perpetuated in the second chalcolithic stage at Ambelikou, near Xeros in the north-west, and in the bottom level at Philia-Drakos in the Morphou plain. Dolichocephalic newcomers from Syria seem to have assimilated the former inhabitants to some extent, but established themselves above all in the eastern areas of the island, where harbour facilities have always been better. The neolithic sites were mostly left deserted, and new settlements, characterised by rectangular, as opposed to circular, buildings, were founded on the white limestone and gypsum which surrounds the red plutonic rock of the southern mountain mass. For the first time a significant number of settlements were established in the Mesaoria and in the Kyrenia passes—then, as now, the key to domination of Cyprus by land. The power, or at least the influence, of Sargon of Akkad (c. 2360–2305) may also have extended

---

[1] Cyprus may take its name from the henna-plant, for which the Hebrew word was *kopher*, rendered as *kýpros* in the *Septuagint*.

as far as Cyprus. If so, we have a very early case of Semitic interest in the island.

The first stage of the Early Bronze Age is represented by finds at Vassilia, near Lapethos, and on the second level at Philia-Drakos. It was introduced in about 2300 by Anatolian settlers with their typical beak-spouted pots of red polished ware. The second and third stages are represented in the rock-cut tombs at Vounous, southwest of Buffavento. During the second stage (*c.* 2200–2100) native culture reasserted itself when the old gourd-shaped pottery displaced the imported flat-base type.[1] The third stage coincides with the arrival of more Armenoid settlers from Anatolia, and is characterised by chamber-type tombs and exuberant pottery, including bull-masked fertility figures holding snakes, symbols of the earth-power, and kneeling figures with their arms outstretched or crossed upon their breasts.

The turn of the second millennium ushers in the Middle Bronze Age at Kalopsidha, on the Famagusta plain, and at Karmi, near Kyrenia. The bronze had come to consist of about 90 per cent copper, 10 per cent tin, and was thus a much harder metal. The copper was now exported in large hide-shaped blocks weighing some eleven stone each. Silver also became commoner, and imports included blue glazed beads, probably from Egypt. The fine red polished ware of the preceding period gives way to a white-painted ware, though a black-on-red type is characteristic of eastern Cyprus. Cypriote pottery of the Middle Bronze Age has been found in Egypt, Syria, and Cilicia. Sailing ships traded frequently with these places, while on the island domesticated draught animals and wheeled carts had become common. Cyprus seems to be mentioned in Babylonian tablets of Hammurabi's time (eighteenth century B.C.).

Contemporary Hyksos irruptions into Egypt created a power vacuum in the eastern Mediterranean which permitted some Minoan influence to grow in Cyprus. This Cretan trade is the first proven case of influence on Cyprus from the West, but it does not seem to have involved any colonisation. It continued into the seventeenth century, when the Minoan civilisation in its turn began to retreat amid the upheavals of the era. It is at this time that the Hittites seem to have established themselves at Nitovikla in the Carpass peninsula, where the massive walls recall the Hittite capital at Hattushash (Boğazköy). Tombs nearby are also in all probability Hittite. These circumstances are particularly interesting for, since Atatürk's time, the Turks have identified themselves with the central Anatolian Hittites, and the Carpass peninsula is always included in

---

[1] Today, at Kornos and Phini, the gourd-shaped type is still made, at Varosha the flat-base type.

their plans for the partition or federation of Cyprus. Another fortress, at Krini on the south side of the Kyrenia range, may well have been built as a defence against the Hittites.

By the beginning of the Late Bronze Age, about 1600 B.C., Cyprus had closer trading connexions with Syria than with Crete, though trade with Mycenaean mainland Greece became important in the late sixteenth and early fifteenth centuries. Meanwhile, the power of Egypt reasserted itself. The Hyksos, who may also have raided Cyprus, were overthrown, and by the reign of Thutmosis III (1501–1447) the island was half-encircled by Egyptian-dominated territory. It is probable that the 'Alashiya' mentioned in a document of this monarch is in fact Cyprus, though whether it was conquered or merely tributary is open to dispute. Other kings of the same line, including the third and fourth Amenhoteps, received letters from Alashiya, mainly relating to copper exports, and it is no surprise to find at Enkomi a copper-smelting house of the fourteenth century B.C. References to Alashiya occur also in Hittite texts found at Hattushash. That Alashiya was Cyprus might be universally assumed, but for puzzling details such as the tribute of elephants' tusks to be sent to Egypt. The elephant was not native to Cyprus, and if Alashiya was only a trading centre for ivory, it may have been for copper also. Still, Enkomi, built at the outflow of the Pedias and Yialias rivers, was the principal Cypriote city during the third period of the Bronze Age, and rich tombs testify to its prosperity. It was an entrepôt of trade for Egypt and the Syrian coast, more particularly the city of Ugarit, east of Cape Andreas and al-Mina on the Orontes. Base-ring and white-slip ware, the latter made in imitation of leather, are typical of the period, though degenerate versions of traditional pottery continue to be produced in quantity. Such items as Asiatic cylindrical seals found in the tombs provide useful evidence of trading connexions. The island's population rose to an estimated 200,000, a figure that was to be halved during the ensuing Iron Age.

A linear script was used in Cyprus from about 1500 B.C., which was either introduced by the Minoans or developed locally under Minoan influence. It is ill-adapted to an Indo-European language like Greek, and may have been used to record the native Cypriote language; but like Minoan Linear A, which it much resembles, it remains as yet undeciphered. Inscriptions in it are found up to the eleventh century B.C., and some almost identical have been discovered at Ugarit. The language of the inscriptions has been claimed by W. Ward as Semitic, but the evidence is not conclusive. In view of the great flood of light thrown on the period by Ventris's decipherment of Linear B, scholars look forward with the keenest interest to the ultimate decipherment and elucidation of these and other linear scripts.

The Arrival of the Greeks

About the year 1400, the Achaean Greeks took and sacked Cnossos, the capital of the Minoan thalassocracy. They had already established themselves at Mycenae and other places on the mainland, and dominated a population of Mediterranean type, on which they imposed their language. From the end of the fifteenth to the end of the thirteenth century the Mycenaean thalassocracy was at its zenith, and Mycenaean traders brought a great deal of pottery to Cyprus, no doubt in return for copper. Indeed, a large proportion of all the Mycenaean pottery known has been discovered in Cyprus, but it was also exported to the Cilician and Syrian littorals, and there is no contemporary Mycenaean influence on the work of Cypriote metal-smiths. So at first the Mycenaeans seem to have been content with trade, like their less aggressive Minoan predecessors. In the second half of the thirteenth century there was a period of diminished commercial activity owing to the troubled conditions of the time (of which mention will be made in connexion with the Phoenicians) but towards the end of the century there was a full-scale Mycenaean invasion of Cyprus, attested by the sudden appearance of many Mycenaean artefacts, including armour, and buildings in fine ashlar masonry. The evidence for this influx is incontrovertible, and more comes to light year by year. Unfortunately, Greek-Cypriote government publications make claims for such colonisation having taken place as early as the year 1500, for which there is no evidence. It might be thought that a back-dating of less than three centuries in the second millennium before Christ was scarcely worth the trouble, but that would be to underrate the importance of political archaeology. The motive for the back-dating is an anxiety to place the coming of the Mycenaeans well before the remotest possibility of Phoenician immigration. The anxiety is, however, not justified. The Mycenaeans and other Achaeans not only preceded the Phoenicians as colonists, they dominated most of the island, which the Phoenicians never succeeded in doing.

The settlement of the Greeks in Cyprus is of the greatest significance; for the ancient Greeks, or Hellenes, were the most remarkable people the world has ever seen. They are the ultimate inspiration for most of what is valuable in the Western tradition. As Francis Galton pointed out in his *Hereditary Genius* (1869) the proportional ability of the Athenians in particular, as shown by the number of outstandingly creative individuals among them between 530 and

430 B.C., places them high above any contemporary human group. And throughout the Greek world such creativeness was associated with vigour of mind and body to an extraordinarily late age. The standard of Hellenic personal beauty is attested not only by the realistic statues of athletes and goddesses, but by many representations of ordinary citizens and their wives. These high physical standards can be attributed to three main factors : preservation of the breeding group, the custom of frequent exercise, and the practice of negative eugenics at birth. Above all, they were distinguished by the quality of their intellect, an intellect no less apparent in their arts than in any of their other activities. As Professor Kitto has admirably put it : 'The greatness of Greek art lies in this, that it completely reconciles two principles which are often opposed : on the one hand control and clarity and fundamental seriousness; on the other, brilliance, imagination and passion.'[1] In a very real sense, every manifestation of the Hellenic genius was a form of art, and was characterised by the same qualities of intellect.

The neighbours of the modern Greeks are not slow to point out that they bear little resemblance, either racially or psychologically, to their ancient predecessors. It is felt with some justice that the notion of 'Eternal Hellas' gives them an unfair cultural advantage. The Hellenes, with their light-coloured hair and their greater stature, were distinct from the slighter, darker people whom they conquered. In other words, they bore more resemblance to present-day northern Europeans than to southern ones. The fact has been obscured, especially since 1945, by assiduous persons who are concerned lest students should draw the obvious conclusion that racial differences among men are as significant as they are in any other species. Moreover, the Hellenes were primarily concerned with human achievement and the enrichment of life, not with a heavenly afterworld or a Communist millennium. They prayed erect before gods who resembled themselves.

But one should add three riders to the foregoing. In the first place, it ought to be remembered that the Mediterranean branch of the European race was responsible for a number of civilisations that preceded the Hellenic, including the Minoan, with all its gaiety and comfort. For some centuries the superiority of the Hellenes lay in their arms rather than their arts, and their vigour was only gradually canalised into civil pursuits. There can be no doubt that they owed a great deal both to the Minoans and to the Pelasgians of Ionia. Indeed they interbred with them before invading Cyprus. The clear beauty of the Mediterranean world had an effect on these warlike northern invaders which may be compared to its effect

[1] H. D. F. Kitto, *The Greeks* (Penguin, rev. edn, 1962), p. 25.

on Goethe during his journey to Italy. It was both a revelation and an inspiration. Secondly, the argument that the modern Cypriotes are not Greeks because they do not resemble the Hellenes does not hold water; for neither do most Greeks of the continent. Thirdly, it is difficult to see what advantage would be gained if the Greeks were to proclaim themselves primarily heirs of the Byzantines rather than the Hellenes. A people's most valuable cultural traditions by no means necessarily derive from those who resemble them.

About the middle of the thirteenth century B.C. an Achaean confederacy, headed by the Mycenaeans, advanced into Asia Minor. Homeric tradition informs us that it was by just such a confederacy that the city of Troy was besieged and burned, but the actual sack of Troy described in the *Odyssey* seems to have taken place at a later date. Homer implies that no Greeks from Cyprus took part in the Trojan War, but in the *Iliad* mention is made of a bronze breast-plate given to Agamemnon by the Cypriote Cinyras of Paphos, a king also sung by Tyrtaeus and Pindar. In the *Odyssey* the goddess Athene speaks of what may well be the mining centre of Tamassus in Cyprus:

So now, going down to my ship and sailing with my companions across the wine-dark sea, towards men speaking strange tongues, I carry shining iron to Temese, in quest of copper.

(I. 182–4)

The cargo of iron is almost certainly an anachronism for the time Homer is describing, not so the copper. To him, writing in the ninth or eighth century, the island is already 'Kypros'.

The evidence of literary legends is not to be despised, because it is so often supported by the findings of archaeology. Thus it is of considerable interest that Agapenor of Tegea, in Arcadia, is said to have been the founder of Old Paphos (Kouklia) after the fall of Troy, and that Telamonian Teucer, of Salamis off Attica, the best of the Achaean archers before Troy, is the person believed by the ancients to have been the founder of Salamis in Cyprus. Salamis, built near the site of Enkomi, and Old Paphos, dominating the south-western coastal strip, were to be particularly important in the history of the island. Other cities too were founded from mainland Greece, and Herodotus, in the fifth century B.C., still distinguished several of them by their mainland origins.

When the power of Mycenae collapsed between 1200 and 1150, probably as a result of Dorian attacks, leaf-shaped swords of continental pattern were appearing in Cyprus, brought by fresh waves of Greeks. In classical times an archaic dialect of Arcadian type was spoken in the island, but it was without the few Doric words

6—C

adopted by continental Arcadian, which is another indication that the Mycenaeans were already well established in Cyprus before the Dorians consolidated their hold upon the Peloponnese. It cannot be denied that Cypriote art and culture are essentially conservative, and it has been argued that this is owing to the absence of any large-scale Dorian invasion of the island, such as made the cultural break in the history of mainland Greece.

The Late Bronze Age cities of Cyprus were destroyed between 1150 and 1050, probably by earthquakes. Foremost among these was Enkomi, which was rebuilt in a poorer fashion, but finally abandoned (perhaps because its harbour silted up) and replaced by nearby Salamis as the principal commercial centre. It was a dark age, for evidence of which we must rely upon weapons rather than pottery to guide us. Most of the twelfth-century swords found in Cyprus are of bronze, but some, like certain of the late Mycenaean lance-heads, are of iron, and the number of iron weapons increases with the passage of time, until in the next century they predominate. The Iron Age had begun.

The invaders' culture was that of a warrior aristocracy, its principal art being epic poetry. They brought with them a concept of law which assumed the paramountcy of local rulers but, while in Greece limited monarchy tended to give way to oligarchy, in Cyprus the trend was towards absolutism probably owing to the existence of a larger subject population. Their religion reflected their concerns as warriors, as exemplified in a fine crater (or cup) found at Enkomi, which represents a chariot group in front of which a human figure in a long robe is holding a pair of scales. The chariot was characteristic of the early Greeks, as indeed of other Aryan invaders throughout Eurasia, and chariot graves with attendant trappings, such as are described by Homer, have been found in Cyprus. The robed figure is no doubt Zeus, who is represented in the *Iliad* as holding the scales of destiny before the warriors as they prepare to depart for battle. Zeus, the principal deity of the ancient Greeks, is the sky-god who sends reviving rain, but he is also essentially violent, wielder of the thunderbolt, like Indra among the Aryans of India and Lugh among the Iron Age Celts of Ireland. Certain Achaean religious customs were introduced in Cyprus, notably cremation of the dead and human sacrifice (of which the immolation of Iphigenia is the classic example). However, the patriarchal mythology of the invaders was influenced both in Greece proper and in Cyprus by the 'mother-goddess' worship of the peoples they found there. Such worship in Cyprus dates back, in some form, to the first half of the third millennium, and had largely absorbed the earlier, theriomorphic cults.[1] Athena of Aepeia and Idalium, Artemis of Citium and Salamis, and Hera of Paphos are merely Hellenised manifestations of the Great Goddess, and the virginity of the two former is no bar to such an identification. (Witness the case of the Virgin Mary, with whom Aphrodite has been identified by simple Cypriotes until the present century.) Curium and Idalium might have their temples of Apollo, Salamis its temple of Zeus, but throughout the island Aphrodite became actually, if not technically, the most important member of the Pantheon. In the *Iliad* (e.g. V.330) she is referred to as Kypris, which might well be translated 'Our Lady of Cyprus', and in the *Odyssey* (VIII. 362–3) mention is made of her famous sanctuary at Old Paphos. There, the high priests of Cinyras's line wielded both spiritual and temporal power, and it was under their aegis that the Aphrodisia were held, with concomitants such as poetic contests and ritual prostitution. It is significant in this context that the architectural plan of Greek temples and the Greek fashion of cult statues were seldom in evidence among the Cypriotes, while oriental influence in artistic matters was much more apparent than in mainland Greece.

Traditions of theocracy have endured in Cyprus from the Bronze Age until now. There also appears to have been biological continuity, for in the *Suppliant Women* of Aeschylus the Argive (Dorian) king refers to the women of Cyprus as being of alien physical type; in his enumeration they are placed between the Egyptians and the Indians. Some ingenious attempts have been made by modern Greek-Cypriote historians to nullify the effect of this passage. For instance, it is correctly pointed out that Curium is said to have been founded from Argos itself and Lapethos from Dorian Sparta. But in view of the large population of Late Bronze Age Cyprus and the fact that the Eteocyprians, or native Cypriotes, continued to be strongly represented at Amathus down to the fourth century B.C., it is easiest to believe that, while the Greeks in the island enjoyed a controlling position as warriors, technicians and traders, they were not a majority in the community, and had become largely intermingled with the remaining subject population by classical times. Evidence for the cultural survival of non-Hellenic elements in Cyprus is not only to be found at Amathus. A good example is the bull-cult, best represented at the sanctuary of Ayia Irini on the western side of the Kormakiti peninsula. This sanctuary was in use from the Late Bronze Age to the end of the sixth century, with a feeble revival in the first century B.C. The bull cult is representative of a theriomorphic stage in religion. The Minoans, for instance, besides their goddess, worshipped a bull god, the Minotaur of classical

[1] Theriomorphic gods are those in the shape of wild animals.

myth. Incidentally, the votive figurines of Ayia Irini from about 650 to 500 B.C. form the most remarkable collection of terra-cottas ever found. Nevertheless, Greek culture was dominant in Cyprus from the Mycenaean settlement onwards.

After the dark age, the colonists in Cyprus were thrown back on their own resources, and developed a modified Mycenaean style of pottery known as Cypro-geometric, which has been much maligned by critics who had only the few examples in European and American museums to go by. Those lucky enough to see the examples at the Cypriote Presidential Palace and the Nicosia Museum will surely agree that they are extremely fine. In this connexion it is apposite to quote a remark of the late Stanley Casson : 'I prefer to see the history and art of the Cypriots as those of Oriental Greeks rather than of Hellenized Orientals. For in many respects Cyprus retained more qualities which are ancient Greek, or perhaps Achaean, than any area of the Greek world'.[1]

About the year 800 the Greeks of Cyprus were reinforced by a new immigration from Hellas, and some of them seem to have helped colonists from Euboea to rebuild the trading centre of Posidium on the Orontes, a city originally founded by the Mycenaeans on the site of al-Mina.

Semitic Influences

As we have seen, Semitic contacts with Cyprus may have been made as early as the third millennium, though there is no evidence of immigration before the Phoenician period. The date and extent of Phoenician immigration are of interest because the suggestion has often been made, usually by opponents of *Enosis*, that the modern Cypriotes are really of Phoenician origin. One should closely examine historical theories that have a bearing on present-day politics.

The original Phoenicians cannot be distinguished from other Canaanites until the latter half of the second millennium. Indeed, the name Phoenician derives from a Greek word meaning 'dark red, purple, or brown', applied by Homer to the brown-skinned Canaanites in contrast to the white-skinned Greeks. An Egyptian fresco of about 1475 B.C. shows sailors of unmistakably Semitic type, evidently Canaanites, but, on the whole, Levantine trade remained in the hands of the Mycenaeans till the end of the thirteenth century, when the flood-gates of the Near East opened to a further influx of northern invaders. The Hittite empire was broken up and the

---

[1] *Ancient Cyprus, Its Art and Archaeology* (London : Methuen, 1937), p. v.

invaders swept down over Syria, where their numbers were swollen by sea-going war-bands, possibly including Mycenaeans from Cyprus. The resulting conglomerate was called by the Egyptians the 'Peoples of the Sea', and Egyptian paintings show that there was a strong Nordic element among them. After the Canaanite cities were submerged, Egypt was threatened on two sides, but about 1191 Rameses III brought the invaders to a halt in great battles by land and sea. Among the defeated were Aegean peoples akin to the Philistines, elements of whom had united with the Canaanites to produce a new people, more Semitic in language than in origin— the Phoenicians proper. This new people combined adventurousness with commercial acumen and rapidly asserted itself. By the turn of the twelfth century the Phoenicians had dominated the commerce of the Levant. Of their chief cities, Sidon is first mentioned c. 1070 B.C., and Tyre arose in the tenth century. However, their colonies at Utica (near the later Carthage) and Gades (Cadiz) seem to have been founded before the turn of the eleventh century.

Iron-workings are to be found in Syria earlier than in Cyprus, and there is a good deal of iron ore on the island. Moreover, bronze continued to be used beside iron, and was superior in some respects (e.g. in making rust-resistant fastenings for ships). The Phoenicians went far afield in search of the tin necessary to harden the copper into bronze, and Cyprus, besides being their main source of copper, was their nearest shelter in the open sea. It can only have been the existence of Mycenaean colonies in the island that prevented extensive Phoenician colonisation at an early date. As it is, they probably had a small settlement at Citium, near modern Larnaca, from about the year 1000. In fact, Citium, despite a previous Mycenaean settlement on the site, is a name of Semitic origin, being a form of the Biblical 'Chittim'. There is a tradition that Elissa (the Dido of the *Aeneid*) fled from Phoenicia to Cyprus in the year 814, and then passed on to found Carthage. Isaiah (xxiii. 1, 2, 12) seems to refer to her flight, and designates the whole island as 'the land of Chittim'.

There is little sign of the Phoenician presence in Cyprus until the eighth century, though this was the time of their greatest activity. By the middle of that century Hiram II, King of Tyre, had a representative at Citium, and Phoenician merchant communities were soon established in other cities also, most notably at Tamassus, with its copper mines. But it is often difficult to be sure that Phoenicians had established themselves in any particular area owing to their tendency to copy the pottery and arts of other peoples. It was the same in religion. At a period when religious similarities were emphasised rather than ignored, the Phoenician Astarte could be identified with Aphrodite, Anat with Athena, Baal with Zeus, Reshep with Apollo, and Melqarth with Heracles. Nevertheless, the Phoenician merchants regarded their interests as distinct from those of the other inhabitants. That they did not succeed in turning the whole of the island into a Phoenician colony is a matter of the greatest importance. In much of North Africa they were successful, and the similarity of their language to Arabic has been regarded as a major reason for the swift consolidation of Islamic conquests there. The Phoenicians, at least as described by their neighbours, seem to have been an unattractive people, gloomy in religion and grasping in commerce. Still, their imitative art sometimes attains to beauty, and they were outstanding in the field of exploration.

The Phoenician expansion took place under pressure from the growing power of Assyria. The terrible advance into Syria of Tiglathpileser III about the year 741, and his subsequent invasion of Asia Minor, left Cyprus in a strong trading position, and Cypriotes took part in the rebuilding of Posidium on the Orontes, destroyed in the Assyrian advance. Josephus reports that Citium successfully withstood an attack by Shalmaneser V in about 727 B.C., but inscriptions of Sargon II set up about 708, one of which was discovered at Citium, record the submission of seven kings of Ya in Yatnana which, if not Cyprus, must at least refer to an area in which it was included. It seems, for instance, that the name 'Lidir' mentioned in the Citium inscription is in fact Ledrae or Ledra, on the site of modern Nicosia. The names of the kings are Greek, Phoenician, and perhaps Eteocyprian. They were to pay a tribute of gold, silver, and various timbers, and kiss the Assyrian monarch's feet in Babylon. In Sennacherib's reign a bull-inscription at Nineveh (c. 702) records the flight of Luli, King of Sidon, from Tyre to Yatnana, probably another instance of Cyprus serving as a Phoenician refuge. If so, it was not under direct Assyrian control. However, the pottery of the period begins to show definite oriental tendencies. A cylindrical seal of Esarhaddon, dated about 670, speaks of ten tributary kingdoms in Yatnana, and two years later the ten kings joined Assurbanipal in his unsuccessful expedition against Egypt. Most of their names are Greek, but one at least is Phoenician. The Phoenician element must have been strengthened by the influx of refugees, for it is about this time that the Phoenician alphabet and language come into general use both in Citium and in the copper centre at Idalium.

Recent excavations by Dr V. Karageorghis have shown that, despite their tributary obligations, the independent kings of Cyprus were extremely rich at this period. Large two-handled amphorae for wine and olive oil show that there were other exports besides metals and timber which contributed to this prosperity. It was also during the Assyrian ascendancy that Cyprian potters settled at Am, near Daphnae, in the Nile Delta.

A new linear syllabary was in use in Cyprus at least from the beginning of the seventh century B.C. Like its forerunner, it was ill-adapted to Greek, but nevertheless a majority of the inscriptions are in that language. Some, however, are in an unidentified tongue, probably Eteocyprian.[1] Most examples of the Cypriote syllabary are of the fifth and fourth centuries, but the script survived until the first century B.C., long after such scripts had died out elsewhere. The continental Greek alphabet, which was inspired by the north Semitic alphabet, of which the Phoenician is an offshoot, was not generally in use in Cyprus until the fourth century B.C. In this, as in other respects, the insular culture shows itself remarkably conservative and slow to accept innovation.

Cyprus Under Egyptian and Persian Control

With the decline of the Assyrian empire, culminating in its overthrow about 612, Egypt reasserted herself under the Philhellenic XXVIth dynasty. By the year 600, the Pharaoh Necho was able to dominate the eastern Mediterranean with a fleet of war triremes, and the Pharaoh Apries (588–569) defeated the combined Phoenician and Cypriote fleets. His successor, Amasis II, invaded Cyprus and found it ruled by a certain Euelthon of Salamis, who exercised control over the island princelings. Euelthon was allowed to become viceroy to the Pharaoh, and tribute was probably light, for Amasis needed the goodwill of the seafaring Cypriotes. Many Egyptian objects of this period have been found in Cyprus, including statuettes of noble Cypriotes wearing the Egyptian kilt and even the serpent crown. But the Egyptians lost control over the island with the death of Amasis.

The early sixth century brought a further strengthening of the traditional connexion of Cyprus with Greece, and this is reflected in the pottery changes of the time, though these are influenced not only from Hellas but also from Hellenic Naucratis, established in the Delta in about 650.

Cyprus was already under Persian influence in the time of Cyrus the Elder. In 525, the island was surrendered to Cambyses. His subsequent conquest of Egypt was aided both by the mainland and insular Phoenician fleets, and probably by Greek Cypriotes also. Cyprus was now absorbed into the fifth satrapy of the Persian empire, which included the eastern Mediterranean littoral, though

[1] That is to say, the language of the indigenous Cypriotes.

there is also evidence that the island paid tribute with the Hellenised Anatolian regions. It is noteworthy that coins of the late sixth century show Cypriote kings without the Persian Great King. Evidently they had been rewarded for cooperation. We may suppose that the Persians did not interfere with conditions in Cyprus, provided the island met their needs.

Control of Cyprus was essential to domination of the eastern Mediterranean, for it is the only island of any size in the whole area. Persia was primarily a land power, and relied heavily upon the Phoenicians for support at sea. In Cyprus, the Phoenicians played the part of a fifth column, exactly as we should expect of an alien immigrant minority, and it was during the Persian period, in the fifth century, that they were permitted to seize the copper centre of Idalium. Afterwards, they gained control of Tamassus and Lapethos, in both of which cities they had previously established groups of merchants. Names such as Praxidemus-Baalsillem of Lapethos testify to that mixing of peoples which was part of the softening-up process. However, despite their best efforts, the Phoenicians never managed to gain permanent control of Salamis, so their hold on the island was not secure.

Under Persian rule a very large area was united and pacified, and trade benefited accordingly. But the burden of taxation was great, and Cyprus, at the seaward limit of the empire, derived little benefit from the great public works on which much of the royal revenue was spent. The year 499 saw the beginning of the Ionian revolt against the Persians. According to Herodotus, Onesilus, a great-grandson of the Euelthon of Egyptian times, urged his brother Gorgus, King of Salamis, to revolt likewise. When Gorgus refused, he was shut out of the city, and Onesilus took control. The other cities of Cyprus, with the exception of Amathus, rallied to Onesilus. The Eteocyprian city of Amathus was under Phoenician influence, but there must have been dissatisfaction among the Phoenicians also, for Citium joined the rebels. Onesilus was besieging Amathus when he learnt of the despatch from Cilicia of a strong Persian relieving force under Artybius. Onesilus already had some Athenian help, and he now turned to the Ionians. Artybius landed his troops on the north of the Carpass peninsula and marched on Salamis over the hills, while his mainland Phoenician allies moved round to attack from the seaward side. In the event, an Ionian fleet arrived in time to defeat the Phoenicians at sea, but Herodotus tells us that Onesilus lost the land battle owing to the defection, at the critical moment, of Stasanor of Curium and the Salaminian charioteers. Onesilus killed Artybius, but was himself killed in the rout. The Amathusians cut off his head and took it home to their native city.

The Ionian fleet, seeing the case as hopeless, sailed home, and Cyprus was reduced in a series of sieges. Excavations of A.D. 1950–57 have shown that during the siege of Old Paphos in 497 B.C. the Persians used large numbers of sculptures to extend their siege-mound, thus revealing a preceding period of Cypriote art and many inscriptions in the native script. Soli was the last city to fall, when its walls were undermined.

In 480 B.C., when Xerxes crossed the Hellespont, 150 of his 1,200 triremes were from Cyprus, among his followers being Gorgus of Salamis. Herodotus describes the Cypriote kings as being turbanned after the Persian fashion, while the rest of the Cypriotes were Greek in dress and equipment. In the battle of Salamis off Attica, the Cypriotes made a poor showing, perhaps out of sympathy for the Hellenic cause. Penthylus, commander of the Paphos contingent, lost eleven of his twelve ships in a storm, was captured off Arte-mision, and gave information to the Greeks. Philaon, brother of Gorgus, was also captured later on. Herodotus relates how Artemisia, Queen of Halicarnassus, another ally of Xerxes, reproached the Cypriotes, among others, before the Great King.

After victory the first Hellenic objective was to secure the trade routes to the East. To this end, possession of Cyprus was all-important. In 478, Pausanias the Spartan sailed for Cyprus with fifty triremes, and within a short time had ousted the Persians from most of the island. During the Athenian invasion of Egypt Cyprus provided a base for the covering squadron, though Citium remained in Persian hands.[1]

The Phoenician fleet played a key part in defeating the Athenians in Egypt, and was then sent to reestablish the authority of Artaxerxes I in Cyprus. About the years 450/49, Cimon, son of Miltiades, laid siege to Citium with 140 vessels, and died before its walls, though the Greeks won victories by sea and land over the Phoenicians and Cilicians at Cyprian Salamis. However, because of the build-up of Persian forces to outflank them, the Greeks could only win these battles by withdrawing sixty vessels which they had sent to aid an uprising in the Delta. In 448, after the Peace of Callias, the Athenians departed, leaving Cyprus to her fate. The island had proved beyond the effective range of their fleet. Yet this did not mean that commercial links were broken. Cypriote luxury wares were being exported to Athens about the year 430, and grain too was a common export. We should not forget that in the fifth century the Piraeus was by far the busiest port in the Mediterranean.

[1] It was during this period of Athenian influence (c. 460 B.C.) that the Chatsworth head of Apollo was made at Tamassus.

As the power of Persia built up against the Greeks, the Phoenicians were quick to seize their advantage. Shortly before Cimon's death the Teucrid dynasty of Salamis was supplanted by a Phoenician one, and the city fell into decay. The Phoenicians also destroyed the temple of Athena at Idalium, thus showing that they were less interested in the fusion of cultures when they had the upper hand.

About 411/10, the Teucrid prince Euagoras, who had fled to Cilicia from the Tyrian Abdemon, returned with a few followers, ousted his rival, and established himself as ruler in Salamis. He showed himself a strong Philhellene, as befitted his family origins, and was the first in Cyprus to use the Greek alphabet on coins, though he also used the Cypriote script for the same purpose. As early as 410, he was made an honorary citizen of Athens for his help against Sparta, and when the Peloponnesian War ended in 404 many Athenians took refuge in his city. In 400, he secured the aid of Artaxerxes II for Athens against Sparta, and remained nominally faithful to the Great King until after the battle of Cnidus (394 B.C.). It was after Cnidus that a statue of Euagoras was erected at Athens beside one of the Athenian admiral Conon, as a token of gratitude for his help to the city. Meanwhile, he had been extending his influence in Cyprus. Soli, Citium, and Amathus combined against him, but he sacked Citium about 398/7 and later other Phoenician cities, including Tyre (382). After Antalcidas's Peace in 386, the Persians were able to concentrate their forces against him and, though he managed to enlist the aid of allies, including Egyptians and Arabs, he was defeated at Citium on land, and then at sea off Salamis. His retention of Salamis under the circumstances was as much a triumph for his diplomatic skill as for the Salaminian defence, for he played off the enemy leaders, Aroandas and Tiribazus, one against the other. In Greece, admiration for Euagoras was expressed above all by Isocrates, who regarded him as an example of the successful autocrat.

Euagoras was assassinated in 374, and succeeded by his son Nicocles, the pupil and friend of Isocrates. Nicocles's sense of Hellenic tradition was only skin-deep, as is shown by the story that he forced Stratonicus, the Athenian jester, to take poison for being over-free in his sallies. Euagoras II, his successor, was also a vassal of the Great King and, when expelled in 351, fled to the protection of Artaxerxes Ochus. The principal Cypriote rulers then revolted against the Persians. According to Diodorus, these were the kings of Salamis, Citium, Amathus, Paphos, Marium, Soli, Lapethos, Kerynia, and Curium; so it appears that the Phoenician colonies were temporarily in alliance with their neighbours. But the Persians were able to exploit dissensions among them, so the scheme had little success. Euagoras II, who had been given a kingdom in Anatolia, returned home only to be killed.

The fourth century B.C. saw the progressive decline of the Greek city-states. In Cyprus and elsewhere an indication of this decline is the deterioration in the quality of exported Attic vases after about the year 380. Internecine conflicts and their attendant plagues had taken a disproportionate toll of the Hellenic citizenry, upon whom the civilisation depended, and the biological loss was never made good. The effects followed inexorably, first in cultural, later in economic terms. The full and satisfying life of the *polis* gave way to the theory of the 'cosmopolis', which meant not a union of all the Greeks, but an unreal world alliance of intellectuals, a notion which inevitably involved a deliberate blurring of distinctions and refusal to discriminate—those unmistakable signs of degeneracy and decay. Hand in hand with this cosmopolitanism, as we might expect, went the cult of selfish individualism, whether in philosophy or in everyday life. The professional cynics, sophists, and hedonists emphasised the transitory rather than the ideal, the exception rather than the rule, and sought solutions in terms of the individual rather than the group. The state was no longer a goddess to be served but a cow to be milked.

Such a condition of affairs was not destined to last. To the north of Greece was a Hellenised people perhaps more like the original Hellenes than the Greeks of the fourth century. Despite the eloquent warnings of Demosthenes, the city-states did not combine before it was too late, and Philip of Macedon was able to dominate the whole country. But it was under Philip's son and successor, Alexander, that the dream of Isocrates was to be realised—the Greeks united under Macedonian leadership to overthrow the Persian empire.

Chapter 3

Cyprus Under the Ptolemies, the Romans, and the Byzantines

Alexander and the Ptolemaic Period

A FTER THE DECISIVE BATTLE of Issus (333), Alexander the Great advanced southwards to secure his flank by destroying the Phoenician allies of the Persians. The Cypriotes sent 120 ships to help in the siege of Tyre, and Arrian tells us that Cypriote engineers cooperated in making the mole which was thrown across the strait separating the city from the mainland. Prominent among the Cypriotes was Pnytagoras, who had taken over the government of Salamis, and Androcles, King of Amathus, previously a Persian sympathiser. Evidently, Phoenician influence in Amathus had not been more than superficial. After seven months, Tyre was taken by assault, and its destruction much reduced Phoenician chances of dominating Cyprus. The Cypriotes also cooperated in the two months' siege of the Phoenician city of Gaza, and Alexander went forward to found the great city in the Delta which bears his name. Pnytagoras was rewarded with the Phoenician copper centre at Tamassus.

When Alexander turned eastwards, Nicocles, son of King Pasicrates of Soli, and Stasanor, of the same city, followed him into central Asia, the latter becoming governor of the Persian province of Drangiana, to which were later added the immense regions of Bactria and Sogdiana. Cypriote shipwrights and oarsmen were among those who built and manned Nearchus's fleet on his return by sea from the Indus to the Persian Gulf, and among those in command were Nicocles of Soli and Nithaphon, son of Pnytagoras. That the Cypriotes were free allies of Alexander is shown by the right of their kings to coin gold, the token of independence.

Alexander was a master of war, with outstanding courage, energy, and imagination. Yet his empire fell to pieces after his death, and the reasons are not far to seek. For more than two centuries the Persians, like the British in India, had held together their empire by keeping themselves aloof, while allowing the maximum of freedom and cultural diversity to their subject peoples. But Alexander

had been infected with the cosmopolitan idea to the point of thinking that the complete fusion of his few Macedonians and Greeks
with the different peoples under his control would promote the
cohesion of his empire. Seduced by the glamour of the East, he
postured in oriental garb, affected the airs of a despot and a god,
tried to insist on the undignified and un-Hellenic practice of prostra-
tion in his presence, and forgot the debt he owed to the fidelity and
fighting qualities of his heroic followers. When he died in his thirty-
third year he left no suitable successor, and his over-extended armies
were left to solve the resulting problems. It was as ruling classes,
concentrated in their strategic cities, and intermarried, especially in
Persia, with the native aristocracies, that Alexander's colonists were
to achieve the salvation of themselves and the Hellenisation of
much of Asia. However, the notion of Isocrates that one could be a
spiritual Hellene without being of Hellenic descent turned out to be
true only to a limited degree.

Cyprus was inevitably a prize in the forty-year struggle among
Alexander's Successors. It is worth giving a fairly detailed account
of the events in which the island was involved, not in order to
'give artistic verisimilitude to an otherwise bald and unconvincing
narrative', but so as to show to what extent its fortunes depended
on those of individual generals.

In the year 321, Ptolemy Soter (the 'Saviour'), one of Alexander's
most trusted generals, who had established himself in Egypt, secured
an alliance with four of the Cypriote kings: Nicocreon of Salamis,
Nicocles of Paphos, Pasicrates of Soli, and Androcles of Amathus.
The subsequent fighting is confused, but within a few years
Agesilaus, envoy of another of the Successors, Antigonus Cyclops,
managed to balance Ptolemy's power in Cyprus with an alliance
consisting of Citium, Lapethos, Marium, and Kerynia. Ptolemy
accordingly sent 13,000 men to Cyprus, commanded by his brother
Menelaus. There Menelaus was joined by yet another of the Successors, Seleucus, who had arrived from the Aegean. Seleucus took
Kerynia and Lapethos by siege, Marium was brought over, and
hostages were taken from the doubtfully loyal dynast of the
Amathusians. Citium was besieged, and presumably taken, for in
312 its king, Pumiathon (the Phoenician form of Pygmalion), was
put to death when proved to be in correspondence with Antigonus.
His siding with Antigonus is explained by the fact that Antigonus
had control of the Syrian coast, including the cities of Phoenicia.
The temple of Heracles-Melqarth, the focus of the life of Citium
as a Phoenician centre, was destroyed, and in 311 a new calendar
era for the city was inaugurated. Marium was razed to the ground,
its inhabitants being transferred to the Paphos area. The confiscated

cities, and the revenues of the dispossessed rulers, were handed over
to the King of Salamis. This campaign struck a crushing blow at
the Phoenicians of Cyprus, and from this time forward they are of
small significance. It is interesting that, according to Antoninus
Liberalis, the Latin rhetorician, Nicocreon refused his daughter in
marriage to Arkeophron, son of Minnyridas, because he was of
Phoenician extraction. This same Nicocreon later fell under suspicion of treating with Antigonus, was surrounded in his palace, and
forced to commit suicide. His brothers fired the buildings, and the
whole family perished in the flames. In this dramatic fashion,
reminiscent of the Norse sagas, the Teucrid dynasty came to an end.

A peace was made between Ptolemy and Antigonus in 309, but
Antigonus's son, Demetrius Poliorcetes (the 'Besieger') was soon
ready to attack Cyprus. In 306, he came from Cilicia with 15,000
foot and 400 horse in more than 190 ships, including 110 fast
triremes, thirty Athenian quadriremes, and fifty-three heavier warships. Landing near Carpasia, he hauled his ships up into an en-
trenched camp, stormed both Carpasia and Urania, and marched
on Salamis. Menelaus sallied from the city with 12,000 foot and 800
horse, but was routed, 1,000 of his men being killed and 3,000 taken
prisoner. Demetrius then prepared to attack the city with a number
of siege devices, including the tower Helepolis (the 'City-taker').
He succeeded in breaching the wall, but Menelaus managed to burn
down his siege-tower before an assault could be made.

Meanwhile, Ptolemy in Egypt had learnt of his brother's plight,
and prepared a large relieving force. He reached Paphos with 140
warships, quinquiremes and quadriremes, and more than 200 transports, containing at least 10,000 mercenaries. Coasting down towards Citium, he sent orders for Menelaus to send the sixty ships he
had in Salamis. But Demetrius was equal to the occasion. Leaving
part of his force to carry on the siege, he put to sea with all his ships
and best men, and anchored off Salamis out of range, thus preventing communication between the brothers. When Ptolemy hove in
sight, he left ten ships to blockade the harbour, and sailed to meet
him with 108 ships, some of them taken from captured cities. The
ensuing battle of Leucolla is graphically described by Diodorus, and
ended in victory for Demetrius. It was a battle between Greeks, as
the sequel shows. Menelaus and Leontiscus, Ptolemy's son, fell into
Demetrius's hands, but were sent back to Ptolemy, together with all
the other high-ranking prisoners, loaded with gifts. This was in return for Ptolemy's generous treatment of Demetrius after the battle
of Gaza six years earlier. Only Lamia, the celebrated courtesan of
Ptolemy's harem, was retained by Demetrius and, though much older
than he, she exerted a strong fascination over him in the follow-

ing years. On receiving news of the victory, Antigonus assumed the diadem and the title of king, conferring the same title on Demetrius, who now took possession of all the cities of Cyprus, adding their garrisons to his own army.

For about twelve years Antigonus and Demetrius ruled over Cyprus and after the battle of Ipsus (301) Demetrius alone. It appears that Ptolemy recognised Demetrius's right to the island, for in 299/8 he granted him his daughter Ptolemaïs in marriage, Demetrius in return sending his brother-in-law Pyrrhus to Ptolemy as a hostage. However, in 295 Demetrius lost a great part of his fleet on the Attic coast, and sent to Cyprus for more ships, thus leaving Ptolemy the opportunity to invade. Demetrius's troubles in Asia Minor prevented him from relieving Cyprus, despite his continuing need for ship-timber, and all the cities of the island surrendered to Ptolemy without a fight, except Salamis, which was taken in 294. Stratonice, Demetrius's aged mother, had held out with her grandchildren in that city, but Ptolemy set them free with gifts and honours.

Under the Persians the Cypriote kings had retained a good deal of independence, for it was not Persian policy to keep too tight a rein on subject peoples; but from the Ptolemaic period until the twentieth century Cyprus was to remain within the grip of empires. True, although the power of the Ptolemies was centred in Egypt, their origins and outlook were Greek, and the yoke of the Greek Cypriotes was the lighter for the fact. The large numbers of mercenaries maintained in Cyprus were also of Hellenic origin, and Hellenic influences reached the island, not only through Egypt, but direct from other parts of the Greek world. The day of the Cypriote kings was over, and Demetrius had suppressed all the mints save that of Salamis, but in the cities the forms of ancient liberties were preserved. That pervading sense of the common interest which was such a feature of the Greek *polis* persisted to a large extent, as is shown by the number of associations for various professions in the island. The Cypriotes participated freely in the regulation of their cultural affairs. Besides, *Tò Koinòn tōn Kyprión,* the League of the Cypriotes, a federation of semi-autonomous communities, was a powerful force making for cohesion. Within it the leading representatives of the cities organised games and artistic competitions, the greatest festival of the year, as of old, being associated with the worship of the Paphian Aphrodite. It was essentially an organisation for the Greek Cypriotes, the other ethnic groups having their own associations. Among these the Phoenicians fell into a special category, for if victory in the struggle just described had gone definitely to Antigonus, Cyprus might have been dominated by them. It is natural therefore that their influence should have suffered a gradual eclipse. An inscription of about 275 B.C. shows that they still administered the district of Lapethos, but their numbers were reduced both by assimilation and emigration. Zeno of Citium (c. 335–263), the founder of Stoicism, is the outstanding Phoenician Cypriote of the Ptolemaic period, though his work was done outside Cyprus. His philosophy has that element of noble resignation which we now associate with the word 'stoic', but his Eastern fatalism and moralism, and his egalitarian cosmopolitanism (which mainly benefits the manipulator and entrepreneur) are typically Phoenician in inspiration.

The achievements of the Greek Cypriotes at this period are not mean. The Salaminians, who had invented the quinquireme in the fourth century, produced the great shipbuilder Pyrgoteles, who flourished under Ptolemy II, and had a statue erected to him by his sovereign. Akesas of Salamis and his son Helicon were the foremost exponents of the art of weaving. The drama was represented by the comic parodist Sopater. Cleon's *Argonautica* served as a model for Apollonius the Rhodian, while Hermias wrote iambic verses. Historians included Aristos of Salamis, Asclepiades the Cypriote, who dealt with the campaigns of Alexander the Great, Hermianax the Cypriote, author of the *Phrygika*, Clearchus the Solian, Demetrius of Salamis (or Soli), and Onasimus the Cypriote. However, the best sculptors tended to be immigrants from continental Greece, the Cypriotes using soft limestone rather than harder materials, and native art traditions weakened under the Ptolemies. The Homeric scholar Aristarchus of Samothrace died in Cyprus in 145 B.C.

Under the Ptolemies the island was divided into four districts: Paphos, which now came to replace Salamis as the capital, Salamis itself, Amathus, and Lapethos, the whole being governed by a *strategos*, corresponding to a viceroy, who was often a member of the royal family. Cypriote taxes flowed into Egyptian coffers, but for most of the period there was comparative peace, and the population continued to increase as the economy flourished. An estimate based on the rate of flow in the aqueduct supplying Salamis gives a population for the city during the Ptolemaic period of some 120,000, as compared with 104,000 for modern Nicosia.

Geographical exploration was encouraged by the Ptolemies and so was scientific enquiry. The founding of the great 'Museum' at Alexandria by Ptolemy Soter led to discoveries which also benefited Cyprus. Plant and animal strains were improved by empirical selection, and the principle of planned economic development, so successful in Egypt, was applied in Cyprus also. Grain became a large-scale Cypriote export, forests were nationalised, and the mines were profitably, though brutally, worked with slave labour. Copper was less plentiful than it had been, but silver continued to be produced in quantity.

The political system of the Ptolemies may be described as a paternalistic despotism, and this was reflected in religion. The cults of Apis and Osiris were combined into a synthetic state cult of Serapis, which did not make much headway in Cyprus. The worship of Aphrodite continued to be an inspiration to mainland Greece, and that of the Cyprian Adonis (ultimately of Syrian origin) was taken to Alexandria by the Ptolemies.

The great period of Ptolemaic rule was its first 150 years, but with the passage of time degeneration became apparent in the ruling family, no doubt owing to the Egyptian practice of incest over many generations, which tends to bring out any defective, recessive genes. The family qualities were exaggerated into vices, and a genius for intrigue led to paranoiac suspicion. At the risk of bewildering some readers with an array of names, it is clearly necessary to give an account of the family fortunes in so far as they affected Cyprus. Ptolemaic family relationships are somewhat complicated, though not without interest, and Cyprus provided a convenient place of refuge for Ptolemies under pressure.

Shortly after the marriage of Ptolemy II (Philadelphus) to Arsinoë II in 277, a half-brother of the king was put to death for stirring up trouble in the island. Philadelphus deified Arsinoë, established an Arsinoeion at Aphrodite's Idalium, renamed Marium after her, and founded three Cyprian cities in her honour, including probably Ammochostus ('Hidden in the sand'), later Famagusta. This last city was destined to replace Salamis, the harbour of which was silting up. After the time of Philopator (221–205) inscriptions recording honours to governors and other high officials become frequent, which argues a certain degree of autonomy. The efficient *strategos* Polycrates (203–197) was the first to put his own mark on the coins issued, and he was probably the first viceroy to bear the title of 'Archierius', or high priest, though it is unlikely that he superseded the high priests at Paphos, who later made similar claims to island-wide authority.

The sixth Ptolemy, Philometor, succeeded as a child in 180. In 168, Antiochus IV (Epiphanes), of the rival (Seleucid) dynasty, demanded the cession of Cyprus, and the governor Ptolemaeus, called Macron, went over to him. After some resistance, Philometor's forces were defeated on land and sea. At this point the Romans, whose power had greatly increased since the second Punic War, saw their chance to intervene. They frightened Antiochus into evacuating Egypt, which he had invaded, and then supervised the evacuation

7—C

of Cyprus. For some five years Philometor then reigned jointly with his younger brother Physcon ('Pot-belly'), who later became Euergetes II; but in 164 Philometor was forced to flee to Cyprus from Alexandria, and then went to ask the help of the Senate. He afterwards returned to Cyprus, while a Roman conciliation committee was sent out. In July 163, the Greek Alexandrians revolted against Physcon, and recalled Philometor. Physcon fled to establish himself in Cyrene, and then went to Rome to ask for Cyprus as part of his share. This suited the policy of *divide et impera*, and Roman envoys were sent to obtain Cyprus for Physcon. However, Physcon's brutalities in Cyrene and Philometor's refusal to cooperate helped to prolong the stalemate. Meanwhile, an attempt was made by Demetrius I Soter, another of the Seleucids, to gain Cyprus by corrupting its governor, Archias. The plot was discovered, and Archias hanged himself. In 154, after again appealing to the Senate, Physcon came with five legates to take Cyprus. But Rome's allies proved uncooperative, the Cretan league supported Philometor, and Physcon was surrounded at Lapethos, where he was forced to make a treaty. Under the treaty, he had to pay an annual tribute of corn in return for acknowledgement as king of Cyrene, but Philometor set him free, promising him one of his daughters in marriage. Cato the Censor praised Philometor's magnanimity in the Senate, and Rome was, besides, too involved in other wars to intervene. After Philometor's death in 145, Physcon succeeded, married his brother's widow, Cleopatra II (who was also his sister) and killed his brother's son, thus continuing to earn his reputation as a *kakergetes* (evildoer). In 131/0 the Alexandrians revolted against him, and he took refuge in Cyprus. Fearing that the Alexandrians might invite his eldest son to replace him, he sent for him and had him killed. The Alexandrians then broke Physcon's portrait statues. His sister-wife had remained in Alexandria and, suspecting her of complicity in the destruction, he killed their fourteen-year-old son Memphites, and sent her his head, hands, and feet as a birthday present. Manners had indeed degenerated since Ptolemy Soter's time. Nevertheless, the native population of Egypt rose in favour of Physcon, who returned from Cyprus in 129. He lived until the year 116, and his *strategoi* in Cyprus grew in power during this time, owing to attacks by Cilician pirates which had to be met independently.

Physcon's successor, his elder son by Cleopatra III,[1] was known by the lengthy name-list Philometor II Soter II Lathyrus ('Chickpea'). He was hated by his mother, who wished her younger son, Alexander, to succeed. As a consolation, Alexander was sent to be

---

[1] Physcon married his niece by his brother and sister, as well as the sister herself.

strategos of Cyprus. The queen-mother forced Lathyrus to divorce Cleopatra IV, a sister he was fond of, and take to wife his younger sister, Cleopatra called Selene. Cleopatra IV accordingly went to Cyprus, where she raised an army, and then to Syria, where she married Antiochus IX, bringing the army with her as a dowry. In 108/7, Cleopatra III staged an apparent attack on her own life, and the mob indignantly drove Lathyrus to Cyprus. His brother Alexander was called to the throne, and Lathyrus was driven for a time to Syria, but reestablished himself in Cyprus in 106/5.

About this time, a new Semitic element makes its presence felt in Cyprus—the Jews. It is not clear when Jewish settlers first arrived in the island, but Ptolemy Soter had transferred large numbers of Jews to various parts of his dominions after his capture of Jerusalem in 320 B.C. Others, no doubt, came out of interest in the copper mines. They were already numerous enough to play an important part in helping Lathyrus to establish his power. Within the same year as that event, the priest-king Alexander Jannaeus succeeded to the throne of Hyrcanus in Palestine, but was resisted by the inhabitants of Ake-Ptolemaïs and Gaza, to whom the Jews of Cyprus sent aid. Cleopatra III meanwhile supported Jannaeus. Lathyrus raised some 30,000 men in Cyprus, and defeated Jannaeus at Asaphon, near the Jordan, with great slaughter. Commanding the opposing army were two Jewish generals of Cleopatra, Chalcias and Ananias. Lathyrus was subsequently prevented from entering Egypt, and by the year 102/1 both he and his mother had returned to their respective seats of power. She died in the autumn of 101, and her younger son, Alexander, then married his niece, Cleopatra Berenice, daughter of Lathyrus. In 95 Lathyrus made another expedition to Syria, and in 88 returned to Egypt after the death of Alexander, who had been expelled and lost his life in a naval battle. Lathyrus then ruled the reunited kingdom until 80 B.C.

From the beginning of the century the Romans had established themselves in Pamphylia and Cilicia, and they treated Lathyrus as a friend because he helped to deal with the menace of piracy. In 86 Sulla's Lieutenant, Licinius Lucullus, visited Cyprus to obtain ships. When Lathyrus died, his widow Berenice, with whom he had associated himself on the throne, was left as ruler of the Ptolemaic kingdom. However, Ptolemy Alexander II, a son of her husband Alexander by a former wife, intervened. He had been taken to Rome by Sulla eight years before, and now, with Roman support, came to marry Berenice and reign in Egypt. Within three weeks he had murdered her (his father's wife and his own) and been murdered in turn by the mob. The Romans claimed that he had left a will bequeathing his kingdom, including Cyprus, to Rome.

The Alexandrians then divided the kingdom between Lathyrus's bastards. The elder, Ptolemy Theos Philopator Philadelphus, who styled himself the new Dionysus, but is better known as Auletes ('the Piper'), was given Egypt; while the younger Ptolemy, for whom no nickname has survived, was awarded Cyprus. In 59 B.C., with much expense in bribes and humiliation, Auletes obtained Roman recognition, but Cyprus was ignored in the treaty owing to its ruler's unwillingness to cooperate. The tribune P. Clodius Pulcher had been captured by Cilician pirates and had appealed to the king of Cyprus to ransom him. Only two talents had been offered, so that the pirates freed him in disgust. In 58, he had his revenge, when he carried a law to annex Cyprus as a province and appropriate its treasury to finance a free distribution of corn to the Roman people. Cato the younger was selected to take over the island, and sent his friend Canidius Crassus on ahead to offer Ptolemy the priesthood of Paphian Aphrodite as compensation for loss of secular power. However, Ptolemy preferred to poison himself. Cato, says Plutarch, was meticulous in his accounts, and realised some 7,000 talents from the sale of Ptolemy's effects, retaining for himself only a bust of Zeno. Such highmindedness in the disposal of other people's property was much applauded, and a lot of the money was used to finance the ensuing civil war.

The annexation of Cyprus was the last stage in the Roman encirclement of Egypt. In 47 B.C., Julius Caesar is said to have restored the island as an appanage for Ptolemy the Younger and Arsinoë of Egypt, who were the two younger children of Auletes, and brother and sister to Cleopatra VII (the Cleopatra immortalised by Plutarch and Shakespeare). Mark Antony later gave the island to Cleopatra as one of his love-gifts, and she drew its revenues, issuing coins on which she is represented holding the infant Ptolemy Caesar, her child by Julius. Her *strategos* in Cyprus at the time of Philippi was Serapion, who was later killed by Mark Antony at Cleopatra's request, Demetrius, a freedman of Caesar's, being appointed in his place. Cleopatra's possession of the island was confirmed by Mark Antony in 36 B.C. and again in 34, but she committed suicide in 30 B.C., and under Octavian Cyprus reverted finally to Rome.

The Roman Period

Despite the change of masters, the Roman period in Cyprus is a cultural continuation of the Hellenistic. Greek remained the language of Cypriote literature, as well as the lingua franca of trade in the eastern Mediterranean. Still, Cyprus was now much more of a province than formerly. The Roman world was too large and powerful for the island to have periods of independence as a refuge for rulers in trouble.

To begin with, Cyprus was associated with Cilicia (Roman since 103 B.C.), and among the early governors of Cilicia was Cicero, who unwillingly left Rome in May 51 B.C., and held office until August 50. He despatched Quintus Volusius to administer justice in Cyprus for a few days, and distinguished himself by attempting to reduce the exorbitant rate of interest on a large loan made by Marcus Brutus to the Salaminians. Marcus Scaptius, supported by the avaricious Stoic Brutus, managed to have the matter left for the next governor to deal with, and thus may have succeeded in exacting the interest; but at least Cicero had made a gesture in the cause of justice. Governors in later periods of Cypriote history were not always so concerned for the financial well-being of the Cypriotes. Cicero's interest in Cyprus remained, and in 47 B.C. he wrote to Caius Sextilius Rufus, who went in that year as first quaestor to the island, warmly praising the Cypriotes, especially the inhabitants of Paphos, which remained the capital. The island suffered exactions during the civil wars from Brutus, Cassius, and Antony and, after the battle of Actium and the death of Antony, reverted, as we have seen, to Rome. When Augustus made his first settlement with the Senate in 27 B.C., his principate included Syria (with Cilicia and Cyprus), and the island was governed by a legate. In 22 B.C., Cyprus was returned to the Senate, and was ruled thenceforth by a proconsul.

Life in Cyprus under the early Roman empire was probably almost unbrokenly tranquil, in common with the other Mediterranean islands. The strictures of the classical Greeks on the luxury of the Cypriotes are added to by the satirist Martial, who speaks of 'Cyprus infamous from too much heat', and by Athenaeus somewhere about the turn of the second century A.D. There were bad earthquakes in and after 15 B.C., when Paphos was ruined and rebuilt as Augusta, but no other disaster of note until Trajan's reign. The big mining centres were enlarged at Marium, Golgoi, Amathus, Tamassus, and Soli (the last of which was visited by Galen about the turn of the second century A.D.). Several million tons of slag remain in the island from ancient times, much of it from the Roman period. In modern times the great slag-heaps near Morphou bay are being reworked with improved methods for extracting the metal. Extensive galleries of the Roman period have been found in several places, with timber supports and oil lamps, together with the remains of foundries for the roasting and smelting of the ore. Cypriote copper was exported as far afield as India, and a brass industry was developed (brass being an alloy of copper and zinc). Umber and asbestos had long been the most important non-metallic minerals in the island, the umber being used in the preparation of paints, and long-fibre asbestos serving for cremation sheets, lamp-wicks, hats, and shoes. Some mica was discovered in the elder Pliny's time (A.D. 23–79), and it was Pliny who thought Cypriote wine superior to all others. As in modern times, agricultural exports were of the first importance, including wine, wheat, olive-oil, and dried fruit. Since the Cilician pirates had been suppressed and communications had improved, the old trade routes revived, especially up the Syrian coast and eastwards through Palmyra. The island's finances and harbour dues were controlled by officials from Rome, but the natives of the island enjoyed a considerable degree of prosperity. There are interesting mosaics of this time to be seen at Paphos, Curium, and Salamis, besides the characteristic coloured Roman glass at the Nicosia Museum, and some fine Hadrianic sculpture, modelled on Greek originals of the fifth and fourth centuries B.C.

The fourfold Ptolemaic division of Cyprus was maintained. Citium had by now quite yielded place to Amathus, but Salamis took on new life, and eventually outrivalled New Paphos (which had grown up on the coast, some ten miles from the Old), attaining once more its ancient pre-eminence. A strip of the Peutinger Table, a thirteenth-century copy of an original map dating from the second to the fourth centuries, shows a good road system in the island, including a circular road near the coasts, which avoided the Acamas promontory and turned southward over the Pentadactylos range to Chytri and Salamis. There was probably also a central road from Salamis to Soli, roads to all the principal cities, and a road from Salamis into the Carpass peninsula.

Perhaps the most important feature of the Roman period is the survival of the Cypriote *Koinòn*, the organism of cultural continuity. From the time of Galba (A.D. 68) onwards it reasserted itself. The coinage came to be stamped in Greek, not Latin. And there are indications that yet older traditions survived. Thus a prominent family in Salamis claimed descent from Teucer, which shows at least that cultural continuity was deeply felt; and not until Hadrian's reign was the Salaminian custom of human sacrifice to Jupiter, a practice said to have been instituted by Teucer himself, officially abolished. The popular games and ceremonies of Aphrodite were celebrated as before, and Strabo gives a good description of these as he saw them at Old Paphos. The *boulai*, or municipal councils, continued to flourish, though the tradition of local autonomy was dead. However, certain distinctions remained. For instance, the

Augustan calendar was in use at Paphos, whereas Salamis retained the Egyptian. Public education was in the hands of gymnasiarchs, and there was the usual close connexion between education and religion. Thus, in the reign of Tiberius, one Adrastus, son of Adrastus, built a temple at Lapethos, and set up a statue to the Emperor, making himself and his descendants gymnasiarchs and priests of Hermes and Heracles, the gods of the gymnasium. There was a fine public library at Soli, set up by local subscription, and a forum of three and a half acres at Salamis. Private citizens went on missions to Rome and elsewhere at their own expense, and fine marble sarcophagi testify to their prosperity. However, few native-born Cypriotes achieved distinction outside the island. An exception was Demonax, the Cynic philosopher of the second century, who successfully vetoed a proposal to hold gladiatorial games at Athens.

The Emperors themselves showed interest in Cyprus. Augustus rebuilt the temple of Aphrodite at Paphos after the earthquake of 15 B.C., following the original plan and identifying her, as usual, with the Roman Venus. Tacitus speaks of a Senate inquiry into the right of asylum in Cyprus, among other places. The temples of Aphrodite at Paphos and Amathus, and of Zeus at Salamis, had established this right. Both Tacitus and Suetonius tell of the Emperor Titus visiting Paphos on his way to the siege of Jerusalem in A.D. 69, when he admired the wealth of the sanctuary and received favourable auguries for his further voyage and his future success. Coins from the time of Claudius to that of Septimius Severus depict this famous temple. Septimius Severus, who reigned from 193 to 211,[1] had particularly close connexions with the island, and a most striking and imposing bronze statue of him has been found at Chytri (Kythrea). It represents him as a naked athlete and now stands in the Nicosia Museum. Another masterpiece of the time is the head of the youthful Dionysus, of the second century, discovered at Salamis.

In religion Cyprus benefited from the tolerance of Roman rule. Despite temple rivalries, we can justifiably say with Gibbon that 'the deities of a thousand groves and a thousand streams possessed in peace their local and respective influence'. There was acceptance of religious, as of cultural, diversity. And the slow growth of a jealous creed from the East was to coincide to a remarkable extent with the spiritual breakdown of the Roman order.

Christianity in its beginnings can only be described as an offshoot of Judaism and, as Doros Alastos has truly said, 'the spiritualised God of the Jews, incapable of being confined, was in itself a potent

[1] This Emperor died at York.

force destined to usher in spiritual totalitarianism'.[1] It was the Jews
also that were to prove the main threat to Cyprus. In the time of
Augustus, Herod the Great paid three hundred talents for half the
revenues of the Soli copper mines, and closer trading ties with
Palestine brought in large numbers of Jewish settlers. The Phoenician pattern of subversion through immigration was being repeated.

The Christian gospel was first preached in Cyprus after the death
of Stephen (*Acts* xi. 19), but to begin with only to the Jews. Soon
afterwards Cypriote Jewish Christians were preaching to the Greeks
of Antioch. About the year 45, Paul landed at Salamis with Joses
the Levite, better known as Barnabas, of Cypriote-Jewish extraction.
Their activities are recorded in the thirteenth to the fifteenth chapters of the *Acts*, Paul's chief success being the conversion at Paphos
of the Proconsul himself, Sergius Paulus. This he effected by the
dramatic expedient of striking his rival, Elymas Bar-Jesus, blind.
Paul and Barnabas fell out later, in Antioch, as to whether they
should take Mark with them on a further mission. Barnabas left
with Mark for Cyprus and, according to tradition, was stoned to
death by a Jewish mob at Salamis in the reign of the Emperor Nero
(A.D. 54–68). This tradition was later to prove of considerable importance to the history of Cyprus.

In the year 70 came the destruction of Jerusalem, and large
numbers of Jews from Palestine began to swell the already considerable Jewish colonies along the coasts of the eastern Mediterranean.
The year 115 saw a terrible Jewish insurrection in Cyrene, which
soon spread to Egypt and Cyprus. By 116, Palestine and even
Mesopotamia were affected. But the destruction in Cyprus was
worse than anywhere else. Led by one Artemion, the Jews committed many atrocities, massacring the entire gentile population of
Salamis. The revolt was put down by the future Emperor Hadrian
and the Libyan consul and cavalry leader Lucius Quinctus. By that
time some 240,000 people had been killed. No evidence has been
adduced to show this number as exaggerated, and Oswald Spengler
gives Artemion's revolt as an example of how 'the inevitability of . . .
reciprocal misunderstanding leads to . . . appalling hatred'.

A decree was passed forbidding any Jew, on pain of death, to
set foot in Cyprus, but within the next few centuries Jews returned
in small numbers. After A.D. 1160 Benjamin of Tudela speaks of
two Jewish sects in the island, and there were rich Jewish communities in the Lusignan and Venetian periods. Their numbers fell
during the Turkish period, dying out by 1738, and they were again
excluded on principle by the end of the eighteenth century. It is said
that as late as the mid-nineteenth century some shipwrecked

---

[1] Doros Alastos, *Cyprus in History* (London: Zeno, 1955), p. 34.

Romanians were killed by the Cypriotes in mistake for Jews. However that may be, there is no doubt whatever, in the words of Sir
George Hill, the island's foremost historian, that the Jewish revolt
'was perhaps as grave a disaster as Cyprus ever suffered'. There was
to be no further threat from that quarter until the 1900s, when
Herzl tried to obtain the island as a stepping-stone to Zion.

Life under the later empire was again uneventful (and therefore
peaceful) in Cyprus. The island suffered, in common with the rest
of the empire, from the great plague of 164; and in 269 the Goths
sailed there among other places, but were decimated by disease and
overcome by force of arms. With the reorganisation of the empire
by Diocletian (284–313) Cyprus came under the diocese of Oriens,
which included the eastern coasts of the Mediterranean, together
with Arabia and Mesopotamia. At first, the diocese was governed
by a prefect, later by a vicar, and from about the year 321 by a
count. The provincial governor of the island was a consular, *vir
clarissimus*. In 324, Licinius collected some ships in Cyprus for his
ill-fated Hellespontine engagement with Crispus, son of Constantine.
A severe drought set in about the same time, but we are assured
that the resulting rapid depopulation was halted shortly afterwards,
when St Helena made judicious use of some holy relics, and caused
the building of more churches in the island. Among her foundations, incidentally, is the small monastery of Stavrovouni on the
highest peak of the Larnaca district. She left a piece of the true
Cross there. Perhaps because of her efforts, Cyprus seems to have
suffered rather less from the drought than its mainland neighbours,
for it was raided by pirates in search of grain. Salamis was badly
hit by an earthquake in 332, and in the ensuing time of further
drought and confusion a once obscure person by the name of Calocerus, who had been sent as governor by the Emperor, attempted
to establish himself as an independent ruler. We have already
noticed several examples of such attempts when the imperial systems
including the island showed signs of weakening, and the same
pattern was to be repeated in the future. Constantine's nephew
Delmatius captured Calocerus, and sent him to an unpleasant death
in Tarsus. In about 345, Salamis was struck by another earthquake,
which was accompanied by a tidal wave. It was rebuilt, though in
an inferior fashion, and renamed Constantia. Paphos also was badly
damaged by earthquakes, and was rebuilt on a notably smaller scale,
doubtless owing in part to its significance as the principal pagan
cult centre. Besides, the early Christian civilisation was technically
inferior to those of the preceding ages, and quite incapable of

replacing all that was destroyed by acts of God. The first half of the fourth century saw a catastrophic decline in population, accompanied by drought and famine, throughout the Roman empire. Mining in Cyprus, already in decline, ceased almost completely, and was not resumed on any scale until the nineteenth century.

Meanwhile, the Christian religion had slowly gained ground. The extravert tendencies of antiquity were replaced by the introversion of those for whom earthly struggles counted for little, except in so far as they determined one's status in the hereafter. The initiates of the goddess, with their symbolic lumps of salt and their imitation phalluses, were superseded by those to whom self-examination and theological argument were the breath of life. Art, in particular, began to reflect the futility of human concerns. The cult of the body was swept away with repugnance and disgust, and surviving statues were deliberately disfigured, especially as regards the genitals. Washing and athletics were regarded with horror, and the baths and gymnasia fell into decay. An ethos which, at its best, was humanitarian superseded one which, at its best, was aesthetic.

The main successes of Christianity were among the disaffected proletariats of the great cities. In the countryside its progress was slower. Thus in Cyprus, while Aphrodite was exorcised, the name of Dionysus anathema, and the wearing of tragic or comic masks forbidden, certain ancient dances nevertheless survived, largely deprived of their sexual significance. A popular sub-culture subsisted in a conservative island. Nor did the clergy see fit to discontinue the ancient traditions of priestly control.

Christianity in Cyprus was no doubt stimulated when, in 310, a number of Christians were transferred to the island from the mines of Palestine. In 313, the Edict of Milan legalised the religion, but under Licinius (314–24) the Bishop of Kerynia, Theodotus, is reputed to have been martyred. By 325 (the date of the Council of Nicaea) there were at least three Christian sees in the island, those of Paphos, Salamis, and Tremithus, of the last of which St Spyridon was bishop, and no fewer than fourteen eparchies are said to have existed in Cyprus under Constantine. It was by Constantine's decision in 333 that Christianity became the official religion of the empire. In 343/4 St Spyridon attended the Council of Sardica with nine other Cypriote bishops. It was a time when the power of the bishops was being consolidated. Despite a setback during the short reign of Julian (361–63), who published an edict granting toleration to all religions and caused the Christians to make restitution for the temples they had destroyed, Christianity continued to make headway. St Hilarion, the founder of Palestinian monasticism, died near Paphos in 371.[1] In 368, St Epiphanius, also from Palestine, had been elected Archbishop of Constantia. Until his death in 403, he was an active rooter-out of those minor heresies which flourished in Cyprus. At the Oecumenical Council of 381 (attended by at least four Cypriote bishops) the thirteenth canon of the Laodicean Synod laid it down that in future laymen should not be permitted to participate in the election of church dignitaries. Thus priestly control was strengthened.

The Early Byzantine Period

In 395 came the final separation of the Eastern and Western Empires, though theoretical unity was maintained until 476. This separation was foreshadowed by Constantine's establishing his capital at Byzantium, which was renamed in his honour, and by the division of the empire at his death in 337. Cyprus, of course, fell to the share of Constantinople. The history of the island under the Byzantines is full of changes in fortune, quite unlike its generally calm existence as a part of the Roman empire proper. The Jewish insurrection, however destructive, had been short in duration but, while technically under the sway of the less masterful Byzantines, Cyprus became for more than three centuries (649–964) a mere no-man's-land. However, the country also experienced periods of considerable prosperity, and it is arguable that participation in a Greek-speaking universal state was more in keeping with the natural aspirations of the Cypriotes. Certainly, Cypriote art remains essentially Byzantine to this day, while in many other parts of the Byzantine empire the inhabitants made use of the Greek *Koiné*, but have retained few Byzantine cultural legacies.

There now begins one of the most crucial struggles in Cypriote history, the struggle for autocephaly, and we are still living with its effects. For some time the patriarchs of Antioch (the capital of the diocese of the Orient) had claimed the right to consecrate the Archbishop of Cyprus. (The great city of Antioch, founded by Seleucus Nicator upon the Orontes, lay in an excellent natural position to influence and be influenced by Cyprus, like Posidium and al-Mina before it.) In Pope Innocent I's time (402–17), Alexander, Patriarch of Antioch, complained that the Cypriotes were ordaining their own bishops, contrary to the Nicene canons. The Pope ordered submission, but the Cypriotes were obdurate. At different times two of the Cypriote Metropolitans, Troilus and Theodorus, were

---

[1] The stronghold overlooking the Kyrenia Pass seems to have been named after another St Hilarion who, according to Leontios Machaeras, lived in that area.

illtreated in Antioch, the latter being struck. In 431, Archbishop Theodorus died, and John, Patriarch of Antioch, induced Flavius Dionysius, Count of the Orient, to order his consular in Cyprus to prevent, if necessary by force, the election of a new archbishop before the matter had been submitted to the third Oecumenical Council, due to meet that year at Ephesus. The Cypriote suffragans nevertheless elected a new Archbishop of Constantia, Rheginus. He and four other bishops then proceeded to the Council of Ephesus to plead their cause. One of their number, Sapricius of Paphos, died shortly after arrival, but Rheginus, with Zeno of Curium, Evagrius of Soli, and the Protopapas Caesarius, argued the Cypriote case so well that the Council made a decision, based on tradition, in their favour. Lists of the bishops at the fourth Oecumenical Council, at Chalcedon (451), show Cyprus as separate. About thirty-seven years later, in the reign of the Emperor Zeno (474–91), the monophysite Antiochian Patriarch Peter the Tiller (a protégé of the Emperor's) revived the controversy. He argued that since Cyprus had been converted from Antioch, and Antioch was an apostolic see, Cyprus should remain subject. But Archbishop Anthemius, the Cypriote Primate, had a providential (and convenient) vision in which the Apostle Barnabas directed him to the invention of his own remains. On the breast of the apostle lay a copy of Matthew's gospel, in Barnabas's own handwriting, just as Mark had placed it more than four centuries previously. It was to prove an event as important for Cyprus as the invention of the remains of St James the Great was later to be for Spain.

In his vision, Anthemius had also been told to appeal to the Emperor, who then referred the matter to a synod summoned by Akakios, Patriarch of Constantinople, and Cypriote autocephaly was confirmed. The significance of this event cannot be over-emphasised. Autocephaly meant a continuation of the ancient pagan Cypriote tradition uniting spiritual and temporal power, and Doros Alastos even claims that it was 'a historical continuation of the *Koinon*'.[1] The fact of autocephaly has had momentous consequences down to our own times, the present Archbishop having attained greater power than any of his powerful predecessors. (If, for instance, Cyprus had remained subject to the Patriarch of Antioch or the Patriarch of Constantinople, considerable Turkish pressure could have been brought to bear for the removal of Makarios III.) After the confirmation of Cypriote autocephaly, the Archbishop of all Cyprus was given the right to sign in the imperial purple (i.e. scarlet), to wear a cloak of the same colour at church festivals, to carry an imperial sceptre instead of a pastoral staff, and to bear the

---

[1] Alastos, op. cit., p. 115.

title of 'Most Blessed'. The Emperor Zeno was gratefully presented with Barnabas's copy of Matthew's gospel, and a church was erected and dedicated to Barnabas over the place of his sepulture. But the Cypriote Archbishop was still not a patriarch, and Hill states that the chrism used in episcopal consecrations had to be obtained from Antioch until 1860, and from Constantinople after 1864.

In the course of time Christianity was profoundly modified by the peoples who adopted it. It was found that the organisational principles of the empire were necessary even to the continuance of a system of belief which enjoined personal salvation before all else. The necessity for the Byzantines to borrow from the past is best exemplified in terms of architecture and painting. Thus, Constantine's Arch already contains materials plundered from the triumphal arches of his predecessors, and the most imposing of Byzantine buildings, the great Cathedral of St Sophia in Constantinople, contains columns looted from the temples of the ancient world. Nevertheless, St Sophia is a beautifully conceived piece of architecture, and was to provide inspiration for the great mosques of the Ottoman Turks. And in the best of Byzantine art, which has its beginnings in the fifth century, Hellenistic grace, beauty, and idealism inspire the oriental hieraticism and severe, abstract formalisation. Cyprus, in common with the rest of the Byzantine empire, benefited from the organisational, architectural and other artistic lessons of the preceding ages.

Even in the fifth century, and increasingly in the sixth and the first half of the seventh, the island appears to have been peaceful and prosperous, at least by comparison with its neighbours. Wine and dried figs were exported, and there was a local craft of jewellery. Sixth-century Cypriote mosaics are still of basically Hellenistic type, though with added oriental influence. The Isaurians (from the Taurus region) ravaged Cyprus in their depredations of 404/7, but the destruction of Antioch by the Persian Chosroes in 540 left the island untouched. The bubonic plague of 542/3 probably affected the Cypriotes, though there is no record of this. In 535, under the reform of Justinian, Cyprus was removed from the control of the Count of the Orient to that of a quaestor whose headquarters were on the Danube. This involved long journeys for the islanders, and they were soon allowed to take their problems direct to the imperial capital. Later in Justinian's reign, about the year 552, two monks managed to smuggle silkworms' eggs through from the Far East, and the silk industry soon began to flourish in Cyprus. The island continued to be a place for the banishment of undesirables, like many other islands the world over. Back in the time of Arcadius, in 399, the eunuch Minister Eutropius had been exiled there, and the tradition was maintained on a large scale. Justinian is reported to have transferred about 3,000 Hyrcanian (north Persian) captives to Cyprus, and about the time of Justin II's death (A.D. 578) the future Emperor Maurice sent some thousands of captives there from Greater Armenia. The only governor of the sixth century whose name is known to us is Epiphanius, father of St John the Almoner. Shortly before 626, the Emperor Heraclius attempted to establish monotheletism in Cyprus when he wrote to the Archbishop Arcadius insisting upon the single will of Christ, but the experiment came to nothing.

The Arab Raids

Also in the reign of Heraclius (610–41) came the rise of another world religion founded upon the Judaic tradition. The Semitic tribes of Arabia swept over the tax-ridden, heretical, and already semiticised southern provinces of the Byzantine empire. In 639, Mu'awiya, chief of the Quraish (the Prophet's own clan), destined to be the founder of the Umayyad dynasty, became Emir of Syria. With the consent of the Caliph Othman, he planned to attack Cyprus and, using the newly-captured naval base at Alexandria, fitted out a fleet of 1,700 ships. It was the first Arab maritime enterprise on any scale. About the year 648/9, Mu'awiya landed in Cyprus and sacked Constantia, massacring most of the inhabitants and dividing the loot with his allies from Egypt. He is said to have filled seventy ships with the proceeds, and the flourishing state of the town which such booty implies is amply attested by the findings of modern archaeology. Before departing, Mu'awiya imposed on the Cypriotes an annual tribute of 7,200 gold pieces, an amount said to be equivalent to that previously exacted by the Byzantine treasury. It was on this expedition that Umm-Haram, daughter of the Lady Milhan, a relation of the Prophet, is said to have died from a fall off her horse. She was buried on the southern side of Larnaca salt lake, a spot to be held particularly sacred during the Turkish period. On hearing that Cacorhizus, the imperial admiral, was coming with a large relieving force, Mu'awiya retired.

In the thirty-third year of the Hegira (A.D. 653/4), the Cypriotes having failed to pay the annual tribute, Mu'awiya sent another force under Abu'l-Awar, who massacred more of the inhabitants and stormed their refuge at Lapethos. He reimposed the tribute, and left behind him an Arab garrison of 12,000, later withdrawn by the Caliph Yazid (680–83). About the year 688 a ten-year 'compromise' was reached, whereby the wretched Cypriotes were to pay equal sums in tribute both to the Arabs and the imperial treasury. Not content with this agreement, the Caliph 'Abd-al-Malik (685–705) later added a thousand dinars to his share of the tribute. The addition was cancelled by Omar II (717–20), but restored by Hisham (724–43). Then the Abbasid Mansur (754–75) returned to the conditions of Mu'awiya. Little wonder that such traditional Cypriote skills as ship-building almost died out during this period. The *stratiotai* (stradiots), soldiers paid for out of the hearth tax called *stratia*, were ineffective in protecting the islanders. But occasionally the Byzantines were able to aid them, as when Justinian II carried off the Arab settlers.

While Cyprus was suffering these exactions, with their concomitant brutalities, attempts were being made to revitalise the empire. In the frontier provinces soldiers were settled to form permanent bulwarks on the ancient Roman model. These were the warriors celebrated in the later, Acritic cycle of heroic poems. The hero of the cycle, Digenes Akritas, also lived in Cypriote folklore. Thus the rock off the south-west coast at the place where Aphrodite emerged from the rich, creamy foam bears the name Petra tou Romiou, the story being that Digenes hurled it at the Saracens when they called him 'Romios' (a pejorative term for a Greek) and a similar tale is told of Petra tou Limniti. Other stories of Digenes (Dighenis) kept continuously alive by Greek ballad-singers associate him with the Troödos and Kyrenia Mountains; so that in the twentieth century, when Grivas began guerrilla campaigns in those very mountains, it was natural that he should take Dighenis as his *nom de guerre*. Dighenis was twice-born in more senses than one.

The latter half of the seventh century was an unfortunate time for the Cypriotes, and their culture suffered in consequence. Sir George Hill has suggested that the seat, though not the see, of the Cypriote Primate was transferred to nearby Ammochostus (Famagusta) because of the destruction of the basilica at Constantia by the Arabs. (Certainly, Ammochostus seems to have been the seat of the Primate by the end of the twelfth century.) However, Leontios (*c.* 590–668), the Cypriote Bishop of Neapolis, became popular as a hagiographer. During the first reign of Justinian II (685–95) the Byzantines proved incapable of defending the island, and a large number of Cypriotes with their Archbishop John were settled near Cyzicus on the south coast of the Sea of Marmora. The name of the settlement was New Justinianopolis, and the Cypriote Primate bears the honorary title of Archbishop of that city to this day. During the same period, in 692, the Trullan Quinisext Council took place, at which the autocephaly of the Cypriote Church was reconfirmed. In 698, when the exile had only lasted a few years,

Tiberius III Apsimarus, Admiral of the Cibyrrhaeote fleet, took the decision to repopulate the island with Cypriotes from all over the empire, and New Justinianopolis was abandoned. The transference of Cyprus from the province of Syria was made by agreement with the Caliph, and in 704 Heraclius, brother of Tiberius, took control of it for the time being. When the Archbishop returned with his followers, many had died through disease, shipwreck, and other causes. St Willibald the Englishman, who called at Cyprus for a few weeks in 723, staying at Paphos and Constantia, described it as 'between Greeks and Saracens'. In 743, some of the inhabitants were transferred to Syria, but were returned the following year. In 747 (the sixth year of Constantine V), there was a recurrence of bubonic plague, and it was then that the Cibyrrhaeote *Theme,* the military command centred on the Pamphylian coast, had its greatest success against the enemy. A fleet of 1,000 dromonds (big, fast ships) was sent from Alexandria by the Caliph Mervan II. It was destroyed by the Cibyrrhaeote Admiral, and a century was to pass before the Egyptian fleet was again an effective force. Prominent among the naval defenders of the eastern Mediterranean during this period were the Christian Mardaites of the Taurus and Lebanon ranges. During the eighth century some alleviation of the Cypriote peasant's lot must have resulted from the Isaurian dynasty's measures to curb the power of the landlords, but their sufferings were not greatly diminished. Cyprus continued to be a place of exile for undesirables, and in 770 those monks and nuns collected at Ephesus who refused to marry were blinded and sent there. Refugees from the iconoclastic persecution also came to the island. At the Oecumenical Council of 787, it was the Cypriote Archbishop Constantine who carried the compromise that icons should be respected though not worshipped.

In 773, the Cypriotes again had need of their fortresses on the Kyrenia range. A Moslem fleet carried off the governor, and in the following years there was a monotonous succession of raids, including two under the Caliph Harun ar-Rashid (786–809). In 806, the *Wali* of the Syrian coast is said to have carried off many captives, including 'the bishop of Cyprus'. Under these circumstances, it is perhaps surprising that the island should have been a refuge for Syrian and Palestinian Christians (as in 813). To such refugees, and to Cypriotes who had been in Syrian captivity, may be attributed the innovation from the eighth century on of the vaulted stone roof for Cypriote basilicas. For some time previously the roofs had been of wood, which shows not only that timber was available in quantity, but also how much standards had fallen since the early Byzantine

period. The most outstanding Cypriote building of the Dark Age
is the Church of St Lazarus, which still stands in Larnaca, and was
built with funds granted by the Emperor Leo on the occasion of the
invention of the saint's remains in 890.[1]

Under Basil the Macedonian (867–86) Cyprus seems to have
become a *Theme* in its own right, governed by Alexius the
Armenian. However, the arrangement only lasted seven years. In
the year of the Hegira 299 (A.D. 911/12) an Arab fleet under the
admiral Dimyana ravaged, burned, and plundered in Cyprus for
four months. But the initiative was passing to the other side. In 961,
the future Emperor Nicephorus Phocas was victorious at sea and
regained Crete. Some three or four years later, after his accession,
Cyprus was finally recovered by the Patrician Nicetas Chalcutzes,
and no longer had to pay tribute to both sides.

It has often been suggested, or hinted, that the successive Semitic
penetrations of Cyprus fundamentally changed its ethnic character. The evidence is conflicting, and is complicated by the mixed
nature of the Semitic peoples of the Fertile Crescent from an early
date. A very small blood-group sample made in the British period
indicates that the modern Cypriotes are more closely related to the
population of the Syrian coast than to that of Greece,[2] but much
more extensive studies of the craniological evidence, both of ancient
and modern times, indicate the exact opposite. A balanced view
would seem to be that, while a majority of the modern Cypriotes
are European in the wider, racial sense of the word, a substantial
minority, especially in the cities, display Hither Asiatic characteristics which can only be the result of Semitic immigration.[3]

In Cyprus during the dark period from the seventh to the tenth
centuries, as in Ireland from the sixteenth to the nineteenth, the
clergy inevitably became the representatives of the people. Their
power had been great before, but at this period the 'Dukes' appointed from Constantinople were mostly reduced to the status of occasional tax-collectors, the traditional upper class suffered loss by
Arab arms or flight to safer regions, and the position of the clergy,
who rose from the people, was correspondingly strengthened. Nicephorus Phocas attempted to curb clerical power in his dominions,
but it was restored under his successor John Tzimisces.

By the end of the period of the Arab invasions, Constantia,
Amathus, Tamassus, Soli, Carpasia, and Curium had passed from

---

[1] This Lazarus is the one raised from the dead in *John*, xi, xii. He is said
to have become first Bishop of Citium.

[2] See A. E. Mourant, *The Distribution of the Human Blood Groups*
(Oxford: Blackwell, 1954), pp. 69–70.

[3] See e.g. Sir Ronald Storrs, *Orientations* (definitive edn, London: Nicholson & Watson, 1943), p. 470 n.

8—C

history save as names. The very name of Citium had been transferred from its site near Larnaca to a village further south. The
ancient city of Lapethos had become the village of Lapithos. The
inhabitants of the port of New Paphos had taken refuge in Ktima,
on the low plateau above the most beautiful coastal strip in Cyprus.
Ammochostus (Famagusta), Leukosia (Nicosia), Lemesos (Limassol),
and Kyrenia (a corruption of Kerynia, formed by analogy with
Cyrene) were emerging as the principal cities. Leukosia in particular
benefited from its inland site, relatively safe from raids.

The Final Period of Byzantine Rule

The pendulum of power that had swung westwards with the onslaught of the Arabs now began to swing slowly eastwards with the
intervention of the western Europeans, led by Latinised Germanic
aristocracies. To begin with, the Byzantines profited from this intervention, though they were later to suffer a good deal at the hands of
their fellow-Christians. The Seljuq Turks, who in 1071 definitively
replaced the Arabs as the chief representatives of Islam, did not
adapt themselves very successfully to maritime warfare, and this
meant they could not control Cyprus. As Shams-ed-Din Muqadassi
says of Cyprus in his *Description of Syria* (written at Baghdad in
985) : 'The island is in the power of whichever nation is overlord in
these seas'. So it became a forward position of the Christians.

From the second half of the tenth to the first half of the twelfth
centuries was the golden age of the Byzantine empire (the period
celebrated for readers of English by the poet Yeats). The social and
organisational aspects of Christianity now predominated over its
basic concern for individual salvation, to the great gain of culture.
Cyprus fully participated in this golden age, and it is the most outstanding period of Greek Cypriote Christian art. The textile industry had revived by the eleventh century, and the prosperity of the
island accordingly increased. There was a vigorous growth of
monastic foundations, including the great monastery at Kykko,
built under the patronage of the Emperor Alexius Comnenus. It
stands high up in the Paphos forest area, and contains an icon of
the Virgin Mary, painted, so we are assured, by the Apostle Luke
on panels presented by the Archangel Gabriel. The present Archbishop was a novice there, and the traditional hospitality of the
monks is still an attraction for hundreds of visitors. Another large
monastery, which was to play a big part in the Emergency of
1955–59, was founded at Machaeras in the central hills, shortly after
Kykko. Other monasteries of the time include those of Trooditissa
and Chrysorroyiatissa, while yet others, like those of Arakas and

Asinou, are no longer in existence. By this time, a church in Cyprus was a symmetrical whole, its dome having a painting of Christ surrounded by angels and prophets, with the Virgin in the semi-dome of the apse, and pictures of saints and biblical scenes in between. Master painters from Constantinople soon found promising Cypriote pupils. Also noteworthy are the works of Cypriote Byzantine silversmiths, working in the same strongly religious tradition.

Life in Cyprus during this relatively prosperous period was by no means without incident. In 1042–43, the governor, who rejoiced in the name of Theophilus Eroticus, led a revolt and imprisoned the collector of taxes. The revolt was suppressed by the Emperor Constantine IX Monomachus, who was content to deprive Theophilus of his possessions and exhibit him publicly dressed as a woman. In 1063, another governor was sent to Jerusalem to obtain a charter whereby the Christians might occupy a quarter of the city. In 1092, Rhapsommates, the governor at that time, leagued himself with Caryces of Crete and even the Emir of Smyrna. The Emperor, Alexius Comnenus, sent a force under John Ducas, with Butumites as its field commander. After fighting at Kyrenia, Rhapsommates fled, was captured and executed. In 1097, we hear of an attack on Laodicea by a Cypriote fleet. Causes for discontent remained, as is evident from the poem by Nicolaus Mouzalon, Archbishop c. 1107–10, testifying to the sufferings of the Cypriotes, owing to the payment of excessive tribute. It was during the eleventh century that the title of Duke for the governor of the island was changed to *Katapan,* or Second Lord.

The Schism between the Roman Catholic and Greek Orthodox Churches had taken place in 1054,[1] and by the time of the First Crusade in 1095 the Byzantines and Westerners regarded each other with suspicion, if not hostility. The main immediate reason for the Schism was a difference of conviction over the important question as to whether the Holy Ghost proceeded from the Father *and* the Son, or from the Father only, but *through* the son; but it is generally allowed that a major part was played by the long-standing refusal of the Eastern bishops to submit to Rome. The less devout have tended to regard the Schism as an expression of cultural differences which go back at least to the division of the Roman empire. However that may be, the protagonists in the dispute pronounced an excommunication and an anathema against each other which were not annulled until 1965. All the same, Western pilgrims continued to call in at Cyprus on their way to Jerusalem. One such

[1] Steven Runciman (*The Eastern Schism,* Oxford, 1955) argues that the process of separation was not complete until the Fourth Crusade. But the Schism of 1054 seems nevertheless to have been a doctrinal turning-point.

was St Lietbert of Cambrai, who was detained there for several days by the *Katapan*, the pretext being to prevent his being taken by the infidels. Erik the Good of Denmark died of fever in Paphos on 10 July 1103 and was buried at the cathedral near the present Church of Chrysopolitissa. The Doge of Venice, Domenico Michiel put in at the island in 1123. Sometimes help was given to Westerners, as when Raymond de St Gilles, Count of Toulouse, was sent ships from Cyprus to help in his siege of Tripoli in 1102. Thus Cyprus continued in her ancient rôle of ship-provider to those attacking the Syrian coast. At the same time the island did not cease to be a place of refuge. When Baldwin captured Beirut in 1110, the Emir and many of the inhabitants fled to Cyprus, which shows that Cypriotes sometimes preferred Moslems to Western Christians. There is evidence also of an influx of Maronites (Syrian Christians who later submitted to Rome), judging by appointments to the abbacy of the Monastery of Ayios Chrysostomos at Koutzoventi in 1121 and 1141. (Koutzoventi was for a long time a Maronite village.) In 1136/7 the entire population of Tell Hamdun in Lesser Armenia, after its conquest by John II Comnenus, was moved to Cyprus. Like the Maronites, and to a greater extent, the Armenians have played a part in Cypriote history. But despite the immigration of Christians from abroad, the native religious tradition continued strong. In 1167, St Neophytus formulated his Rule at the famous *encleistra*, or enclosure, seven miles from New Paphos. It involved ten to eighteen monks (no female animals allowed), and was modified in 1189 and 1209. During the course of his long life he wrote voluminously, and his rock-hewn chapel and cell, decorated with paintings under his personal supervision, became a popular place of pilgrimage. At the beginning of the twelfth century, especially good artists had come to Cyprus from Constantinople, and by the end of the century there were more churches of the period with paintings to be found in Cyprus than in any other part of the Byzantine empire.

The influence of the West meanwhile grew. Sigurd Magnusson, King of south Norway, called at Cyprus on his return from Jerusalem in 1110/11, on his way to visit the Byzantine Emperor. Many of his men were to remain in the Emperor's pay as Varangian mercenaries. In 1148, the Venetians were given commercial privileges in Crete and Cyprus by Manuel Comnenus, in return for their support against the Normans in Corfù. Thus did the Venetians gain their first precarious foothold in Cyprus. The Normans were of the same north Germanic origins as the Varangians, but the latter usually arrived in the Mediterranean via the Viking kingdoms of Russia, and were much less Latinised in culture. According to Abbot Nicholas of Thingeyrar in Iceland, who returned from his travels in

1154, there were Varangians in the Byzantine garrison at New Paphos. (Incidentally, there was a fortress at New Paphos, which had evidently recovered to some extent.)

Renaud de Châtillon, the Frankish adventurer, made an expedition to the island in 1156, apparently with Armenian help, accompanying wholesale pillage with murder and mutilation. He was forced to humiliate himself before the Emperor in 1159, but a threat now revived from another quarter. In 1158, the Emir of Egypt made a raid in which the governor's brother was carried off. Two years later, Raymond III of Antioch sent pirates to attack Cyprus after the Emperor Manuel had failed to marry his sister Melissendra. And, as if Eastern and Western enemies were not enough, in 1166 large sums of money were extorted from the island by Andronicus, the newly-appointed governor of Cilicia. However, he deserted his post in the following year. In 1184, Isaac Ducas Comnenus, great-nephew of Manuel, established himself in Cyprus, after the fashion of relatives of royalty in times of decay, and declared himself Holy Emperor of the island. The new Byzantine Emperor, Isaac II Angelus, sent a fleet against him, but the usurper, with the help of the Spanish-Sicilian admiral Margarito, defeated it. In addition, the simultaneous Norman advance made a diversion in the usurper's favour, for he had married a sister of William III of Sicily. Another Frankish raid took place in 1191, which would have advertised the weakness of the island as an independent state.

Chapter 4

From the Conquest by Richard the Lionheart to the End of Venetian Rule

THIS CHAPTER of Cypriote history falls naturally into three periods: government by a Frankish aristocracy, partial control by the Genoese and the Mamelukes, and domination by the Venetians.

The establishment of the Crusader kingdom of Jerusalem in 1099 proved unfortunate for the Byzantines. Under Saladdin, a vigorous leader of Kurdish extraction, the Seljuq-Turkish and Arab Moslems mobilised their superior numbers and effectively checked the Crusaders. Frustrated, the warlike adventurers of feudal Europe fell upon the 'schismatic' Christians in their rear. Cyprus, situated on the main sea-route to Palestine, was an early and obvious prize.

In 1187, Saladdin destroyed the Crusaders' forces at the Horns of Hattin, west of the Sea of Galilee. Among the captured was Guy de Lusignan, King of Jerusalem and future King of Cyprus. He had gained his title to Jerusalem by marrying Sibyl, heiress to the throne. The following year he and his brother Aimery were released in exchange for the town of Ascalon and a promise, later broken, that they would never again bear arms against Islam. In the meantime, Saladdin had taken Acre and Jerusalem. Soon only the coastal towns of Tyre, Tripoli, and Antioch remained in Christian hands, though they also retained a few strongholds such as al-Marqab, Tortosa, al-'Arimah, Chastel-Blanc, and Krak des Chevaliers.

News of these disasters inspired the Third Crusade, in which Philip Augustus of France and Richard of England played a prominent part. They were held up for a time by contrary winds, and spent the winter of 1190/91 in Messina. Berengaria, daughter of the King of Navarre, was brought there by Richard's mother, Eleanor of Aquitaine, to be his bride. When Richard's fleet sailed on 10 April 1191, one of the ships contained his sister Joanna of Sicily, and Berengaria. Driven by one of the violent storms which are common in Cyprus waters, their ship sought shelter at Lemesos. Others were wrecked. Benedict of Peterborough tells us that Isaac Comnenus, who was in league with Saladdin, prevented the royal ladies from obtaining supplies in Cyprus, and robbed the wrecked crews. Isaac's demand that the ladies should land was rejected, and after two survivors of the wrecks, Roger de Harcourt and William du Bois of Normandy, had cut their way through his forces to the ladies' ship, he set up fortifications on the beach and put to sea in pursuit.

At this point, Richard arrived from the Gulf of Adalia (Antalya). He landed, and Isaac fled. As might be expected, the Latin merchants resident in Cyprus welcomed the English king. Groups of alien merchants are not noteworthy for their loyalty to the countries in which they prosper, unless of course their interests are involved. However, we have it on the authority of one Neophytus (who is perhaps the saint of that name writing at an advanced age) that the native Cypriotes, disgusted with the rule of Isaac, also welcomed Richard.

To begin with, Isaac promised to help with the Crusade, but then fled and sent a message to Richard demanding his withdrawal. Richard landed horses and took Isaac's camp, gaining great booty and the 'imperial' standard. He was now joined at Lemesos by a reinforcement from Syria, including Guy de Lusignan, whose right to the Kingdom of Jerusalem had been contested on the death of his wife. On 12 May 1191, in the chapel of the fortress at Lemesos, Berengaria became Richard's wife and was crowned Queen of England. Meanwhile, Isaac's wife and daughter had retired to Kyrenia, where there has been a stronghold throughout so much of Cypriote history. Richard sailed for Famagusta, disregarding messages from Philip Augustus urging him to come to Acre, and marched on Leukosia. After a skirmish at Tremithoussia, near Athienou, Isaac took refuge in the Pentadactylos range. At Leukosia Richard fell sick for a time while Guy took Kyrenia. After some more fighting, notably at St Hilarion above the strategic Kyrenia Pass, Richard moved to attack Buffavento Castle, and Isaac surrendered. The booty was immense, and the native islanders gave up half their possessions. A Frankish garrison replaced the Greek, and two justiciars were appointed by Richard to send supplies to the Crusaders in Syria. Thenceforth, Cyprus was to be a Crusaders' base of operations for over a century. Isaac was handed over to one Ralph Fitz Godfrey and, on Ralph's death, was passed on to the Knights Hospitallers, who took him to Margat, near Tripoli.

The conquest of Cyprus by the King of England was a matter of great importance. Isaac, however unpopular, was the last independent Greek ruler of the island until 1960. Domination by Richard also provides an interesting historical precedent for the period of British rule after 1878.

Having made his arrangements for provisioning from Cyprus, Richard sailed for Acre with Guy, and reached it after a sea-fight. When he had gone, a Cypriote monk, a relative of Isaac Comnenus, gathered his adherents for a rebellion. As so often, the clergy provided political leadership for a subjugated people. Richard had shown humanity, but to the Cypriotes he was a foreign despot, rather than the figure of romance he is to us. The rebellion came to nothing, for Robert de Turnham, who had been left in charge by Richard, struck quickly and hanged the monk.

Clearly, Cyprus was proving something of a liability, and Richard sold control over it to the Knights Templars, a fighting order originally founded in 1118 for the protection of pilgrims to the Holy Land. The price was 100,000 gold dinars, of which 40,000 were to be paid immediately and the rest was to be raised by taxing the Cypriote population. No wonder Neophytus, writing in 1196, spoke of the aggravated sufferings of the people and the exodus of the rich over the preceding few years. Resentment against the exactions of the Templars crystallised in a plan to massacre them and their dependants. With only fourteen mounted Brethren, twenty-nine other mounted men, and seventy-four footsoldiers, their leader Bouchart first took refuge in Leukosia Castle, and then made a surprise sally, spreading destruction throughout the island. But it was obvious that their position was untenable in the long run.

After the recapture of Acre by the Christians in July 1191, Richard's negotiations on behalf of Guy de Lusignan for the retention by Guy of his title to Jerusalem were unsuccessful. Now the Templars were glad to make an arrangement whereby Guy compensated them for their investment and gained another realm. Guy did homage to Richard for his new realm, as a fief to be retained during his lifetime, but on Guy's death in 1194 Richard failed to claim the reversion and Constantinople was too feeble to do more than protest. Yet, up to the early sixteenth century, the English still regarded Cyprus as rightfully theirs, and in 1879 W. Hepworth Dixon was to reassert this claim on page 139 of his *British Cyprus*.

The Government of the Lusignans

The Lusignan period began with Guy in 1192 and lost much of its power after the assassination of Peter I in 1369. Relative stability was maintained, despite the rivalry of the Frankish nobles, because society was organised on a hierarchical basis. Egalitarian systems, in so far as they are egalitarian in practice and not just in theory, break down much sooner.

The period was one of great prosperity, in which the native

population shared to a comparatively small extent. However, this prosperity was dependent on the ability of the Franks to hold the island by force of arms, and at least no tribute was being sent abroad, for the first time in twelve hundred years. In addition, the Franks were reasonably humane.

The feudal system of the west European Middle Ages is most perfectly exemplified in the kingdoms of Jerusalem and Cyprus, and Cyprus retained the system long after it had crumbled elsewhere, indeed up to the Venetian period. Government was in the hands of an *Haute Cour,* comprising the entire body of barons, possessing executive, legal, and judicial powers, and presided over by the King or his representative. Most of the barons, like Guy himself, were Franks who had been forced out of Palestine or Syria.[1] All holders of fiefs were technically liegemen to the King, so that the latter could not punish a liege except by judgement of the *Haute Cour.* In matters of religion, marriage, and testaments the nobles came before church courts, and all cases involving non-noble Franks, including those which also involved noblemen, came before the *Cour des Bourgeois,* or *Basse Cour,* from which there was no appeal to the higher court. A Viscount appointed by the King presided over the *Basse Cour,* and his lieutenant, the *mathesep,* or *mactasib* (a word of Arabic origin), kept strict control over the markets. Commercial honesty was enforced much more strictly than it was when the society came to be dominated by the merchants themselves. The whole system of law was regulated by the Assizes of Jerusalem, a composite work of different dates, much of it from the pen of John d'Ibelin (*c.* 1268).

In the thirteenth century at least, the King's officers were the Seneschal, who supervised the court mercenaries, the finances, and the fortresses; the Constable, who commanded the army in the King's absence; the Marshal, the Constable's lieutenant, who was in direct charge of the mercenaries, carried the royal banner in battle, distributed spoils, and replaced horses; the Chamberlain, who personally attended the King and was steward of the royal household; and the Chancellor, an office of less importance in Cyprus than in the West.

Apart from his lieges and the mercenaries, the King could call upon the fighting orders established in the island and, in times of national emergency, the *arrière ban* (i.e. all citizens capable of bearing arms). The Knights of the Temple, of St Thomas, and of the Hospital of St John of Jerusalem all owned castles, of which the most outstanding example is the Commandery of the last-named at Kolossi, controlling the Akrotiri peninsula. Castles were also built,

---

[1] 300 knights and 200 *sergents à cheval* were initially settled in Cyprus.

or rather rebuilt, along the northern range, from Kantara (literally the Arabic word for bridge)[1] westwards.

Under the Lusignans, the capital city grew in circumference to some nine miles, as opposed to the present three-mile circuit of the Venetian walls, built in 1567. It contained some eighty churches. Owing to their difficulty in pronouncing Lefkosia (still the Greek form) the Franks called the city Nicosia, as they called Larnaca Narnaka. Owing to the converse confusion, they called the Byzantine Nemesos Lemesos, and the new name stuck.[2]

The chief glory of Lusignan Cyprus was Famagusta (originally Ammochostus, and still so called in the Greek form). It had been a town of some importance in the seventh century, but did not rise to prominence until about the end of the thirteenth century. It became the greatest emporium in the eastern Mediterranean, and there were said to be 365 churches within its walls, one for each day of the year. The fall of Acre in 1291 enhanced its prosperity because many Christian merchants took refuge there and trade with the Moslem world continued as before. As in ancient times, the Syrian ports were the land terminals for caravans coming from as far afield as China, and since the eighth century trade with the Far East had also been carried on via the Indian Ocean and the Red Sea, so that goods arrived in Cyprus from Egypt also. What remains of Famagusta's one-time magnificence can still be seen in the present-day Turkish quarter, within the Venetian walls.

But Cyprus was not just an entrepôt for spices and other Eastern goods. Episkopi, for example, was a very important centre for sugar production.[3] Other exports included wine,[4] olive-oil, salt, the cotton goods for which the island was famous, and embroidered vestments. The best-known of Cyprus wines was *commandaria*, named after the Grand Commandery of the Knights of the Hospital of St John of Jerusalem, and so perhaps the oldest named wine in the world. It was a favourite with the Plantagenets, and Raleigh was to obtain from Elizabeth the monopoly on its sale. The vine of Champagne was introduced from Cyprus by Theobald IV, Count of that province and King of Navarre, after visiting his cousin Alice, for some time Queen of the island. The vine of Madeira was introduced

---

[1] Another Arabic place-name of note is Komi Kebir.
[2] I suggest that the Middle French 'l' was pronounced with the tongue in a dento-alveolar position, as in Modern French, and that the Franks confused the Greek pre-palatal 'l' with 'n' because it was made with the tongue in a similar position to that adopted for the articulation of 'n'.
[3] Sugar was introduced from Egypt in the tenth century. (see F. Brandel, *La Méditerranée et le monde méditerranéen à l'époque de Philippe II*, Paris, 1949, p. 122.)
[4] Richard had drunk Cyprus wines in 1191.

from Cyprus in the fifteenth century, and both Marsala and Tokay are said to be of the same provenance. The Cyprus wine was reckoned powerful, and the natives mixed it with water in the proportions common among the ancients, one to four. Some English knights died of drinking it neat, and their tombs were on view in 1344/5.

In the brilliant and warlike Frankish scheme of things, the Cypriote Greeks held lowly positions, outshone by the nobles and the rich merchantry of many nations. It is true that the native laws and customs were only abrogated when they conflicted with those of the conquerors, but we have the description of miserable conditions attributed to St Neophytus, and in 1211 Wilbrand of Oldenburg speaks of the Franks ruling a population of debased, ill-clad serfs, much given to wine-drinking. It is at least good to know that they had the wine to drink, and it seems that their position improved somewhat as production rose over the first two centuries of Lusignan rule. New plants and cultivation methods were introduced, and cereals seldom had to be imported.

According to Philippe de Mézières, writing in 1389, the lowest class of Cypriote serfs, called *Parici* in Latin (*Paroikoi* in Greek), rendered a *corvée* (i.e. unpaid labour) to their lords of two days each week, and their lords took one-third of their produce, excluding seed, as had been the custom under the Byzantine dukes. It is worth remarking that these terms are less disadvantageous than those obtaining in many underdeveloped agricultural areas of the world today. In addition, the *Parici* paid a poll tax, which was increased under the Lusignans. Lords could not inflict mutilation or death upon their serfs, but there were regulations governing the marriage of serfs belonging to different lords. A second class, of 'freemen' called *Perperiarii* (*Perperyarioi*), performed the same *corvée* and paid the same tribute, as well as an annual tax; and a third class, consisting of those who had been emancipated, and called *Francomati* or *Eleutheroi* (*Lefteri* in its demotic form), held their lands free and were paid some wages, though they had to render from a tenth to a fifth of their crops to their lord. Marriage between the *Francomati* and the serfs was frowned upon, and the former came under the jurisdiction of the magistrate, not the local lord. In time a native bourgeoisie re-arose, entering commerce, the administration, or the army, and enjoying higher living standards than they could have done at the end of the Byzantine period. Those who are shocked at the notion that the feudal period had something to be said for it should reflect that the rise in the standard of living of the masses, where it has occurred, owes more to changes in techniques than in the structure of society.

The Principal Events of the Period

As in the case of the Ptolemies, the continuity of the Lusignan dynasty was a factor making for stability, and individual monarchs had considerable influence on events. The family was a typically Frankish one, previously settled in Poitou, and its origins are evident when chroniclers specifically refer to the fair hair of Hugh I, Peter I, and Janus. Of course, a majority of those in between, including the queens, must also have been fair, for otherwise the recessive characteristic would not have survived. The separateness of the Franks was long maintained by a ban on intermarriage with the subject people. As in all such situations, loss of distinctiveness in the dominant group coincided with the break-up of the system. This is by no means to imply that subjected peoples are incapable of creating lasting systems of their own, but such systems will be different because the peoples themselves are.

Aimery (1194–1205)

Guy had derived his authority from his title to Jerusalem, but was not officially King of Cyprus; whereas his brother Aimery, elected to succeed him by the *Haute Cour,* managed to gain both crowns. In 1192, Richard had transferred his rights over Cyprus to Henry, Count of Champagne; and Aimery, before his election, aroused Richard's ire by intriguing with the Pisans. The Italian city-states were expanding trade in the rear of the Crusading armies, and their activities were of steadily increasing political importance.

Aimery soon established his *de facto* control, and in 1197 Henry of Champagne ceded his rights over Cyprus, foregoing the 60,000 dinars still owing from Richard's deal with the Templars, but gaining the County of Jaffa, which Aimery had held as of right. The same year saw the culmination of Aimery's efforts to obtain recognition as King from a competent feudal authority. He did homage to the Bishop of Hildesheim as representative of the Emperor Henry VI, and received in return the crown, sceptre, and sword of kingship. After many presents had been exchanged, the warlike bishop and his companion-in-arms, Count Adolf of Holstein, left Cyprus on their ill-fated German Crusade. A year later, Aimery became King of Jerusalem too, through marriage to Isabel, thrice-widowed Queen of that city. Thus he repeated his brother's marital success.

Isaac Comnenus gave the Lusignans little trouble. He was released in about 1195, but died soon after, perhaps of poison. His wife and daughter then became political pawns of no lasting significance. However, the Greeks could still produce individuals with initiative. One such, Kanakis, known to the Franks as Cannaqui, established himself at Antioch and made raids on Cyprus, carrying off the Queen, Echive d'Ibelin. She and other captives were released at the command of Leo II (the Great) of Cilician Armenia. She died soon afterwards. In 1210, Leo was to marry Sibyl, daughter of Aimery, thus cementing an alliance useful to both.

None of the neighbouring continental territories has ever remained uninfluential for long on the history of Cyprus. Aimery suffered piratical raids from Egypt, which the Sultan, al-Malik al-Adil, was unable to restrain. In retaliation, he seized an Egyptian fleet and in 1204 raided the Nile Delta, returning with considerable booty to his mainland city of Acre. But such plunder was trivial compared with that taken at the sack of Constantinople in the same year. The warriors of the Fourth Crusade were more interested in despoiling the Byzantines than the Egyptians, and many of the Syrian Franks joined them.

Aimery was both a strong and prudent ruler. He forced the restitution of lands which had been given away by Guy with too liberal a hand, built fortresses, and continued the Cathedral in Nicosia. At his death the annual revenue stood at 300,000 white besants (Byzantine silver coins). His death was caused by a surfeit of fish, which brings to mind the death of Henry I of England from a surfeit of lampreys. After Aimery the crowns of Cyprus and Jerusalem were not to be united again until 1269, in the person of Hugh III.

Hugh I (1205–18)

Hugh, Aimery's son, was a minor at his accession, and Walter de Montbéliard (Mümpelgard), Constable of Jerusalem, took over the Regency. Aimery had made a six-year truce with the Sultan of Egypt. The threat now came from the north. Ghiyas ad-Din Kaikhosrau, the Turkish Sultan of Iconium (Konya) in central Asia Minor, attacked the Christian stronghold of Adalia (Antalya) on the south coast. Walter went to its aid and raised the siege. However, there was mutual suspicion between Greek and Frank, as well there might be after the taking of Constantinople. The local Greeks collaborated with the Turks, and the Frankish-Cypriote garrison was forced to capitulate in March 1207. Walter was back in Cyprus within the year.

On attaining his majority, Hugh accused Walter of misusing his office. Walter promised an account of his stewardship to the *Haute Cour,* but decamped the day before with his family and following, together, it seems, with 200,000 gold besants. He took refuge with the Templars at Gastria, on Famagusta Bay, crossed to Acre, and was welcomed by the King of Jerusalem, Hugh's rival. The Regent's lands were then confiscated despite the protestations of Pope Innocent III. Until the Fifth Crusade in 1217, Cyprus had no official relations with Syria and Palestine, but Hugh took part in that campaign and died at Tripoli.

Henry I (1218–53)

Under Henry 'the Fat' Cyprus entered the main stream of European politics. The son of Hugh I, Henry was only eight months old at his accession. Of course, long periods of minority rule were agreeable to the nobility, at least in time of peace, because they established legality without tying their hands. Henry's mother, Alice, was made Regent and guardian of the King. In this capacity, probably because of the weakness of Cyprus at sea, she granted commercial privileges to the Genoese, thus beginning a relationship which was ominous for the future.

Shortly after Alice was appointed Regent, Leopold VI, Duke of Austria, made an attempt to take over the kingdom, but he was foiled by the barons and by Pope Honorius III, who took Alice and the King under his protection. Perhaps as a result of this crisis, Alice agreed to associate with her in the Regency her uncle Philip d'Ibelin, younger brother of John, the powerful Old Lord of Beirut. In effect the two d'Ibelins then governed Cyprus, and did it well.

When King John of Jerusalem sailed for the Delta, Cyprus supplied provisions for the venture, and Eustorge, Archbishop of Nicosia, went with him. Damietta was captured in March 1220 with a little help from the Cypriote Franks. In revenge, the Saracens raided Lemesos, and killed or made captive more than 13,000 people. Damietta had to be evacuated in 1221, and a peace of eight years was made with the Sultan al-Malik al-Kamil.[1] Another disaster of that time was not of human agency. Paphos suffered badly in an earthquake of May 1222, and did not recover until the end of the Venetian period.

Queen Alice was one of those high-spirited ladies who had such an influence over the fortunes of Cyprus in both Lusignan and Ptolemaic times. After falling out with Philip d'Ibelin, she married Bohemund, later Bohemund V of Antioch and Tripoli, and tried to have him replace Philip as Regent. Philip, however, was retained until his death in 1227, when the Old Lord of Beirut officially took over his duties. At this juncture, there occurred a serious threat to the island's independence.

In 1228, Frederick II Hohenstaufen sailed for Lemesos to re-

[1] The recurring 'Malik' means, of course, 'King'.

assert the Imperial claim to Cyprus, which derived from Aimery's homage to Henry VI. Three years before, Frederick had married Yolande, heiress to Jerusalem, and he intended to administer Cyprus in the name of their infant son, Conrad IV. The *Haute Cour* reacted by having Henry I crowned, long before his majority. John d'Ibelin had to give hostages to Frederick, but later ignored his summons and sent the noble women and children to the castle of Dieudamour (St Hilarion). As Frederick marched on Nicosia with his Lombard forces, d'Ibelin retreated to Dieudamour himself. A great deal of diplomatic and military campaigning followed, in which d'Ibelin showed himself both resourceful and chivalrous. The heavy Lombard cavalry devastated the Mesaoria, but were of little use in the northern range. Eventually, the bailies to whom Frederick had farmed out the island were defeated, and the last Lombard stronghold, at Kyrenia, capitulated in 1233. Genoese seapower had been an important factor in reversing the fortunes of war to the advantage of the Cypriote Franks, and Genoa had to be rewarded with trading concessions. In 1236, John d'Ibelin died, and his son Balian, as Constable of Cyprus, took his place in the King's confidence. Ten years later, Henry was to be released by Pope Innocent IV from the fealty he had been forced to swear to Frederick.

When Jerusalem was threatened by the Khwarazmians in 1244,[1] an appeal to Henry (as also to Bohemund V of Antioch) was without avail, and the city fell in August of that year. In the ensuing disaster at Gaza a Cyprus contingent of 300 men was wiped out. The whole fabric erected by the Westerners in the Near East was crumbling, but the only European monarch to respond to the call for a new Crusade was St Louis of France.

By the time the French armies and the Genoese fleet had arrived in Lemesos, in September 1248, Tiberias and Ascalon had also fallen. In May 1249, St Louis sailed for Egypt. Henry of Cyprus was with him on his entry into Damietta in June of that year, but then returned home. However, the Cypriote Franks distinguished themselves at the Battle of al-Saghir in February 1250. After failure of the Crusade, St Louis called in at Cyprus on his return to France.

Hugh II (1253–67)

Henry's first wife was Stephanie, sister of Hayton of Armenia and daughter of Leo and Aimery's daughter Sibyl. After her death,

---

[1] The Khwarazmians were central Asian Turks (from Chorasmia) who had ruled a large empire in Iran. They had been pushed west by the Mongols, and their soldiers were now homeless and dangerous plunderers.

he married Plaisance, daughter of Bohemund V of Antioch, and before his own death she had borne him a son, Hugh. Queen Plaisance was accepted by the *Haute Cour* as Regent and guardian of the King, and the succession of minors over three consecutive generations goes far to explain why the baronage in Cyprus remained so influential. Shortly afterwards she contracted a union with Balian d'Ibelin, namesake and nephew of Henry I's adviser. Balian, eldest son of John of Arsur, Bailie and Constable of Jerusalem, was then in his teens. Pope Alexander IV objected to the match on the grounds that it was within the prohibited degrees, and ordered Hugh of Fagiano to declare it null and void. Queen Alice's marriage to Bohemund V of Antioch had also been annulled. In these cases, the Popes were probably in the right. For dynastic reasons, there is a strong tendency among hereditary rulers to inbreed. If, for example, the fatness which characterised Henry I, Peter II, Janus, and John II of Cyprus was inherited, inbreeding over generations might well have produced another Physcon!

Queen Plaisance did not separate from Balian until 1258, and the same year saw the chief success of her Regency. Her brother, Bohemund VI of Antioch-Tripoli, persuaded the Masters of the Temple and the Teutonic Order, the Communes of the Venetians and the Pisans, and the Frankish knights of Palestine to declare young Hugh II heir to the Kingdom of Jerusalem as well as that of Cyprus. The Grand Master of the Hospital of St John of Jerusalem, together with the Communes of the Genoese and the Spaniards, backed Conradin (successor to the claims of Henry VI and Frederick II), but to no avail. When Plaisance died in 1261 she was succeeded in the Regency of both kingdoms by her cousin Hugh of Antioch. Hugh II died childless at the age of fourteen, and the first Lusignan dynasty came to an end. A couple of years before, Aquinas had dedicated his *De regno* to him, no doubt with a view to supporting him against his powerful barons. When Hugh died, this treatise on absolute monarchy remained unfinished.

Meanwhile, the power of the Italian city-states was growing in the Levant. Outstanding among them were Genoa and Venice, which had been opposed in the fratricidal 'War of St Saba' in Palestine as they had been over Hugh's inheritance. Venice was on the winning side, but the Genoese redressed the balance by helping the Paleologi to retake Constantinople in 1261. The new Byzantine Emperor, Michael Paleologus, wished to regain Cyprus, and was on friendly terms with Baibars Bundukdari, Mameluke Sultan of Egypt from October 1260.

Hugh III (1267–84) and the Mamelukes

Hugh of Antioch-Lusignan was the son of Prince Henry of Antioch and Isabel de Lusignan, deriving his claims to the crowns of Cyprus and Jerusalem through descent from Alice of Champagne. Hugh took his mother's maiden name and his successors followed his example. The *Haute Cour* supported him against more powerful rival claimants, Conradin, last of the Hohenstaufen, and Conradin's supplanter, Charles of Anjou. Its privileges would have been impossible to maintain within a more consolidated monarchy. Another claimant was Mary of Antioch, Hugh III's first cousin once removed, who was a grand-daughter of Isabel I of Jerusalem. In 1277, she was to transfer her rights, or rather claims, to Charles of Anjou in return for an annuity.

Since the conquests of Jenghiz in the first quarter of the thirteenth century, much of Islam had been overrun by the Mongols. The Mamelukes were to redress the balance. They constituted a Praetorian bodyguard of Turkish slaves in Egypt,[1] whose function was to protect the successors of Saladdin. It was they who had repulsed the French invasion and held to ransom St Louis himself. In the following year they overthrew the Sultan Turanshah and set up one of their number, the Emir Aibek, in his stead. They resembled the Franks in that they too were vigorous, turbulent intruders from the north, and also resembled them in their aptitude for the arts of government and in their munificence as patrons of arts and letters.

Attempts by the Christians to cooperate with the Mongols were mostly unsuccessful, though in 1260 Hulagu took Damascus and was meditating capture of Jerusalem with the object of giving it to the Christians. At that juncture, the Khakan Mangu died, and Hulagu started towards Mongolia; so that pressure was relieved for the time being, and the Mamelukes could advance up the coast. They took Caesarea, Haifa, and Arsur in 1265; and the Bailie of Cyprus, as Hugh III then was, led a small force against them. But one after another the Christian fortresses fell, until in 1268 Bohemund was left as Count of Tripoli only, with fiefs at Sidon, Beirut, and (nominally) Tyre. Nor was the tale of fortresses stormed by any means complete even then. However, in 1271 Baibars suffered a set-back, when he sent fourteen galleys to Cyprus painted black like Christian ships and flying the banner of the Cross. The fleet was wrecked near Lemesos, and 1,800 of the crews captured.

---

[1] They mostly came from southern Russia, being shipped from the Crimea by Genoese and Venetians, to whom they were sold by the Mongols of the Golden Horde.

9—C

At this point, Prince Edward of England, shortly to become Edward I, one of the greatest of English kings and a kinsman of the Lusignans, was intervening in Palestine. His plan for an alliance with the Mongols resulted only in a raid by 10,000 Mongol horsemen. With his mere thousand men, he made a raid of his own towards Lydda in July 1271, but his troops suffered from the heat and from over-indulgence in fruit and honey. He then made a more successful raid in company with Hugh of Cyprus, as far as Caco, south of Caesarea. During this campaign Edward almost equalled the ruthlessness of Baibars, when he slaughtered all the Moslems in Nazareth. Because Hugh's knights, led by James d'Ibelin, argued that they were under no obligation to serve outside Cyprus, a truce was arranged with Baibars at Caesarea in April 1272. After an attempt to assassinate him had failed, Edward sailed for England in the same year.

Baibars died in 1277. Kalaun soon emerged as Sultan, and in 1281, having protected his rear by making truces with the Temple, the Hospital, and Bohemund VII, he just managed to stop the Mongols of Iran, together with their ally, Leo III of Armenia, at Homs. A few Franks participated, but the King of Cyprus, whose treaty with Baibars had been of purely local application, was unable to arrive in time.

King Hugh, in the meantime, had been engaged in a struggle with William de Beaujeu, Grand Master of the Temple, who supported the claim to Jerusalem of Charles of Anjou. Hugh was forced to retire to Cyprus, where he seized the Templar houses at Paphos and Lemesos, destroyed their fortress at Gastria, and seized their revenues throughout the island.[1] The Sicilian Vespers, of March 1282, were the beginning of the end for Charles, and Hugh then attempted without success to restore his authority on the mainland.

John I (1284–85), Henry II (1285–1324) and the End of Frankish Syria

Hugh's son John was crowned King of both realms, but it was barely a year before he died. His younger brother Henry succeeded him at the age of fourteen. Henry was an epileptic, though he recovered later in life.

The first half of Henry's reign was disastrous for the Lusignans. After the Mongols had been stopped at Homs, the way was clear for the Mamelukes to reconsider their truces with the Christians. Theologians on both sides had enunciated the principle that faith

---

[1] The Order was to be abolished in 1312 by Clement V, backed by Philip of France.

need not be kept with infidels, thus overriding the natural tendency of warrior-élites to maintain a code of honour. In 1291, Acre, Tyre, Sidon, Beirut, Haifa, and all the remaining Christian outposts on the mainland fell one after another. Henry gave some help through Acre, and came in person for a time, but his efforts were insufficient. By the end of the year only the small island stronghold of Aradus (Arwad or Ruad), north of Tripoli, was left in Christian hands. A slight revival of hope came in 1299, when Ghazan, the Mongol Khan of Persia, invaded Syria with 100,000 men. Together with Hayton II of Armenia, who brought 3,000, he routed the Mameluke forces near Homs and took Damascus. The Franks failed to send help, owing to a squabble between the Temple and the Hospital. Small forces eventually sent from Cyprus were cut up by the Mamelukes, and a raiding expedition to Egypt, led by the King in person, had little more success. In February 1300, the Mongols went back to Persia, and did not return, owing to their wars with the Mongols of Russia and central Asia. Aradus, held by the Templars, fell in late 1302 or early 1303. King Henry, who was ill at the time, made no move to aid them.

The Franks who escaped from Syria took refuge in Cyprus, where they suffered the destitution and misery reserved for those who lose their grip and try to evade their problems by bickering among themselves and making concessions to the enemy. The King did what he could to relieve their distress. Throughout the fourteenth century the Frankish ladies of Cyprus wore mourning for the loss of Syria, but that century has been called the most prosperous in the history of the island. Indeed, the loss of Syria may be said to have benefited Cyprus, which then became the main base for Christian merchants in the Levant; and the Lusignan kings were no longer under the necessity of mounting costly expeditions to the mainland. The King's Greek subjects suffered for a time even more than the Syrian Franks, and some of them fled to Saracen lands to escape starvation.

With the humiliation of the Syrian Franks came an increase in the power of the mutually suspicious Genoese and Venetians. Hill acknowledges their contribution to the fourteenth-century prosperity of Cyprus, but rightly regards them as a 'parasitic growth'. Alone among the merchants, they paid no tolls and, once out of control, their greed was to undermine the prosperity to which they had previously contributed. Fortunately, they spent much of their time at each other's throats. The Venetians were defeated by the Genoese in a naval engagement off Cyprus in 1292, and suffered a more serious defeat off Lajazzo (Ayas) in 1294. The latter action followed a raid by the Venetians on the Genoese in Cyprus. In 1299 and subsequently, there was a great deal of friction between the King and the Genoese, which seems to have led to his favouring the Venetians as a counterweight. The Genoese raided Episkopi in 1302, and their pirates were often active thereafter, for instance in 1312 and 1316. When the Hospitallers left Lemesos to take Rhodes from the Byzantines in 1310, it was a Genoese pirate, Vignolo de Vignoli, who gave them valuable help. The reality of that medieval piracy is brought home to us in Flecker's 'Old Ships' :

> The pirate Genoese
> Hell-raked them till they rolled
> Blood, water, fruit and corpses up the hold.

Other pirates were active too, in particular the Catalans, who raided the island in 1307, among other dates. Both the Catalans and the Pisans obtained rights from Henry II in 1291, and there were also German traders at Paphos. But none of these caused the same amount of trouble as the Genoese, against whom Henry had to take severe measures.

The King's younger brother Amaury, who had been among those left to their fate on Aradus, gathered about him a party of those (including several Ibelins) who felt that the King had badly mismanaged the island's affairs. In 1306, he was elected governor by the *Haute Cour*, which overrode Henry's protests. Amaury also had the backing of the Genoese, and granted the Venetians the privilege of trade without toll which was confirmed by Henry on his restoration, by Hugh IV in 1328, and by Peter I in 1360.

The quarrel between Henry and Amaury was brought before the Pope in Avignon. Among the King's adherents were the Franciscans, and in Nicosia on St George's Day, 1309, one of them, an Englishman, gave a sermon in which he praised the King under the guise of St George. Later, another friar minor likened him to St Peter. In January 1310, Amaury decided to exile Henry to Armenia, for which he was roundly cursed by the Queen Mother (Isabel d'Ibelin) in French, Arabic, and Greek. Amaury diminished his popularity by raising forced loans from the burgesses of the major cities, and in June was stabbed to death by his favourite, Simon de Montolif, who then escaped. A train of events had been set in motion which led to Henry's restoration. The occasion was celebrated most colourfully in both Famagusta and Nicosia, the Frankish burgesses wearing white and red, the Syrians red and green, the Genoese yellow and violet, the Venetians yellow and red, and the Pisans red only. The Palio at Siena gives an idea of what the processions must have been like. Henry was not a strong king, but Dante's reference to him

as a beast in the *Paradiso* (XIX, 145–8) cannot be regarded as justified.

Hugh IV (1324–59)

All prisoners were released at the coronation of Hugh IV, Henry
II's nephew. Though vindictive in private, he was a pacific and
successful king, and the dedication to him of Boccaccio's learned
De Genealogia Deorum libri XV was a fitting tribute.

The chief threat to the Cyprus trade was piracy, which had become as much a menace as in Cicero's time. Occasionally, pirates
were caught and hanged, as in 1325, but Cyprus had no powerful
navy of her own. It even seems that in 1329 the King had to pay a
big indemnity to the Genoese for the destruction of one of their
pirate ships. The Catalans, operating from Cagliari, now began to
outdo the Genoese themselves in piracy, and their destructiveness
must have been partly motivated by resentment at Hugh's ill-treatment of Ferdinand II, Infante of Majorca, who had married Isabel
d'Ibelin, and whose claims constituted a threat to Hugh's security.
Ferdinand had formerly been commander of the Catalan Company,
the terror of whose name still lives in the folklore of Greece.

Prosperity was unaffected by quarrels over the succession. Ludolf
of Sudheim, who was in Famagusta from 1336 to 1341, speaks of
the Cyprus nobility with their falcons, hounds, and even leopards
(for hunting the moufflon), their jewels and fine garments, as the
richest in Christendom. The two main setbacks of Hugh's reign
were the great floods of 1330 and the Black Death of 1348, in which
over half the population seems to have died. Prosperity nevertheless
continued.

Meanwhile, another branch of the Turks was beginning to make
its mark on history. Othman (1289–1326), eponymous leader of the
Ottomans, and Orkhan (1326–59) were dominating Asia Minor.
This was of great concern to Hugh, for the cities of Scandelore,
Anamur, Siki, and Satalia (Adalia) all paid him tribute. In 1334 he
joined the Venetian league against the Ottomans, whose fleet was
largely destroyed. Another victory over them, apparently by the
Cyprus fleet alone, was won in 1338. Cyprus also belonged to the
Holy Union headed by Pope Clement VI which took Smyrna in
1343.

Peter I (1358–69)

Towards the end of Hugh IV's reign, his adventurous son Peter
upset him by travelling to the West in order to recruit for a new

Crusade. To that end, Peter founded the Order of the Sword, with its motto : 'C'est pour loïauté maintenir'. This chivalrous principle contrasts with the treatment by King Hugh of Sir John Lombard, accused of assisting the departure of Peter and his brother John of Antioch in 1349. Sir John was tortured and had his hand and foot cut off before being hanged. At last the princes were pardoned at the intercession of Clement VI, and Hugh allowed Peter to be crowned a year before his own death in order to forestall any attempt by Peter's nephew, also called Hugh, to dispute the succession.

The royal treasury had become exhausted under Hugh, and Peter needed considerable sums for his Crusade. Thus the *Perperiarii*, many of whom had become civil servants and rich burgesses, were allowed to buy themselves off the poll-tax, the price falling from 2,000 to 1,000 white besants.

Rioting was very much a feature of the time, especially at Famagusta between the Genoese and Venetian factions. In 1360, on reconfirmation of her privileges, Venice refused Cypriote traders reciprocal exemptions on the grounds that all would then demand them. After a good deal of unpleasantness, including the cutting out by the Genoese of the tongue of a Pisan in service with the King, a treaty with Genoa followed in 1365. One of the main difficulties in dealing with the Venetians and Genoese was that so many Levantines had obtained recognition as belonging to those nations, and therefore claimed their rights—a somewhat similar situation to that which was to obtain in the nineteenth century as regards the British empire. Such 'naturalised' persons were called White Genoese and Venetians, and there was a category of Black ones too, mostly manumitted slaves.

Peter has been called the last of the Crusaders, whereas that title really belongs to King Sebastian of Portugal (killed at al-Qasr al-Kebir in 1578). However, it is true that conditions were less propitious for such activity in Peter's time than they had been in the century before. To begin with, Peter turned his attention to Asia Minor. When Gorhigos was offered to him by its Armenian population he sent an English knight there, one Sir John, with four companies of archers as a garrison. A later assault by the Grand Karaman was to be repulsed by Peter's brother John, and the place was to remain in Lusignan hands until the reign of John II.

Next, Peter attacked the league of Turkish emirates which had coalesced against him. Adalia, the centre of the emirate of Tekke and the Satalie of Chaucer's Knight, was taken by storm in 1361, and Froissart states that all in the city were slain.

Between 1362 and 1365, Peter was in the West gathering support, while raids and counter-raids went on around Cyprus. In 1363, he visited Edward III of England, and was honoured by him with a splendid tournament at Smithfield and other entertainments. Peter was robbed by highwaymen on his way back to the English coast, but Edward paid all his expenses and gave him a fine ship called the *Catherine*, which Peter left behind, presumably because he wished to return overland. Like other monarchs, Edward wanted no part in the new Crusade, except the island of Cyprus itself, should Jerusalem be retaken!

In France once more, Peter visited the Black Prince in Aquitaine and witnessed the anointing of Charles V at Rheims, before visiting the Emperor and the kings of Poland and Hungary on his way to Venice. On account of his help in suppressing a rebellion against them by the Cretans, the Venetians were willing to provide him with ships, men, and artillery. One hundred and forty vessels assembled at Rhodes, and Cyprus merchants were withdrawn from Syria as a feint, but the real objective was Alexandria, which was taken in October 1365. After three days of massacre and looting, the Christians withdrew. The event is celebrated in the epic *La prise d'Alexandrie* by Guillaume de Machaut. Seventy ships were laden with the plunder, and the 5,000 captives included Eastern Christians. The Genoese prudently took no part in the fighting, but secured 800,000 florinsworth of loot.

Amadeus, Count of Savoy, and the King of France were now ready to take the Cross, but the Venetians, anxious for their commercial interests when they heard that Egypt had stopped all trade with the West, sent out the false news that Peter had made peace, and the project came to nothing. Venice also forbade the export of arms and horses to Cyprus.

Peter sent emissaries to the Emir Yalbugha al-Khassik, ruler of Egypt and guardian of the Sultan, offering to meet him in single combat or decide the issue by a combat of champions. However, the Cypriote Franks so impressed the Mamelukes with their prowess in a jousting display that the challenge was not taken up. In this connexion, it should be remembered that the Franks in battle were nearly always opposed to superior numbers. Another incident illustrative of Peter's character occurred later at Rhodes, where a knight called Rochefort dared him to a duel. Peter came to meet him, but Rochefort failed to arrive. Another quarrel, with a friend of Rochefort's called Lesparre, had to be reconciled by the Pope. Pope Urban V called Peter an 'athlete of Christ', but the spirit of *Nemo me impune lacessit* cannot be reconciled with the cheek-turning of the Christian.

Peter's forces succeeded in sacking Syrian Tripoli but, under pressure from the trading states, including the Catalans, he came to an agreement with Yalbugha. Yalbugha was then murdered on account of his desire for peace, the young Sultan Sha'ban being especially hostile, and Peter made several more raids on the Moslem mainland. On a visit to Italy some time afterwards, he was offered the crown of Armenia, which he eventually accepted; but he never ruled his new kingdom.

King Peter's athletics were not confined to those in which he participated for the greater glory of religion. Though fond of his termagant wife Eleanor of Aragon, whose shift he took with him on his travels, he also had two mistresses. The first of these, Joanna l'Aleman, was brutally treated by the Queen in his absence, but the Queen herself seems not to have been blameless as regards extra-marital activities. As time went on Peter was becoming more morose, no doubt over the failure of his plans. His persecution of the Giblet family because he coveted a pair of their greyhounds is a case in point. The *Haute Cour* took alarm at his growing absolutism, and in January 1369 some nobles, including Philip d'Ibelin and Sir Henry de Giblet, decided to act. They waited until his second mistress, Echive de Scandelion, had gone out of his room, and then stabbed him to death. The Turcopolier, or master of light horse, Sir James de Nores, then came in and castrated the King's already headless body, making a remark appropriate to the occasion. It was not so much violence as the very personal expression of it that characterised the Middle Ages. Peter's own brothers, John, Prince of Antioch, and James, Constable of Jerusalem, later James I, were held back during the killing, but later joined in persecuting Peter's adherents.

Whatever Peter's faults, we should keep in mind the great impression he made on his time, as exemplified in laudatory references by Chaucer in *The Monkes Tale* and by Villon in his *Ballade des Seigneurs du temps jadis*.

Peter II (1369–82) and the Genoese

Peter I's son and namesake succeeded at the age of fifteen. Unlike his father, he was mild and lethargic, so that his realm offered a standing temptation. His uncle, Prince John of Antioch, acted as Regent.

There was little friction with the Moslems during Peter II's reign, but the Genoese were another matter. Trouble arose when he was crowned King of Jerusalem at Famagusta in October 1372. There was a quarrel as to whether a Genoese or a Venetian should hold the right-hand rein of the King's horse as he rode out of the

Cathedral, and the Frankish gentlemen sided with the Venetians. The Genoese were plundered and some were defenestrated. There was a truce, but many Genoese then left secretly with their treasure. The Pope, Gregory XI, attempted to mediate, without success. In the spring of 1373 the Genoese Cattaneo arrived off Cyprus with seven galleys supplied by the Mahona, a Genoese financial organisation,[1] and demanded the Pope's award of compensation and the handing over of Venetians guilty of killing Genoese. The Venetians were too much occupied with the war of Chioggia to intervene. The Cypriote Franks withdrew their garrison from Gorhigos and allowed it to fall into the hands of the Bey of Tekke in return for tribute, rather than let it become a Genoese base. It made little difference. After making further, more exorbitant demands, the Mahona fleet burned Lemesos, and invited the slaves, serfs, and criminals to join them. Among those they incited to rise were Bulgars, Greeks from Romania, and Tatars, the last bought from Latin or Turkish merchants or else descendants of some brought in during the Crusading period. The Genoese took Paphos and, after the arrival of a further fleet, which increased their forces to 14,000 men, Famagusta and Nicosia. The struggle was fierce for a time, but the King provided no decisive leadership, and the enemy were able to loot the cities and maltreat the people. Among those they robbed were two Nestorian brothers Lakha, from whom they took two million ducats, and the Prince of Antioch, from whom a hundred thousand were taken. They also killed some of those who had taken part in Peter I's murder, a gesture which cost them nothing.

The Constable James retired to Kyrenia, and the leader of the Genoese expedition, Campo Fregoso, boxed the King's ears when forcing him to instruct the Constable by letter to hand over the stronghold. This missive had no effect, but Queen Eleanor, who now began to meddle in earnest, ordered the Constable back to the Kyrenia Pass when he was advancing on Nicosia. However, he surprised a Genoese train of camels and wagons on its way to Famagusta. Later, after the Queen had managed to trick the enemy and reach him with a supply of money he defeated a Genoese force sent against him. In another series of attacks, the Genoese succeeded in outflanking the Constable's Bulgarian mercenaries in the Kyrenia Pass, when a Greek priest was induced to show them a path round their position. Basically, it was the same tactic as the Persians had used at Thermopylae. The Genoese made attacks on Kyrenia by land and sea, using siege-towers (reminiscent of Demetrius Poliorcetes) and a mangonel (the middle syllable of which gave us the

---

[1] One is reminded of the East India companies' rôle in extending Dutch and English power in the East.

word 'gun'). They were repulsed with other missile weapons, together with Greek fire, and backed down when the Cypriote Franks
responded to the suggestion of a fight in the open. On their way
back to Nicosia, the main body of besiegers was decimated by
Bulgars who had reestablished themselves in the Pass. However, an
attack by the Constable's forces on Nicosia failed. Since the Genoese
held the trump card—the King—a settlement had to be arrived
at. The Genoese did not keep their side of the bargain, and took
the Constable James back with them to Genoa as a prisoner, as
well as many Frankish-Cypriote knights, some of whom were married to Genoese ladies. They began by insisting on an indemnity
of 900,000 ducats, and by a treaty of October 1374 they gained a
perpetual tribute from Cyprus of 40,000 gold florins a year, plus
a fine of 2,012,400 more to be paid over twelve years. But the
greed of merchants masquerading as statesmen is seldom good
business in the long run. Imposition of the exorbitant tribute was
one thing, collection quite another. It is true that they gained
Famagusta as 'security', and Hill has estimated that in about 1395
that city had double the trade of all Cyprus about 1855; but monopoly drove away the merchantry of other nations, and the city
actually became a liability in the fifteenth century. An important
point is that the Genoese, despite their superiority in heavy weapons,
had failed to dominate the island as a whole.

An interesting development of Peter II's reign was an attempt,
backed by Margaret of Lusignan, Despotissa of the Morea, to
promote a marriage between the King and Irene, daughter of the
Byzantine Emperor John V Paleologus. But there was to be no such
Franco-Greek union until the time of John II. In 1376, Peter was
betrothed to Valentina Visconti, daughter of the Duke of Milan.
Queen Eleanor hated her as a rival, and so had to be sent back to
Aragon for good. Eleanor's greatest triumph had been in procuring the assassination of the Prince of Antioch, in revenge for his
presumed complicity in the murder of Peter I. She first persuaded
him of a plot against him by his Bulgars, so that he had them
thrown one by one from St Hilarion Castle. He was then defenceless.

After the Visconti marriage, the Milanese, Venetians, and Catalans agreed to help against the Genoese, but an attack on Famagusta was unsuccessful. In 1381, Venice made peace with Genoa
and agreed not to interfere in Cyprus.

James I (1382–98)

Peter II died without issue, and was succeeded by his uncle, the
Constable James. He had suffered a great deal during his imprison-

ment in Genoa, and his wife, Héloïse of Brunswick, had to support them both for a time with her needle. However, they had certain Genoese friends, and when their son was born in 1374, he was given the name of Janus, after the mythical (but appropriate) founder of Genoa. James returned in 1383, under a treaty whereby Genoa retained Famagusta and two leagues round it, besides gaining Kyrenia as a 'pledge' and 852,000 florins in instalments down to 1394 (one florin equalling four gold besants). This left only Salines (Aliki) and Lemesos as major ports which the Cypriotes might use without restraint.[1] Janus was only released after a new treaty in 1392. In spite of the continually extended Genoese impositions, the crushing salt tax in a land which exported salt in great quantity, and the evil custom of farming out the collection of revenues, not to speak of the plague in 1392/3, Thomas of Saluzzo (in 1395) still speaks of the love of the Cypriotes for luxury. The submission of Genoa to France in 1396 meant that some of the pressure on Cyprus was relieved.

James I was a handsome and hospitable man. He entertained Hotspur and Bolingbroke when they visited the island in 1392. After the rout of the Christian forces by the Ottoman Sultan Beyazit in 1396, he contributed a large sum towards a loan for ransoming the captives.

Janus (1398–1432) and the Mameluke Invasion

Despite his corpulence, Janus was a tall, strong, good-looking man, like his father or his uncle Peter I. In 1399 he was crowned King not only of Cyprus and Jerusalem but also of Armenia. As successor of Peter I, James had claimed this last crown in 1393, on the death of the exiled Leo VI Lusignan. Before 1401, Janus married Héloïse, sister of Valentina, Queen to his first cousin, Peter II.

Janus tried to take advantage of the growing friction between Genoa and Venice, but his attempts to capture Famagusta in 1402 and 1404, the first with Catalan naval backing, came to nothing. On the second occasion both sides made use of cannon obtained from Venice, the first time that they had been used in Cyprus. Inequitable treaties were broken, and frictions with the Genoese continued, such as the violent disturbance of 1421 in Nicosia.

Meanwhile, the ills of Cyprus multiplied. There was bubonic plague in 1409, 1419, 1420, and 1422, and a plague of locusts from 1409 to 1412. Locust eggs and hoppers were collected and burned in pits, a method used in the island until 1884.

[1] The rise of Larnaca dates from about this time.

There was no threat from the north, for Teimur the Lame had destroyed the armies of the Ottomans in 1402 and set them back at least twenty years. To the south, raids up the Nile and into Alexandria harbour by Cypriotes and Catalans irritated the Egyptian sultans. In 1414 came a truce and a mutual exchange of captives, but from the time of Sultan Barsbai's accession in 1422 raids and counter-raids began again. Two years later, Barsbai, who had been angered by raids on Syria mounted from Lemesos and Aliki, sent a fleet which plundered the whole of Lemesos except the castle and did damage at Kouklia. Janus's counter-stroke, against Tyre, had only limited success. In 1425, two fleets, one from Damietta, the other from Syria, both under the command of one Jerbash, raided places in the areas of Famagusta and Larnaca. Lemesos suffered again. It is pleasant to record that Barsbai would not allow separation of the families of those captured when they came to be sold. In 1426, the friendly Sheikh of Damascus, Muhammad ibn Kokaidar, sent warning to Janus of the Sultan's intention to destroy Cyprus on account of the piracy, but no heed was taken. The Byzantine Emperor, Manuel Paleologus, tried to soften Barsbai's heart with presents, also to no avail. The badly-defended island was too big a temptation. The Genoese wished to relieve the pressure on Famagusta, and both they and the Venetians refused Janus aid.

In the summer of 1426, 180 sail, with a Mameluke force of some 5,000 men, left Rosetta. The force landed in Cyprus under the command of Taghribardi al-Mahmudi, took Lemesos once more, and ravaged the countryside. Janus, together with the Antipope John XXIII, had persecuted the Hospitallers, but now had reason to be grateful to them. Their strongholds at Episkopi and Kolossi held out against the Mamelukes. Janus was defeated by the Mamelukes near the Hospitallers' tower at Khirokitia when his infantry broke and fled. The King and those who stood by him, including the Catalan Carcerán Suárez, fought desperately, but Janus was captured. The Mamelukes then ravaged at will, appropriating, among other things, a massive gold cross at the Orthodox monastery at Stavrovouni. The turn of Nicosia came next, and 5,000 captives were taken there alone. The records, including the laws, were burnt. One of Janus's brothers, Hugh, Archbishop of Nicosia, sent the royal treasure to Kyrenia, the inevitable refuge in time of trouble, and followed with the rest of the royal family. Over most of the island, robbery and rape were the order of the day. The Italian mercenary leader Sforza led Spaniards to plunder the countryside, and peasants turned on the landowners. A Greek called Alexis proclaimed himself King at Lefkonico. After the Mameluke departure, Archbishop Hugh was made Regent, and dominated the situation with the aid of the Hospital. Alexis was hanged in May 1427, the month of Janus's return from Egypt.

King Janus had been humiliated at a triumph in Cairo, taking part shackled and riding on a lame ass, though he did better than some of his followers, who were tortured to death for not apostatising. His ransom came to 200,000 ducats, with an annual tribute of 8,000 more. This was less than the Genoese had extorted (the gold ducat and florin being about the same weight), but constituted a terrible burden on the ravaged island. Part of the tribute was to be paid in camlet, an expensive cloth of mixed silk and camel hair manufactured at Famagusta. Almost needless to say, the Genoese Office of St George (which incorporated the old Mahona) did not bate a stiver of its own tribute. However, Benedict Parnessini, a Genoese, and John Podocataro, a Cypriote noble of Italian origin, gave all or most of their wealth towards the King's ransom. The Hospital contributed largely, and the Pope, Martin V, raised money from the sale of indulgences and redirected church revenue to the same end. Freedom was sold to the *Perperiarii* for a mere twenty ducats, fifty times less than in the middle of the previous century. Janus, now a broken man, placed his affairs in Archbishop Hugh's hands. He was paralysed in 1431, and had his final stroke a year later. With all his qualities, he had not had the character to control the situation in which he found himself as king.

John II (1432–58) and Helena Paleologa

John II was to all appearances somewhat like his father Janus, very tall and fat-legged, but physically active and a fine horseman. However, he was effeminate, and carried the irresoluteness of his father to an extreme. He succeeded at the age of eighteen, with Peter of Lusignan, Count of Tripoli, as Regent and Constable, backed by a council of forty, including Carcerán Suárez, who had been made Admiral of Cyprus by Janus. Yet the King's aunt Agnes seems to have been his principal adviser to begin with. In the year of John's accession the Cypriote historian Machaeras was sent as ambassador to the Sultan of Iconium. He was a Greek with a fair knowledge of French, and thought that Cypriote dialect had become barbarised through the influx of French words (some of which it still retains). His importance is an indication of the rising status of his people.

The new King faced the burdens of tribute to both Genoese and Mamelukes, a repetition of the seventh-century situation in which the Cypriotes had to pay tribute or taxes to both Arabs and Byzantines, without protection from either. With Catalan help, John brought pressure to bear upon the White Genoese, and in 1441/2 made three unsuccessful assaults on Famagusta. In 1447, Genoa handed over the city, as well as colonies elsewhere, to the Office of St George because bad administration and a fall in population had led to its becoming a liability. A tax on foreign merchants was rescinded in 1449, but this had little effect, as is shown by the frequent refusals of prominent Genoese to take the Captaincy of the city. A German pilgrim, Stephen von Gumppenberg, who was there in 1449/50, found fine buildings but mostly a waste within the walls. In 1476, a Venetian admiral was to describe it in similar terms.

Difficulties arose with the Venetians as they had with the Genoese, partly with regard to debts, partly as regards the taxing of the White Venetians, whom the King claimed to be all of Syrian origin, no one of them ever having seen Venice. The year 1434 saw an Egyptian attack on Kolossi, perhaps in reprisal for Catalan raids on Syria, and in 1440 the Egyptian fleet revictualled in Cyprus on its way to attack the main base of the Hospital of St John at Rhodes. In 1448, Gorhigos fell completely under control of the Grand Karaman. Cyprus now had no continental interests. The most important event of the period was the taking of Constantinople by the Ottomans in 1453.

John's first wife, Medea, daughter of John James Paleologo, Marquess of Montferrat, died in 1440. Two years later he married another member of that important clan, Helena, daughter of Theodore II Paleologus, Despot of the Morea, and grand-daughter of the Byzantine Emperor Manuel. Though always ailing, she had a very strong character. The hand of this rather terrifying lady was strengthened by the death of Archbishop, now Cardinal, Hugh within the same year. A mistress of intrigue, she dominated the government for sixteen years, and secured official recognition as Regent from the *Haute Cour*, thus illustrating the decay of baronial power. Aeneas Sylvius (Pius II) says that she kept her husband happy the while by pampering him with delights. Only in the last two years of her life was she challenged, by James the Bastard, John's son by his mistress Marietta of Patras. Helen hated Marietta, and assaulted her, biting off her nose. Stephen de Lusignan tells us that the King witnessed the struggle with the greatest of pleasure, flattered that the Greek Amazons should contend for his affections.

To the Cypriote Greeks Helena was something of a heroine. Among the Greeks she had promoted to high positions was Thomas of the Morea, her foster-brother, who became Chamberlain. The King favoured his own teen-age son James for the Archbishopric, but although James obtained the revenues the Pope would not confirm the appointment. The King's only legitimate offspring, Charlotte, another forceful lady, was the hope of the Latin party, and instigated James to arrange the assassination of Thomas of the Morea. James was then deprived by the King of the revenues of his see, went to Rhodes for some months, returned secretly to Nicosia, killed some partisans of the Queen (including the brothers Gurri, from whom he took 6,000 ducats), and established himself in the archiepiscopal palace. The *Haute Cour* then agreed to reinstate him in his see and revenues.

Charlotte, *en secondes noces*, married Louis, Count of Geneva. Helena, as a Greek Orthodox, was scandalised by this first-cousin marriage, but died before it took place. John's death followed three months later.

Charlotte (1458–60) and James II (1460–73)

Charlotte and her ladies scandalised not only Helena but also Rome and the Court of Savoy with their licence and extravagance. It had been agreed by the *Haute Cour* that she should be Queen and that Louis should succeed if she died without male issue. Technically, she was to reign for six years, though only in authority for the first two. James took the oath of allegiance to her, but did not perform the crowning as Archbishop, the Bishop of Lemesos officiating instead. Soon he attempted a *coup d'état*, was betrayed, and fled to Egypt, where the Sultan Inal received him well. Later, it was to be claimed by the Venetians that James was the true sovereign of Cyprus in that the Sultan, as suzerain, had legally granted the island to him. A fleet was raised in Egypt and accompanied James to Cyprus in September 1460. On landing, he increased his popularity by freeing many serfs, while Charlotte and her rather weak-willed husband retired to Kyrenia like so many before them. The Mamelukes besieged them there until the winter, when they returned to Egypt, leaving behind two hundred of their number at James's entreaty. James now had Savoy, Genoa, Pope Pius II, and the Hospital ranged against him. Kolossi held out, and Charlotte and Louis received help from Rhodes. They controlled some castles in the Paphos district for a time, but had to retire again to Kyrenia. In March 1461, James attacked Famagusta, and failed to take it because his scaling ladders were too short. A Genoese attack on the Carpass was repelled, as previous ones had been. James's adherents soon included the Catalan John Pérez Fabregues, later Count of Jaffa, and the Sicilian Muzio Costanzo, later Admiral of Cyprus. He badly needed them because most of the barons had sided with Charlotte.

As a bastard and usurper, James also needed recognition as King, and went to Italy to obtain it. He was refused by Pius II, partly on account of his association with the Sultan, but was recognised by Florence. In such matters, one recognition is usually enough to crack the dam. Seeing which way the wind was blowing, Charlotte induced the Dominicans to hand over their treasure, and went west herself. The Pope gave her horses and a shipload of provisions, though he refused to excommunicate James, and she received little other help except from Savoy.

James took Famagusta in early 1464, after it had been a running sore in the side of Cyprus for ninety years. He then turned his attention to Kyrenia, where the garrison was reduced to eating horses, dung, cats, and mice. That stronghold was never to be taken by storm, but its commander in this case, Sor de Naves, capitulated and was rewarded with the hand of the King's natural daughter and the office of Constable.

Some apprehension was occasioned by the fact that James had massacred most of his Mamelukes. They had behaved extremely well, but later plotted against his life. The Sultan accepted James's explanation, though the sister of Janibeg, the dead Mamelukes' leader, did not. She sent a Saracen assassin who tried to stab James in the neck on the mole at Famagusta. Being very strong, he managed to shake the Saracen off into the water, where he was dispatched.

King James now took control, sending runaway serfs back to their villages and punishing his enemies. Charlotte and Louis continued to press their claims from Rhodes for several more years, but their efforts came to nothing, except that James had to suppress a peasants' revolt in their favour the year before he died. In 1485, three years after Louis's death, Charlotte was to cede her rights to the House of Savoy, which maintained its ineffectual claim to Cyprus until the late seventeenth century. Indeed, the claim was not extinct until Italy became a republic in 1946.

Although James, who was half-Greek himself, discouraged marriage between the classes, he abolished restrictions in 1468 on marriage between serfs from villages owned by different masters. When he died, of dysentery, he gave orders that the slaves in his galleys should be released, which was done. All the same, conditions deteriorated during his reign. In 1469, there was a famine, brought on by drought, which led to the importation of grain. Over the next two and a half years, three-quarters of the population are said to have died of the plague, and the King took refuge at Akaki. In 1473/4, the locusts returned.

By James's death the nobles of Cyprus were a commixture of

adventurers from every part of the Mediterranean, including a number of non-noble origin. Some were brave men, in particular the Catalans, but the baronage now lacked that cohesion against any outside threat which had characterised the Franks, whatever their internal dissensions. Such cohesion takes centuries to achieve, even when very similar peoples are intermixed.

Individual Greeks benefited from the changed situation. Some Byzantine families seem to have survived and been counted among the nobility, while more were to come in via Venice. Nobles risen from the bourgeoisie were quite often Greeks, and those of Frankish-Cypriote or Gallo-Peloponnesian origin mostly had Greeks among their forebears. It is significant that many Cypriote nobles had now come to refer to themselves as Cypriotes and to distrust the 'Franks', by which was meant western Europeans in general. George Bustron, a Roman Catholic and the close associate of James II, was to write his chronicle in the Cypriote vernacular, and Charlotte spoke only broken French. Greek was, in fact, the normal language of social intercourse, though Italian was common among the merchants. Frankish influence remained in the Cypriote vocabulary and to a certain extent in the local architecture, which had been cut off from Byzantine models.

During the lifetime of James the Bastard the Venetians were becoming increasingly concerned about the expansion of Ottoman power, and needed a base from which to aid its enemies and protect their own trade-routes. A parallel was to occur in the nineteenth century with regard to Russian expansion and British trade-routes. Cyprus was the obvious base in both cases, though other interests were also involved. James, as an enemy of the Genoese, naturally inclined to the Venetians. In 1468, he was married by proxy to Catherine Cornaro, a noble Venetian lady, and agreed that Venice should inherit his kingdom if there was no heir. Catherine was then declared to be the adopted daughter of St Mark, patron of Venice. (Thus Mark intervenes for the third time in the history of Cyprus.) The bride was very beautiful, though this did not prevent James from indulging in gallantries which provoked certain gentlemen to engineer a plot that nearly resulted in his death two years later. James's marriage to Catherine was consummated in 1472.

King Ferdinand of Naples wished his natural son Alonzo, adopted son of Charlotte, to marry James's natural daughter Charla and claim the succession. Prominent in the anti-Venetian party which supported such a match were the Catalans. Lewis Pérez Fabregues, younger brother of John Pérez, was to lead them after the death of James.

10—C

James III (1473–74) and Catherine Cornaro (1474–89)

The Venetian Senate had promised James the Bastard that it would treat his realm as if it were its own. It was true to its word. The Venetian admiral Mocenigo, commander of the 'Sixth Fleet' of the day, was at his death-bed, promising that Catherine would be protected.

Within the year before James's death, Catherine had borne him a son, also called James. The Catalan party now reacted vigorously, with the backing of two Neapolitan galleys. The Queen was forced to agree to the marriage they desired, and the child James was taken away from her. The Venetians then landed, and the people rose in their favour under one Stephen Kaduna. Having failed to capture the fortresses, in particular Kyrenia, their opponents had to flee to the West, where their intrigues proved unsuccessful. Once in control, the Venetians behaved with some leniency, though all Catalans, Sicilians, and Neapolitans were banished from Famagusta, and Venetians were appointed to all the key posts in the government. The infant James died within a short time, thus removing another obstacle to Venetian designs. Among those to be deported in 1476 were Marietta of Patras, to whom the infant king had been confided, and James II's natural children, one of whom, Eugene, was popular and of a winning disposition. The last throw of those in league with Charlotte occurred in 1479, when Sir Mark Venier, a captain of crossbowmen who had been put in charge of the Famagusta garrison, conspired in complicity with Naples to kill Catherine and take the island for Charlotte. He and his fellow-conspirators were hanged.

Queen Catherine seemed content with the 8,000 ducats a year allowed her, while two Venetian 'counsellors' ran the kingdom. Efforts were made to repeople Famagusta, with little success. In 1478, when Scutari, on the Asiatic shore of the Bosphorus, was given up to the Turks, the Scutariotes refused an invitation to settle in Cyprus. In 1486/7, benefice holders were forced to settle there.

The Sultan Kaitbai of Egypt became restive over arrears of tribute, but was mollified with substantial payments. In 1488, when the fleet of the Ottoman Sultan Beyazit made an attempt to capture Famagusta on his way to Egypt, it was sent back to the Dardanelles by a demonstration of twenty-five Venetian galleys. The following year saw an Ottoman raid on the Carpass, and the Venetians responded by increasing the number of stradiot mercenaries. Under these circumstances, the Egyptian Sultan remitted two years' tribute, 16,000 ducats, to help his Venetian allies. This remission did not benefit the Cypriotes, and some of them fled from Venetian exactions to the Ottoman dominions.

The decision of Venice to remove Catherine as a figurehead was precipitated by an attempt in 1488 to interest her in marriage with Don Alonzo of Naples. Two conspirators, Rizzo di Marino and Tristan de Giblet, were captured on the coast of Cyprus. The latter killed himself and the former was hanged in prison three years later. Since there was a possibility that Catherine was implicated in the affair, she was forced to abdicate 'voluntarily' in 1489 and go to Venice. Her brother George helped the Venetian emissary to persuade her, for otherwise the Cornaro family would have suffered. Later, the Grand Commandery of the Hospital of St John became attached to that family. George himself was amply rewarded, and Catherine was allowed to retain her 8,000 ducats a year. She was received with honour in Venice and granted the estate and town of Asolo, where she lived for many years.[1]

The Venetian Period (1489–1571)

Venice had steadily extended control over her main trade routes. In 1206 she had occupied Crete, which she kept until 1669, in 1207 the Cyclades, held until 1566, in 1215 Euboea, held until 1470, in 1386 Corfù, held until 1797, and in 1483 the rest of the Ionian islands. Rhodes, an essential link in the chain, was held by the Hospital until 1522, when its fall to the Ottomans, coupled with the Ottoman conquest of Egypt in 1517, meant that Cyprus was isolated in an Ottoman sea. For the Cypriotes, the only item on the credit side was the overthrow of the Mamelukes, who had been contemplating a descent on the island owing to arrears of tribute and the worsening quality of the camlet in which much of it was paid.

Under Venice, Cyprus was governed by a Lieutenant in Nicosia and two Counsellors. There was also a 'Captain of Cyprus' in Famagusta, who commanded the army in time of peace, while a Proveditor-General took over in time of war. The Lieutenant was always a noble Venetian elected by secret ballot for a two-year tenure of office, and he and his colleagues were continually watched by the spies of the Council of Ten in Venice. The whole system was based on mutual suspicion and counter-checks. As with the Genoese, great difficulty was experienced in finding suitable men to serve as Captains in Famagusta. From this time forward until the twentieth century, Cyprus was not an active political factor in international affairs, and the governors, with few exceptions, are not of sufficient importance to merit special sections in a history.

[1] See Browning's *Pippa Passes.*

The *Haute Cour* was abolished by the Venetians. Indeed, in matters of dowry and marriage settlement the nobles were put under the jurisdiction of the court of the Cypriote Viscount of Nicosia, the old *Cour des Bourgeois*. The Assizes of Jerusalem were still in use,[1] though an Italian translation by Florio Bustron had to be authorised in 1531. Famagusta, a shadow of its former self, was still governed by Genoese laws. A *Reis's* (judge's) court was set up to deal with the affairs of the Christian minority groups, while the Jews were treated separately. By the sixteenth century there were also Gypsies in the island.

Many of the nobles were reduced to complaining about the law of primogeniture or appealing to the Venetians for pensions. Fewer than sixty received stipends as feudatory soldiers. Others emigrated, while yet others contrived to remain rich through compromise. Certain families survived for a very long time, notably the 'Kalimeri', a branch of the de Nores who, like the Lusignans, lasted into the nineteenth century. As in other such cases, there was nothing tragic about the slow decline of the Cyprus aristocracy. Had they resisted more it might have been otherwise.

At first sight, it might seem that the goodish revenues the Venetians obtained from Cyprus were entirely the result of squeezing and exploitation. Malpractices were common, and in 1497 two inspectors were sent out from Venice to investigate them. Francis Contarini, Captain of Paphos, and Troilo Malipiero, Captain of Cyprus, were both found guilty of tyranny and corruption. Martin von Baumgarten, who visited the island in 1508, spoke of all the inhabitants as slaves to the Venetians, paying them 'a third part of their ground, or corn, wine, oil or of their cattle, or any other thing'. This is exaggerated, as Turkish estimates show, though it is true that many serfs still left the island for Rhodes and other places in the Ottoman dominions, driven out by tax-farmers' exactions and petty tyranny as much as by official taxation. A fine of 2,000 ducats had to be imposed on any ship carrying a serf without licence.

Nature also was unkind. Locusts were regarded as a divine visitation, scarcely to be combated. Plague came in 1494, 1505, and 1533. There were floods in 1547, a severe earthquake in 1491, in which part of Nicosia Cathedral was shaken down, and others in 1542, 1546, 1567, 1568 or 1569, as well as a tornado in 1568. In 1490, the population was only about 106,000, as opposed to about half a million in the best of the Lusignan period and more in the Roman period. Nevertheless, it rose to about 197,000 by 1570. In 1562, it was about 180,000, including 50,000 serfs and 90,000 *Perperiarii*.

---

[1] In 1507, a Norman traveller commented upon the Frenchness of the Cypriote nobility.

Sugar production declined under the Venetians and export of it ceased around 1600 owing to competition from Madeira and other places. However, cotton production was expanded. It is to Lefkara that Leonardo is said to have come in 1481 to buy fine cloth for Milan Cathedral, and the well-known modern Lefkaritika embroideries show the influence of sixteenth-century Italian needlework.

Cypriote wine and salt were still held in high regard, and flax, hemp, indigo, and saffron were also produced. Famagusta might be largely in ruins, but Salines took its place to some extent. Nor can the Venetians be blamed for the decline in trade after about 1470, a decline for which the Ottoman severance of trade routes to the East was initially responsible. The most just assessment of the Venetians as rulers is to say with Bernard Sagredo, their Proveditor-General, that their interests were not bound up with the island as those of the Lusignans had been. To the Venetians it was more of a base and a dumping-ground for undesirables, as it had been for much of the Byzantine period.

There was a small rich class of Cypriotes still, and though Dietrich von Niem might speak of Cyprus as an island where French pride, Syrian effeminacy, and Greek flattery and fraud came together, Stephen de Lusignan describes the Cypriotes' love of hospitality, hawking, music, gaming, fencing, and feats of arms. The lowlier people he specifically describes as delighting in games, quail-fighting, dancing, and poetry. Their dirges, in particular, were such as to move the listener to tears. The Venetians temporarily returned the *Parici* to servitude, but in general they and the *Francomati* could buy their freedom and their taxes were not increased. A loophole for the serfs existed in that foundlings were classed as *Francomati*, so that a number of serf children were 'found' in this way.

After the Ottomans had attacked the Carpass again in 1500 and 1501, a treaty was made with the relatively peace-loving Sultan Beyazit II in 1503. Beyazit's successor, Selim I, conqueror of Egypt, made difficulties over the Cyprus tribute, insisting that the arrears of five years should be paid in uncoined gold and not in goods. In 1519, this was agreed to. Ottoman power was increasing by leaps and bounds. Selim's successor, Süleyman the Magnificent, ruled from Algeria to the Caucasus. His armies overran the north Balkans and Hungary, and obliged Austria to pay tribute, while his corsair admiral, Hayrettin Barbarossa, was active in the Aegean and the Mediterranean at large. In 1539, the Ottomans destroyed Lemesos, ending the treaty of 1503. The following year saw a treaty between the Venetians and Ottomans but, despite Venetian bribery of Ottoman officials, a major assault on Cyprus was only a matter of time.

In 1562, Sagredo warned the Signory that the Greek-Cypriote

lower classes would rise if there was no remedy for their grievances. In the autumn of that year one James Diassorin, cousin of the Despot of Moldavia and founder of a school in Nicosia, plotted with Megaducus, a Greek captain of horse, to take over the island, and communicated with the Turks in code. Through a Cretan agent of Venice in Constantinople the plot was discovered. Diassorin was taken, quickly tried, and strangled when the people demonstrated. He had had considerable success in stirring up the Cypriote Greeks with references to ancient glories, and persons to the number of 8,000 who had come into the capital had to be ordered to leave. Secret emissaries sent by the Cypriotes to Constantinople in 1566 were made to disappear by the Venetians. It was said that 50,000 serfs were ready to rise. Nor were the nobility more trustworthy from the Venetian point of view. At one time it was planned to shut them all up in a fortress built for the purpose on the Akrotiri peninsula.

The Ottoman Grand Vezir, Mehmet Sokolli, was consistently friendly towards Venice. However, the most influential adviser of Selim II was the anti-Venetian Joseph Miques, or Nasi, a Jewish banker who was made Duke of Naxos and Count of Andros by Selim. He was one of those Marlowe had in mind for *The Jew of Malta,* and it was he who countersigned the order in 1563 which directed an agent to persuade the Duke of Savoy to revive his claims to Cyprus. The Duke of Savoy would have nothing to do with the Turks, and revealed all to the other Catholic powers, but Miques continued his intrigues. There was one widespread story that Miques excited Selim's desire for Cyprus by plying him with the island's wine[1] (which accords with Selim's nickname, 'the Sot') and another that Selim promised him the kingship of Cyprus if his designs were successful. Whatever the methods by which Miques persuaded the luxury-loving Selim (and worse stories, on no better evidence, have been believed of other royal advisers) there can be no doubt that the acquisition of Cyprus was to the advantage of the Ottomans; so that Miques, like Disraeli, was serving the interests of the empire as well as his own.

The Ecclesiastical Struggle

In northern France, the British Isles, and Sicily a Norman aristo- cracy became gradually assimilated into the native populations and continued for a long time to supply a large proportion of their

---

[1] Robin Parker (*Cyprus: a handbook of the island's past and present,* Nicosia: pub. by the Greek Communal Chamber, 2nd edn, 1964, p. 245) tells a similar story with particular reference to *commandaria.*

leaders. The Frankish aristocracy of Cyprus differed no more in race from the natives of the island than the Norman aristocracy from the natives of Sicily, but in Cyprus there was an added difference in point of religion.[1] The situation of the Protestant English ascendancy in Ireland does not afford a very close parallel because in that case racial differences were much smaller and intermarriage more frequent. However, the native Cypriotes resembled the Irish of the sixteenth century and onwards in that they regarded their Church as a bulwark against cultural domination and gave more allegiance to their priests in political matters once the native secular leaders had been killed, driven out, or forced to compromise with the invaders. From the native Cypriote viewpoint, the Lusignan period was basically one of struggle between the Greek Orthodox and Roman Catholic Churches.

A papal Bull of 1196, issued by the aged Celestine III, organised and established the Roman Catholic Church in Cyprus, much to the disadvantage of its Greek Orthodox counterpart. In Cyprus the Latin Church was not the Church of the people but, given the circumstances, its record is not discreditable. St Francis of Assisi visited the island in the years 1219/20, and shortly afterwards Franciscan friars arrived. Other religious orders also had their representatives in Cyprus.

After the fall of Acre the seat of the Patriarch of Jerusalem was transferred to Cyprus, and in the fourteenth century, partly on this account, partly because of its geographical position, visiting the island became an occasional substitute for pilgrimage to the Holy Land. This had the advantage of not putting money into the purse of the infidel. Shortly after Peter I's murder in 1369, St Bridget of Sweden arrived in Cyprus and pleaded for the murderers with his filial namesake and successor.

As has been remarked in connexion with the Byzantines, Christianity was profoundly modified by the peoples who adopted it, and as the western Europeans differed from the inhabitants of the Byzantine empire, so they produced a form of religion which differed in essential respects from the Eastern Orthodox, and bore even less resemblance to the primitive Church. The feudal society of the West had to accommodate a vigorous class of nobles, whose collective power balanced that of their monarchs, whereas the power of the Byzantine Emperor was limited only by inefficiency or the necessity to compromise. In effect, the war-bands of pagan Europe were still in being, though their energies were more or less canalised in organisational patterns influenced by the example of the Roman world. Further, there was in the West, particularly in the Italian

[1] One might add that Cyprus is as Greek as Sicily is Italian.

city-states, a balance (however uneasy) between secular and clerical power, quite unlike the symbiotic relationship of Church and State in the Byzantine feudal system. This balance made possible the development of specifically secular modes of thought. It is no accident that the Renascence and Scientific Revolution took place in the West.

To some extent the Greeks benefited from the balance of power between the Lusignan state and the Latin Church. The interests of their political and religious rulers were liable to conflict, as when trade with Egypt was carried on or the King laid taxes upon the Latin clergy, despite a papal prohibition in each case. The nobles showed a cordial dislike to too much interference with their Orthodox subjects, on whom they depended for rent money and other feudal dues. In 1223, for instance, Philip d'Ibelin, as co-Regent, objected to the fleecing of Greek priests by their Latin counterparts, and in 1264 the then Regent, Hugh of Antioch, excused himself from helping the Latin Archbishop to inflict punishment on the Greeks, insisting that the permission of the *Haute Cour* was necessary in such a case. Nor was the Latin Church always cast in a punitive rôle. The Popes sometimes restrained the more bigoted of the Latin hierarchy, as in 1243, when Innocent IV told his legate to prevent religious persecution of the Cypriote Greeks. In 1330, when there were twenty-eight days and nights of rain, together with a terrible storm on 10 November, the Pedias rose and inundated Nicosia, drowning thousands. Lemesos (Limassol) was also badly affected. The Latin Archbishop, John del Conte, helped the King's relief measures by throwing open to the destitute not only the churches but also his own house.

The regular establishment of the Latin Church in Cyprus took place five years after Richard's conquest, in the time of Aimery, who had succeeded his brother Guy as ruler of Cyprus in 1194. Under an arrangement made by the papal commissioners, including the Chancellor of Cyprus, the new Latin Archdiocese of Nicosia was to cover the whole central area of the island from north to south, incorporating the former dioceses of Nicosia itself, Tremithus, Citium, Lapithos, Kyrenia, Chytri, Soli, and Tamassus. The Orthodox bishops were not expelled from their sees as yet, and in 1211 Wilbrand of Oldenburg found they had thirteen of them. Alan, Archdeacon of Lydda, one of the papal commissioners, was elected first Latin Archbishop by the new chapter in Nicosia, and the third commissioner, the Bishop of Laodicea, became first Latin Bishop of Paphos. It is hard to believe that these elections caused much surprise.

An interesting example of historical parallelism occurred when Thomas Morosini, as Latin Patriarch of Constantinople after its sack in 1204, made a claim to Cyprus reminiscent of that made under the Emperor Zeno by the Patriarch of Antioch. The Pope, who wanted direct control over the island, refused the claim in 1206 on the grounds that when the Latin Church was established in Cyprus Constantinople was not yet in the Roman communion.

The year 1220 saw the Convention of Lemesos, organised by the papal legate, Pelagius. By this Convention, tithes on Greek church lands were all to go to the Crown and the barons, except where the estates of the Latin Church were concerned. The Greek clergy were freed from the poll-tax and *corvée,* and they were not at first under Latin control as regards dogma, but their movements were strictly controlled and their bishops were subordinated to Latin ordinaries. The Syrians, Jacobites (Monophysites), and Chaldeans (Nestorians) were to be obedient to the Latin Archbishop of Nicosia. Two years later the terms were made more severe, and the Orthodox Archbishop was expelled from Famagusta, where his line had resided since the seventh century, and sent to remote Rhizokarpaso, inland from the ancient port of Carpasia. Only three other sees were to be left to the Greeks after the deaths of their then incumbents : the Paphos diocese, with its centre at Arsinoë (Polis tis Chrysochou); the Lemesos one centred at Lefkara; and the Nicosia one centred at Sóli (Solía). The estates and tithes of the other Greek bishops were to revert to the Latin Church at their death. Thus it was that in the early sixteenth century the revenues of the four Latin bishops were five to ten times greater than those of the Greek. In this respect the Latin Church very much resembled the Protestant Church of Ireland. In the course of time, the Latin clergy became pleasantly accustomed to their lotus land, so that concubinage and hawking were common among them. However, in 1412 the Constantinopolitan monk Joseph Bryennios tells us that the failings of the Cypriote Orthodox clergy in such respects were equal to those of the Latins.

The Greek Church of Cyprus remained in bondage to the Latin until the Turkish conquest, and during that period was the centre of passive resistance to the overlords, although native Cypriote hopes for independence did not truly revive until the time of John II's second Greek Queen, Helena Paleologa. The Orthodox Archbishop Neophytos agreed to the terms of the Convention of Lemesos, but later changed his mind and fled to Nicaea. Having changed his mind once again, he returned to Cyprus, but the Cyprus Orthodox Church did not as a whole submit to the Pope. In 1230, the Cypriote Orthodox bishops, together with some abbots and priests, were exiled, and in 1231 the Patriarch of Constantinople, Germanos, denounced those who cooperated with the Latin Church. In the latter year, thirteen monks of Cyprus (including two who came from

Asia Minor) suffered martyrdom by order of Pope Gregory IX because they upheld the Eastern teaching that leavened bread, as opposed to unleavened, should be used in the Eucharistic service. On this important matter of principle they were put in prison, where one of them died. The remaining twelve were then dragged over the ground and burned alive. The Syrian Jacobites and Nestorians likewise refused obedience to the Roman Church, despite measures taken by the Vatican. The conciliatory measures of Pope Innocent IV from 1243 onwards led to the return of certain of the priestly refugees, and his legate, Eudes de Châteauroux, who arrived in 1248, turned out to be lenient. The Greek Archbishop did him homage, though Greek demands were not met. The next Latin Archbishop, the Tuscan Hugh of Fagiano, who succeeded in 1251, was the reverse of conciliatory, and had a fairly free hand after the death of Innocent IV in 1254. When opposed, Hugh retired in a huff to Italy. When in Cyprus, he bandied excommunications with the Orthodox Archbishop Germanos Pesimandros, although the latter had formally put himself and his Church under the protection of the Holy See. Such were the edifying relations of the two principal Christian Churches.

In 1260 came Pope Alexander IV's *Bulla Cypria*, whereby the four Greek-Cypriote sees were made conterminous with those of the Latins and their bishops had to take oaths of obedience, while all their tithes went to the Latin Church. The elected Greek-Cypriote Archbishop, called Germanos like the Patriarch, was to hold a relatively independent position, but it was intended that there should be no Greek Archbishop after his death. The Greek-Cypriote clergy were severely criticised in the Orthodox world for accepting the Bull and yielding up their independence. However, Hugh de Fagiano deplored what he regarded as excessive leniency, and retired to Tuscany for the second time, while retaining his archbishopric. In 1263/64, the Pope accused the Cypriote Orthodox clergy of blasphemy, sexual perversion, magical practices, etc. One of Hugh de Fagiano's major irritations was the refusal of the civil authorities to punish Greek and Syrian schismatics and heretics. There was also dissension between the Latin Church and the authorities in the matter of tithes, and still more dissension between Archbishop Hugh and the Patriarch of Jerusalem.

Absenteeism among the Latin archbishops was not rare. They were outside the island for thirty-six of the sixty-nine years between 1291 and 1360. For instance, Gerard, who held the position from 1295 to about 1312, was in Cyprus only from 1297 to 1299. During his sinecure there were various irregularities, such as the embezzlement of the funds for the building of the Cathedral of St Nicholas in Famagusta by the treasurer Saurano. Gerard was succeeded by the noble Roman John del Conte, of the Order of Preachers. John was elected in 1312, but only came to Nicosia in 1319. The treaty of 1328, with Genoa, was named after him. His successor, in 1332, was the Franciscan Elias de Nabinaux, who gave up the archbishopric in 1342, when he became a Cardinal and Patriarch of Jerusalem. Elias came into conflict with the canons of Bellapaïs and is noted for an attempt to make Greeks, Nestorians, and Syrian and Armenian Monophysites conform with the Roman Church. They were to retain their rites provided they became Uniates. Nothing came of the plan. The Maronites, by contrast, had allied themselves with the Crusaders, and about the year 1182 had united with the Latin Church, under the jurisdiction of Amaury, Patriarch of Antioch. With their craft and mercantile skills, Syrians were given special inducements to settle in Cyprus, including tax exemptions and a separate *Reis,* or judge, to decide minor cases among them. There were also non-Christians in the island : the Moslems, who since the Lateran Council of 1215 had had to wear distinctive dress, and the Jews, who had to wear a yellow sign on their heads at the insistence of John del Conte. Of course, such distinctions in dress were also enforced upon Christians in the Moslem world.

The Latin Archbishop Philip inserted in the constitution of 1350 two clauses against intermarriage between Greeks and Latins, providing that when such a marriage took place the children were to be brought up in communion with Rome. This action arose out of complaints that some Roman Catholics, especially women, were frequenting the Greek churches. In 1358, the papal legate, the Carmelite Peter de Thomas, caused a riot when he tried forcibly to convert the Orthodox clergy of Nicosia, who had been herded into the Cathedral for that purpose. The mob broke in, and the civil authorities showed no disposition to intervene. The riot was only put down when the Prince of Antioch,[1] brother of the King, arrived with some dignitaries and a number of soldiers. The legate was ordered to leave the island, and though he later regained the confidence of King Peter I and died at the conquest of Alexandria, the riot was a turning-point in the history of Cyprus. Subsequently, Greeks became officers of state, and nobles of Byzantine origin later became soldiers, examples being Sir John Lascaris under Peter I and George Monomachos under Peter II.

On the death of Pope Gregory XI in 1378 occurred the Roman schism. Two popes were elected, Urban VI and Clement VII, and the Cyprus authorities, together with the Hospitallers of Rhodes, threw in their lot with the latter, who was subservient to French

[1] Not the Patriarch of Antioch, as Alastos has it.

interests. However, the Dominicans and Franciscans in the island sided with Urban.

The fifteenth century was a time of decay in religion, and consequently of 'oecumenism' and attempts to rationalise the structure of individual Churches. In 1405, an approach was made by the Cypriote Orthodox clergy towards union with the See of Constantinople, which would presumably (though not certainly) have meant abandoning the autocephaly of the Cypriote Church. Only the Bishop of Lemesos stood aloof from this move. The monk Bryennios was sent from Constantinople to Cyprus in the following year. Some of the Cypriote bishops agreed to submit to the Patriarch of Constantinople, but failed to keep their agreement. What they wanted was a secret compact whereby they might submit while outwardly maintaining conformity to Latin rule.

Before March 1412 Hugh of Lusignan was elected Latin Archbishop of Cyprus, though he was not actually appointed until 1426. The Mameluke invasion of the latter year ousted many of the religious orders established in the island. In 1442, Queen Helena tried to arrange the election of the nephew of her foster-mother (a Greek Orthodox) to the Archbishopric of Nicosia, and was only forestalled by Pope Eugenius IV, who chose Gelasius of Montolif for the post. She managed to remove Gelasius, who was not reinstated until 1446, and died in the following year. In 1456, the see was given by Pope Nicholas V to Cardinal Isidore of Kiev, who kept it until 1462, though in title only. Pope Pius II (1458–64) remarked on the degree to which the Cypriote Latins were influenced by the Greek Church. J. Hackett, in his *History of the Orthodox Church of Cyprus,* remarks that the Latins tended to become Orthodox (in the Eastern sense) when they saw which way the wind was blowing.

At the 'Council of Reunion' held in 1438 and 1439 at Ferrara and Florence, the prelates of the Eastern Orthodox Church, with the exception of the Archbishop of Ephesus, acknowledged the Double Procession of the Holy Ghost and the supremacy of the Pope. The reunion was not formally repudiated until 1472 (by Gennadius II, Patriarch of Constantinople), but it remained a dead letter, like the reunion which had been signed at Lyons in 1274. Such agreements, prompted as they were by the political exigencies of the Byzantine Emperors, and redounding mostly to the advantage of the Roman pontiffs, were fated to non-implementation from the beginning. Further attempts at reunion, under Leo X in 1521 and Clement VII in 1526, were similarly unsuccessful.

James II of Cyprus had Greek as well as Latin support. However, his nomination of William of Goneme to the archbishopric was not accepted until 1467, and two years later the nominee resumed life as an Augustinian friar. He was succeeded by Lewis Pérez Fabregues, a Catalan representing the Catalan party. In 1476, the Venetian Senate successfully supported the candidacy of Victor Marcello.

The restrictions placed on the Greek bishops in 1222 were gradually broken down in the fifteenth century, especially owing to the efforts of Helena Paleologa. In 1458, one of them, Bishop Nicholas, was permitted in Nicosia. The following year the Latin Bishop Peter de Manatiis admitted that the Greek bishop appointed by him had legitimate cure of Orthodox souls. A Bull of Sixtus IV in 1472 revealed irregularities in the Latin Church of Cyprus. The Greek Bishop of Soli was acting as Bishop of Nicosia, and technically unfit persons, such as illegitimates, were having holy orders conferred on them.

The late fifteenth century saw severe depopulation of the island, and the general demoralisation was nowhere more apparent than in the Latin Church. Simony flourished under the Venetians. In 1483, Felix Fabri complains of Latin sees being bought and sold, and of one bishop in particular, a beardless youth with effeminate manners. Other anomalies he noticed included a priest who served both the Latin and the Greek churches at Stavrovouni : 'On Sundays he first said Mass in the Latin church, and consecrated the Host, as do the Westerns, in unleavened bread. This done, he went over to the Greek church and consecrated as do the Easterns, in leavened bread.'[1] The Church of St John Lampadista at Kalopanayiotis had a Latin chapel and a Greek church under the same roof, without any separation of the two. Such examples of cooperation were unacceptable to the Latins, the fact being that oecumenism inevitably involves one Church benefiting more than another, and in this case it was the Eastern Orthodox which was slowly digesting the Latin.

Under Venice, absenteeism among the higher Latin clergy became rife, and strong support was given to Venetian nominees. Indeed, the patronage of the See of Nicosia was finally placed in the hands of the Signory by Pius IV in 1560. The last Latin Archbishop, Philip Mocenigo, was elected under this dispensation. He made some reforms, but his attempts to make the Latin secular clergy conform to the rules were mostly failures. Certain of them, for instance, had followed the Greek practice of taking wives. According to Bernard Sagredo, a contemporary of Mocenigo's, some priests had as many as three. There were men who avoided fast days by professing first one cult, then the other, and the relaxation of the Roman ban on mixed marriages had resulted in persons professing different creeds

[1] Quoted by Hill, vol. III, p. 1097.

within the same family. All this had its colourful side, as is shown by yet another contemporary, the Dominican Stephen de Lusignan, a descendant of the former royal house. He speaks of festival processions in which Greek and Latin clergy would take part, accompanied by a gaily-dressed assortment of other sects : Armenians, Maronites, Copts, Jacobites, Ethiopians, Nestorians, Iberians, and Georgians, all chanting in their respective tongues.

Long before the Turkish conquest, the position of the Latins in Cyprus had been eroded. Sagredo tells us that by his time the great abbey of Bellapaïs was in ruins, and the fact is symbolic. As in Rhodes, Crete, the Principality of Athens, and the Duchy of Achaia, only the foreign conquerors, whether Frankish, Catalan, Genoese, or Venetian, had been Roman Catholics, and even in their heyday they made few Greek converts. In the course of time, they themselves tended to emigrate or become assimilated into the Orthodox fold. An obvious parallel, in this respect also, occurs in Ireland, where a once dominant Protestant minority, constituting over 9 per cent of the population of the twenty-six counties in 1861,[1] has dwindled to but 4 per cent of the present population of the Republic. We may smile at any claim that one form of Christianity prevailed over another because it was intellectually more convincing. The truth is that in each case the indigenous people's will to survive as a distinct cultural entity could only be demonstrated by adherence to the one organised native body left, namely the Church. Concern for the interests of their own ethnic group, and hatred of an apostasy which was equated with treachery towards that group, kept many inside the native Churches who might otherwise have been tempted by the economic advantages of joining the sect of their overlords.

Medieval Architecture

Nothing more strikingly represents the idealism of the medieval Roman Church and the feudal system of checks and balances than Gothic architecture, and Cyprus is well provided with examples. Those who regard the doctrines of Christianity as largely irrelevant may still admire the organisation and artistry which could produce a Gothic cathedral.

The building of St Sophia at Nicosia was begun about the year 1209 by Archbishop Thierry, a Parisian. The basic pattern was one prevailing at the time in the Ile de France, and includes a choir, an ambulatory, and two transeptal chapels. The treasury, with its two storeys and eastern apse, recalls the Sainte Chapelle in Paris. St

[1] Calculation based on the denominational census figures for that year.

Louis's master-masons worked on it when he visited the island. Archbishop John del Conte, who came out to Cyprus in 1319, was able to consecrate the more or less completed Cathedral in 1326. It has suffered at the hands of the Genoese in 1373, the Mamelukes in 1425, and also from earthquakes at various times, most notably in 1491, but still retains its grandeur. Yet grander, to one's own mind, is the Cathedral of St Nicholas in Famagusta, which was begun at the turn of the fourteenth century. Like its counterpart in Nicosia, it has suffered at the hands of the Turks, who stripped it of its ornament, stained glass, and sculptures; but the magnificent façade, with its triple doorway, great west window, and twin towers, overlooking what was once the largest square in Europe, gives a clear idea of what the building must once have been. After its completion each Lusignan king was crowned in it as King of Jerusalem after having been crowned in the Cathedral at Nicosia as King of Cyprus.

The beautiful abbey of Bellapaïs, which figures in so many descriptions of the island, stands near Kyrenia in an outstanding position overlooking the Caramanian Sea. Its church was founded at the end of the twelfth century, probably by the Augustinians, but in 1206 the resident canons were permitted to join the Premonstratensian Order of St Norbert. The monastic buildings seem to have been constructed in the reign of Hugh IV. Most remarkable of these is the refectory, perhaps an indication that residents in Cyprus grow to love luxury. Its spacious vaulting is supported by clusters of slender colonnettes, which gives an effect of lightness. The heavy zig-zag moulding and dog-tooth ornament on the arch of the western door of the south wall[1] are features deriving from the Romanesque and early Gothic styles respectively. In architecture too, Cyprus is an island of survivals. The massive buttresses reinforcing the outer walls of Bellapaïs may be taken to symbolise the determination of the embattled West to maintain the products of its genius. But this is not a guide-book, and one must be content with these few words describing the three most important of the many buildings of the Lusignan period.

It has been stated that for the Greeks it was not a good period as regards architecture because their hierarchy had too little money to build for aesthetic effect; but that does not seem to be the case. From the thirteenth and fourteenth centuries we have some good Byzantine churches, like Ayios Kirikos at Letymbou, Chryseleousa at Emba, Chrysopolitissa at Kato Paphos, and Ayios Dimitrianos at Dhali. In the thirteenth century, a simple type of church, with a

---

[1] According to the present Curator of Ancient Monuments. Hill says these motifs are to be found on the doorway opening into the refectory from the north cloister (vol. III, p. 1126).

steep roof of flat tiles against the snow,[1] developed in the Troödos range. Sometimes it was divided internally into a nave and three aisles, like a miniature early Christian basilica. Later on, the Byzantine dome was combined with the Gothic basilica, as in the case of St George of the Greeks at Famagusta and the Cathedral of St Nicholas in Nicosia (now the Bedestan).

The relative unimportance of Cyprus under the three following imperial systems is evident in terms of surviving architecture. The Venetians built great defence works, it is true, but the sole important surviving remnant of Venetian domestic architecture is the Captain's *loggia* opposite the Cathedral in Famagusta. Even the Catalans have left more of a mark on architectural style. The British, who ruled for exactly the same length of time as the Venetians (eighty-two years), were to leave little more of architectural value. Turkish buildings of merit are rather more numerous, but the Turks' showing is not good when one reflects that they ruled for three hundred and seven years.

---

[1] This type of roof was a Western feature. Those interested should consult Andreas and Judith A. Stylianou, *The Painted Churches of Cyprus* (Stourbridge, Worcs, 1964).

Chapter 5

The Turkish Period

The Turks Prepare

U NDETERRED BY THEIR FIRST SERIOUS SET-BACK (their repulse
from Malta by the Hospital and its allies in 1565) the Turks
went ahead with preparations to invade Cyprus, and built
a base for the purpose at Fineka, just east of Castellorizon. Their
historical justification for the invasion was that Cyprus had paid
tribute both to Mamelukes and Arabs, and was thus naturally
subject to the Moslem caliphs. The execution of Turkish corsairs in
Cyprus and the harbouring of Christian corsairs who raided the
Moslems provided subsidiary justifications, reminiscent of those for
the Mameluke invasion.

In 1569, a terrible explosion in the Arsenal at Venice was thought
to be the work of Miques's agents, and in early 1570 the Turks
seized Venetian vessels and goods. These and subsequent losses precipitated a financial crisis at Venice. However, when the Porte
formally demanded the cession of Cyprus, the Signory, despite the
existence in its midst of a peace party wishing to exchange the island
for commercial privileges, returned defiance.

The man selected to lead the Turkish forces was the Fifth Vezir,
Lâla Mustafa Pasha, while Piale Pasha, Third Vezir, was made
Captain-General of the fleet. The ships collected at Rhodes and
sailed to Fineka Bay, where janissaries and cavalry were taken on.
In all, there were 350 sail, with 50,000 foot, 2,500 horse, thirty
heavy artillery pieces, and fifty small cannon. In Cyprus, some
prisoners from a Turkish raiding party gave news to the stradiots
of the immense invasion to come.

Venetian Preparations

Apart from the galleys, the defence forces of Cyprus were utterly
inadequate. Some of the stradiots were of poor quality,[1] and the
peasant companies of *Francomati* and *Parici* were in the habit of

[1] Under the Lusignans the *stratia* had been collected, but no stradiots
raised, for none were needed.

fleeing when they saw enemy ships. The coastguard of Arnauts, mostly Albanians, was little better.[1] In 1562, there were only 1,769 in the military force, plus 4,500 Greeks under Italian captains. These last proved good soldiers, and some 3,000 of them were to perish at the siege of Famagusta. In the event, the Cypriote noblemen also fought well.

The Venetians dismantled the fortifications of the Kyrenia range and elsewhere for lack of defenders. However, they had strengthened the defences of Famagusta with a two-mile circuit of fortifications cut from the local tufa. Particularly strong was the Martinengo bastion on the north-west side, designed by Girolamo Sanmichele. The citadel, including the 'Othello' tower, dates from 1489.[2]

The Nicosia fortifications were designed by Julius Savorgnan in 1567, 60,000 ducats for the work being provided by the Cypriote nobles and 50,000 by Venice. The four-mile circuit of the Lusignan walls was pulled down and replaced by a circuit of one mile only. This involved destroying most of the Lusignan city. The eleven Venetian bastions, named after noble Cypriotes and Venetian officials, still stand. Savorgnan's inferior successor shelved the plan for a moat, the fosse was not made deep enough, and there was not enough revetment on the sloping walls. Even so, the work was not finished in time, partly because of the laziness of the labourers, four of whom were said to be worth only one in Lombardy, partly because unpaid artisans were used in the later stages, and partly because of the incompetence of Nicholas Dandolo, the Venetian Lieutenant.

The defence of Famagusta was conducted by Mark-Antony Bragadin, in company with the brave and experienced Astorre Baglione of Perugia. Baglione, as Commander-in-Chief, improved fortifications all over the island, and took prudent measures, such as the internment of aliens (Armenians, Jews, Maronites, Copts, Syrians, and Indians), though in this respect he was not thorough enough. Thousands of Armenians were to aid the Turks in the conquest of both Nicosia and Famagusta. Some of the peasantry were taken into the cities, trees and crops were burnt, and wells poisoned around Famagusta. However, too much grain and livestock was left for the Turkish foragers. The *Parici* were liberated to give them some incentive to resist, but not the serfs proper (despite the Signory's order) because the Rectors did not wish to lose those of the Real. Little wonder that some of the serfs also welcomed the Turks. Another measure taken by Bragadin was to establish a mint

---

[1] Sons automatically succeeded Albanian fathers in the profession.
[2] One Christopher Moro was Lieutenant from 1505 to 1507.

of copper besants, to be accepted on pain of death and reclaimed after the war in silver (the 'war bonds' of the time).

In Venice, Jerome Zane was made Captain-General of the expeditionary fleet, though he had to take into consideration the views of three other Venetian leaders. In response to Pius V's appeal, Philip II of Spain agreed to supply ships for the relief of Cyprus, though he did so only after intolerable delays. The Emperor and the King of Poland gave their treaty with the Turks as their reason for not participating, while Catherine de Médicis declared that Turkey was France's friend.

The allies joined the Venetians at Crete, and the combined fleet consisted of 205 sail. The Venetians provided 126 galleys, a galleon, eleven galeasses, and six *navi*, but they were short of some 20,000 men owing to disease and desertion. Twelve of the ships were papal, under the command of Mark-Antony Colonna, and forty-nine were Spanish, under the command of John Andrew Doria, Prince of Melfi, Don Álvaro de Bazán, Marquis of Santa Cruz, and Don John of Cardona. Philip II, who was jealous of Venetian power, had given Doria overall command of the Spanish fleet. Doria proved an inferior, procrastinating leader, as well as a poor seaman.

The Turkish Conquest

On 1 July 1570, the Turkish fleet was sighted off Paphos. Lemesos, Akrotiri, and other places were sacked, though the stradiots, under Italian officers, drove the Turks back from Polemidhia. Unfortunately, Dandolo decided not to oppose any landing in force, and Baglione's pleading could not move him. So Mustafa was able to land unopposed at Salines, with 20,000 foot and 3,000 horse, at a time when attack by a force drawn from over 3,000 regular foot and 3,000 horse under Venetian command, together with some of the several thousand Cypriote militia, might have weakened him decisively. By the time Mustafa invested Nicosia his army had risen to 100,000 men, and his expulsion was almost impossible with the forces available. The stradiots massacred all the men of Lefka for collaborating with the Turks, as well as other renegades who had offered themselves to the Turks as guides. However, some of the peasants carried on guerrilla warfare against the invaders, and one leader of mainland Greek origin, John Sinklitico, is said to have been responsible for the deaths of 500 of them.

At Nicosia, Dandolo and his two advisers refused to permit any major sortie and ordered economy in the use of gunpowder, while the Turks built commanding bastions in zig-zag pattern (against enfilade fire) within three hundred paces: the four southern bastions of

Tripoli, Davila, Costanza, and Podocataro. Otherwise, only the Caraffa bastion at the Famagusta Gate suffered a major assault.

The Turkish artillery now hammered at the largely unrevetted walls, so that more and more débris fell into the fosse. The Costanza bastion was captured by the Turks for a short time, and messengers bearing letters in cypher to Famagusta were also caught. At last, in mid-August, the timid Rectors were prevailed upon to allow a sortie under Piovene of Vicenza. Attacking during a siesta, he took two Turkish forts and spiked their guns, and this despite the indiscipline of many of his Greek and some of his Italian followers. Dandolo, however, showed that resentment of initiative which is the prerogative of the small-minded. He closed the gates to prevent a sally by horsemen who wished to go to Piovene's aid, so that Piovene and his few men were surrounded and killed. The Turks admitted that the sortie could have succeeded had it been in sufficient force. Another display of Dandolo's ineptitude came when he dismounted the cavalry, who might have made damaging sorties.

The Turks kept up their constant bombardment, so that by the end there were only 400 of the original Italian force left in the city. Mustafa's emissaries who came to demand surrender were killed by an irresponsible gunner. After the arrival of large Turkish reinforcements, the final assault came on 9 September 1570. After a stout resistance, in which many Greeks were also killed, the remnant of the besieged retired into the courtyard of the Lieutenant's palace. There they laid down their arms on a promise of clemency by the Beylerbey Derviş Pasha, but were slaughtered notwithstanding. Dandolo also died, despite an apparent attempt to obtain special terms for himself. A drunken Greek hauled down the standard of St Mark and hoisted the Turkish flag in its stead.

Over the next eight days, more plunder was taken in Nicosia than at any time since the sack of Constantinople. Among the captives was the daughter of John Sozomeno, a narrator of the siege. Her beauty was the cause of a chivalrous adventure reminiscent of the Moorish tales in Spanish literature. In November, a handsome Turkish cavalry captain, who had killed a rival to obtain her, deserted with her to Famagusta with the intention of becoming a Christian. However, he was treated with petty suspicion, given an interpreter to instruct him in Christianity, and confined in the Castle away from his lady. In despair, he killed the interpreter and hanged himself.

At the sack of Nicosia attractive youth was offered for sale, and the flower of both sexes were kept, according to custom, as presents for the Sultan. These were loaded on a galleon, but all were blown up, it is said, by a Cypriote lady who put a flame to the powder magazine. Thus chastity overrode the traditional Cypriote licence.

In mid-September, the Pasha Mustafa entered the Cathedral, henceforth a mosque. The stronghold of Kyrenia had fallen without a shot fired, so on 16 September all artillery was moved to Famagusta, arriving on the following day. Only 4,000 janissaries[1] and 1,000 cavalry were left in Nicosia.

The allied fleet reached a point beyond Castellorizon in the same month, and there received news of the fall of Nicosia. Hearing of the enemy's strength, they decided to turn back, the decisive voice being Doria's.[2] He was later promoted by Philip II, but Venice regarded the affair in a different light. Zane was tried for disobeying his orders, and died in prison before the verdict was known.

At Famagusta, the whole population had taken an oath to Christ and the Doge, and the defence was brilliantly and bravely conducted. Baglione cut up the Turkish cavalry in a sortie, and was to make twenty-six more sorties in the course of the siege. Another good attacking soldier was Nicholas Donato. In addition, the highly-trained Italians (including Baglione himself) were usually to prove more than a match for their adversaries when they met them in single combat outside the walls. On men like these the gift of Dandolo's bloody head made no impression, and Bragadin was in no mood to surrender.

The defence consisted of 3,600-700 Venetian infantry (2,800 of whom did not survive the siege), 2-300 stradiot horse, and about 4,000 Greeks, with ninety guns and supplies of wildfire. Thus, about 8,000 defenders were confronting about 200,000 Turks, including some 6,000 light cavalry, with up to 145 guns, including those of the fleet. Four of these guns, called basilisks, hurled balls 200 lb in weight. Nevertheless, the Venetian artillery was more accurate, and accounted, among others of note, for Mustafa's chief engineer.

But even the above disparity does not reflect the true position, for Mustafa was constantly being reinforced from Anatolia by persons who had been attracted by the rumours he disseminated concerning the great wealth of Famagusta, so that the Turkish numbers rose to 250,000. In all, some 80,000 of them died at the siege, which relieved pressure on central Europe for another twenty years. The inefficiency and pusillanimity of Dandalo and others cannot obscure the glory of the defence of Famagusta. Even the epic Venetian defence of Candia, which was to last twenty-four years, could not eclipse it.

---

[1] Lit. 'new soldiers' (from *yeni çeri*), recruited from boys taken from Christian parents in the Balkans.

[2] He had already been defeated by Piale Pasha at Los Gelves (Jerba) in 1560.

The Turks quickly built forts, which were replaced by Armenian sappers and peasant labour whenever destroyed by artillery fire. At night, zig-zag trenches were dug, deep enough for cavalry.

A noble Venetian named Mark Quirini succeeded in reaching the beleaguered garrison at Famagusta towards the end of January 1571 with a dozen galleys and four transports loaded with provisions and munitions. On arrival he destroyed three Turkish galleys and captured a transport. In mid-February, he sailed for Crete with the children and other non-combatants. In April, when the remaining useless mouths were expelled, the Turks allowed them to disperse to their villages in peace.

Piale Pasha, who had proved ineffective against Quirini, was replaced as naval commander by Ali Pasha, who arrived on 30 March with thirty more galleys. On 12 May, a great Turkish bombardment began, to which the Venetian reply was initially effective; but later, owing to lack of ammunition, only thirty guns were allowed to fire back thirty shots apiece each day, and the defenders fought on against impossible odds. A Turkish despatch was sent to Constantinople reporting that Famagusta was defended, not by men, but by giants.

On 28 May, a Venetian frigate came with a message of hope from Crete, which proved illusory. On 21 June, a large hole was blown through the defences by a mine, and an assault through it was thrown back. The next day another Venetian frigate arrived, promising help within eight days. Half a dozen more assaults were made through the breach, so that the few defenders had to fight with scarcely any sleep, day after day. The clergy and the women toiled at the débris and brought up arms, stores, and water. Women also fired the arquebuses of the dead, and Serafino Fortebraccio, a Milanese Dominican who had become Latin Bishop of Lemesos, exhorted the defenders with vigour, just as Francis Contarini, Bishop of Paphos, had done at Nicosia. This was no time for the turning of cheeks.

A huge Turkish fort now overtopped the Venetian arsenal, so that the defenders fought without cover. The Turks spread poison on the great salient outwork, or ravelin, captured it, and mounted guns on it. Soon the two sides were close enough to talk and jeer, so that silence had to be imposed on pain of death. Mining and countermining were rife. By mid-July resolution had weakened, largely owing to lack of sleep, but Bragadin said he could send a frigate to plead for help in Candia, and attack after attack continued to be repulsed. On 20 July, a Christian captive told the Turks that a Christian fleet was coming, and on 28 July Bragadin still refused to surrender. Horses, donkeys, and cats were all eaten, and only some bread, beans, and water remained. On 31 July, the Christians, defended only by casks and sandbags, threw back a great assault three times in six hours, with a loss of 5,000 men to the besiegers. On 1 August, there were only seven barrels of powder left. Bragadin urged resistance to the last, but terms were nevertheless sought, and an armistice was declared on that day.

Mustafa, full of compliments, agreed that those who wished might leave in borrowed Turkish ships, while those left behind might keep their property and within the space of two years have safe passage anywhere they pleased.

On 5 August, the Christian leaders went to surrender. Mustafa raged over the fate of Turkish prisoners allegedly killed after the armistice, to which Bragadin replied that his fifty prisoners had either been sent to Venice or were alive in Famagusta. Moslem historians allege that some of the prisoners had been tortured, and they are probably right. The extraction of information by torture is characteristic of all but the most secure societies. However, Mustafa's allegation was almost certainly unfounded, as is shown by his not commenting upon Bragadin's answer but changing the subject to express his indignation that the Christians had dared to hold out with so few resources and kill 80,000 of his best men. Bragadin was bound, and Mustafa cut off his right ear and his nose. Baglione abused the breaker of faith and was beheaded. A slaughter of the Christians then began, and was tardily checked by Mustafa, who needed prisoners for his triumphal entry on 8 August. Girls and boys were raped, and the city was sacked. A vessel carrying most of the Italian women is later said to have foundered. Among the Italians who escaped death was Angelo Gatto of Orvieto, who finished his detailed account of the siege in the Black Sea Tower at Constantinople in November 1573.

With wounds festering, Bragadin was forced to carry sacks of earth and kiss the ground as he passed the Pasha. On Friday 17 August, he was hoisted in a chair on the yard of a galley for all to see, and brought down to be flayed alive. Mustafa's offers of clemency and honours if he became a Moslem were of no avail. Bragadin bore the torture unflinchingly for half an hour, dying only when the knife reached his waist. Other flayings also took place, but it is worth recording that some Turks condemned the treatment of Bragadin. The different parts of his body were put on view in prominent places, while his skin was cured and stuffed. It was presented to the Sultan, but eventually abstracted from the Ottoman Arsenal and brought back to Venice in 1581.

Mustafa returned to a gloomy Constantinople. On 7 October 1571, Don John of Austria, with the ships of the Holy League, mostly Venetian, and disciplined troops, largely Spanish, had destroyed the Turkish fleet at Lepanto. Doria, characteristically, had nearly lost the battle through his mistaken and timid manoeuvres. The battle effectively stopped the Turkish advance in the Mediterranean area. Even so, the Venetians, under the terms of their treaty with the Porte of March 1573, had to renounce all claim to Cyprus and pay an indemnity of 300,000 ducats.

The fall of Cyprus captured the imagination of Europe as few other events have done. The classical associations of the island were in such artistic contrast to the grimness of war. When Thomas Jordan wrote that 'Dame Venus, love's lady,/Was born of the sea' all educated readers knew that her habitat was Cyprus. Ronsard had written a plea to Venus in sonnet form asking her protection for the island as the Turks made their warlike preparations :

> Belle déesse, amoureuse Cyprine,
> Mère du jeu, des Grâces et d'Amour...

In the English drama Cyprus was a typical never-never land. Dekker's *Old Fortunatus* depicts it as a place of luxury, revelry, and langour. In Act III, scene i, of that play Andelocia says : '... 'tis the fashion of us Cypriots to yield at first assault'. Thomas Heywood's *The Four Prentices of London with the Conquest of Jerusalem* recalls the medieval riches of the island; and in Markham and Machin's *The Dumb Knight* there is a 'King of Cyprus', seen as a sort of knight-errant 'led on/By the divine instinct of heavenly love', which is perhaps a reminiscence of Peter I. In several plays Cyprus is only a convenient name, though in Fletcher's *The Beggar's Bush* (I. iii) it is mentioned as a source of wine. However, the English were well informed on the Turkish conquest by Richard Knolles in his *Generall Historie of the Turkes* (1603), culled from various continental sources. Shakespeare's *Othello*, acted in 1603 or 1604, comes nearer to history than any other Elizabethan play dealing with Cyprus.

In Spanish literature a similar contrast is evident, between Cyprus as the romantic setting for Richard the Lionheart and his Crusaders in Lope de Vega's *Jerusalén conquistada* and the reference by the Captive in *Don Quixote* (I. xxxix) to the 'lamentable and unfortunate loss' of the island.

Attempts to Regain Cyprus

The power of the Lusignans had long passed, but not the claims of those with Lusignan connexions. One such was Guy de Saint-Gélais, son of the Sieur de Lanzac, who planned an expedition in 1578. It came to nothing. Another was Charles Emmanuel I, Duke of Savoy from 1580. Unlike his predecessor, he considered the idea of holding the island as the Sultan's vassal, but in 1600 we find him planning revolt with Archbishop Benjamin of Cyprus through the Rhodian Francis Accidas. He promised safeguards for the *Parici*, also that no Spanish-type Inquisition would be instituted. By 1608 he is said to have spent more than 30,000 *scudi* in gifts, but to no avail. In 1632, at a time of bad relations between Savoy and Venice, the Cypriote Abbot Theocletos wrote to Victor-Amadeus of Savoy for help, and in 1664 Archbishop Nicephorus again offered the island, this time to Charles Emmanuel II.

In 1607, Ferdinand I, Grand Duke of Tuscany (another con-nexion of Queen Charlotte's), sent an expedition to Cyprus which, according to Sir Henry Wotton, contained many English pirates. It arrived at Famagusta having outsailed its provisions, and after some engagements was forced to retire. Four hundred Paphiotes who rose in its favour, or who refused to cooperate against it, were massacred by the local Turkish soldiery.

In 1572, some Cypriotes were put to death for intriguing on behalf of Venice, and the Turks in Cyprus grew concerned over their lack of means to repel an assault, so that a reinforcement of 500 janissaries was sent. In 1578, when Moslem garrison troops re-volted over lack of pay and killed the Beylerbey, Arab Ahmet Pasha, they were supported by Cypriote Greeks, but the revolt collapsed despite Venetian interest. In 1605, the Governor was concerned over the possibility of attack by the Spanish and Maltese fleets, but noth-ing came of it. A Greek-Cypriote rebellion in favour of Venice was put down before 1617, and her intrigues continued thereafter, though there was little she could do once Crete had fallen.

The Ottoman Administration

For the first year of the Turkish period Cyprus was ruled by Muzaffer, a Pasha of three tails,[1] who established his residence at Nicosia and became Beylerbey, or lord of lords, over a province which included the mainland sanjaks of Alaya (Scandelore), İçil, Zulkadir, and Tarsus. Thus the ancient connexion with Cilicia was re-established, and lasted for well over a century.

About the year 1670, the province centred on Cyprus had be-come of less importance and was placed, together with Rhodes and the archipelago, under the *Kapıdan* (or *Kaptan*) Pasha, the Otto-man High Admiral. He was represented in Cyprus by a *Müsellim*, or governor, an arrangement reminiscent of seventh- and eighth-cen-tury control by Cibyrrhaeote admirals. In 1703, the island became

[1] i.e. of the highest rank.

a private source of revenue for the *Veziriazam*, or Grand Vezir, and the office of *Müsellim* was combined with that of *Muhassıl*, or chief tax-farmer, for the absentee landlord. In 1745, the island again became a Pashalik of three tails in its own right, but only three years later was returned to the Grand Vezir. The year 1785 saw the retransfer of Cyprus to the *Kapıdan* Pasha. About the year 1849, it was attached to the Pashalik of Rhodes, and the *divan* came to include representatives of the Christian communities. In 1856, the *divan* became a *Meclis-i-Kebir*, of which the Archbishop was an *ex officio* member, though the Christians were in a small minority. In 1861, Cyprus was detached from the Pashalik and became a *Mütesarriflik*, or governorate, directly under the Porte. Then the pendulum swung again towards subordination to the mainland, and in April 1868 the island was made part of the Vilayet of the Dardanelles. The *Vali's* headquarters were at Chanak, south-west of Gallipoli, and thither witnesses at trials were constrained to travel. But this clumsy system, reminiscent of sixth-century rule by a quaestor on the Danube, lasted only two years and four months. Kibrish Mehmet, the Grand Vezir, was a native of Paphos,[1] and Archbishop Sophronios II, with a deputation consisting of two Moslems and two Christians, was able to persuade him to make Cyprus an independent *Mütesarriflik* again. In 1876, the island was given the right to send one deputy to the new constitutional assembly, inaugurated in Istanbul by Midhat Pasha as Grand Vezir. By 1878 the island was back under a *Vali* at Rhodes.

The island was initially divided into sixteen subdistricts, or *kadılıks*, each ruled over by a *kadı*, or Koranic judge. However, as the power of the Christian bishops grew, in the eighteenth century, the administrative districts came to correspond with the four episcopal sees: Nicosia and the Carpass, Famagusta and the Mesaoria, Kyrenia with Chrysochou and Pendayia, Paphos and Soli, Citium and Limassol (as Lemesos was now generally called by Europeans). By the nineteenth century the administrative districts were six in number, each ruled by a *Kaymakam*, or local governor. The district centres were at Nicosia, Kyrenia, Famagusta, Larnaca, Ktima, and Limassol. This arrangement, in its essentials, was perpetuated by the British and still obtains.

The Turkish governors ruled through a *divan*, or advisory committee, made up of officials; although the Cypriote-Turkish *Ağas*, or rich notables, were to exert their influence throughout the period.

A notable feature of the earlier Ottoman period was the separate control of finance by a *Hazine Defterdari*, or director of the trea-

---

[1] He was three times Grand Vezir. Kâmil Pasha, four times Grand Vezir, was born at Nicosia in 1833 and died there in 1913.

sury, assisted by two other officials, who was also appointed by the Porte.

The governors were backed by a naval force and garrison of varying size. By the eighteenth century the latter seems to have become fixed at 1,000 foot (janissaries)[1] and 2,666 horse (spahis), maintained by indirect taxation. The quality of the troops degenerated with time, and in 1806 the garrison, though nominally 4,000-strong, was actually much below that figure. In 1841/2, there were only 840 men. Indeed, at scarcely any time during the Turkish period were there enough soldiers in Cyprus when order was threatened.

The Koranic law was administered by a chief *Kadı*, appointed by the Sublime Porte, that is to say, by the central office of the Sultan's government in Istanbul.[2] The Mufti (*Müfti*) of Cyprus was the official interpreter of that law. In the Tanzimat, or reform, period after 1839, the *Kadi's* powers were progressively reduced, and *Mukhtars*, or headmen, were locally elected. However, it seems from a charter proposed by the Cypriotes to the Duke of Savoy in 1600 that they could elect their elders at that time too. A Dragoman (*Tercüman*), or 'interpreter', by custom a Greek, acted as link between government and subject population.

In 1858, the Turks adopted a Western-inspired penal code, which continued to be administered in Cyprus during the British period. An English judge, Walpole by name, who dispensed justice on the basis of the code for many years, regarded it as somewhat inelastic (an understatement), but 'based on principles of common sense, common morality, and common justice'. However, there was frequently a great discrepancy between Ottoman justice in theory and its practical administration in the provinces. For instance, on 9 June 1873, when sixty-three out of 600 poorly-guarded inmates of Nicosia prison tried to escape from their appalling conditions, eight of them were murdered by the Turkish mob with the connivance of the authorities and fifty-five were seriously and repeatedly wounded, of whom another eight later died.

The Christian Churches Under the Ottomans

It had long been the Turkish custom to exercise control over the *rayahs* (literally, human cattle) whom they conquered through the spiritual leader of the *millet* (ethnic religious group) concerned. Those who are disturbed by the thought should reflect that when fifteenth- and sixteenth-century Christians captured territory from

---

[1] These were exempt from taxation.
[2] This word, derived from the Greek εἰς τήν πόλιν (lit. 'into Town') is preferred by the Turks to Constantinople.

the Moslems they did not allow Islam to survive. In 1453, a few days after the fall of Constantinople, the young Sultan Mehmet II had invested George Scholarios as the Patriarch Gennadius II, and recognised him as the Head of the *Millet-i-Rum*, or (Orthodox) Greek community. Such recognition was useful, for the Ottomans organised taxation on a denominational basis, the Christians paying the *kharaj*, a tax for the free practice of their religion, and a military exemption tax, because they did not have to serve in the army like the Moslems.

Initially, the Eastern Orthodox Church in Cyprus gained a good deal from the Turkish invasion. Its bishoprics were restored and its autocephaly recognised, while the Roman Church was abolished in the island. Of the Latin bishops, only Archbishop Mocenigo, who was in Venice, survived. A few of the nobles, a Lusignan, a Sinklitico, a de Nores, ransomed themselves and regained certain estates. Others were enrolled in the spahis, as in the Venetian period. Some of the Latins temporised, after the fashion of persecuted minorities in the East, while others were absorbed into the Orthodox Church, like the Heptanesian Venetians.[1] Gradually, pressure on the Roman Church was relaxed, owing to the resumption of trade, and in 1650 the traveller Tavernier records that the Latins of Cyprus were dressed like Italians. Titular bishops were appointed to the Lusignan sees, which became subject to the Apostolic Vicar in Constantinople. From 1762 they were subject to the papal representative in Aleppo, and from 1848 to the Latin Patriarch of Jerusalem. The lot of the Latins improved greatly in the nineteenth century, owing to the patronage of the French consuls.

For ethnic reasons, the Uniate Maronites, whether in the Lebanon or Cyprus, fared better under the Turks than the Latins proper. The Nuncio Jerome Dandini found nineteen Maronite villages when he visited Cyprus in 1596, with as many as three churches to a village, all provided with priests. By 1700 the number of their villages had fallen to ten at most, largely because of emigration and economic decline. There are lists of Latin priests for the Maronite villages over the period 1690–1759, and it appears that the Maronites produced none of their own in Cyprus.

From 1736 the Cypriote Maronites were again under the technical jurisdiction of Mt. Lebanon, but about the middle of the eighteenth century they, like the Latins, were subjected to direct Orthodox control, and both the Orthodox Archbishop Chrysanthos and the Dragoman Hajigeorghakis persecuted them.

Some of the Maronites forced into Islam in 1821 seem to have managed to revert later, under French protection. By 1845 the

[1] i.e. those who settled in the Ionian islands.

French had obtained a *firman*, or order, removing them from the control of the Orthodox Bishop of Kyrenia (with all the present-giving that entailed) and restoring them legally to the jurisdiction of Mt Lebanon. Estimates of their numbers in Cyprus vary from as few as 450 in 1842 and 709 in 1868 to twelve or thirteen hundred in 1844 and 1872. There were about 3,000 of them in 1931.

The Armenian Gregorian Church was also subjugated to the Orthodox Archbishop, though the Armenians were given a church-building in Nicosia for their help to the Turks during the siege. In 1738, Pococke speaks of them being few and poor in Nicosia, but as having an Archbishop of their own, as indeed they had had in the Venetian period. Their numbers in Cyprus were to be swelled in 1907/8 as a result of Abdül Hamit II's massacres, and again in 1915, owing to Talât Pasha's massacre.

From an early stage in the Ottoman period the Orthodox Arch-bishop was elected by the whole Greek-Cypriote community, and the monastic order seems to have provided a number of able men to fill the post. The Holy Synod consisted of the Archbishop and the Metropolitans, the number of which varied with the number of sees.[1]

About the end of the sixteenth century, the Patriarch Joakim of Antioch revived an age-old struggle when he laid claim to juris-diction over the Church of Cyprus in accordance with the forty-second canon of the Council of Nicaea, but the move came to nothing.

The hierarchy collected the taxes from the people, and are very much in evidence in the section on taxation which follows. In 1660, the Archbishop Nicephorus was permitted, on that account, to make direct appeals to the Grand Vezir. In the time of Niceph-orus (1660–74) the doctrines of Calvin were considered and rejected by the Orthodox Church, and his successor, Hilarion Kigala (1674–79), was forced out of office for favouring union with Rome.

A very important Archbishop was Philotheos, who was deposed in 1744 for exactions allegedly made in the previous year, and re-stored to office in 1745, after his unworthy supplanter had been deposed. In 1754, he was officially accepted by the Ottomans as Ethnarch, or subsidiary ruler of his people, a dignity which, the Turks rightly point out, was not accorded to the Orthodox Arch-bishops of the Lusignan or Venetian periods. The Church attained great dignity under Philotheos and his two successors. The first of these, Païsios, succeeded in 1759. The great Codex of the

[1] Nowadays, several abbots, as well as the Archimandrite (dealing with the internal affairs of the Archdiocese) and the Exarch (dealing with its external affairs) are likewise members of the Synod. As late as 1917 a bishopric, that of Salamis, was revived, but without the incumbent becoming a Metropolitan (as the bishops with power of election had come to be called).

Archiepiscopate is largely in his hand. Though forced to take refuge in Beirut in 1761, he returned as Archbishop in the following year, and died at Larnaca in 1768. Chrysanthos, who succeeded in that year, was notable for his restoration of churches and monastery buildings. Though temporarily replaced in 1784 by the Abbot of Machaeras (as Joannikios I) through the intrigues of the Governor Haji Baki, Chrysanthos was reinstated in the same year. He was exiled in 1810, after the fall of Hajigeorghakis (of which more later), and died at Chalkis. Kyprianos, the Turkish nominee who succeeded him, paradoxically became one of the principal martyrs of the Cypriote Church. After murdering the Archbishop and bishops, the ill-famed Governor Küçük Mehmet appointed his own nominees in their places. The first of these, the monk Joakim, was admonished by the Oecumenical Patriarch and forced to resign in 1824. He was succeeded by another of the nominees, Damaskenos of Kyrenia, who was, however, freely elected. Damaskenos was unjustly banished to Sparta in Pisidia in 1827. Then came the turn of yet another of the nominees, Panaretos, who managed to obtain some alleviation of taxation, but was too subservient to the Turks. He was forced to resign, through an intrigue, in 1840. His successor, Joannikios II, was described by the British Consul, Niven Kerr, as 'a common swindler' who raised money among rich Philhellenes in England and kept it. Yet Reşit Pasha was willing to accept him as a friend. Cyril (Kyrillos) I (1849–54) will be mentioned later. Makarios I (1854–65) was highly esteemed by both Greeks and Turks. He died of cholera when he refused to leave his flock (as Païsios, for one, had done under similar circumstances). Sophronios II then continued as Archbishop until 1900.

In the 1830s the power of the bishops and abbots was to some degree offset by reforms giving laymen a greater voice in church affairs. Sophronios II received wide powers in relation to religious matters and church revenues (including those from holy wells and marriage licences) under a *berat* issued by Abdül Aziz in 1866, but he did not regain the administrative power wielded by the Archbishops before 1821. Restrictions imposed on the Orthodox Church had been considerable. For instance, there had been severe limitations placed by the Turks on the use of church-bells, and in 1857/9 the French Consul championed the Greeks in their desire for relaxation in this matter, as provided in the reformist declaration called the *Hatt-i-Hümayun* (Imperial Rescript) of 1856.[1] Several churches confiscated by the Turks in earlier days had now been regained by the Greeks for financial considerations, and more were now built.

[1] A wooden *semantron* was in use at Stavrovouni into the twentieth century.

When one considers the diuturnity and resilience of the Cypriote autocephalous Church, one realises to what an extent Macaulay's famous essay on the Roman Catholic Church is also applicable to the Eastern Orthodox.[1]

Taxation Under the Ottomans

The history of Cyprus under the Ottomans is very largely a record of trouble over taxation. Since, after the conquest, all the Christian inhabitants were *rayahs* and technically equal, the complex taxes on different social classes, ranging from one-sixth to one-third of their produce, could be simplified; and the reasonable proportion of one-fifth was imposed upon all. Only one day's *corvée* a week was required, instead of two, and then only in certain areas. Poll-tax and land-tax, together with livestock, salt, grape-yield, and wine taxes were all abolished. The military exemption tax and the *kharaj* were far less onerous than these, and the overall relief on cash taxes is said to have been about 50 per cent. Lefkara, in particular, was compensated for its sufferings by the grant of immunities, rather as Cretan Greeks were to be rewarded for helping in the conquest there. In theory this was all very well, but in practice the Cypriotes were soon suffering from added exactions, so that some even longed for the return of the Venetians. In 1585, partly owing to natural causes, there was a deficit of 68,000 ducats (revenue 208,000, expenditure 276,000). Such discrepancies brought inspectors from the Porte, but the root cause of corruption, namely tax-farming, remained. The Moslem *zaptiehs*, or tax-police, were often of the lowest type, and as late as the beginning of the nineteenth century the French Consul Regnault describes the cruel methods used to extort money.

As a result of the visit made by an inspector of the Porte in 1641, emigrants were offered tax relief for a year if they would return. However, within twenty years the old abuses revived, and many *rayahs* escaped to Syria. In 1665, the Governor, İbrahim, was executed after Cypriote complaints had been investigated, and his successor was removed for a similar reason. Under the *Kapıdan* Pasha the *Müsellim* received £3,000 a year, a big sum for those times, and the *Ağas* of Nicosia who, together with the bishops, controlled the collection of tax, cooperated with the Dragoman Markoulles to falsify the census.

Under Mehmet Boyacıoglu (of whom more below) the capitation tax was regularly sent to Istanbul, but without any mollifying effect. The position under the Grand Vezir may be readily understood

[1] See his review of von Ranke's *History of the Popes*.

when it is learned that the taxes were farmed out yearly to the highest bidder, who legally received only about £75 a year, and who had control of the executive.

Trouble in the early 1750s led to Archbishop Philotheos sending emissaries from Beirut, who managed to persuade the Grand Vezir to moderate his demands on Cyprus. This led to his recognition as Ethnarch, but Mariti in the 1760s was to describe Cyprus as among the most heavily taxed parts of the Ottoman Empire. In 1764, Çil Osman Ağa became *Muhassıl*, and attempted to recoup himself for the large sum his post had cost him by imposing upon the Christians a sum more than twice the normal *kharaj*, and upon the Moslems half that sum. A complaint was made to the Grand Vezir, who sent out an official bearing an order for alleviation of the burden. When the notables were assembled at the *Saray*, or palace, to hear the declaration read out, the Governor reproached Archbishop Païsios for accusing him, and Païsios replied that he was merely begging mercy for the *rayahs*. Thereupon, that part of the floor upon which the Christian bishops and many others were standing collapsed, and the beams were found to have been sawn through. The Veziral official, or *Cokedar,* was served with poisoned coffee, but saved by an antidote. The mob reacted in fury, and when fired on by the Governor and his followers, killed him and eighteen or nineteen others. The palace was then looted. The *Ulema*, or Moslem religious dignitaries, and the *Ağas* sent a report detrimental to the dead Governor, and the Sultan, Mustafa III, was persuaded by the Grand Vezir not to punish the rioters. Nevertheless, restitution was demanded for damage at the palace (as in 1931).[1] Little of the loot was returned, and the Turks would not pay even half the sum fixed for the Christians. This situation led to Halil's rebellion, described below. After four years the depleted population was left to face famine and a big debt.

In 1772, when Sadık Mehmet Pasha was sent with three hundred men to defend Cyprus in case of Russian attack, the Governor Ismail Ağa refused them pay or provisions, so that the population had to borrow money to maintain them for eighteen months. The Porte, however, refused to make any reduction in tax.

There now appears, or rather reappears, on the Cyprus scene, a remarkable picaresque figure whose history reminds one of macabre fiction, and who was all too much involved in the tax affairs of the island. Haji Baki began his career as a one-eyed, illiterate woodcutter at Klavdhia in Cyprus. After some time misbehaving as a volunteer irregular, he gained the favour of an *Ağa*'s odalisque, or concubine, and became *Müsellim* of Antalya. Dismissed for irregu-

[1] Cf. below, p. 210.

larities, he returned to Cyprus and became chief magistrate at Larnaca, where he distinguished himself by his extortions. When Christophakis, who had been Dragoman since 1737, observed this, he had Baki dismissed. But he had misjudged his man. Baki murdered him on Easter morning 1750, thus anticipating in little the excesses of 1821. Seventeen years later, Baki re-emerged into the light of history when he was removed from some official position for his misdeeds, stripped of his possessions, and reduced to beggary. Yet in 1771 he became *Defterdar*, or head of the Treasury! He managed to get rid of the Dragoman Haji Joseph, who stood in his way, and then set his sights higher still. A new *Muhassıl* who wished to get rid of Baki was poisoned, and so was his successor, probably at Baki's instigation in both cases. With his remarkable powers of persuasion, he then managed to induce the Cypriote Turks and the bishops to ask the Porte for his own appointment as *Muhassıl*. Thus he obtained the post for a period of eight months. His successor was a drunkard of no account, and when the *Kapidan* Pasha visited Cyprus, Baki made him the customary present of money and persuaded him to procure his own reappointment as *Muhassıl*.

Baki ruled from 1777 to 1783, and though he behaved well to begin with, he soon began to take taxes in kind and re-sell the goods at high prices. Finally he placed a crushing eight-piastre tax upon the *rayahs*, regardless of a bad harvest. Archbishop Chrysanthos and his three suffragans (who may not have been blameless themselves) departed secretly for Istanbul, whereupon Baki warned his patron the Admiral. An attempt was made to have four nominees consecrated in the place of the Cypriote bishops, but the Patriarch of Antioch refused to cooperate. The Archbishop and his party, after staying with the Dutch Consul in Smyrna and suffering a shipwreck, gained an audience with the Grand Vezir and managed to have Baki put on trial. The irrepressible adventurer was removed from office and condemned to loss of all his wealth, but managed to collect together another large sum, went to Istanbul, and secured his reappointment as Governor from the Grand Vezir's successor. At this, a deputation of Moslems and Christians hurried to the Porte, and raised such an outcry that he was not permitted to go. He died of the plague as a customs officer in Jaffa. Amusing as his story may appear, he left Cyprus saddled with an enormous debt and suffering from famine.

For twenty-five years after Baki's overthrow, Cyprus was ruled on the advice of Archbishop Chrysanthos and the Dragoman Haji-georghiakis Kornesios. It seems undeniable that the island's nadir of misery coincides with the greatest influence of Greek dignitaries. Their exactions and those of the *Muhassıl* led to a rising of the

Turks in 1804, while the Greeks took refuge in emigration. There is evidence that trade expanded slightly during that time, but that taxes more than offset any resulting advantage. Certainly, the population seems to have fallen lower in numbers than at any time since the early Iron Age. In 1809, anger at the irregularities of Hajigeorghiakis caused him to take refuge, first with some Turks and then with European consuls, before escaping to Istanbul. There he was beheaded, after the Grand Vezir had promised not to hang him, a characteristically Turkish joke which was to be repeated, in reverse, a dozen years later. Kyprianos, on his accession to the Archbishopric, found that Chrysanthos had left a debt of over £400,000, which he ascribed to the extravagance of his predecessor. William Turner, the ex-diplomatist who visited the island in 1815, expressed his utmost contempt for the extortionate Greek clergy, and gave vent to a bitter comment much quoted since by the Turks : 'For a Greek, as he seldom possesses power, becomes immediately intoxicated by it when given him, and from a contemptible sycophant is changed instantaneously into a rapacious tyrant'. Some account must be taken of bias here, and of the part played in the extortion by the Turks, and to a lesser extent by the foreign consuls, who lent money at interest rates up to twenty per cent; but three years later Sibthorp likewise regards the tax-burden as crushing.

After 1821, though they had lost much of their power, the clergy continued to collect taxes from the *rayahs*, and also, for a time, from the Turks. Peasants were fleeing as far afield as Leghorn and Marseilles, and the Archbishop joined the Turks in complaining of help given to the emigrants by European consuls. 'Tithes' of up to one-third of an individual's produce were collected, and over-evaluations of the property of the dead were made by assessors, almost all of whom were Greeks. In bad years the peasantry fell into debt with these extortionate tax-collectors, and the moneylending evil became deeply rooted. In 1833, there was one of several outbreaks of unrest against the exactions of both Governor and Archbishop. The following year there was some alleviation for the *rayahs*, but from 1838 to 1840 the farmed taxes were guaranteed by an Armenian banker in Istanbul, which led to a debt of 2½ million piastres being added to the tax burden. In 1841, Talât Efendi came out to suspend the old system of taxation, but was opposed by the Christian moneylenders and clergy, who were indeed the principal opponents of reform. Some of the Turks were also against reform, and armed themselves, pretending that an uprising was imminent. Taxes now came to be collected for the Sultan's personal account, which lessened the episcopal power. In 1845, the Archbishop and Greek *demogerontes,* as also the popular Turkish Mufti, were exposed as embezzlers. From 1851 to 1853 *rayahs* were still fleeing to the consuls for protection. In 1856, tax-farming was officially abolished, though in 1867 the British Vice-Consul Sandwith was to find it still in operation. On the credit side, the stipends of the clergy were fixed, much to their annoyance. The Governor Halet Bey introduced a system whereby the collection of tithes was rented out to the villages rather than the middlemen, but the system was inefficiently operated by the clergy.

One important point to notice is that very little of the tax-money collected remained in the island. Thus, in 1858 only one million piastres out of 14 million collected were used for salaries, etc., and in 1867 Sandwith says that of £230,000 collected £200,000 went to Istanbul, leaving a residue of only £30,000 for use in Cyprus. In 1869, he says, 2,512,936 piastres were spent on the administration, while 14,323,938 were remitted to the Sultan's treasury.[1] However, the Turks did not collect the taxes in full,[2] so that foreign estimates of the revenue were usually exaggerated.

The Ottoman Economy

Although the Ottoman advance had been responsible for severing trade routes to the East, that alone does not account for the stagnation and decline of the Cyprus economy during the Turkish period. The principal trouble was that Bartholomew Diaz had found a route round the Cape in 1488, thus eliminating the Middle East as the world's main entrepôt of trade. Little wonder that the Mamelukes threatened to destroy the Christian holy places if the Portuguese did not abandon their Indian voyages, and that the Venetians supplied them with ship's timber so that they might drive the Portuguese from the seas. The discovery of America aggravated the problem because a flood of gold and silver from that source caused inflation of the Ottoman currency. So trade declined in the Middle East, while money was worth less.

The year 1572 saw a terrible famine in Cyprus, with lack of seed for the harvest, and bad years of drought and locusts followed. It is to the credit of Sultan Selim that he issued a decree ordering justice for the Greeks on pain of punishment. Serfs were given the right of succession, and other improvements in their lot, to be enumerated below. Unfortunately, as in the case of the law, Ottoman economic measures were better in theory than in practice.

The evidence regarding the prosperity of Cyprus at the beginning

[1] The exchange rate in 1878 was 120 piastres to the pound sterling (see Hill, vol. IV, p. 463 n).
[2] See below, p. 212.

of the Turkish period is somewhat contradictory. The Mesaoria
had been described as a waste in the mid-sixteenth century, yet the
1579 edition of the great atlas of Ortelius (fol.71ʳ) still speaks of
the abundance of the island in wine, corn, olive-oil, and cane-sugar,
as also of its profitable trade. Sir Anthony Sherley, who visited
Cyprus in 1599, speaks of its desolation, and so does the Dutchman
Cotovicus shortly afterwards. In 1605, the Portuguese Jew Pedro
Teixeira made a visit, and reported that exports included much
cotton and wool, though trade had fallen off since the conquest and
both Nicosia and Famagusta were shadows of their former selves.
Incidentally, he remarks that only in Cyprus does one see the
Christian subjects of the Porte wearing hats.

As time goes by, the evidence for economic decline is unmistakable. For one thing, Nature continued unkind. Eighteen years of
locusts culminated in 1628. In 1633, the Porte prevented interference by local Moslems with a procession carrying the icon of
Panayia[1] through the island. However, the relief gained in this
way was insufficient, and the Cypriotes fled in ever larger numbers
to Crete, the Morea, and Corfù. The year 1640 brought a great
famine, and 1641 plague, so that, according to an inspector sent
out by the Porte, only 25,000 *rayahs* over the age of twelve to fourteen years were left. This represents an enormous drop from the
85,000 *rayahs* recorded in the census taken after the conquest, but
that number is probably exaggerated, as assessments of population
for tax purposes are wont to be. What is obviously a gross exagger-
ation is the total population figure of 250,000 given by Accidas in
1600. The figure was designed to impress the Duke of Savoy with
the desirability of owning so prosperous an island. A frequently
quoted figure is given by Archbishop Kyprianos, who states that
in 1764 there were only 7,500 *rayahs* (excluding 1,500 of the crippled, the blind, the aged, the destitute, and children ten or eleven
years old)[2] to pay the *khuraj* estimated for 10,066 in 1754. But those
responsible for collecting taxes on behalf of third parties have good
reason to impress the world with the fewness of the tax-payers, and
the same author records a total population of 84,000 from a census
of 1777. Other figures will be quoted in connexion with the numerical proportions of Greeks and Turks. Suffice it to say that there is
a tendency in the eighteenth century to give the total population
as about 80,000. There may have been a fall in numbers by 1814,
when Gordon gives an outside figure of 70,000. The population then
rose to some 180,000 by the end of the Turkish period.

---

[1] The birthplace of the present Archbishop.
[2] Small children were seldom counted in those days of high and varying
mortality rates.

Owing to the inadequacy of Turkish records, the testimony of foreign observers is of great importance during the Turkish period. The observers include the Italian Pietro della Valle in 1625, the Frenchman Noël Hurtrel in 1670, the Dutchmen van Bruyn in 1683 and Heyman in the early eighteenth century, the Britons Richard Pococke in 1738 and Alexander Drummond in 1745 and 1750, the Swede Hasselkvist in 1751, the Italian priest Giovanni Mariti between 1760 and 1767, and various British and continental travellers and consuls in the late eighteenth and early nineteenth centuries.[1] They give the usual lists of Cyprus products, laying special emphasis on the resinous gums. Heyman informs us that the growing of sugar cane had long ceased (perhaps partly owing to slave-supported competition from the West Indies). Drummond is apparently the first to give detailed estimates of exports. The general picture presented is one of comparative desolation, but the comparisons are nearly always with ancient or medieval times, when trade had prospered, and we must take account of a frequent bias against the Turks. Besides, the desolation was sometimes the result of Maltese pirate raids, and in contemporary Mediterranean terms the picture was not always so dismal as over-taxation would lead us to expect.

From the darkness of the eighteenth century the rule of Bekir Pasha (1746–48) shines out like a beacon. It was he who, as a pious endowment and at his own considerable cost, built the large aqueduct at Larnaca and lined it with vineyards and mulberry plantations, besides building flour mills nearby. Nor was this done out of mere ostentation, for previously the poor of Larnaca had had to carry water on their backs from a place two hours away.[2] The aqueduct fell into disuse, but was restored in the mid-nineteenth century. Bekir also encouraged trade at Salines and built twenty-three shops in Nicosia.

Only after the intervention of Napoleon in the Levant was the Ottoman empire stimulated to a painful and ultimately abortive revival. The system was saddled with inequitable trade capitulations, the imposition of which by the European powers made fundamental economic reform almost impossible and was a major cause of over-taxation. Over-taxation, in its turn, made for improvidence and dishonesty. In addition, the Christian *millets,* supported by individual powers, were largely out of control and formed cancers in the body politic.

The mainly political reforms of the 'infidel' Sultan, Mahmut II,

---

[1] See C. D. Cobham's *Excerpta Cypria.*
[2] Drummond, in 1745, comments on the unpleasant saltiness of the Larnaca water.

were continued by his successor, Abdül Mecid, who in 1839 issued the *Hatt-i-Şerif of Gülhane* (the Noble Rescript of the Rose Chamber). This inaugurated the Tanzimat period, or Reform period proper. Many of the measures adopted were improvements, though often inefficiently introduced and administered. In 1841, Talât Efendi was sent out to Cyprus as Governor, and had some success in improving communications and destroying locusts. In 1845, Niven Kerr, a British Consul, considered Cyprus the most oppressed of the Ottoman dominions; yet Ethem Pasha, who was Governor from 1843 to 1845, had straightened the channel of the Pedias and undertaken other useful public works. Measures for the destruction of locusts taken by Osman Şerif Pasha in 1855 were condemned as impious by Moslem religious dignitaries who regarded locusts as a divine visitation, just as many medieval priests had done. Religious attitudes must also bear part of the blame for Ottoman unpredictability and arbitrariness. If use of the future tense without a prefixed 'Inshallah' (D.V.) be regarded as impious, it must inhibit longterm planning.

The island's trade suffered set-backs during the Reform period also. Prices began to rise in the Ottoman dominions after about 1834 and, especially after the Crimean War, the depreciation of the piastre led to much immigration. There was a blight on the vines from at least 1853.

It is noteworthy that even during the time of İshak Pasha, a drunken and lethargic Governor, an energetic Commander of Artillery called Ali Pasha took what measures he could to remedy the devastation caused by the flooding of the Pedias in the autumn of 1859.[1] One Governor who almost demands mention is Ziya Pasha, who ruled energetically for six months in 1862/3, draining marshes, encouraging the cultivation of cotton, and trying to organise a fifteen-day fair for each September. He liked to play Harun-ar-Rashid on his tours of the island, and on one occasion, disguised as a dervish, captured a dangerous gang of criminals. Ziya Pasha had some success in keeping down the locusts, by destroying them in funnel-shaped pits. His successor, Halet Bey (1863–64) was officially of opinion that water from the holy well of Zem-Zem (at Mecca) was the thing to keep off locusts, but took the added precaution of having their eggs collected. Unfortunately, the next Governor allowed them to multiply once more. Halet Bey was also responsible for improvements to the harbour-service and in market hygiene. It was the Governor Sait Pasha (1868–71), backed by the *Vali*, Ahmet Kaisarlı Pasha, who took the most effective anti-locust measures,

---

[1] One is reminded of John del Conte's behaviour during the floods of 1330 (see above, p. 152).

and who completed the road from Larnaca to Nicosia, the only proper highway in the island at that time. However, on his second visit, in 1870, Kaisarlı Pasha found famine, drought, and locusts, which lasted until 1874. He suggested the sinking of artesian wells, and there were elementary relief measures, such as the supply of seed-corn to the very poor in bad years.

By 1871 carobs, or locust beans, had become the island's chief export, and the revenue from the salt monopoly had risen to £20,000. Trade had flourished since the Anglo-Turkish Commercial Treaty of 1861, which reduced export duties. But local manufactures could not compete with foreign goods, often imported almost free of duty under the capitulations.

A major point in favour of Ottoman government in Cyprus is that under it vaccination led to disappearance of the plague. Also, in contrast to the judgement of Niven Kerr, quoted above, one should in fairness recall that of Hamilton Lang, who was British Vice-Consul four times in the 1860's and Consul in 1871. He speaks of Ottoman misgovernment, but reckons that 'of all the Turkish provinces, perhaps Cyprus was the best administered'.[1]

Inefficiency was often manifest under Ottoman rule, but the effect of that inefficiency was to produce the kind of backward yet interesting and hospitable island for which the tourist seeking a simpler (and cheaper) way of life may soon have to sigh in vain. The Turks have never regarded business very highly, and in the decline of their empire the Ottomans retired into the Arabian Nights of a Persianised culture. An excellent illustration of this is the account by 'Ali Bey el Abbasi' (Don Domingo Badía y Leyblich) of his meeting with the Governor-General at Nicosia in 1806 : 'He is a man of intelligence, full of life, and said to be well educated . . . He was splendidly dressed, with a superb fur coat. His Persian pipe was brought and he offered it to me . . . Six pages, fifteen years old, all of the same height, beautiful as angels, and richly clothed in satin with superb cashmere shawls, brought us coffee and then incense and sprinkled me with rose water. On my taking leave the governor escorted me to the door of the room'.[2] Of course, there were drawbacks. Ali Bey is displeased, for instance, by the concealment of women, and he makes some astringent comments on the economic and political situation, but it is above all the fascination of the island which is conveyed to the reader. Similarly, Kinglake, in his *Eothen* (1844), is struck by the extreme poverty of a Greek priest with whom he stayed the night, but also by the beauty and sweet scents of

---

[1] R. H. Lang, *Cyprus: its history, its present resources, and future prospects* (London, 1878), p. 190.
[2] Cobham, op. cit.

Cyprus; and the impression made on him by the graceful bearing of Cypriote women may be set against the unfavourable comments of other travellers. In 1862, Horace White, the British Vice-Consul, speaks of the Cypriotes as quiet, sociable, idle, and frequently drunk on cheap wine.[1] He also notes that they are keen on business, and that there is hardly any brigandage, burglary, or opposition to authority. The plain fact is that an overtaxed people resorts to emigration, barter, and subterfuge, so that its living standards fall less than might be expected.

Architecture, Art, and Archaeology in the Ottoman Period

So much of Ottoman culture is Byzantine in origin : baths, seraglio, veiled women, the crescent, the domed shapes of the mosques, even the title Efendi; yet the Ottoman spirit is as different from the Byzantine as the Byzantine from the classical.[2] Standing in the Blue Mosque at Istanbul or in the great mosque at Edirne which commemorates the conquest of Cyprus, one is lost in admiration of the beauty and originality of Ottoman art and architecture.

With the decline of trade, Cyprus became an insignificant part of the Ottoman empire, and it has been said that the Turks did not build in the island, but merely made use, cuckoo-like, of the buildings of others. Makarios III, for instance, has committed himself to the statement that the Turks did not even build a mosque for themselves before 1878. That is not so. In Nicosia alone are to be seen the caravanserais called the Büyük (Great) Han, built by Muzaffer Pasha in the sixteenth century, and the smaller seventeenth-century Kumarcılar Hanı; the seventeenth-century *Tekke* of the Mevlevi dervishes (which has been a museum since April 1963); the small but perfect Arab Ahmet Pasha mosque, built in the eighteenth century, together with half a dozen others of various dates;[3] and the attractive library of Sultan Mahmut II. Other mosques of the Turkish period are to be found in Larnaca, Limassol, Dhali, Lefka, Lapithos, Kyrenia, and Famagusta. There are several *tekkes*, or dervish convent buildings, of that period, of which by far the most famous is that of Hala Sultan. A tomb, incorporating a solid meteorite weighing fifteen tons, was built in 1760 by Sheikh Hassan, the custodian of her grave, and both mosque and *tekke* were added in 1816 by Seyid Mehmet Emin Efendi, at that time *Muhassıl* of Cyprus. The

[1] One is vividly reminded of Wilbrand of Oldenburg's description in 1211 (see above, p. 123).
[2] Similarly, Gothic architecture bears resemblances to the Seljuq-Turkish, but not in spirit.
[3] See Cevdet Çağdaş, *Kıbrısta Türk Devri Eserleri* (Nicosia, 1965).

minaret and dome are to be seen from afar through the haze over the Larnaca salt lake, amid the surrounding palms, citrus trees, and cypresses. Nor is the magic in any way lessened as one approaches. It is the third most holy place in the Moslem world, after the Kaaba at Mecca and the shrine of the Prophet at Medina, and has been much visited by pilgrims. The architecture combines with the setting to convey an impression of tranquillity. A number of other tomb-buildings of the Turkish period are to be seen in Cyprus, as well as tombstones, some of marble, engraved with flowing patterns and calligraphy. Finally, one should mention the castle rebuilt at Paphos by Hafiz Ahmet Pasha in the sixteenth century, the one at Larnaca built by Mehmet Pasha in 1625, the Larnaca aqueduct, and a number of ornate well-heads. There are also remaining examples of Turkish houses, with their characteristic, projecting upper floors.

From the architectural point of view, the Turkish period was less happy for the Greeks than that of the Lusignans. The Orthodox Cathedral became a *bedestan* or grain store, and for most of the period the building of new churches was forbidden. However, the Turkish refusal to allow work on any but existing churches may have saved many which might otherwise have been pulled down. There is a series of mid-eighteenth-century frescoes at the old Arch-bishopric Church of St John (which are sometimes held to represent a decline in quality), but the tendency of Greek-Cypriote artists was to paint icons, often of high standard. A good iconostasis (screen separating the sanctuary from the main body of the church) is an impressive sight. The art is still carried on today at the monasteries of Stavrovouni and St Barnabas.

Like the Greeks, the Turks have in the past shown little concern for historical remains other than their own. At Famagusta, Christian churches were torn down and sold to make hotels and quays at Port Said. However, as we shall see, the British themselves were not blameless in this respect.

Archaeological digging, as opposed to mere tomb-robbing, began in 1862, when Vogüé dug at Golgoi and Idalium, sending his finds to the Louvre. The science suffered a severe set-back owing to the depredations of General Luigi Palma di Cesnola, who was United States Consul at Larnaca for many years. With the help of his brother Alexander he plundered the island. His finds, collected quite without method, and without any official *firman,* were bought by the Metropolitan Museum in New York, and when the arrival of the British finally put a stop to his activities he became Director of that museum. Strange to relate, he held the post from 1879 to his death in 1904.

The Racial Results of the Ottoman Conquest

Cypriote Greeks are fond of quoting an opinion of Sir Ronald Storrs : 'A man is of the race of which he passionately feels himself to be'.[1] That seems to be true for all practical purposes in that the desire for union of genetically similar people can override economic disadvantages and upset political settlements made by aliens. What is false in Storrs's proposition is the assumption that proclamations of belonging made by alien minorities in their own interest should be taken at their face value.

While disclaiming any belief in race (that is to say, genetic make-up) as a determining factor, Greek apologists from Makarios III downwards have found it necessary to impugn the Turkishness of the Cypriote Turks. For those who see the force of Disraeli's remark that 'race is everything' the matter will be of more than academic interest.

Cyprus was much depopulated during the conquest, so that by imperial decree the surplus population of central Anatolia, as well as some essential craftsmen, was settled in Cyprus. The first Turkish census shows a taxable Moslem population of 20,000, as opposed to 85,000 taxable Christians. Of course, not all the Moslems were necessarily Turks. In April 1964, Makarios referred to Greek villages, especially in the Paphos district, where some or most of the population embraced Islam after the conquest, as did Maronites at Marona, and Armenians at Armenochori. Many of these changed religion in order to escape the *kharaj*, some as late as the nineteenth century. Among the descendants of those who did so may be assumed to be the *Linovamvakoi,* or 'Linsey-woolsies', who gave themselves Moslem names and outwardly acknowledged Mahomet, while secretly practising the rites of the Greek Church.[2] Presumably most of these persons rejoined the Greek Church when it was safe to do so, and so were lost to the Moslem community. One cultural effect of mixing is change of language, but in 1911 it appears that only 1,191 Moslems gave Greek as their mother-tongue and only 139 Greek-Orthodox gave Turkish. More important is the statement of Pococke that the Moslem men 'very often' married Christian women, but as against this there is evidence that immigrants con-

---

[1] In a footnote Storrs admits a friend's argument that pro-German feeling did not make the Jews German, any more than pro-British feeling makes a 'Rock-scorpion' British. He then goes off the rails in speaking of the 'intense British loyalty' of the French-Canadians.

[2] See the whole article by L. H. Dudley Buxton, 'The Anthropology of Cyprus', *Journal of the Royal Anthropological Institute,* vol. L (1920), pp. 183–235. It seems that in 1902 there were as many as 10,000 *Linovamvakoi* (see *Cyprus Today,* vol. VI [1968], no. 1 [Jan.–Mar.], p. 29).

tinued to drift across from Anatolia (rather as did the Lowland Scots after the Ulster plantation), and so helped to maintain the Turkishness of the Moslems. True, the Turks did not systematically drive out the indigenous population, as was done in parts of Ulster, but difference in religion helps to maintain separateness, and it takes a very large influx of different genes (or a big selective shift) fundamentally to alter the character of a breeding-group.

Nor will the argument hold water that most of the Turks in Cyprus were a mere garrison. In any case, garrisons breed (as, for example, in the case of the British one in India). According to Evliya Efendi's *Siyah Name,* a travel narrative, Cyprus in about 1670–75 contained 30,000 'Moslem warriors' and 150,000 'infidels'. The reference to warriors is misleading, for the garrison is known to have been very much smaller. In 1696, Coronelli says there are about 28,000 Christians and 8,000 Turks in the island, excluding women and children, but he may have taken these figures from the obvious underestimate of Cotovicus in 1600.

In the eighteenth century, estimates of relative proportions are sometimes flatly contradictory. On the one hand, Pococke tells us that in 1738 two-thirds of the inhabitants were Christians; on the other, Drummond says that in 1745 there were only 50,000 Greeks as against 150,000 Turks. On the face of it, Hill thinks Drummond's figures have been inverted. The difficulty is that Kyprianos quotes from a census of 1777 which showed 37,000 Christians, as against 47,000 Turks. Kyprianos adds that there are grave doubts as to the number of Turks, but in 1792 de Vezin says there are 60,000 Turks in a population of 'over 80,000'. Modern Turkish propagandists have made great play with these figures, but the author is inclined to believe that the Archbishop, the Dragoman, and (perhaps) the *Muhassıl* deliberately underestimated the number of *rayahs* in official returns so that less money would have to be sent out of the island. The truth seems to be revealed in a perceptive passage by 'Ali Bey' : 'The government has never succeeded in learning how many Greeks there are in the island. They own to a total of thirty-two thousand souls : but well informed persons raise this number to a hundred thousand. Last year a commissioner was sent to make an exact enumeration of the Greek families, but he was "got at", loaded with gold and went away—his task unfulfilled. This handling the taxes brings enormous gains to the spiritual heads of the people, who suffer in silence lest a worse evil befall them.' The figure of 100,000 is probably exaggerated, not so the rest.

If we take the figures showing a majority of Turks at their face value, a most astonishing change takes place within twenty years or so. In 1815, Turner says there are 40,000 Greeks as against

20–30,000 Turks, and in 1821 Tricoupis estimates 80,000 Greeks as against 20,000 Turks. Frankland estimates the population as five-sixths Greek in 1827. In 1841, the Governor, Talât Efendi, says there are 76–77,000 Greeks and 32–33,000 Turks, besides minorities. Lilburn, in 1842, estimates 70,000 Greeks and 30,000 Turks; Niven Kerr, in 1846, 75,000 Greeks and 25,000 Turks; and Ross, in 1845, 85–90,000 Greeks and 25,000 Turks. It seems that the proportion of Greeks rose in the nineteenth century because conditions were being created in which their business ability had more outlets, but it is very likely that they were always a majority.

The most recent study of race in Cyprus, by M. Robert-P. Charles,[1] is as much a propagandist as a scientific document. His sample is too small (486 persons), there is no mention of the community to which each person studied belongs, and there are astonishing omissions in the list of racial types. For instance, he characterises four-fifths of his sample as 'autochthonous' to Cyprus, and we are led to believe that they are generally Mediterranean in type, and of the same kind as the majority in Greece. Most of them are, but there is no mention here of the Hither Asiatic element so often remarked on by observers (and not only by the British, who had an axe to grind). That element is ignored, presumably because it points too clearly to a subordinate connexion with the Semitic world. Nor is there any mention of the smaller Negro element, which is particularly strong among the Turkish population of Scala, but is to be found among the city Greeks also. In 1668, Peter Senni of Pisa reckons 1,000 black slaves, male and female, among the booty to be taken in Cyprus, and in 1845 Ross reckons what seems to be an exaggerated proportion of 5,000 Negro slaves among the 25,000 Turks.[2]

But Charles is more suspect as regards the conclusions he draws from his evidence. Thus, he makes the quite unwarranted assumption that only the few Turcoman types (0.65 per cent of the whole sample) are 'Turcs proprement dits'. The same assumption is implicit in Makarios's statement that only at Bey Keuy and in a few of the çiftliks (hamlets), where Mongoloid types are to be found, can it be said that the Cypriote Moslems are of Turkish origin. The truth seems to be that the Turks were not originally Mongoloid, though they intermixed with the Tatars, as they did with other peoples of the Eurasian plains. The nomad Turkish tribes of Persia show a higher proportion of fair characteristics than the settled population,

---

[1] 'Considérations sur le peuplement moderne de Chypre et ses origines', *ΚΥΠΡΙΑΚΑΙ ΣΠΟΥΔΑΙ* (1965).

[2] The Governor-General Aziz Pasha, who arrived in 1871, was particularly strong against the slave-trade. No slaves were sold in Cyprus for many years before the British took over.

and at places like Manisa, in western Turkey, where the invaders did not intermix to any extent with the conquered, the same pheno-menon is observable. True, the Turcoman type is most frequently found among the 'classe dirigeante', as Charles observes, but so is the fairer type (e.g. Kemal Atatürk), which was reinforced by the custom, continued over centuries, of marrying the exceptionally beautiful Circassian women. More important still is the point that the Turks are heirs to Anatolia, which, like Spain, is a great land bridge, and like Spain has come to contain a varied assortment of peoples. Charles claims that only 0.16 per cent of the 16.49 per cent he characterises as Anatolian (i.e. 'Ionian') or sub-Anatolian (i.e. Armenoid) in type are to be considered as autochthonous Anatolians. Of course, Anatolian immigrants have been arriving in Cyprus from very early times, but Charles's statement does not square with his admission that among the Turkish invaders the Turcoman type was in a proportion of only one in ten. On that assumption we should expect the proportion of autochthonous Anatolians in the sample to be at least 5.85 per cent, and in reality it is probably a good deal higher. One is willing to believe that there is in Cyprus a racial overlap more considerable than that between Turkey and Greece, but it is not possible that it should be as large as M. Charles suggests.

A group of Cypriote Turks is usually easily distinguishable from a group of Cypriote Greeks, and when *L'Express* (3 December 1967) distinguishes 'des Grecs au profil angulaire' it is presenting the general truth.[1] In Turkish cartoons the Greeks are represented as sharp-featured Mediterranean types (especially the irregulars) or else as Hither Asiatic (especially the politicians). Some Turkish propagandists have tried to impugn the Greekness of the Cypriote Greeks by exaggerating the Hither Asiatic element, but the *Special News Bulletin* (29 September 1967) speaks of them as 'people of the same race as . . . in Greece'.

Unrest Among the Cypriote Turks

In a conquered, colonised country it is the settlers, not the subject population, from whom most trouble is to be apprehended, at least until such time as the occupying power has become internally weak-ened. Then the indigenous inhabitants reassert themselves, if still in sufficient numbers, and the settlers become more and more depen-dent on their parent nation. So it has been in Cyprus.

In the 1680s, a time of crisis when the Ottoman power, hitherto geared to expansion, was stopped before the walls of Vienna and

[1] In many Turks the nose is striking, but it seldom goes with sharpness of feature.

driven out of Hungary, a certain Cypriote *Ağa* called Mehmet Boyacıoğlu, with much Moslem and some Christian support, began a revolt which lasted seven years. The Porte sent one Çolak (Armless or Paralysed) Mehmet Pasha to restore order, but when he tried to assert himself he was reduced to a labourer's status. Then Çıfıtoğlu Ahmet Pasha was sent with a force from Caramania. He seized the Kythrea flour mills, where he was joined by Çolak Mehmet, and blockaded Nicosia for two months. Mehmet Ağa was given safe-conduct to leave the city, but was nevertheless hunted down, his small band dwindling, to be hanged himself, while his few remaining followers were suspended alive on hooks under their chins. Modern Greek-Cypriote attempts to depict such revolts as risings of Greeks and Turks in a common cause should be treated with the greatest reserve.

Turkish punishments continued extremely severe, indeed cruel. In 1712, when some Turkish sailors kidnapped about twenty Nicosiote *Ağas*, they were tricked by their captives, and executed by hanging, impalement, and strangling. Less painful elimination would have been far preferable, but one should not forget that similar punishments were in use in the West.

In 1765, owing to their unwillingness to pay the fine levied on them in the previous year, some three hundred Turks seized the strategic flour mills at Kythrea. Others came to terms with them, and soon Halil Ağa, commandant of Kyrenia Castle, became leader of a new outbreak. For a while he ruled most of the island from Kyrenia, but failed to take Famagusta or Nicosia. Meanwhile, the Porte, which had been apprised of the seriousness of the situation by Archbishop Païsios and the bishops of Paphos and Kyrenia (who had gone to Istanbul), sent over İbrahim Bey, with only 150 men, to deal with Halil. He and Süleyman Efendi, despatched for the same purpose, succeeded in persuading Halil that they had brought his appointment as Governor, and the bishops sent him financial testimony of their allegiance from the relative safety of Larnaca. However, Halil was not to be trapped so easily. Eventually, Kör (Blind, Careless) Ahmet Pasha was sent over with 2,000 foot and five hundred horse. A Turkish privateer and a leader of irregulars, each of whom had two hundred men, did a good deal of damage during the period before Halil was betrayed at Kyrenia and bowstringed.

In 1804, when the local Turks under İsmail Ağa rose with the Turkish garrison of Nicosia against the exactions of the Archbishop, the Dragoman, and the *Muhassıl*, 2,000 troops were sent from Caramania to put them down. Nicosia was besieged and taken, three of the ringleaders were impaled, and others were sold to Barbary corsairs. Two years later, a *Binbaşı* (Major) called Altıparmak (Six-Fingers) came over from Tarsus with some seventy or eighty followers to attack the Christians. He landed in the Carpass, where he was joined by some of the former rebels. They were dispersed by 500 regular troops, and the captured Altıparmak was flayed alive. By this time such punishments were viewed in Europe with abhorrence. A further scare was caused in 1808, when a Turkish officer sent over from Antalya made the Limassol fortress into a base for marauding. The Greeks cooperated with government forces against him, though these behaved badly towards the local population. After a month's siege the rebel died at the stake.

In 1833 came the revolt of the Imam of Tremithoussia, the second of three in that year, the others being Greek. His followers were not above using stray Christians as targets for shooting-practice, but he nevertheless attracted a number of Christians to follow him owing to the eighteen-piastre tax levied in that year. On this account he was nicknamed the *Gâvur* (Infidel) Imam. He tyrannised for three or four months in the Paphos district, which because of its poor communications was especially liable to such outbreaks. Then government troops arrived, who behaved badly themselves. The Imam escaped to Alexandria, but was eventually caught and impaled.

Sometimes, the Turks seem to have behaved with remarkable personal, as well as judicial, ferocity. Thus, in 1835 the consular agent of France in Limassol reported that government troops under the command of Hüseyin Ağa had not only killed eighteen or nineteen *rayahs,* but actually drunk their blood. This was not a Turkish custom, and other peoples have much worse evidence against them. It is best explained in terms of the indignation felt by poorer Turks at the disintegrative effects of Greek nationalism. They saw around them Christians who were much more prosperous than most Turks, but with no inner allegiance to the state. Thus when the first Governor-General of the Pashalik of Rhodes, Musa Savfet Pasha, declared that Christians and Moslems were to be treated alike, it had little practical effect. Still, Turkish troops were not usually ill-disciplined; 800 men sent from the Dardanelles to Cyprus in order to put down the mutiny of an artillery detachment in 1838 behaved very well.

Among the settlers, antagonism towards the Greeks grew somewhat as the Porte made concessions to its Christian subjects. A move to make Larnaca the capital was resisted by them, for Nicosia had a much higher proportion of Turks (12,000 of them, and only 4,000 Christians). Besides, the European consuls in Larnaca would certainly favour the Greeks. In 1860, when an inspector was sent out from the Porte to inquire into conditions, Christians were forced to sign whitewash statements; and in the same year Turkish and Negro Moslems at Episkopi, persons 'of the worst description', were said to be a threat to the surrounding countryside. All the same, in 1862 the British Vice-Consul Horace White describes the Turks as having little of the Arabs' fanaticism, and as being slightly over-bearing only in Nicosia.

Towards the end of the Ottoman period in Cyprus there came into prominence a group of idealists who made it their mission to rejuvenate the empire. Prominent among these were Ziya Pasha and the playwright Namık Kemal. The latter was exiled to Famagusta from 1873 to 1876. The efforts of these 'Young Turks' were not successful in the long run, but they provided a springboard for the achievements of Atatürk.

The Beginnings of Enosis in Cyprus

The ties of religion and language which bound Cyprus culturally with other Greek areas had never been broken. Indeed, the expansion of the Ottoman empire facilitated communication between them. With the rise of nationalism, the Greek variety expressed itself early. The concept of 'Hellenism', that is to say the *Enosis*, or union, of all territories which either had, or had had, Greek majorities, found political expression in the Έταιρία τῶν φιλικῶν or *Philiké Hetaireia*, founded by Constantine Rhigas at Bucharest in the early 1780s. He propagated his ideas with the encouragement of a sympathetic Turkish officer named Pasvanoğlu, a person who may be regarded as the prototype for large numbers of intellectual Britons in the nineteenth and twentieth centuries. The movement received a check with the execution of Rhigas in 1798, but was revived at Odessa in 1814. From 1818 onwards, *Hetaireia* emissaries were visiting Cyprus, and the part of the island in the coming struggle was determined. Surrounded by predominantly Moslem territory, Cyprus was in no position to rise, any more than the Greek minorities in Anatolia and its adjacent islands, but the Archbishop agreed to supply funds and provisions.

The revolt in Greece broke out in March 1821, and the Turks of the Morea (Peloponnese) were massacred. This aroused understandable indignation among Turks elsewhere. In Cyprus the authorities collected enough information to connect the Archbishop with the movement, and from literature distributed by the Archimandrite Theophilos Theseus, the Archbishop's nephew, had reason to fear that a revolt was brewing there too. The evidence for the Archbishop's complicity in planning an actual uprising was shaky, though it would have been in the tradition of his Church. In June, the Greek revolutionary naval commander Constantine Kanares was to come to Cyprus and stock up with three shiploads of provisions near Ayios Serghios and at Asprovrysi, near Lapithos.

Under these circumstances, the Governor, Küçük Mehmet, suggested to the Porte that troops be sent and that the leading Greeks of the island should be executed. Some 4,000 ill-disciplined troops were sent over from Syria, and fired on the flags of the foreign consuls, especially the French. Méchain, the Consul of France, demanded and obtained satisfaction. The Sultan, Mahmut II, hesitated to permit the slaughter of Cypriote Greeks but, with a Russian attack on Istanbul imminent, ordered the disarming of the empire's Christians. The disarming was carried out in April and early May, and the Turkish historian Vergi Bedevi states that a search of Greek-Cypriote churches and houses revealed large quantities of arms,[1] though Hill (by far the most accurate of Cyprus historians) makes no mention of this. Even the knives of the butchers were taken, and the troops began a reign of restricted terror, killing several monks and other Greeks. Meanwhile, the Governor sent the Porte a list of 486 influential Greeks whom he wished to kill. Having hanged the Patriarch Gregorios on Good Friday, the Sultan saw no reason for hesitating further, and agreed to the Governor's suggestion. The property of the dead was to be confiscated and their families enslaved, unless they should apostatise. When secretly informed of this, the *Ağas* were eager to appropriate the Christians' wealth.

The Governor took measures to allay suspicion, and summoned the doomed persons to Nicosia, apparently so that they might express their gratitude to the Sultan for his fatherly care. A few Greeks were wise in time, and took refuge with the consuls, especially the French, British, and Russian. Kyprianos comes well out of the affair, for he had a premonition of death, and might perhaps have escaped. The Governor had sworn on the Koran that he would not behead Kyprianos, and he kept his word (as did the Grand Vezir in the case of Hajigeorghakis). After the three Metropolitans had been beheaded in the palace square, Kyprianos was hanged from a mulberry-tree, while his secretary Meletios was suspended from a plane-tree nearby. On the next day came the turn of the Abbot of Kykko and many others. A majority of those proscribed were killed, though a few were saved by Turkish friends and a number reached safety through the consuls. Those of Prussia, Austria, Naples, and the United States took advantage of the refugees' helplessness to exact money and valuable goods from them. Indeed, the Mediterranean

[1] *Kıbrıs Tarihi* (Nicosia, 1966), p. 143.

13—C

businessmen commonly employed as consular officials by European powers were involved in not a few shady deals and downright dishonest enterprises, and their privileged position inevitably aroused resentment, especially on the part of the Turks.

At most, forty people embraced Islam during the terror, and most recanted later with the help of responsible European consuls. Monasteries, churches, and houses were looted, upper floors were forbidden to Christians, and the killing of Greeks, proscribed and otherwise, is believed to have continued for about a month. Some of the leading churchmen, including the future Archbishop Joannikios, escaped to Rome, and issued a manifesto for the liberation of Cyprus. Nicholas Theseus, brother of the Archimandrite, was appointed to collect a force to effect the liberation, but he was not to take action in Cyprus until a dozen years later. Both Theseus brothers became Lieutenant-Generals in the Greek army.[1]

Since so many Greek sailors had deserted, the Sultan had to call on Mehmet Ali, Pasha of Egypt, to come to his aid. In April 1822, troops under Salih Bey arrived in Cyprus and took to plundering. They did not get on well with the troops of the Kapıdan Pasha, an enemy of Mehmet Ali's. Towards the end of the year, Küçük Mehmet was replaced by Mehmet Bey. In 1827 came the destruction by Admiral Codrington at Navarino of a fleet commanded by Mehmet Ali's son Ibrahim; but the Greek fleet was not powerful enough to take Cyprus. It could only make a couple of ineffectual forays, in 1823 and 1826. In 1829, after the Treaty of Adrianople, which ended the Greek War of Independence, Egyptian troops withdrew from Cyprus, and a subsequent attempt by Mehmet Ali to acquire the island failed.

In 1830, Count Capo d'Istria came to power in Greece, and expressed a desire for the *Enosis* of Cyprus. Three years later, two Greek-led revolts took place there, in addition to the one led by the *Gâvur* Imam. One of these, based partly on dissatisfaction over taxation, was led by Nicholas Theseus. But he did not have the Archbishop's support and, after agreeing to disperse his followers, who were assembling to the number of three to four thousand men at Stavrovouni, he escaped with the help of the French Consul, Bottu. The poet Lamartine took him on from Rhodes to plead his case in Istanbul. Eventually, Nicholas Theseus left the Ottoman dominions, as it seemed the French Ambassador could no longer protect him.

[1] When, on 30 April 1964, the Turkish *Special News Bulletin* published a photograph taken at Aytotoro of a Greek priest firing a rifle, it need not have occasioned much surprise. After all, the French used priests as soldiers in the Great War.

The other rebellion also had a strong Enotist element. It was led by a monk called Joannikios, who is said to have fought in the Greek War of Independence, and who is stated by Archbishop Panaretos to have been incited principally by Theophilos Theseus, then at Larnaca as Exarch of the Holy Sepulchre, and by the French Consul. He managed to gain a following of Albanian ex-prisoners of war, who were returning from Egypt after the Treaty of Kütahya between the Sultan and Mehmet Ali (for the latter had been forced back from Istanbul by the powers). Joannikios established himself in the Carpass, and seems to have intended collaborating with the *Gâvur* Imam. He was joined by a few poorly armed Greek peasants, but eventually he and his Albanians were taken and executed.

In 1847, the old Governor, İsmail Adil Pasha, a moderate man, found it necessary to order the lowering of the Greek flag, which was flown at the Consulate established in the previous year. The Greek Consulate was long to be a focal point for Enotist agitation. In 1854, eighteen copies of an Enotist pamphlet were found in Archbishop Cyril's palace. They belonged to a protégé of his, Epaminondas Phrankoudes, a school-teacher from Greece. Phrankoudes was expelled, along with all other Hellenic subjects in Cyprus. Turkish anger was extreme, and the Archbishop felt it necessary to make the reading of seditious literature an excommunicatory offence. The worry undermined his health, and he died shortly afterwards. In 1867, the authoress Erato Karyke, who had taught at the Nicosia Girls' School from 1859 to 1863, sent from Athens many copies of a pamphlet reclaiming Constantinople and Cyprus. They were seized on arrival, and a Turkish warship showed the flag in Cyprus waters as a result.

It cannot be too much emphasised how much the rapid successes of pan-Hellenism depended upon outside pressure on the Turks. Turkey's need was Greece's opportunity, and every concession made by what was then the 'Sick Man of Europe' was regarded as another sign of weakness.

In December 1862 occurred a typical instance of the Greeks' desire to involve the powers on their behalf. Despite the bullying of Palmerston in the Don Pacifico affair and the allied occupation of the Piraeus in 1854, they elected Alfred, future Duke of Edinburgh, as their monarch by an overwhelming majority in a plebiscite. He was not permitted to take the crown because that would have upset agreement among the powers. Then Prince George of Denmark was chosen for the post, and given the title of King of the Hellenes (not King of Greece like his predecessor Otto) so as to underline Enotist aspirations.

Enormously helpful to the Greeks in gaining the support of the European powers was their common Christianity. In Cyprus, when a Turkish mob desecrated a European cemetery in 1848, when outrages were committed by Turks during Ramazan 1858, or when the *Kadı* of Nicosia dressed up as a Christian priest and spat on the Cross in 1874, the Greeks could be sure of the consuls' sympathy; whereas the destruction of mosques and Moslem cemeteries in Greece aroused no comparable reaction.

Greek-Cypriote Education in the Ottoman Period

In the Middle Ages the Byzantine Greeks had some claim to be considered the most literate people in Europe, but educational standards among the Greeks had fallen by 1571, especially in Cyprus. For a long time only a few Cypriote Greeks stand out as in any way educated.

Leontios Eustratios, born at Kilani in about 1565/6 and dying between 1600 and 1602, travelled much in western Europe and, having acquired both considerable knowledge and Roman Catholic views, returned to teach in Cyprus. That other Romaniser, Archbishop Hilarion Kigala, was a patron of learning, and Archbishop Sylvester (1718–33) wrote a manuscript description of Cyprus. His successor, Archbishop Philotheos, started a school of Greek letters and music in Nicosia, and brought over Ephraim of Athens, later Patriarch of Jerusalem, to teach there. Occasionally, too, bishops made independent efforts to foster teaching. However, both Pococke and Drummond speak of priestly ignorance. Archbishop Chrysanthos was to some extent a patron of learning, and the Dragoman Hajigeorghiakis contributed towards turning a house into a school. In 1812, Archbishop Kyprianos, having heard reproaches of Cypriote ignorance while abroad, founded the Hellenomouseion for the teaching of classics. It was closed in 1821 and reopened in 1830. Kyprianos also founded a school at Limassol. Archbishop Cyril I tried to set up a training school for the clergy at the suggestion of the Russian Consul-General in Beirut, but it came to nothing owing to his troubles in 1854. Makarios I did quite a lot for education, opening the Nicosia Girls' School in 1859, and sending two young men to study theology and philology in Athens. One of these was Sophronios, who was to be next Archbishop, and the other Kyprianos, later Archbishop of Citium (Kition). It was Sophronios, in 1893, who reconstituted the Hellenomouseion in the Pancyprian Gymnasium, and so created a training-ground for Enotism.

Throughout the Ottoman period the rural clergy remained largely illiterate, and registers of births, deaths, and marriages were seldom kept in the parishes. Nor was there any education for the Turks other than purely religious training and private reading, the habit of which grew in the nineteenth century.

European Designs on Cyprus

To begin with, those states with serious designs on Cyprus (Savoy, Tuscany, and Venice) were too weak to confront the Ottoman power; but in the course of time three nation-states became interested in Cyprus, either from the commercial or political point of view. These were France, England, and Russia.

About the year 1630, Henry, Duke of Rohan, leader of the Protestants under Louis XIII, seems to have become interested in buying Cyprus to settle his followers there; but in 1638 both the Duke and the Oecumenical Patriarch, with whom he was negotiating, died. After 1669 a plan for taking Cyprus in the interests of the French and the Duke of Savoy was made by Bernardin Gigault de Bellefonds, one of Louis XIV's marshals; but it came to nothing. So did the plan of the French consuls Laffon and Dubreuil for settling displaced Alsace-Lorrainers there in the 1870s. Meanwhile, the French consuls had been extending their influence in the island and often came into conflict with the English. De Mas Latrie's great work on the Lusignan period, produced between 1852 and 1861, underlined the one-time Frankish control of Cyprus, and Napoleon III, while mainly intent on extending his influence in Syria, had his eye on Cyprus too.

In 1580, the English acquired the same privileges in the Ottoman empire as the French, and in 1587, on the eve of the Armada, Queen Elizabeth asked for the Sultan's help against Spain. The English Levant Company, set up in 1592, traded with the Ottoman empire, and in 1603 an Englishman called Pervis was farming the revenue of the Salines, or salt-pans, of Larnaca. In 1605, Teixeira records the existence of an English consulate in Cyprus, together with Venetian, French, and Flemish ones. In 1626, it appears that there was an English Vice-Consul in Cyprus, who was subordinate to the Consul in Aleppo, and ten years later came the first regular appointment of an English consular official in the island. In 1722, the Cyprus vice-consulship became an independent post. In 1754, the books of the British consulate in Cairo were transferred to Cyprus, and from 1786 there was a full British Consul in the island, with large business interests. However, the post was demoted to a vice-consulship, perhaps about the turn of the century, was placed under the Consul at Rhodes from 1849 to 1861 (when Cyprus was subordinate to the Pashalik centred there), and then became independent again, except between 1865 and 1870, when it was under the Consul in Beirut.

During the Napoleonic wars the naval importance of Cyprus became evident, for example to Captain J. M. Kinneir in 1814. In May 1799 Commodore Sir William Sidney Smith, commander of the *Tigre*, an eighty-gun ship of the line, raised the siege of Acre, and so prevented Napoleon from returning to Europe via Asia Minor. Then, in Cyprus, the Turkish Vice-Admiral was assassinated in a mutiny of janissaries, Arnauts, and Albanians. Sidney Smith intervened to put down the rising, and was embraced by the aged Archbishop Chrysanthos, who put an episcopal cross round his neck.

The British empire, having few land-links, was especially dependent upon sea-power, and there was a special need to protect the routes to India. In this connexion, the younger Pitt drew attention to the danger from expansionist Russia. A new overland route to India via Mesopotamia was suggested from about 1836 onwards, but would have conflicted with French interests in Syria. The British Admiralty made a survey of Cyprus in 1849, but the lack of harbour facilities was a big disadvantage in days when ships were being made bigger and bigger, and the unhealthiness of the marshy port areas was an added drawback. Still, to shore up the Ottoman empire, as Palmerston had determined to do from 1840 onwards, Cyprus was the obvious base, Malta being too far away and Alexandretta within the French sphere of influence. Other possible bases on the mainland or in the Aegean were rejected owing to their vulnerability. The opening of the Suez Canal in 1869, and the consequent dramatic shortening of the through sea-route to India, increased fears that Russia might strike in that direction, and underlined the need for a convenient base. Salisbury originally favoured Crete, but was won round to Cyprus. In 1875, Disraeli bought from the Khedive a controlling share in the Canal. Thus was fulfilled the aspiration of Goethe,[1] not only that the Canal should be built, but that it should be in British hands. From then on the assumption of control over Cyprus was a logical step.

Russian pretensions to influence over the Greeks in the Ottoman empire followed from their common membership of the Eastern Orthodox Church, just as French pretensions to influence over the Maronites and Latins followed from common membership of the Roman communion. In the seventeenth century Russia was solely preoccupied with extending her power over the Eurasian heartland, but as early as 1714 a Muscovite monk called Vardom was said to

---

[1] See David Hotham, 'Building a Waterway across Europe', *The Times*, 2 March 1968, p. 9.

be stirring up the Greeks in Cyprus. Such action was certainly compatible with Peter the Great's proclaimed ambition to rule over the Greeks.

Turkey declared war on Russia in 1769, and in the following year Russia's naval victories extended her influence into the eastern Mediterranean. Also in 1770 came a Russian-inspired Greek revolt in the Peloponnese, a mere fifty-five years after that part of Greece had been taken from Venice. Under the Treaty of Kuchuk Kainarji in 1774 Russia not only gained a great deal of territory, but also the right to keep warships in the Black Sea and sail them through the Dardanelles. In 1788, after other gains, the Russian army advanced to destroy the Ottoman power, but was held back by trouble over Poland and by the French Revolution. At Tilsit in 1807, after France had saved Istanbul from a Russian fleet, Napoleon and the Tsar discussed partition of the Ottoman empire. In the continuing Russo-Turkish conflict the Cypriote Greeks were on the Russian side, if only in spirit.

The Turks gained a respite after 1815 owing to the rivalry in the Balkans of Austria and Russia, notwithstanding their participation in the Holy Alliance. However, Russia soon renewed her pressure on the Turks, first through the Greek revolt, then directly. By the Treaty of Unkiar Skelessi in 1833, Russian ships gained the sole foreign right to use the Straits, but Western disapproval made such an arrangement unworkable. Another Russian privilege which aroused ill-feeling was her right to pay only 3 per cent export duty, as opposed to 12 per cent paid by other nationals. During the Crimean War the consular agent in Cyprus for Sweden and Norway, one of two Anthony Vondizianos,[1] became the focus for pro-Russian feeling among the Cypriote Greeks. In April 1853 the latter were cowed when two Turkish warships showed the flag at Larnaca, but were delighted when the Turkish fleet was destroyed by the Russians at Sinop, on the Pontic coast. The Cypriote Turks began to arm, and were restrained by the British and French Consuls. When Russia was defeated, Turks in Nicosia gave themselves up to eight days of drunken rejoicings.[2]

When the Russo-Turkish War of 1877 broke out there was again tension in Cyprus, and the Archbishop was called a dirty dog by

---

[1] The former Anthony Vondiziano, of Cephallonian origin, was British Vice-Consul from the first decade of the nineteenth century until his death in 1838, when P. Paul Vondiziano, his son-in-law, became Vice-Consul. Another Paul Vondiziano was an Enotist agent sent by the Cypriote Greeks to Capo d'Istria in 1830.

[2] The Turkish partiality for strong drink, despite the prohibition of 'wine' in the Koran, ranks with their reticence and their friendliness in explaining why they often get on well with northern Europeans.

little Turkish boys.[1] The Treaty of San Stefano on 3 March 1878 set the scene for the subsequent British take-over of the island, for the other European powers refused to accept its provisions.

The designs of Germany on Cyprus were far less serious than those of the powers already mentioned. In 1849, Prince Chlodwig von Hohenlohe-Schillingsfürst had the idea of occupying Cyprus and Rhodes, as well as Crete, if possible; and just before the British occupation von Löher spoke of Cyprus as a one-time imperial fief, harking back to the days of the Hohenstaufen. Germany did not properly extend her influence in the Ottoman empire until the 1890s.

[1] It should be understood that animal appellations are very offensive to the Middle Eastern mind.

Chapter 6

The British Period

Disraeli and the Acquisition of Cyprus

THE ACQUISITION of Cyprus was clearly in the interests of the empire, and the third Marquess of Salisbury, then Minister for Foreign Affairs, was particularly enthusiastic for it. Gladstone, as leader of the Opposition, called the secret convention by which it was effected 'insane' and the result of 'an act of duplicity not surpassed, and rarely equalled, in the history of nations'. 'The immortal Gladstone', as the Greeks are wont to refer to him, also expressed himself in favour of *Enosis*, but in April 1881, after he had returned to power, he refused to violate the Convention by handing Cyprus over to Greece. Instead, he took the next logical step and occupied Egypt. Yet in 1897 he was again to express support for *Enosis*. Such are the flexible principles of politicians.

Salisbury's Prime Minister, Disraeli, could certainly claim to be serving British interests in securing Cyprus. Nevertheless, he had long been interested in the island, and not only for British reasons. He had actually visited 'the rosy realm of Venus' in 1831, and his *Tancred* (1847, Bk. IV, Ch. 1) has a reference to the desire of the British to acquire it, as a recompense for such services to the Ottoman empire as their part in turning back Mehmet Ali, the expansionist Pasha of Egypt. But it should not be forgotten that Disraeli was a representative exponent of the Zionist idea and that Cyprus is an obvious stage on the road to Palestine.

The poorly informed are often under the impression that Zionism came into being only with Herzl, as a result of the Russian reaction against the Jews; but Herzl merely gave the idea new life. Joseph Miques, for example, had obtained from Selim II a grant for the settlement of Jews at Tiberias, and also wished to establish a colony of Jews in Cyprus.[1] Nor is Disraeli's British nationality irrelevant. Manasseh Ben Israel (1604–57) had cooperated with English millenarians to bring about the re-establishment of the Jews in England

---

[1] See F. Brandel, *La Méditerranée et le monde méditerranéen à l'époque de Philippe II* (Paris, 1949), pp. 909–10.

as a prelude to their resettlement in Palestine, and had paid large sums to Oliver Cromwell in furtherance of this end. Fernández Carvajal, another Jew, had been contractor to the New Model Army. From the 1850s onwards there was agitation in England for a Jewish state in Palestine guarding the route to India, and when Disraeli spoke to Queen Victoria of Cyprus as 'the key to Western Asia', we may be sure that he had more than the passage to India in mind. Besides, the holders of Ottoman bonds were anxious to acquire a pledge for a safe return on their investment. Cyprus had been suggested as security for loans since the 1840s.

The Convention of 1878

With the Russians at the gates of Constantinople, the Turkish Sultan was in no position to argue with Great Britain. The secret Convention whereby the British 'occupied and administered' Cyprus was signed on 4 June 1878 by the Right Honourable Austen Henry Layard (British Ambassador to the Porte and famous archaeologist) on behalf of Queen Victoria, and by Savfet Pasha on behalf of the Sultan. The terms were that if Russia should fail to restore to Turkey the eastern provinces of Batum, Ardahan, and Kars (invaded in the previous year) or make any further attempts to take over Turkish territory, England undertook to support the Sultan by force of arms. In return, the Sultan agreed to take measures for the reform of his government and the protection of his non-Ottoman subjects, while at the same time ceding Cyprus *de facto* if not *de jure*. In an Annex of 1 July, signed by Layard and the Grand Vezir, it was agreed that a religious tribunal (Mekhéméi-Sheri) should continue to regulate Moslem religious affairs on the island, and that there should be joint administration of *Evkaf*[1] property by Ottoman and British appointees; also that England should pay the Porte the excess of revenue over expenditure to be calculated on the average of the previous five years, and that the Porte might retain control of its own land at a fair price for public uses. Furthermore, if Russia restored Kars or any of her other conquests made in Armenia during the foregoing war, England was to evacuate Cyprus and the Convention should be at an end.

Sir Ronald Storrs has intimated that the Turks broke their side of the bargain by massacring the Armenians,[2] but the British

---

[1] Transliterated (wrongly) as 'Evkraf' in both the English and French versions.

[2] Sir Ronald Storrs, *Orientations* (definitive edn, London, Nicholson & Watson, 1943), p. 462.

government never officially expressed that view. Turkey's joining the Central Powers, which prompted Great Britain's annexation of the island in 1914, was rightly thought to have been against the spirit of the Convention, though it was not in direct contravention of it. In 1918, after the Russians had agreed to a plebiscite in Ardahan, Kars, and Batum, and 97 per cent of the population had voted for restoration of the provinces to Turkey, some Turks hoped to regain Cyprus. At the Armistice, the Allies (no doubt on the principle of self-determination!) took away the three provinces from Turkey. Ardahan and Kars, though not Batum, were retaken by Mustafa Kemal in 1920, but Cyprus was not forthcoming. In effect, the Convention had been unilaterally abrogated by Great Britain, but Mustafa Kemal, in his desire for peace, did not make an issue of the matter. At the Treaty of Lausanne in 1923, Turkey recognised Great Britain's annexation of the island and gave up all claim to it.

Disraeli's *marché oriental* was not complete in its details for some time. The 'average' excess of revenue over expenditure, plus the value of the other Ottoman interests, was eventually calculated, with what Storrs was to call 'the scrupulous exactitude characteristic of faked accounts',[1] at £92,799 11s 3d yearly. Of the whole, not a penny reached the Sultan. It was all used to pay off the Ottoman Guaranteed Loan of 1855, and at times the British government had to make up large deficits in the tribute money. At least the Romans, by contrast, had seen to it that most of the money extracted from Cyprus became the property of the state. The only financial advantage gained by Great Britain was the Supplementary Agreement with the Sultan of 14 August 1878, giving her the power to regulate 'commercial and consular relations and affairs'. She used this to free the island of the iniquitous capitulations with which the Ottoman empire was burdened.

The British acquisition of Cyprus aroused considerable interest and resentment, especially in nations with Mediterranean interests. German reactions were on the whole approving, but the French, who had already been outbargained over the Suez Canal (which they themselves had built) had to be compensated with a free hand in Tunisia; while the Italian *Bersagliere* reported that the 'divine island' had been 'sold by the eunuchs of Constantinople to the usurers of London'.[2] Speculators, including rich Constantinopolitan Greeks, descended upon Cyprus and bought up property which was to appreciate enormously in value. Among these was Zacharios Vasilios Zachariades, later to be known as Sir Basil Zaharoff.

1 Ibid., p. 464.
2 Hill, vol. IV, p. 291.

The British Land

The actual occupation of the island was effected with a few blue-jackets and Royal Marines under the command of Vice-Admiral Lord John Hay. Contemporary accounts of it have something of a musical comedy atmosphere. The first landing took place at Larnaca on 9 July, and by the time 400 Indian troops arrived from Malta on 17 July the Union Jack had been flying for five days at Nicosia. The Governor, Besim Pasha, handed over his power without making any difficulties, and there was no opposition from any other Turks in government employ, perhaps partly because the British granted them their arrears of salary in full. All the same, two events took place which were ominous for the future. The first occurred on Friday 12 July during the flag-raising ceremony attended by the Vice-Admiral at the Paphos Gate of Nicosia. A Greek provoked a Turkish officer, and had to flee into the crowd when the latter drew his sword. George Kepiades, historian of the 1821 massacre, made a speech of welcome on that occasion. The second ominous event happened on 22 July, when Sir Garnet Wolseley, the first British High Commissioner, landed at Larnaca. In welcoming him, the Bishop of Citium, Kyprianos, expressed the hope that Cyprus would be united with 'Mother Greece' as the Ionian islands had been.[1] A deputation also expressed Enotist sentiments when Wolseley visited Limassol.

The Greeks were given the impression, apparently by *The Times* Correspondent (who happened to be Wolseley's private secretary) that their taxes were to be abolished, but they were to be disabused of the notion. For the Turks, the emphasis of the official Ottoman *firman* on the temporary nature of the British occupation proved equally illusory.

Nicosia was found by the British to be a dirty place, its only attraction being a clean water supply. Wolseley was reduced to living two miles outside it under canvas. Early in 1879, these quarters were replaced by inadequate wooden buildings, originally intended for the military commander in Ceylon. They were erected in sections, the work being done under contract with Zaharoff, and constituted 'Government House' until the 1930s. In addition, the High Commissioners were to have summer quarters in the Troödos, and by May 1880 the poet Arthur Rimbaud was at work on this second

---

[1] The Ionian islands had all been taken from the French by the Royal Navy during the period from 1809 to 1814. The granting of democratic institutions to their Greek inhabitants had led to Enotist unrest in 1849, and in 1864 they had been ceded to Greece, thus affording a hopeful precedent for the Cypriote Greeks.

residence as a contractor's foreman. The Troödos was to be a favourite hot-weather area for Anglo-Egyptians as well, there being no such heights in Egypt.

Gradual British Reforms

The Berlin Treaty of 13 July 1878 established peace for the next thirty-six years. Great Britain had succeeded in forming a coalition to maintain a shrunken Ottoman empire, and so preserved the power balance in the Middle East. But the Cypriotes did not share to any marked extent in the rapidly increasing prosperity enjoyed by many peoples.

Cyprus has been referred to as Great Britain's Cinderella colony, and there is truth in the charge. The main reasons are three in number. First, until 1914 Great Britain did not claim to own the island, and so had less incentive to develop it; while the uncertainty of its status in the long term discouraged private capital investment. Second, the tribute represented a considerable burden at a time when colonies were expected to pay for themselves. Third, control over a good harbour at Alexandria made it unnecessary for the British to develop the shallow ones in Cyprus. Indeed, possession of the island by a power which also has control over better ports on the nearby mainland has always meant that the Cypriote ports played a less important economic rôle than would otherwise have been the case.

But if the achievements of the British in Cyprus were slow, they were none the less sure. Population rose from 186,084 in 1881 to 274,108 in 1911, 450,114 in 1946, and 574,008 in 1960. More important, the increase in population was accompanied by a rise in living standards.[1]

Kitchener's survey of the island between 1880 and 1883 provided good maps and much information upon which to base administrative improvements. The standard of the administrators themselves was not, it seems, as high as was the case in, say, India; but then the Indian Civil Service attracted men of a higher calibre than the Home Civil Service. One reason for the lower standard in Cyprus was the cheese-paring attitude of the elected members of the Legislative Council with regard to official salaries, an attitude conditioned by resentment over the tribute. Nevertheless, the administrators in Cyprus were very much more honest and energetic than the average

---

[1] In certain countries, more especially since 1945, the failure of the economy to keep pace with the increase in population brought about through advances in disease control has led to an actual drop in living standards, despite increases in the G.N.P.

in any Middle Eastern country outside the British empire. High Commissioners and (after 10 March 1925) Governors involved themselves in the life of the island. In 1897, for instance, the High Commissioner, Sir Walter Sendall, gave money to the Girls' High School in Nicosia to enable graduate pupils to pursue their studies abroad, and a marble bust of him was set up there in gratitude. Most of the British rulers, and notably perhaps Sir Ronald Storrs, made a number of lasting friendships in the island.

It has sometimes been said that the chief psychological fault of the British in Cyprus was that they remained aloof from the people, but the charge is ill-considered. It is quite true, as Storrs says, that 'the reciprocal bitterness engendered by social slighting is progressive and cumulative'.[1] However, it is better not to present too many opportunities for such social friction to occur. It is relatively easy for a high official, or a person with deep knowledge of the language and customs, both to rule and to deal with the people on a basis of easy familiarity. It is quite another matter for minor officials, whose knowledge of culture is probably not so profound, and who soon discover that familiarity either breeds contempt or else provides opportunities for the exercise of the subtler social pressures. Storrs concedes that in general the relationships of British officials with their Cypriote subordinates were of the best.

Fortunately, the British in their empire usually followed a policy of not permitting a large number of colonists to settle in already populous countries. Some of the difficulties which result from the settlement of even a few such immigrants are apparent in the case of Cyprus. Thus, ex-Indian army officers, on fixed pensions, who had chosen the island as a cheap and pleasant place of retirement, were naturally opposed to any improvements which would result in a cost-of-living increase. Again, after the Second War a number of persons emigrated to Cyprus who had no interest in the local culture, some of whom did not even bother to learn Greek. Inevitably, they were resented, especially by the better-educated Cypriotes. It is one thing to be ruled by a Brahmin, quite another to be placed in a position of social inferiority to a box-wallah.

One definite achievement of the British was in the administration of justice. Whereas before 1878 total expenditure on justice was £250 a year, and judges received 14s per month (with results which may easily be imagined), judges now received adequate salaries and the cause of impartiality benefited enormously. Security also was greatly increased. For instance, rape, a not infrequent crime in the Ottoman period, now became very rare. Difficulties, however, were still occasioned by the scrupulous niceties of the Ottoman law

[1] *Orientations*, p. 476.

regarding land tenure and the right of succession. Cases were cited in 1914 of a carob tree owned by more than a hundred co-heirs, of a one-fifth share of a single room purchased from 132 persons, and of a well in the Carpass divided into 2,903,040 shares, held in varying proportions by nine individuals.

In 1878, Lord Gifford, Wolseley's A.D.C., had tethered his riding-camel[1] to a gate of Nicosia and returned to find it eaten up by pariah dogs. Now the disease-ridden strays were exterminated.[2] Sanitation was made better than at any period since ancient times, and villages were increasingly supplied with clean water.

In the twentieth century the pace of improvement was accelerated, especially after the tribute was lifted; and the slow progress of years came to fruition. In 1901 there were 10,000 wage-earners, in 1941 20,000. By 1912, use of the pit-and-screen method had led to the almost total extermination of the locust, though it had taken time to convince the people that such a result was possible and, owing partly to peasant negligence, another £20,000 had to be allocated for a new anti-locust campaign in 1948. Still, by the end of the British period the age-old locust problem was completely under control.

On the basis of scientific discoveries, mostly British, which had been made in the 1890s, a campaign was also launched to exterminate the malaria-carrying anopheles mosquito. In 1914, the spleen rate was still over 20 per cent and up to 1939 there were still 17,000 cases of malaria a year, but by 1949 the disease was eradicated. Leprosy too was almost wiped out, and the island benefited in general from advances in the field of medicine, so that it came to have one of the lowest mortality rates in the world.

At the beginning of the British period the island's wines were receiving an unexpected boost owing to the scourge of phylloxera on the continent. *Commandaria* became popular in Paris itself, where de Musset drank it. Rimbaud acquired a taste for it while he was in Cyprus, just as his predecessor Lamartine had done. In the early 1890s, protective tariffs on the continent hit the wine industry badly, but before 1914 sixty thousand sultana vines introduced from Crete were proving fairly successful. Cyprus wines were

[1] Camels were not first introduced by the Turks, any more than turbans were (see above, p. 89). Gjerstad found camel remains dating from the Bronze Age.

[2] There is a strong objection in the East to taking an animal's life 'unnecessarily'. For instance, the Ottomans used every now and again to exile the stray dogs of Istanbul to one of the Prinkipo islands, where they ate one another and finally starved. The author has aroused horror in Persia by his desire to put down diseased stray animals. Incidentally, in Cyprus today it is a vociferous minority of British residents who make the biggest outcry when the police round up strays.

not to regain widespread popularity until the Second World War, when British drinkers were cut off from the continent. In 1955, the vine-industry received a subsidy, and in the following year Mr F-J. Rossi, Managing-Director of a London wine firm, made a report which resulted in the procurement of better vines and French advice.

The problem of rural poverty was tackled very slowly, as is shown by the *Survey of Rural Life in Cyprus,* prepared at the direction of Sir Ronald Storrs. But the better-off Cypriotes must bear much of the blame for the slowness of progress in agriculture, as the degenerate practice of unproductive usury was rooted not only among businessmen and the higher clergy, but also in the professional class. (Of course, it is arguable that the bondholders of the Ottoman Loan did not set a very good example.)

In 1929, Lord Passfield (Sidney Webb), then Colonial Secretary, was able to point with pride to the contrast between Cyprus then and its situation when the British had taken over. Under the Turks there had been no hospital, only twenty-six miles of road, fewer than 7,000 children at school, no organised effort to develop mineral resources, agriculture, or forestry, and excessive taxes. All that was now changed. Hospitals had come into existence, there were 870 miles of road (720 of them asphalted),[1] and 46,000 children went to school. The salt-pans at Larnaca and Limassol were much more productive, and the mining of asbestos had been revived. Since 1913/14 (when only one copper mine had been in operation) there had been increased exploitation of other minerals not mined by the Turks. Attempts had been made at farm and stock improvement, and credit had been made available to farmers on reasonable terms. Trades unions and cooperatives were being encouraged. Reforms in the fields of finance and forestry, as well as British encouragement of archaeology, will be described below.

Cyprus suffered economic set-backs in the early 1930s, in common with the rest of the world, but in the near-famine conditions of 1934 the peasants received government relief. Also, certain advances were made, especially as regards communications. Storrs knew of no air traffic via Cyprus between the end of the First War and his own time as Governor. He managed to establish an emergency landing ground near Nicosia, and in September 1930 Imperial Airways began an experimental summer service between Cyprus, Palestine, and Egypt. In 1932, flying-boats began to land on the Akrotiri salt lake on their way from England to Palestine. The service was later discontinued. In 1935, the Nicosia aerodrome, where only

---

[1] By 1914 there were also 61 miles of railway across the Mesaoria, and an extension of ten miles was later added, but the line is now disused.

twelve aeroplanes had landed in the previous year, and which had no hangar, was seen to have potential; and in 1936 civil air transport began in Cyprus. True, this involved only one 6-8-seater DH 89 Dragon-Rapide aircraft, but already a few military thinkers were beginning to realise the increasing importance of air power, and to see the island as an unsinkable aircraft-carrier. Meanwhile, road-building proceeded, so that by the end of the Emergency Cyprus was to have the best road-system in the Middle East, 3,300 miles of it, 800 of which were asphalted.

The Second War stimulated demand for Cypriote exports in general, and the Korean War of mineral exports in particular. The distortion of the economy owing to the recession after the Korean War and the overemphasis on the services sector (supplying the British forces) did not become apparent until half-way through the Emergency. In view of this, and of the large sums disbursed by the British in aid,[1] it would be wrong to suppose that the Cypriote Greeks reacted against the British on economic grounds, however strong feeling may once have been over the Tribute issue.

In terms of culture in its wider sense, the main British legacies to Cyprus were better administrative techniques and fairly widespread technical and legal education. Cypriotes still study for British examinations. Of culture in its more restricted sense the British left little. There is not much doubt that the imposition upon the Cypriotes of a régime like that of the Italians in Rhodes would have suppressed Enotism as a political force and perhaps resulted in more efficient administration, but it was the healthier tendency of the British in Cyprus to permit the development of local cultural traditions. In India, by contrast, Macaulay's contemptuous rejection of Sanskrit and, by implication, Persian, and his insistence upon English as the educational medium, led to the creation of a large class of babus, whose general alienation from their own culture was only equalled by the general superficiality of their acquaintance with English culture.[2] Greek-Cypriote poets like Vassilis Michaelides (1849–1917) and Demetris Lipertis had no reason to write in any other idiom than their own.

In the course of time, the authorities began to participate (or 'interfere') in the development of education. By 1953 there were fifty Greek and ten Turkish secondary schools, with a total of 16,536 pupils, an increase of five times over 1930.

A word should be added concerning British contributions to the architecture of the island. Most of these were of a severely practical nature, though a few of the private houses (as opposed to the

---

[1] See below, pp 215, 311.
[2] Exceptions like Rabindranath Tagore do not disprove the rule.

accommodation for service families perpetrated by the Ministry of Works) reflected the good taste of their British designers. A number of the administrative buildings are at least pleasant, and there is also Government House, which the author admires. It was designed by Maurice Wells, and the plan was executed by J. V. Hamilton and L. F. Weldon. Cypriotes were responsible for details of the design. The main structure is of Yerolakko sandstone, with the harder Limassol limestone for staircases and other internal features. The attractive Cyprus hardwoods, then unreliable owing to faulty seasoning and felling at the wrong season, have been incorporated in the form of panels into more reliable timbers from elsewhere in the empire. The whole is a happy marriage of Lusignan, Greek-Orthodox, and Turkish motifs, though it is a pity that the architect did not have enough confidence in his own culture to incorporate characteristics of traditional English architecture.

Sir Ronald Storrs has been criticised for approving the imposition on the Cypriotes of a £25,000-plan for replacement of the wooden building burnt down by them in 1931, but he described the imposition on them of the £70,000 cost of the substitute plans as 'unjustifiable, inexcusable and unforgivable'.[1] One can answer that the finished product is certainly more suitable for a Presidential Palace, but that was not its original purpose. Government House is one more exemplification of the Parkinsonian principle that a grand headquarters is built just as the organisation is going into decline.

The Zionist Plan for the Colonisation of Cyprus

Despite the achievements of their governing officials, it cannot be claimed that the British in their heyday regarded Cyprus as an essential part of their empire and, as the Orontes began to flow into the Tiber, the Cypriotes were in more danger than they realised. The following facts have not, to the author's knowledge, been referred to by any previous historian of the island.

The year after publication of Theodor Herzl's Zionist manifesto, *Der Judenstaat* (1896), over two hundred representatives of world Jewry assembled at Basle and elected Herzl President of the Zionist organisation. By 20 June 1896 he was thinking of 'acquiring' Cyprus in order to offer it to Turkey, with additional payment, as a trade for Palestine. On 1 July 1898, he confided to his diary: 'Perhaps we can demand Cyprus from England, and even keep an eye on South Africa or America—until Turkey is dissolved.'[2]

---

[1] *Orientations*, p. 515 n.
[2] *The Complete Diaries of Theodor Herzl*, ed. Raphael Patai, tr. Harry Zohn (New York, London: Herzl Press and Thomas Yoseloff, 5 vols, 1960), vol. II, p. 644.

Because the Ottoman Sultan, Abdül Hamit II, was adamant over Palestine, other Zionists soon became interested in Cyprus also. In January 1901, a proposal in the *United Services Magazine* that Great Britain should exchange Cyprus for German East Africa led Herzl to speculate : 'Germany would then have to welcome a Jewish settlement in Cyprus with delight. We would rally on Cyprus and one day go over to Eretz Israel and take it by force...'[1] Several times in July 1902, Herzl discussed with Lord Rothschild his scheme for Jewish settlement of the Sinai Peninsula, Egyptian Palestine (El Arish), and Cyprus. His Lordship was very much in favour. The Sultan's offer of Mesopotamia, although refused, was to be held in reserve, for Herzl was sure it was still open.[2]

The following 23 October, Herzl had an interview with Joseph Chamberlain, the Colonial Secretary, and put the same plan to him. Chamberlain answered that the proposed mainland settlements were a matter for the Foreign Office, and that, as regards Cyprus, Greeks and Moslems already lived there and the British government had a duty to stand by them. Besides, 'there would be real difficulties' if the Cypriote Greeks resisted with the support of Greece and Russia. He feared a 'trades union' problem in Cyprus, such as already existed in London's East End. However, if Herzl 'could show him a spot in the English possessions where there were no white people as yet' they could talk about that. The 'Greeks would resist the Jews in Cyprus', just as the Australians were then opposing Indian immigration. Fear of being swamped was the reason, 'and in his office he couldn't do anything against the will of the indigenous population : "In our country everything is out in the open, and if Cyprus were discussed in this way a storm would break out immediately" '. Herzl replied that 'not everything in politics is really disclosed to the public—only results, or whatever may happen to be needed in a discussion'.[3] He then outlined his plan for 'having a current created in our favour in Cyprus'. As he said later to Lord Rothschild, he 'planned to despatch six men to Cyprus and have them create a popular demand for inviting in the Jews'. To Chamberlain Herzl put the same idea in a modified form, and said that 'golden rain' would overcome all opposition : 'The Moslems will move away, the Greeks will gladly sell their lands at a good price and emigrate to Athens or Crete'. Chamberlain gave his blessing to the Sinai settlement plan, provided Lord Cromer (Evelyn Baring) recommended it. On the next day, stimulated by the desire to divert Jewish immigration from the East End of

---

[1] Ibid., vol. III, p. 1023.
[2] Ibid., vol. IV, p. 1294.
[3] Ibid., p. 1361.

London, he told Herzl 'the Cyprus part of it is *my* affair' (whatever
that might mean), and advised Herzl to deceive the Foreign Secretary, Lord Lansdowne, as to his intention to use El Arish as a
vantage-point for taking over Palestine, well knowing the opposite
to be the truth.[1]

The Sinai settlement project came to nothing, owing to lack of
water, and several attempts which had actually been made to establish Jewish agricultural settlements in Cyprus had met with little
success by the time Herzl died in 1904. But those who are tempted
to regard the threat to the Cypriotes as unreal should reflect that
the Balfour Declaration was obtained through very similar
manoeuvres to those of Herzl, with the help of another Lord
Rothschild, and that room was made for Jewish immigrants in
Palestine by buying land and housing from better-off Arabs and
systematically evicting the Arab tenants. Meanwhile, interested
parties in authority ensured that the ring was held, and the press
denigrated those who resisted.

The Island's Finances Under the British

Wolseley put an end to the *zaptiehs'* enforcement of the collection of episcopal dues, and to Sir Robert Biddulph (High Commissioner from June 1879 until 1886) must go the credit for eradi-
cating the curse of tax-farming. A large number of tithes were
abolished in 1880, including that on carobs. A locust-tax was imposed in 1881, but the tithe on grape-yield was abolished in 1883,
and by 1901/2 fifty-five articles were freed from tithes. The Turkish
tax on trades and professions was done away with early, and the
military exemption tax (previously reduced) was abolished in 1906.
The tithes on cereals did not go the same way until 1926, but
meanwhile a number of other taxes were reduced. On the debit
side was the scandal in 1885, when the Chief Inspector and other
officials of the Revenue Department were charged with 'corruption,
forgery, embezzlement and under-assessment of tithes'.[2] However,
the elimination of corruption led to the complaint that the taxes
were now collected in full, as they had not been under the Turks.
Also, the British, to begin with, made insufficient allowance for
losses through earthquakes and floods, and in 1887 there were anti-
tax demonstrations after a bad harvest.

The usury problem was tackled slowly, owing to opposition from
influential Cypriotes. Not till 1914 was the legal interest rate
reduced to 12 per cent (the rate obtaining under the Ottomans in

[1] Cf. ibid., pp. 1362, 1368–9.
[2] Hill, IV, p. 498.

the eighteenth century), and not till 1949 was it further reduced
to 9 per cent. The turning-point came with the setting up of the
Agricultural Bank in 1925, in the teeth of opposition from the
moneylenders. On his arrival as Governor in 1926, Storrs found
three moneylending lawyers among the elected members of the
Legislative Council and a landowner who was also a moneylender,
besides an Orthodox bishop and a merchant whom he places by
implication in the 'numerically insignificant class of parasites' who
made a living out of the peasant producer. Storrs estimated that
70 per cent of the peasantry (who then comprised three-quarters of
the population) 'were chronically indebted to usurers and merchants
whose actions for recovery (more than half the cases in the District
Courts) afforded employment to the numerous advocates, who
derived the major part of their professional income from that
source'.[1] It was a classic case of the treachery of the clerks. No
wonder Storrs wished to exclude moneylenders from his proposed
Council of Administration.[2]

The growth of the Cooperative Movement, encouraged by the
authorities, provided the peasantry with a means of escape from the
stranglehold of debt. The first cooperative credit society was set up
in 1909 at Lefkonico, and 1914 saw the first law regulating cooperatives. In 1923, legal provision was made for non-credit societies.
This law was revised in 1939 and is still in force. By 1937, when
a Cooperative Central Bank was established, there were 333 cooperatives. Sir Charles Woolley, Governor from 1941 to 1946 (who is
unjustly ridiculed by Percy Arnold in his account of journalistic
experiences in Cyprus), was especially favourable towards the
cooperative movement. In 1940, there were 37,000 people in cooperatives, by 1954 as many as 115,000, and the number of societies
had grown to 734.

The 'Tribute', which in the beginning amounted to nearly fifty
per cent of the gross revenue, remained a major issue for forty-nine
years, and all the High Commissioners and Governors over that
period protested against it. The burden during the nineteenth century was crushing and a bar to progress, but things were not so bad
as might appear. Thus, in 1889 Sir Henry Bulwer (then High Commissioner) was able to point out that, while an average of £92,686
had been sent to the Porte before 1878, now only an average of

[1] *Orientations*, p. 473. In February 1968, a house-painter had to be dis-
suaded (through disqualification of one of his sponsors) from standing for the
Presidency of Cyprus on the simple platform of the abolition of interest.
[2] Ibid, p. 500. In 1934, the total agricultural debt in Cyprus seems to
have been as much as £2 million (see N. C. Lanitis, *Rural Indebtedness and
Agricultural Co-operation in Cyprus*, Limassol, 1944, p. 25).

£50,469 was sent, that is to say, the difference between revenue and expenditure. The balance, some £40,000, was made up by a British grant-in-aid. But grants-in-aid were not automatic, and in 1899 Chamberlain claimed that it was merely an accident that the Tribute had been 'hypothecated' to the Ottoman Loan. When Winston Churchill, as Colonial Secretary, visited the island in 1907 he expressed the hope that the grant-in-aid, which then stood at £50,000, would become permanent. He also attacked the whole principle of the Tribute. In 1910/11, the grant-in-aid dropped to £40,000, but in 1910 was definitely fixed at £50,000 a year, so that the actual amount paid by the Cypriotes was about £42,800. By this time the burden of the Tribute was much less, and in 1914 there was a net balance of revenue over expenditure of £181,318 (i.e. after the Tribute had been paid).

In 1925, Churchill, as Chancellor of the Exchequer under Baldwin, was encouraged by Storrs effectively to abolish the Tribute by increasing the grant-in-aid to an exactly equivalent amount. The Tribute was not abolished in name because of the existing Egyptian debt. As a *quid pro quo* suggested by Storrs, £10,000 or 1.4 per cent of the total Cyprus revenue, was set aside for Imperial Defence. Other colonies had already agreed to make similar contributions. The resulting compromise was welcomed by all fifteen elected members of the Legislative Council (i.e. including the Turks), who handed Storrs a document stating : 'The happy answer of the Imperial Government has fulfilled all Cypriot aspirations concerning this burden . . .'. Later, Storrs was cheered in Egypt by 800–900 Cypriotes, when he went there to raise loans in aid of the Cypriote economy. However, the euphoria was short-lived, and agitation was renewed because, in the years since 1878, over £2 million had been paid by the Cypriotes towards the Tribute, and they (backed by British officials) thought that an equivalent amount should be spent by the British government in Cyprus itself. Eventually, very much more than that amount was given by Great Britain in aid, but not openly to offset the Tribute, so that rancour was unassuaged. In March 1926, before Storrs's arrival, all the elected members had demanded that the annual surplus of £11,000 on the Ottoman Loan, plus the sums paid into it out of Cyprus revenue since the annexation of the island in November 1914, in all £923,000, should be spent in Cyprus; but this was not done.

In 1929, Lord Passfield argued that the 1855 loan was made when Cyprus was part of the Ottoman dominions, and that, had it been considered as a successor state of the Ottoman empire at the Treaty of Lausanne, its share of the loan payments would have been greater. More reasonably, he felt that a yearly sum of £42,800 between 1907 and 1927[1] was not an excessive price to pay for British administration, in view of its achievements. Nor was the Tribute such a burden as formerly, for revenue had risen from £176,000 to £750,000 a year.

After 1931 the British government paid much more attention to the island. Revenue in that year was £862,796, while expenditure was £877,476, the balance being made up by Great Britain. In the following year, the figures were £779,449 and £872,749 respectively. By an Act of 1940, colonies no longer had to be self-sufficient, and this principle was to have unfortunate consequences in several countries when British officials handed over to native ones, but not in Cyprus.

In 1941, income tax, long a burden to the British, was at last introduced in Cyprus; and taxes, light before, continued to rise until 1944. Between 1940 and 1943 the island received £1,071,000 in the form of grants-in-aid, and in 1944/5 £827,490. In 1946, the British introduced a ten-year development plan, and contributed about £6 million towards it. The *per capita* G.N.P. rose from £80 in 1950 to £158.6 in 1957. Owing to the inflation of sterling, this does not, in real terms, represent a 14 per cent average rate of increase, but 4.8 per cent. Still, that is a respectable growth rate; more than Great Britain herself was able to manage. Annual expenditure on public administration and defence rose from £3.4 million in 1950 to £14.4 million in 1957, and Britain contributed £2 million more towards development.

Forestry Under the British

Apart from such inadequate protective measures as those taken in 1873, the Ottomans did little to preserve the woods of Cyprus. Indeed, one of the gravest charges which can be made against Islam is that, wherever it has penetrated, the trees have tended to disappear.[2] In Ottoman Cyprus, fires had not been controlled, and goat-grazing over centuries had led to continuous erosion. In one way, the lack of communications, especially in the Paphos area, had been a blessing; for it prevented exploitation of the larger areas of forest.

The first forestry studies were carried out in 1879, and demarcation was begun, using beacons, in 1884. British forestry officials were brought in from India, and the forester's uniform today remains

---

[1] In 1910/11, it was £10,000 more (see above).
[2] It is all the more to Atatürk's credit that he introduced a tree-planting cult into Turkey.

essentially the same as that worn by those officials. Within a short time, burnt areas were being planted.

The struggle against the goat (on which many people depended) was long and hard. Not until 1913 was there a law restricting these animals to non-forest areas. Some forest roads had been constructed, but resources were limited, and large areas had to be clear-felled during the First War, owing to lack of roads.

As early as 1920, Cypriotes were being trained at forestry schools in England, and in 1928/9 two Cypriotes were sent to take a university degree-course in forestry.

The greatest name in Cyprus forestry is undoubtedly that of Dr A. H. Unwin, a contemporary of Sir Ronald Storrs. Storrs is clearly describing him when he writes that 'the principal Forest Officer loved his trees like human beings, only a good deal more.'[1] His long-distance walking and his vigorous denunciation of the goat will long be remembered; and if he aroused resentment in the sentimental and the small-minded, that merely helped to circulate his ideas. It was Dr Unwin, in 1929, who founded the Cyprus Forestry Association. It was open to all, and promoted much interest in the subject. Professor R. S. Troup of Oxford made a visit to Cyprus in the same year. In his report of 1930 he referred to minor state forests as a source of friction, suggesting concentration on planting in highland areas. As a result, in the mid-1930s the low-lying minor forests were made over to the District Commissioners. This was unfortunate, for the D.C.s were much more likely to give way to local pressure. However, a beneficial side-effect of depriving the Cypriotes of representation after the 1931 outbreak was that the goatherds' influence now counted for little, and a number of improvements in the forest law could be put into effect. Storrs tells us that by 1938 forests covered 17.35 per cent of the total land area. Gradually, the peasantry came to see how much harm the goat was doing, and towards the end of the Second War a law was passed enabling village areas to vote in favour of tethering goats. Many villages did so, and the goatherds, who had previously bullied the peasantry, were successfully defied with police help. In 1950, the government published a policy statement on the forests which has been described to the author by a senior Cypriote forestry official as 'one of the best in the world'. The following year came the founding of the Forestry College at Prodhromos, with the help of Oxford University and Forestry Commission schools in the United Kingdom.

[1] *Orientations,* p. 486.

The Progress of Archaeology and the Protection of Antiquities

After 1878, depredations such as those of Palma di Cesnola, undertaken, to use his own words, 'with the countenance and indulgence of the authorities and public officers', were at last brought to an end. In reaction, the Legislature restricted the maximum exportable proportion of an archaeologist's finds at one-third, and a law of 1905 further restricted the export of antiquities. Unfortunately, these measures merely encouraged tomb-robbing among the villagers, so that in 1927 the law was modified to permit more archaeological exports and make smuggling easier to deal with. The model legislation of 1935 was drafted by Sir George Hill himself.

The first archaeologist of distinction to excavate in the British period was Max Ohnefalsch-Richter, who in 1880 was empowered to dig at Salamis. In the days before Cambridge liberals began to reject the experience of the past as incompatible with their ideology, the learned world was united in its desire to learn from antiquity; and educated Britons, then as now, were particularly interested in archaeology. The museum in Nicosia was founded in 1883 and maintained by private subscriptions, largely British. In 1888, the British School of Athens dug at Kouklia, and 1899 was a landmark in Cyprus archaeology, when Max Ohnefalsch-Richter and John L. Myres published their catalogue of the Cyprus Museum. The present museum building was not erected until 1908. It was dedicated to the memory of Queen Victoria.

The British, however, were not blameless in respect of the monuments of the past. Bellapaïs was used for a time as a rifle-range by British troops, and the government appears to have filled in the marshy site of Citium with ballast from its own acropolis.[1] In 1885, nothing was done to prevent the robbing of tombs at Marium, and not until 1891 was it forbidden to use buildings at Famagusta as quarries for Port Said. Soli was similarly used. At that time, scholars in Cyprus were mainly interested in the classical period. Later, Rupert Gunnis, who was made A.D.C. and private secretary to Storrs, showed considerable interest in medieval antiquities, but not until the time of A. H. S. Megaw, Director of the Department of Antiquities from 1935 to 1959, can it be said that Byzantine buildings were properly protected.

For a long time, archaeology in Cyprus was held back by lack of funds, and Sir Hamilton Goold-Adams, who ruled from 1911 to 1915, has been called the first in his position to show 'a really intelligent interest' in the subject, as opposed to a merely benevolent

[1] Bekir Pasha also made use of rubble from Citium.

attitude. For instance, in 1914 a grant of £450 was made to Myres, then a Professor at Oxford, in respect of excavations carried out in the previous year.

To begin with, the poverty of most Cypriotes naturally made them more concerned over economic matters than anything else but, stung by references to their ignorance,[1] they became actively interested in the findings of archaeology. However, their enthusiasm was selective. Storrs reported that in his time none of the recorded Phoenician remains had 'survived the determination of the Greek majority that Cyprus shall possess proofs of none but Hellenic origin'.[2] Nor did they share the British interest in the monuments of the Lusignan period. A typical cultural struggle developed, with the British discounting the undoubted Hellenic influences and the Greeks admitting the existence of little else. As in most such cases, the scholars on either side did not declare their interest, and may not even have admitted it to themselves.

Mr G. H. E. Jeffery, who was Curator of Ancient Monuments from long before the First War, and Curator again after the war until his death in 1935, was allowed only £600 a year in all, which included his own salary. He did a great deal with this, but it was a derisory sum. Storrs's suggestion that a ten-shilling landing-tax for archaeological purposes should be imposed on each tourist was unfortunately turned down, and lack of funds made it impossible to pay guards to collect entrance fees at so many remote monuments. Between 1934 and 1942, Lord Mersey and his committee raised thousands of pounds in support of archaeological investigation in Cyprus, and after the war much more money was made available.

After the 1927 legislation the learned world became very interested in Cyprus, and a number of excavations took place, especially noteworthy being those carried out by the British Museum, by the Swedish Cyprus expedition under Gjerstad from 1927 to 1931,[3] and by Schaeffer at Enkomi in 1933. Several British, French, and American universities sent expeditions between 1935 and 1959. And native Cypriotes now began to make their own very considerable contributions to knowledge. It was in 1933 that Porphyrios Dikaios discovered the large site at Erimi which turned out to be of the Copper Age.

---

[1] The expression Βοῦς Κύπριος was not unknown in Athens.
[2] *Orientations*, p. 470.
[3] Dr Karageorghis considers the record of this expedition as a turning-point in Cyprus archaeology. The reader should consult Einar Gjerstad, *Studies on Prehistoric Cyprus* (Stockholm, 1926).

The Cypriote Orthodox Church Under the British

Under the British the Archbishop was no longer officially recognised as Ethnarch, and the Greek hierarchy were resentful of losing powers which they had wielded under the Turks. Also, the property of the Church had previously been exempt from tax, which was now no longer the case.

Kyprianos, Bishop of Citium,[1] was elected to the first Legislative Council, and the clergy were very much to the forefront in agitating for *Enosis*. On occasion, they saw the need to influence elections, and both in 1891 and 1906 there were cases of elections voided owing to their interference. Storrs goes so far as to call the Orthodox Church in Cyprus 'a political rather than a religious institution'.[2]

In 1879, a memorial was addressed to Wolseley by Archbishop Sophronios, Bishop Neophytos of Paphos, and Bishop Kyprianos, in which they prayed that priests should not be imprisoned for debt or be made to work on road gangs. There was also a Pancyprian memorial signed by fifty-four local representatives. Both memorials complained of the difficulty of maintaining the Church (now that it was harder to enforce the collection of tithes). In the same year, the people demonstrated when two priests sentenced to a month's imprisonment at Famagusta were shaven like the other convicts.[3] The practice was discontinued.

In the time of Sophronios, relations were good between the Cypriote Church and its relatively unobtrusive Anglican counterpart. In 1889, the Archbishop was well received by the Archbishop of Canterbury, and a doctorate of divinity was conferred upon him at Oxford. He made no objection to the distribution of bibles, which was at that time a major activity of Protestant missionaries. But when the mild Sophronios died in 1900 the atmosphere became more heated. In that year the Holy Synod was refused a government grant towards the setting up of a training school for the clergy. In 1906, a mob attacked the American Presbyterian mission in Famagusta, which was under suspicion of proselytising.

Between 1900 and 1909 occurred what Hill has described as a 'squalid schism' in the Church of Cyprus over who was to be the next Archbishop. The patriarchs of Alexandria, Jerusalem, and Greece were all involved, though not he of Antioch. The Bishop of Citium, Cyril Papadopoulos, was the more violent and Enotist

---

[1] Kyprianos was particularly incensed at being made to pay taxes.
[2] *Orientations*, p. 474.
[3] A parallel is to be found in Richard the Lionheart's insistence that the Cypriote magnates should be shaven.

candidate, and had tried to found an organisation to further
his aims in 1899. He naturally had the support of the people. His
opponent, Cyril Basileiou, Bishop of Kyrenia, was a less forceful
character, and more mildly Enotist, but he had the support of the
rich. The High Commissioners, Sir W. F. Haynes Smith (1898–
1904) and Sir Charles King-Harman (1904–11), wisely kept out of
the dispute. In 1908, the demonstration of a pro-Papadopoulos
mob led to the temporary imposition of martial law in Nicosia, but
order was restored by half a company of the Green Howards, who
were brought up from Polemidhia. Eventually, a compromise was
arrived at. Cyril Papadopoulos became Archbishop as Cyril II from
1909 until his death in 1916. Then Cyril Basileiou succeeded as
Cyril III, and held the position till he died in 1933.[1]

The power of the people directly to elect their Archbishop was
to some extent neutralised in 1914 by an ecclesiastical charter
whereby sixty-six elected delegates voted jointly with the Holy
Synod. In 1943, an attempt by Major John Clerides to secure
election by the people of the entire Ethnarchic Council came to
nothing.

Between 1933 and 1947 there was no Archbishop because the
troubles of 1931 had led to the exiling of Nicodemus Mylonas,
Metropolitan of Citium,[2] and Makarios Myriantheus, Metropolitan
of Kyrenia. The opinion of the patriarchs was that they might
vote from abroad, but the Cypriotes would not allow it, insisting
that both bishops be allowed to return. That forceful Enotist,
Leontios Leontiou, Metropolitan of Paphos and nephew of Cyril
III, had been out of Cyprus during the riots. He had been refused
permission to land in November 1931, but was permitted to do so
in June of the following year. On the death of his uncle he became
Locum-tenens.

In 1937, three laws were enacted by the British for regulating
the affairs of the Cypriote Church. The first provided for investigation and auditing of the accounts of churches and monasteries.
The second disqualified from election to the Archbishopric any
deportee, any person not a native of the Colony, and anyone convicted of an offence punishable by two or more years of imprisonment. The third made the election conditional on the Governor's
approval. These laws were repealed in 1946. At that time there
were again two aspirants to the Archbishopric. The political Right
was represented by Makarios Myriantheus, the Left by the *Locum-*

---

[1] Storrs, perhaps harshly, was to call him 'the only spiritually-minded
Orthodox . . . priest' he discovered in Cyprus (loc. cit.).

[2] Storrs (*Orientations*, p. 505) refers to his power of contracting the pupils
of his eyes to fascinate or overawe an opponent (cf. above, p. 36).

tenens. The latter was elected in June 1947, but died in July. His rival then succeeded as Makarios II, dying in June 1950. Makarios II's successor, Makarios III, is the most important of all Cypriote archbishops, and requires a section to himself.

The Struggle Over Representation

The British High Commissioners were effectively governors, while District Commissioners took over the six Turkish *kazas,* or administrative districts. It has been said that, apart from some municipal administration towards the end of the Turkish period, the Cypriote Greeks had little experience of governing. That is to ignore their long tradition of church and tax administration, but memories of the latter did not predispose the Cypriote Turks in favour of government by the majority.

In the first year of their rule the British established a new Legislative Council, to consist of four to eight members, with official and unofficial appointees in equal proportions. In 1879, the Archbishop and the Greek district representatives presented a memorial to the High Commissioner asking for a representative assembly. In 1882, a Legislative Council was set up, with twelve elected members (nine Greeks and three Turks, elected separately) and six official ones, the H.C. or presiding senior official having a casting vote. This vote was usually decisive, for the three Moslem (viz Turkish) members nearly always voted with the officials.

In the winter of 1887/8, the Greeks demanded more extensive rights, through abolition of the H.C.'s power of veto. Nothing came of their agitation, and Sir H. E. Bulwer,[1] for his part, complained of the caucus system whereby Greek members decided by a majority at a previous, private meeting how they would vote at a Council meeting. The Turks were to make the same complaint for a very long time.[2] Yet the caucus is inevitably an adjunct of any multiethnic elective system, and is also characteristic of many elective systems in relatively homogeneous societies. In 1897, three additional advisory members were added to the Council, two Greeks and one Turk.

The Legislative Council had no powers in the matter of the Tribute, the H.C.'s salary and expenses, those of the six official members, those of the judges, or those of the courts. However, the elected members had control over other expenditure, and occasionally the H.C. had to exercise his power to rule by Order in Council so as to restore cuts in appropriations.

[1] H.C. 1886–92.
[2] See below, p. 314.

In 1902, the Turkish elected members voted with the Greeks in opposition to the H.C.'s right of veto, and proposed an extension of their power. The cooperation was shortlived, as the Turks could not see eye to eye with the Greeks over the Tribute without alienating the Porte and, in effect, trusting their political future to the Greeks. Later in the year, the alliance came apart, precisely over the Tribute issue. In 1903, owing to the absence of a Turkish member, the Greeks passed a motion reflecting the deceased Mr Gladstone's expressed desire that the Cypriotes should participate to a greater extent in the administration, the object being to prepare them for *Enosis.*

When Churchill visited the island in October 1907, the Greeks suggested that the Council be composed exclusively of elected members in proportion to the Christian and Moslem populations, but Churchill, who was otherwise sympathetic, pointed out that this would be tantamount to surrender by the British and the Turks. At the end of 1911 the demand for proportional representation was repeated, with added demands that the Council should have complete control over finances, that official members should have no part in it, and that all administrative and judicial appointments should be filled by Cypriotes. The Colonial Secretary rejected these proposals. In January 1912, the now customary demand was made for *Enosis,* the lifting of the Tribute, and proportional representation; to which the H.C. replied that the Turks must have their safeguards; and on 17 April all the Greek members resigned in a body as a protest. This was the signal for indignant meetings. A small deputation waited on the Colonial Secretary (Harcourt) in London. He considered their proposals, but rejected them. The members who had resigned were later re-elected.

The settlement of the archiepiscopal succession led to energies finding a new outlet in anti-government agitation, and by the beginning of the First War a new problem was causing concern in Cyprus, as elsewhere. A government report of 1914/15 remarked on the surplus of secondary-school graduates who despised manual labour and were 'fit for nothing but clerical work', of which there was not enough.[1] The existence of such a group is always a factor making for instability. There was little popular discontent during the Great War, when 11,000 Cypriotes found employment with the British as colonial auxiliaries, chiefly muleteers; but afterwards the dissatisfaction of the intellectuals found a ready outlet in the press, and the people, who had expected easy *Enosis,* were readier to respond. The year 1921 saw the introduction of a Seditious Publi-

[1] The problem of finding such people employment still remains (see above, p. 68).

cations Law, and in 1928 as many as five publications were prohibited. A good deal of the subversive literature was printed in
Athens.

In 1919, some Greeks were taking the line that meliorative legislation was a waste of time because *Enosis* was near, but such an
expectation was shown to be over-sanguine. In December 1920, the
Greek elected members again resigned in a body, and the Council
was boycotted by most Greeks until 1923. In 1922, two elections
were held. The only ones elected by the Christians in the first of
these were two Maronite priests, which is an example of how a
minority tends to identify its interests with those of the power
counterbalancing the majority. In the second election, after the
disaster to Greek arms in Asia Minor, seven Greeks were elected,
including four anti-Enotists, but only 2,000 voted, out of an electorate of 50,000. As time went by, the long-term effects of the Asia
Minor set-back became apparent, and more Cypriote Greeks turned
their attention to problems of self-government, rather than the
short cut to *Enosis*.

In December 1922, the Archbishop presented a memorial
demanding full self-government and proportional representation,
but it was answered with the statement that the Cypriotes were not
politically ripe for such liberties. Spyros Araouzos, an able lawyer,
now wrote to the Colonial Secretary (the Duke of Devonshire) on
behalf of his people. He cogently argued that in no British dependency did the Whites have less part in the administration than was
the case in Cyprus. He admitted that the Cypriotes were excitable
and irascible, but so were all Greeks and Latins, and he pointed out
that others not superior in intellect had been granted more political
liberty. (Greeks were much incensed over the fact that Cyprus was
behind the Caribbean and African colonies on the road to self-
government.)[1] Further, the Greeks were now four-fifths of the
population, and should be represented accordingly. The Colonial
Secretary replied that the interests of the Turks must be safeguarded, and added, rather weakly, that he was in favour of
appointing Greeks to the higher administrative posts if they were
free from 'racial prejudice'. A memorial to the Labour government
in February 1924, demanding self-government pending *Enosis*, was
also rejected, by J. H. Thomas, the new Colonial Secretary.

When Cyprus became a Crown Colony in 1925, the number of
Legislative Council members was raised to twenty-four (12 Greek,

[1] Lawrence Durrell, in the 1950s, speaks of 'a mountain of [government]
posters showing pictures of the Queen decorating coal-black mammies with
long-service medals—the very thing to make Greeks and Turks, with their
colour-bar, dance with rage' (*Bitter Lemons*, London: Faber, 1967 edn,
p. 152).

3 Turkish, and 9 official). The Governor's separate, advisory Executive Council also contained Cypriotes. But in November 1925 the Colonial Secretary, then L. S. Amery, still felt that the Cypriotes were not advanced enough for further constitutional powers.

The day before Storrs landed as Governor, in November 1926, the Council rejected the appropriations bill, so that government had to be by Order in Council, and in 1928 the Bishop of Citium, together with other Greek elected members, withdrew altogether from discussion of the budget. Incidents like these go far to explain Storrs's opinion that the Council was 'an exasperating and humiliating nuisance'.[1] As its President, the Governor was expected to be both partial (on behalf of imperial interests) and impartial. Storrs resisted internal autonomy as an obvious first step towards *Enosis*, but he was nevertheless a Philhellene and devoted to the interests of the island. This he showed by the part he played in the abolition of the Tribute, by his active promotion of Cyprus products, by his securing the appointment of Cypriotes as judges, by his encouragement of technical education, by his improvement of communications, and by such cultural measures as the opening of a public library in 1927. Indeed, many Enotists saw his improvements as threatening their cause.

When the Labour Party came to power in 1929, delegates led by the Bishop of Citium, among them Zenon Rossides, went to London and requested that all local matters should be under Cypriote control. They circulated Members of Parliament, and had reason to hope from past Labour pronouncements that their request would be granted. But the promises of politicians are one thing, their performance quite another. On 28 November, Lord Passfield replied astringently to the Greek-Cypriote memorial, saying, *inter alia*: 'There is much to be said for the view that what Cyprus needs at present are fewer occasions for political discussion and more occasions for constructive work', and he pointed to the existence of partial, municipal self-government. A Royal Commission of Inquiry (re *Enosis*) was refused, and the subject treated as 'definitely closed'. Lord Passfield's words were rather abrupt and undiplomatic, and the sense might well have been conveyed differently, but there can be no doubt that as Colonial Secretary he genuinely tried to do what was best for the peoples under his care.

There were, of course, indignant reactions in Cyprus to Lord Passfield's *obiter dictum*. However, he was not responsible for creating the general climate of dissatisfaction before the riots. The economic slump was responsible for that.

It was in 1927 that Storrs, just in case, recommended transfer of

---

[1] *Orientations*, p. 472.

1. A Cyprus moufflon or wild sheep. The only wild animal still found in the island.

2. Troödos pines under snow.

3. Bellapaïs Abbey. The most beautiful of medieval monuments in Cyprus. Situated on a rock escarpment halfway up the Kyrenia Mountains.

4. Kolossi Castle. Crusader castle dating back to 1210.

5. Icon painting in St Barnabas' Monastery.

6. Kykko Monastery from the air.

7. The Tekke of Hala Sultan, seen across Larnaca Salt Lake.

8. Cyprus is one of the oldest vine growing countries in the world.

9.   Sir Ronald Storrs, Governor of Cyprus 1926–32.

10. A Greek-Cypriote demonstrator is arrested by a Turkish-Cypriote policeman and a British civilian (August 1955).

11. Turks in Nicosia demonstrate after the killing by EOKA of a Turkish policeman in Paphos (13 January 1956).

12. Greek students in Athens demonstrating in favour of *Enosis*. They are on their way to the British Embassy (April 1955).

13. Cypriote Greeks being searched before being taken away for questioning. Chief Inspector Donald Thompson has just been killed in Ledra Street, Nicosia (September 1958).

14. Field Marshal Sir John Harding, Governor of Cyprus 1955–57.

15. Sir John Harding visiting the Turkish village of Elea, near Lefka.

16. Sir Hugh Foot returns to London to make a report (December 1957).

17. British troops of the Lancashire Fusiliers patrol Hermes Street, on the edge of the Greek half of Nicosia, after the killing of Sergeant Reginald Hammond (3 August 1958).

19. Greek-Cypriote irregulars manning a road-block outside Nicosia (December 1963).

18. Colonel George Grivas arrives in Athens at the end of the EOKA campaign (17 March 1959).

20. Tea at Government House during the Constitutional talks (February 1960). From left to right: Dr Küçük, Mr Amery, President Makarios and Sir Hugh Foot.

21. Turkish-Cypriote women and children flee before the Greek-Cypriote irregulars during the troubles.

22. Cypriote Turks manning the battlements of St Hilarion Castle during the troubles. Beyond is the Kyrenia coastal plain.

23. At the U.N. Secretariat. From left to right: Zenon Rossides, President Makarios, U Thant, and Spyros Kyprianou.

24. A United Nations unit on patrol.

25.   President Makarios with Mr Harold Wilson during the Commonwealth Prime Ministers' Conference at Marlborough House (September 1966).

26. Nicosia, the capital of Cyprus.

27. The new Archiepiscopal Palace, Nicosia.

28.   Kyrenia, small harbour town sixteen miles from Nicosia.

29.   The Morphou Dam, which helps to irrigate an area famous for its citrus fruits.

the garrison from Limassol to Nicosia, but this was not done. In 1929 and 1930 he proposed modifications of the constitution, so that the Council should be reorganised on the lines of the Turkish *Mejlis* (*Meclis*) *Idare*, with three-quarters of the members representing the peasantry. Having got rid of the patronage system under which teachers had formerly been appointed, he now proposed restrictions on Enotist agitation and a rise in teachers' salaries. He also urged the expulsion of Alexis Kyrou, the Greek Consul, who provided a focus for the agitation, but nothing came of the suggestion until after the 1931 riots had taken place.[1] If all the measures suggested had been adopted there would probably have been no riots, and Lord Passfield must be held responsible for rejecting any restrictive amendment to the constitution. Meanwhile, a boycott of British goods by the Enotists came to nothing, as was to happen again during the Emergency.[2]

The outbreak of October 1931 was preceded by the resignation from the Legislative Council of Greek elected members, headed by the Bishop of Citium. The elective seats were afterwards abolished, and the surviving Advisory Council was nominated. It included four Greeks and one Turk, but none of the higher clergy. (In January 1934, one of its number, A. Triantaphyllides, was assassinated.) Village headmen (*mukhtars*) also came to be appointed by the government.

Meetings of more than five (later fifteen) persons without permission of the local District Commissioner were banned in Cyprus, but in 1937 the Committee for Cyprus Autonomy was founded in London, and the same year saw another fruitless deputation, which included John Clerides, later Mayor of Nicosia. In 1939, yet another memorial was presented, and questions were asked in Parliament, with similar unsuccess. The Cypriote Greeks were nothing if not persistent, and in this they resembled the Irish Home Rulers of the late nineteenth and early twentieth centuries.

Meanwhile, the British in Cyprus encouraged the growth of the trades union movement, especially under the governorship of Sir Herbert Richmond Palmer (1933–39). Union activity had begun about 1920, and in 1931 the registration of unions was legally provided for. In 1932, there was still only one union in existence, whereas by 1940 there were sixty-two (with 3,389 members). In 1941 came the establishment of a minimum wage and a trades union and trades disputes law, which also regularised peasant economic associations. By 1944 there were some ninety unions,

---

[1] Kyrou, a native Cypriote, reappears as Permanent U.N. Representative of Greece from 1947 to 1954.
[2] See below, pp. 291–2.

16—C

with a membership of about 10,000 (including 702 women). By 1954 the number of trades-unionists had doubled.

From October 1941 onwards, political meetings were allowed in Cyprus, and both K.E.K. (the Cypriote National Party for Enosis) and P.E.K. (the Pancyprian Rural Union) began to attract support. The Soviet Union had now been forced into an alliance with Britain against Germany, and another political factor came into prominence, namely the Communist AKEL (Reform Party of the Working People). There had been a Communist organisation in Cyprus since 1924, with leaders such as Placatis Servas (later Mayor of Limassol) who had been trained in the Soviet Union. In 1933, Palmer made Communist Party membership an offence. However, during the war, with the tide of propaganda running strongly in its favour, AKEL gained strength. In 1943, at the first municipal elections in twelve years, the party gained control of both Limassol and Famagusta.

In March 1944, there was a twenty-three-day strike of Cyprus government employees. It is interesting to note that Hugh Foot, who had held the post of Colonial Secretary in Cyprus since the previous year, and who even acted as Governor in the absence of Woolley, was particularly antagonistic towards the strike. Later, he was to become prominent as something of a left-winger himself, and was appointed Governor during the Emergency. In this case his main concern was that the strike might damage the war effort. On 25 March, there was a serious outbreak of trouble at Lefkonico, in which two persons died and a number were injured.

Towards the end of the war, official tolerance of AKEL wore thin. In January 1946, eighteen members of the left-wing P.S.E. (the Pancyprian Trades Union Committee) were sentenced to one year for sedition, while another twelve were sentenced to eighteen months, and the organisation was banned.

The social policies of AKEL were largely disruptive or short-sighted. In 1945, it opposed a scheme put forward by Captain L. S. Greening, District Commissioner of Nicosia, for forty-two villages to send in elected representatives. As elsewhere, the party was more interested in the deterioration of conditions than their betterment. Contented workers make bad revolutionaries. In Limassol and Famagusta, AKEL even refused to cooperate in an excellent scheme to control the marketing of perishable produce. The K.E.K. supported the scheme, and gained by it.

In October 1946, a Labour peer, Lord Winster, became Governor, and over the next year and a half developed proposals for Cypriote self-government. A consultative assembly was to be established, with responsibility for internal affairs, but it would not be permitted to discuss any alteration in the island's status as part of the Commonwealth. In explanation of this condition, the British referred to the unstable political situation in the eastern Mediterranean. The Governor's consent was to be required for the introduction of bills affecting defence, external affairs, minorities, finance, or the constitution. The assembly was to consist of twenty-two elected members (eighteen from a common electoral roll, four from the Turkish communal roll), plus twelve Greeks, four Turks, and four British officials, who, together with the chairman, were to be chosen by the Governor. In 1948, an election was held, but it was boycotted by the Enotists, under the leadership of Leontios, Bishop of Paphos, and disapproved of by AKEL, which was opposed to the wide powers retained by the Governor. Of the Greeks elected several withdrew, so that when the constitutional proposals were put to the vote, in May 1948, they were passed by only eleven votes to seven. True to form, six Turks and one Maronite, together with four Greek independents, voted in favour, while five Greek left-wing mayors and two Greek trades union representatives voted against. The opposition then withdrew. In August, a general strike was organised, and the assembly was dissolved.

In 1949, AKEL, which had lost support through its anti-Enotism, went technically Enotist itself. In the same year most of the other Greek political forces were united under the Ethnarchic Council, which was created by Archbishop Makarios II. In 1954, the British again proposed a legislative council, but the Enotists would not cooperate, and fear of consequent domination by AKEL led to British insistence that there should be an official, nominated majority. So the plan came to nothing. Subsequent proposals are best considered as responses to the Emergency.

The Struggle for Enosis

The British began by badly underestimating the strength of Enotist feeling. In his *Cyprus* (1878) Hamilton Lang, an otherwise intelligent writer who had been British Consul in the island, spoke of the Cypriotes as unlike the Greeks in that they were 'deficient in liveliness and nervous activity and . . . not infected with the monomania of Hellenic aspirations'. The peasantry, in particular, were supposed to be unaffected by Enotism, but this was to disregard the unremitting propaganda of the village priests, who were the leaders of the people. The half-truth (dear to conservatives) that trouble is always the work of a few agitators ignores the fact that people may be predisposed to listen to them.

Though under the Colonial Office from 1880 onwards, Cypriotes were officially described as Ottoman subjects on their passports until 5 November 1914, when the British annexed the island; and not until 1917 did they officially become British subjects. In practice, Cyprus was a Crown Colony from 1878, not from 1 May 1925, when it officially became one. The Ottoman connexion, however, provided an excellent excuse for not considering Enotist demands.

Religion and language were supposed to be the only links between Cyprus and Greece, as if these alone were not significant. But religion was also an ethnic distinguishing mark, and the linguistic link was strengthened by tying the education of Orthodox Cypriotes to that of Greece. The examinations for the Pancyprian Gymnasium, to give an example, were set in Athens. Storrs complained that while at school the Cypriote Greeks learned a great deal about Greece and very little about their own island.

It was not the Hellenic past that truly inspired Enotism. Homer, Aeschylus, and Sophocles might be invoked, but 'it was their names rather than their verses that were cited'. Both pupils and teachers studied the classics, not in the original, but through modern renderings in the vulgar and monotonous fifteen-syllable 'Political' rhymes. Storrs quotes an excellent parody in English :

'If that is what you mean to say I can no more behold you.
I told you so, I told you so, I told you so, I told you.'[1]

Classics in the original presented to the Central Training College for Boys remained for years with their pages uncut. As Storrs put it : 'The only Greek scholar I ever found was the Archbishop, and even His Beatitude would have been defeated by an average Sixth Form boy in a competition in classical Greek prose or iambics'.[2] In truth, the Hellenic ethos was alien to the Byzantine, which inspires Enotism. Enough has now been said to show why it is no accident that the Orthodox Church is so closely associated with Greek irredentism. Grivas might talk grandly of Marathon and Salamis, but the *nom de guerre* he chose was that of a legendary Byzantine frontiersman, and among his models were men like Pavlos Melas, the best-known of the Greek irregular leaders in Macedonia (killed in 1904). References to the accomplishments of the Hellenes merely

---

[1] To paraphrase Andrew Lang, the present author thinks of the *Odyssey* in this metre as 'The splurge and blunder of the *Oddity*' !
[2] *Orientations*, p. 469. Leaving aside the question as to whether the writing of Greek iambics serves any useful purpose, the position has changed since Storrs's time. The average British Sixth Former no longer learns Greek (nor indeed, does he have any penchant for the objective Sciences). In Cyprus, however, there is more interest in the classics. The author had occasion to make use of the Xenophon tag, θάλασσα, θάλασσα and this was corrected by the son of Mr Stylianakis to the Attic form, θάλαττα, θάλαττα.

serve to fill the modern Greek with a vague and exaggerated sense of cultural superiority.

Proof of enduring Greek-Cypriote enthusiasm for 'pan-Hellenism' came in 1880, when the Greek army mobilised against the Turks. Archbishop Sophronios expressed solidarity with Mother Greece, and 107 mules were given to Greek army officers by Cypriotes, in addition to the ones they bought. When they sailed, 150 volunteers accompanied them. In 1897, the Greek Consul, Philemon, recruited volunteers for the Thirty Days' War, and the government did not prevent him. That war went badly for the Greeks, though the Cypriotes fought well at Velestino. Philemon was to be removed from his post in 1900, on account of his Enotist activities, which embarrassed the Greek government. His temporary replacement, the merchant and historian Philios Zannetos, proved equally Enotist.[1] In 1912, the Mayor of Limassol and about a hundred volunteers left to fight in the First Balkan War. It cannot be maintained that Enotism was all talk.

Agitation for *Enosis* was continuous throughout the British period, though it had greater success at some periods than others. As Hill put it before his death in 1948 : 'Hardly a year has passed since the Occupation without the "Hellenic idea" finding expression in some form or other'.[2] Indeed, there were so many expressions of Enotism that only the most important will be mentioned here. The notion that the Greeks of Cyprus remained under British rule for many years without complaint is as groundless as the notion that the Turks were not antagonistic towards *Enosis*. In the threefold struggle for abolition of the Tribute, representation, and *Enosis*, the last aim was regarded by a majority of Greeks at any given time as the most important. Almost any excuse was good enough for agitation. The Greek flag was flown and the Greek National Anthem played, not only for visiting officials from Athens but on all Greek national occasions. Sometimes the Greek Consuls were much more extreme in their approach than the Greek government, which was anxious not to alienate Great Britain.

In 1887, Queen Victoria's Golden Jubilee celebrations were boycotted, so that they failed for lack of attendance. Sports were organised as a counter-attraction, and all over the island the clergy gave Enotist sermons. The 'disloyalty' of the Cypriote Greeks was frequently remarked on by British observers, but the charge was unjustified. They had loyalties of their own. It is true that Greek elected members broke their oaths of loyalty to the Crown, and

[1] Zannetos was to be deported in 1922 under the previous year's Aliens Law for refusing to apply for a permit to practise medicine.
[2] Hill, vol. IV, p. 496.

that cannot be wholly condoned, but if entry into a privileged group is conditional upon taking an oath, that oath will often be taken in vain. This is not to say that British governors were not wholly justified in taking action against those who threatened the system they represented. As it happens, the Diamond Jubilee, in 1897, was not boycotted, partly perhaps because of Sendall's popularity. The British did not make the mistake of punishing people for what they believed, but only for actions which threatened security. There were many Cypriotes who did not regard their pan-Hellenism as incompatible with a high regard for the British. Byron would have been surprised at his canonisation by Cypriote schoolteachers.

In 1895, when Sir William Harcourt, as Chancellor of the Exchequer, admitted that he thought Cyprus was useless to Great Britain, there were demonstrations or resolutions in favour of *Enosis* in several Cypriote towns. In 1897, Cypriote Enotists and their sympathisers held a meeting at St James's Hall in London. The placing of Crete under a Greek High Commissioner in the following year caused much emotion, and a Patriotic League was founded in Athens to bring about a similar result in Cyprus. Its founder was George Phrankoudes, described by the Oecumenical Patriarch Joakim as 'a stirrer-up of trouble in Athens about many things'. The Metropolitan of Athens came to a League exhibition of Cyprus products in 1901, but the Greek government prudently sent no representatives.

Greek-Cypriote euphoria over the Diamond Jubilee was short-lived. In 1899, there were cheers at the Limassol Olympic Sports for King George of the Hellenes, but not for Queen Victoria, and only Greek flags were flown. At the Pancyprian Games, held at Larnaca in the following year, the Metropolitan of Citium began the proceedings' in the name of God and Hellenism', thus politely giving precedence to the Deity. The accession of Edward VII brought renewed demands for *Enosis*.

There was without doubt a strong idealistic element in the *Enosis* movement. In 1902, when Chamberlain suggested that the Cypriote Greeks perhaps preferred to be administered by a rich Great Britain, rather than by a poor Greece, there were prompt protests from Cyprus.

The year 1903 brought resolutions from Nicosia, Larnaca, Limassol, and Kyrenia, demanding, as was now customary, the abolition of the Tribute, the protection of antiquities, and *Enosis*. Abolition of the Tribute had a definite Enotist aspect (as it meant severance of the Turkish link), and so did the preservation of (Greek) antiquities. A moving spirit was Andreas Themistocleous, Director of the

Limassol Gymnasium, who gave a speech in April of the same year, at the opening of the Pancyprian Games, in which he emphasised the value of target-practice. In 1906, the visit of a Greek training-ship provided yet another opportunity for demonstrations.

Right up to the end of the Second War, the Orthodox Christians of Cyprus were officially described as non-Mohammedans, so they were particularly pleased in 1907, when Churchill referred to them as being of Greek descent and showed a sympathetic understanding of their Enotist aims. Enotist activity now went off the boil for a time, though it was kept simmering by the activities of such men as Theophanes Theodotou, the lawyer and politician. The coronation of George V in 1911 prompted Enotist telegrams of 'congratulation' from the Archbishop and Greek mayors.

Venizelos, the Greek Prime Minister, was largely responsible for bringing about the *Enosis* of his native Crete, and had similar ambitions for Cyprus. In December 1912 or January 1913, Lloyd George (in the presence of Prince Louis of Battenberg and Churchill) suggested to Venizelos that Cyprus be exchanged for a base at Argostoli, in Cephallonia. Venizelos accepted in principle, but there was opposition from Streit, the Foreign Minister of Greece (on the grounds that this would tie Greece to Britain), and the matter dropped. The annexation of Cyprus in 1914 was seen, apparently by Venizelos among others, as a necessary stage on the road to *Enosis*. At one time it had been felt by most Greeks that the British Occupation was a step in the same direction.

The war gave opportunities for *Enosis* which were badly handled. After Gallipoli, on 12 September 1915, Bulgaria declared war on Serbia, and the Allied expeditionary force to Salonica was in peril. Accordingly, on 16 October, the British Foreign Minister (Sir Edward Grey) offered Cyprus to the Greek Prime Minister (Zaimes) in return for Greece's fulfilment of her treaty obligation to go to war on the side of Serbia. In Cyprus there was, as usual, much agitation for *Enosis,* but Great Britain's offer was not taken up, and within a few days it lapsed.

Enotist demonstrations took place at Larnaca and Limassol in 1916. In May of that year the secret Sykes-Picot agreement provided that Great Britain should not alienate Cyprus without the consent of France. That consent was unlikely to be forthcoming, for bondholders in France received half the Ottoman Tribute without the French government making any outlay. In 1917, there were more Enotist resolutions and memorials, and it was in that year that Greece, under Venizelos, finally joined the Allies.

In December 1918, Archbishop Cyril III led a delegation to

London. Ramsay MacDonald, among others, was favourable to their demands, and so was a section of the press. As for the Cypriote Greeks, they declared that they did not wish to prejudice British interests in the island. However, strategic counter-arguments prevailed, and the delegation's efforts came to nothing, as did those of another deputation in 1920, which included Zannetos. It is interesting to note that T. P. O'Connor, editor and M.P. (for an Irish area of Liverpool), was in favour of a plebiscite in Cyprus. At that time a temporarily defeated Turkey was in no position to object, and would almost certainly have done nothing to reverse a *fait accompli* later on.

While the Archbishop's deputation was still in London, in October 1919, Malcolm Stevenson, the Officer Administering the Cyprus government,[1] was able to forward to London a letter from Michael Pantelouris, a Cypriote schoolmaster in Athens. Pantelouris denounced 'the incompetence and corruption of the Greek Government' and prayed for 'continuance of British rule in Cyprus'. He also called for the teaching of English in Cypriote elementary schools and for more constitutional liberties.[2]

There were demonstrations in 1920, when Cypriotes were prevented from joining the Greek army, and more in the following year, which was the centenary of the Greek declaration of independence. Stevenson forbade processions, but the Archbishop nevertheless organised one, and rioting, chiefly by students, ensued.

The defeat of the Greeks in Anatolia in 1922 led to a cooling of Enotist fervour and greater concentration on constitutional issues. There was a rumour that the minority populations of Smyrna and Cyprus might be exchanged, but it came to nothing. Fridtjof Nansen, a great European, organised an exchange of populations under the auspices of the League of Nations, but unfortunately the minorities of Cyprus and Istanbul remained.

The official change in the island's status to that of Crown Colony led to the inevitable protest and appeal for *Enosis* by the Archbishop. Rejection was by now expected, but the object of the memorials and letters was to keep the issue alive, and in this they succeeded.

In 1928, the jubilee commemoration of the British Occupation was boycotted by order of the bishops, the Greek elected members, and the mayors; though Venizelos, pro-British as usual, advised participation. Tension rose in 1930, when the 'National Assembly', consisting of the Greek elected members and other lay and clerical representatives, organised itself for *Enosis* under the leadership of

[1] He was H.C. from 1920 to 1925, and then Governor until 1926.
[2] See Hill, vol. IV, p. 531.

the Archbishop. A resolution was passed, and was signed by a majority of the village notables, though a large minority stood out against ecclesiastical pressure, and some of them were not later renominated. With the passage of the Village Authorities Law in the following year, the minority was protected but, as so often happens, this was only done by restricting the liberty of the majority.

The elections of October 1930 strengthened the Enotists still more. Their guiding light was Nicodemus, Bishop of Citium, who had made no secret of his hope that he would see Kyrou (the Greek Consul) Governor of Cyprus. On 17 October, two days after the departure of the British Mediterranean Fleet from the island, he issued an Enotist manifesto. Apart from the usual points, this contained much abuse of the British régime and the claim that no obedience was due to the laws of a foreign ruler. On the 18th, he resigned from the Legislative Council, and the other Greek elected members followed suit over the next few days. Also on the 18th, a 'Cyprus National Radicalist Union' was founded, with the object of encouraging 'fanatical' Enotism, and the Bishop made a speech at Larnaca which was not extreme enough to warrant prosecution. That could not be said for his speech at Limassol on the 20th, when he incited his audience to disobey the laws.

On the following evening came the riots. Dionysios Kykkotis, chief priest of the Phaneromeni Church in Nicosia, kissed the Greek flag and declared *Enosis*. He then led on the rioters, who smashed the windows of Government House, and then threw in combustible materials so that it burnt to the ground. The police were insufficient in numbers to dominate without firing, and in any case young students were deliberately thrust to the front of the crowd to embarrass them. In the end they fired, and the mob broke up. At Limassol the D.C.'s house was set on fire with petrol, though his wife, his twelve-year-old daughter, and his two servants were known to be inside. They escaped, but their house also was burned down. This rather indicates that the burnings were pre-planned.

Two ships of the Royal Navy now arrived, and troops from Egypt were landed. Storrs decided to deport ten ringleaders of the insurrection: the two bishops, Kykkotis, two elected members of the Council, three leaders of the Radicalist Union, and two Communists. The deportation was effected without warning, as in the case of Makarios III and his three companions in 1956. The Bishop of Citium took it well, fastened episcopal jewels inside his hat, and endeared himself to the officers of H.M.S. *Shropshire* by calling for a stiff whisky and soda. Many, including Storrs, were of opinion that the sudden deportations cracked the insurrection, and they were almost certainly right. Even so, the same measure was not to work in 1956.

Storrs states that of 598 villages in Cyprus 389 took no part in the disturbances, which implies that the others did. In all, six rioters were killed, some thirty wounded, and some 2,000 imprisoned for a time. Thirty-eight policemen were also wounded. In view of the extent of the unrest the casualties were not excessive, and Lloyd George congratulated Storrs on his handling of the situation. The Cypriote Greeks had to pay £66,000 for property destroyed in the towns and in nearly seventy villages.

Of the deportees, Nicodemus Mylonas was to die in Jerusalem in 1937, and Kykkotis in Alexandria in 1942, while Makarios Myriantheus was to return after the war and become Archbishop. Also among the deportees were the brothers Savvas and Socrates Loizides. The former managed to get away from the Bayswater (London) boarding-house where they were all kept for a time, reached Athens, and set up a small office to propagandise for *Enosis*. In 1947, he and his brother were established in Athens as a link between the Greek government and the Cypriote Ethnarchic Council. Savvas established himself as a Member of the Greek Parliament, and was to be very active on the Greek delegation at the United Nations during the Emergency. Socrates, meanwhile, helped Grivas to prepare his campaign.

The Athenian press, true to form, came out with unsubstantiated accounts of torture and bloodshed by the British, accounts which owed more to the influence of Christian hagiographical literature than to any observation of reality. Such fabrications do more damage than their perpetrators realise, for though the Greek is not one to bear malice and will readily greet his enemy within a year or two of slandering him, the latter may be inclined to respond with the cold contempt which inevitably creates more resentment. Venizelos, on the other hand, showed the statesmanship which rarely deserted him. Deep as was his sympathy for the Enotist cause, he condemned the riots as harmful and untimely, and prevented any dangerous demonstrations in Greece. His own plans for *Enosis* included a base in Cyprus for the British, and he saw clearly that the British were in no mood to make any concession that could be interpreted as yielding to pressure.

In London, Zenon Rossides, the representative of the 'National Organisation', had kept up a letter-writing campaign in the *Manchester Guardian* since January 1931, and he was now supported by various persons, including Robert Byron (in the *Week-end Review*), Arnold Toynbee (in the *New Statesman*), and Harold Nicolson (on the B.B.C.).

In Cyprus a number of rather draconic laws made the régime more like that of the Italians in Rhodes. The constitution was withdrawn and the Governor ruled by decree. The flying of the Greek flag without licence was prohibited. This law was not allowed to lapse until the Greek victories in Albania in 1940, and was not repealed until 1946. The police were given the right of search. The use of bells was forbidden, except for regular services, and they were not heard in Nicosia until June 1934.[1] Censorship of the press was introduced and earlier restrictions on publication were strengthened. The Boy Scouts, whose scouting activities were as limited as their political ones were not, were no longer allowed to be under external auspices. Some restrictions were also placed on Enotist propaganda in the schools. In the elementary ones English was made compulsory, and Greek history, Greek national songs, and Greek portraits were all banned, though the curricula continued to be largely as in Greece. Cypriote schoolmasters later protested against these restrictions.

The repressive legislation was continued until 1937, and remained in effect after that. Undoubtedly, it damped down Enotism by denying it expression. In 1934, one Dendias published a book favouring a Commonwealth solution for Cyprus, and the Committee for Cyprus Autonomy was officially in favour of a similar solution. When under pressure most Enotists fall back on independence, but only as a step towards their goal. The accession of George VI brought the usual Enotist telegrams. By this time the Cypriotes had another grievance, which was hard to explain away. Both Iraq and Egypt had been granted bilateral treaties, but not Cyprus.

Throughout the 1930s there was Enotist activity both in Athens and London, but the coming to power of General Metaxas in 1936 led to the curbing of the Greek press. In America a 'Pancypriot Brotherhood' celebrated the fifth anniversary of the 1931 insurrection, and a New York 'Committee for the Self-determination of Cyprus' was to be active during the Second War. A Cypriote petition to Neville Chamberlain in 1938 was given prominence in a German broadcast, but Germany could not properly exploit pan-Hellenism for the same reason that she could not exploit pan-Arabism, namely that Italy's imperial interests would have suffered.

On 28 October 1940, Greece was forced into the war. In all 30,000 Cypriotes were to join the British forces, this time in more varied rôles. Cypriote propagandists were active in London, and among those who favoured the granting of *Enosis* after the war was

---

[1] One is reminded of Turkish restrictions on the use of church-bells (see above, p. 174).

Compton Mackenzie (*Reynolds News,* 12 January 1941). In view of Eden's later inflexibility, it is worth recording that while in Athens in February 1941 he suggested that 'the future of Cyprus would be settled after the war in talks between the two governments'.[1] The anniversary of Italy's attack on Greece provided Churchill with an opportunity to write a typically vague and grandiose message to the Greek Prime Minister in which he referred to a future 'Pan-Hellenic Army of liberation'. Nothing came of the idea, if indeed it *was* an idea and not just a phrase. After the fall of Crete, the Germans could have taken Cyprus too, for it was only defended by a small force, but they drew the wrong conclusion from their parachute drops on Crete, considering rather their heavy losses than the brilliant success of the mission. Cyprus (unlike Crete) provides excellent landing areas for parachutists, as indeed the Turks have since realised. The German threat led to British wives being evacuated from the island, but some forty cabaret-girls, mostly Hungarian, were released from detention to do voluntary and vital war-work in their place.

Towards the end of the war, the Churchill government began to think in terms of a Commonwealth solution for Cyprus. Sir Cosmo Parkinson was sent in August 1944 to sound out Cypriote opinion. The *Locum-tenens* organised the presentation of a Pancyprian Enotist memorial, but Parkinson refused to discuss the matter. Eventually, Lord Winster's constitutional proposals followed. There is no doubt that the natural airfields of the Mesaoria played a large part in British thinking on the Cyprus question. Its value as a *place d'armes* and unsinkable aircraft-carrier goes far to explain why it was not given independence at the same time as India or the Middle Eastern states. For their part, the Enotists saw the growing prosperity and economic reforms as a threat to their cause.

In October 1945, members of the Cyprus Regiment demonstrated in sympathy with the Jews, who were detained in Cyprus camps from the end of the war until 1948 (in order to prevent their illegal entry into Palestine). During the demonstration they killed a Cypriote police-sergeant.

The *Locum-tenens* led an Enotist delegation to London in December 1946, which included Rossides and John Clerides, Mayor of Nicosia, but its hopes were definitely dashed in the following February by Arthur Creech Jones, the Labour Colonial Secretary. The refusal was followed by more demonstrations in Cyprus.

There was considerable bad feeling in Cyprus in 1947, when

---

[1] Stephen G. Xydis, *Cyprus, Conflict and Conciliation, 1954–1958* (Columbus, Ohio: Ohio State Univ. Press, 1967), p. 6.

Italy formally ceded Rhodes and the Dodecanese to Greece. Turkey, which had entered the war on 22 February 1945, and then only because it was the condition of entry into the United Nations Organisation, would have been in no position to oppose the *Enosis* of Cyprus.

The chief success of the Enotists before the Emergency was the organisation of a plebiscite by Makarios II and the Ethnarchic Council. The lists were open from 15–22 January 1950, and of 224,747 Cypriote Greeks eligible to vote, 215,108, or 96 per cent (out of 79 per cent of the adult population), opted for *Enosis*. Civil servants, school-teachers, and government employees did not vote, and the Greeks, on the basis of district returns, claimed that a number of Turks went to make up the large percentage. The British, of course, challenged the methods by which the referendum had been conducted, and especially pointed to undue clerical influence but, having refused to conduct it themselves, their position was not strong.

Though AKEL had become technically Enotist, the party was alienated by the result of the Greek civil war of 1947 to 1949, and even more by Greece's joining NATO in 1951. In Cyprus, the party continued to have considerable influence (as in 1952, when some 100,000 signatures against the British bases were collected) and certainly did not wish to unite with monarchist Greece. As usual, the political differences were reflected culturally. *Haravghi,* for instance, is written in the local demotic dialect, not in the classicising *Katharevoussa* dear to the Enotists.

The persistence of the Enotist spirit over so long a period goes far to demonstrate its ineradicability. That same persistence and rigidity of aim have long been a subject for mirth among pragmatic Britons, but pragmatism is the philosophy of those who still benefit from the idealism, however self-interested, of their forebears; it is not suitable for a people which no longer controls its own affairs. That Enotism is idealistic in essence should by now be clear, whatever the amusing idiosyncrasies and exaggerations of its partisans. But it also contains a base element, which is well exemplified in the passage for which Polycarpos Ioannides was sentenced to eighteen months imprisonment in 1950 : 'Political assassination is not murder ... The only condition of subscription [to this newspaper] is for every reader to bring in the head of a "European".' This spirit was to be very much in evidence during the Emergency, and deserved more punishment than it received.

The Cypriote Turks Under the British

The Greeks have worked hard to convince the world that the Turks of Cyprus have lived in harmony with them for centuries. However, the antagonism evident during the Ottoman period was carried forward into the British, and almost every Enotist memorial led to an expression (less well publicised as a rule) of Turkish opposition. The Turks also opposed any moves towards majority rule. In 1882, when the Legislative Council was set up, they presented a petition pointing out that in Anatolia, which had a large majority of Moslems, the Christians were allowed to have equal numbers and votes on the administrative councils. They naturally wished the same (inequitable) systems to apply to them in Cyprus.

The Cypriote Turks frequently called attention to inflammatory articles in the Greek-Cypriote press, which exulted over every Ottoman defeat. In 1893, they protested at the plan of Sir Charles Dilke and Henry Labouchère to cede Cyprus to Greece for a cash payment. Two years later the Turks had cause to complain of Christian insults on Greek Independence Day, such as the torchlight procession of schoolchildren who paraded through the predominantly Turkish Tahta Kale quarter of Nicosia singing about slaughtering the hated Moslems. The Mufti of Cyprus, Hacı Ali Rifki Efendi, complained of Christian insults to Moslem women and notables, and of Christians using the words 'boom, boom' to imply that the Moslems would be shot. At Tokhni, a mixed village on the Limassol road, there had lately been a disturbance, and even the women were now insulting one another. In Nicosia, Moslem children had reacted when Christian ones threw stones into their school, and Greeks in the market-place were calling Turks 'Dogs and Donkeys'. In a fashion typical of leaders, the Mufti added that he had persuaded many Moslems not to be present at the coming Christian (Enotist) meeting, but probably some would go, and he anticipated a disturbance if the meeting were not forbidden.[1] A report by the British Commissioner B. Travers in the same year speaks of Greeks deliberately provoking the Turks at Vitsadha and Vatili. In 1902, Canon F. D. Newham, Chief Inspector of Schools, recorded that when he asked to hear Greek schoolchildren sing, they usually responded with a war-song, 'Forward, follow the drum that leads us against the Turks'. The same year saw a number of Moslem meetings protesting against Enotism, one of which produced a petition with 600 signatures, and Ahmet Raşid, ex-member of the Council, asked the British not 'to deliver peaceful people into the hands of wild beasts and ruin and destroy

[1] Public Record Office document C.O. 67/91, 3 May 1895.

them'. In common with the vast majority of Moslems, he felt that
if Cyprus were ceded to anyone it should be to its nominal suzerain,
Turkey. In 1903, the Moslem elected members moved an amendment and a resolution in the same sense. There were frequent
complaints of Christian insults and Enotist activity. For instance,
in 1904 the Greek schoolmaster of Kalavassos paraded his pupils
carrying Greek flags and chanting, 'the heads of the Turks must be
cut off and their bodies thrown into filth'. Other insults were
evidently regarded by the Turks as unrepeatable, for they referred
to them as 'indecent words' causing 'precipitancy and boiling
anger'. In 1911, the editor of *Kypriakos Phylax* was fined for a
violently anti-Turkish article. Later in the same year three thousand
Turks passed a resolution of protest against possible *Enosis*. In
1912, the Balkan War and Italian successes against the Turks in
Tripolitania exacerbated ill-feeling in Cyprus. The Greeks of
Limassol insulted local Turks, who retaliated. Police had to fire
on the rioters, and on 27 May troops were called out. By the time
all was calm, five persons had been killed and 134 wounded.
Eighteen persons, mostly Greeks, were sentenced to prison terms
ranging from nine months to fifteen years.

As is commonly the case with non-commercial minorities in
imperial situations, the Cypriote Turks were generally liked by the
British, and examples of friction between them are hard to find,
especially before the First War. In 1882, the Moslems had reason to
protest when the Society for the Propagation of the Gospel tried to
turn the Bedestan into a church. The project was given up. In December 1912, the Moslem elected members prayed that, if the status
of the island were changed, it should be either ceded to Great
Britain or annexed to Egypt. Both the *Kadı* and the Mufti favoured
the annexation of 1914.

Before and during the First War, the Cypriote Turks were essentially on the defensive, complaining of provocations and combating
Enotism. Greco-Turkish antagonisms were above all stimulated by
the Cretan question, which came to a head in the 1890s. Its history
bears resemblances to that of Cyprus in the twentieth century. In
response to Enotist activity, the Turks had begun to persecute the
Orthodox majority in Crete from 1859 onwards. In 1866, the
Christians rebelled under the leadership of Abbot Mareses of
Arkadion. By 1868 the rebellion was under control, though it did
not peter out until the following year. In 1878 and 1889 there
was more unrest, and a new rebellion in 1896 led to the Thirty
Days' War. Despite set-backs in the north, the mainland Greeks
succeeded in invading Crete. Subsequently they withdrew, under
pressure from the protecting powers, but left arms for the Cretans.

Guerrilla warfare was renewed, and the powers prevented the Turks from reinforcing their garrison. On 6 September 1898, the Moslems of Candia rose, killing the British Vice-Consul and some British soldiers, as well as many Greeks. In December, the four protecting powers reacted by making the island 'independent', placing it under a High Commissioner from Greece, Prince George, and setting up a militia to be trained by the Carabinieri. Left with nothing but paper guarantees, a number of local Turks wisely emigrated when the British forces withdrew from Candia. Many others were massacred by the Greeks, but the well-publicised massacres of secessionist Armenians by the Turks, from 1894 onwards, told against them. Those who had been outraged by the atrocities of bashi-bazouks in Bulgaria raised hardly a peep when the same things were done to the Cretan Turks.

In 1905, Venizelos took to the hills with his Enotist following, and in the following year Prince George resigned as High Commissioner, to be replaced by Alexander Zaimes. Zaimes took the Italian-trained militia under his control, and in October 1908, after the powers had withdrawn all their troops, Cretan *Enosis* was proclaimed.

Meanwhile, intelligent Turks had realised that a purely defensive policy must result in the breakdown of their empire and the humiliation of their people. The first newspaper setting forth the views of these Young Turks had been started in London in 1868 by the Committee for Union and Progress. In 1894, the Committee moved to Paris. Its propaganda made many converts among Ottoman officials, and above all among the army officers, of whom Mustafa Kemal was one. In 1908, the Young Turks seized power in Istanbul, and in 1909 deposed the Sultan, Abdül Hamit II. Among other things, they demanded repudiation of Cretan *Enosis* by Greece. But it was too late. In the ensuing chaos, Venizelos became Prime Minister of Greece (a portent for the Cypriote Archbishop Makarios III), and Greece, Bulgaria, Serbia, and Montenegro united against Turkey. At the Treaty of London in May 1913, which ended the first Balkan War, the Turks had formally to cede Crete and other European territory to Greece.

As in the case of Cyprus, the Turks make the doubtful claim that they were once a majority in Crete. Incontrovertible is the fact that of 88,000 Cretan Turks in 1895 hardly any now remain. Massacre and, still more, social pressure have done their work. A further similarity to Cyprus is that in Crete the Turks were strongest (proportionally) in the towns, while the Greeks dominated much of the countryside. The mountain ranges of both islands provide excellent cover for guerrillas.

The Cypriote Turks lived through a period of great apprehension in 1915, when Cyprus was offered to Greece, but in 1917, when they were given the choice of becoming British subjects or leaving the island, only one-eighth of their number left. Others went later, but many returned after 1923. In March 1964, Archbishop Makarios was to claim that in the 1930s Turks went to Anatolia from Galatia (in the Carpass) but afterwards returned. The Turkish claim that there are 300,000 persons of Cyprus origin now in Turkey would seem to be considerably exaggerated, especially since the Turkish proportion of the Cyprus population does not seem to have dropped more than seven per cent during the British period. In 1881, the number of Moslems was 46,389 (as opposed to 136,629 Greek Orthodox, and 3,066 others), that is to say, 24.9 per cent.[1] At the census of 1911 there were 56,428 Moslems,[2] 214,480 Greek Orthodox, and 3,016 others,[3] so that the Moslem percentage of the population was 20.1, as opposed to a Greek-Orthodox percentage of 78.8. At the 1951 census there were 81,000 Moslems (17.9 per cent), 362,000 Greek Orthodox (80.2 per cent), and 8,500 others (1.9 per cent). In 1960, the percentage of Turks was 18.1 per cent, of Greeks 78.3 per cent.

During the First World War the Allies heavily emphasised the principle of self-determination, their object being to weaken the Central Powers by disrupting the Austrian and Ottoman empires. The French and British empires then expanded, and the principle of self-determination was not, of course, applied where Turks, Arabs, Hungarians, or Germans were concerned. The Treaty of Sèvres, signed on 10 August 1920, was a Versailles Treaty for the East. It gave the Greeks a free hand in the Smyrna region, which they had occupied with Allied approval. It is true that the Turks had forced some Greeks and Armenians out of the area since 1914, but they had been a majority in the area for a long time, and were now subjected to humiliation, maltreatment, and murder on a very large scale. The atrocities were perpetrated with the blessing of Papa Chrysostomos of Smyrna. In November 1920, Venizelos was voted out of office, and King Constantine returned from exile to put into practice his plan for the re-establishment of the Byzantine empire. This was the *Megalo Idea*, or Big Idea, arising out of the creation of 'Greater Ionia'. The victorious Greek advance was held up in late 1920 by the Allied Supreme Council, for the territorial

[1] Makarios claims that many of the Greeks, a large proportion of whom were country dwellers, were left out of the census. Some may have been omitted, but the number is unlikely to have been large.

[2] According to Dudley Buxton, this figure included 1,036 Arabs.

[3] These included 1,073 Maronites, 588 Armenians, 397 British residents plus 144 in the garrison, and 193 Jews.

17—C

interests of the French and Italians conflicted with those of the
Greeks. Then, in the spring of 1921, the Greeks launched their
great offensive.

But the Turks reacted as one people. Under the leadership of
Mustafa Kemal (later to take the name of Atatürk, Father of the
Turks) they had begun to reorganise their political life. They now
regrouped their forces in central Anatolia and struck back at the
Greeks. Their men fought with desperate courage and their women
carried heavy shells and supplies for extraordinary distances over
the most difficult terrain. The Greeks also fought well, and the
turning-point came in August 1921 with the Battle of Sakarya. It
lasted twenty-one days, and was said by Atatürk, perhaps with
justice, to be the longest battle in history. The Greeks, falling back
on Afyon and Eskişehir, continued to fight, but eventually their
retreat became a rout, and the collapse of discipline had terrible
consequences. Seeing the mutilated bodies of their people in the
villages along the way, the Turks responded in kind. On 10 September 1922, they entered *Gâvur* Izmir (Infidel Smyrna) and the
war was brought to an end. At the Treaty of Lausanne in July
1923, which abrogated the Treaty of Sèvres, the Turks also made
concessions. They accepted without reserve the British annexation
of Cyprus, and agreed that western Thrace, with its Turkish
majority, should be retained by Greece for strategic reasons.[1]
Inevitably, when the Turks revived their claim to Cyprus they
argued that strategic considerations had overridden demographic
ones in the case of western Thrace.

The exchange of populations eased the ethnic problems of Greece
and Turkey, so that on 10 June 1930 Venizelos and Atatürk were
able to sign a Convention. It settled, among other things, the value
of property left behind by the refugees. As a conciliatory gesture
Atatürk transformed St Sophia from a mosque into a museum.

The phoenix-like resurgence of the Turks in Anatolia had its
effects in Cyprus also. As early as 1919, Dr Esat, Dr Behiç, and
Hasan Karabardak invented the rumour of a Greek attack in
Easter week so as to inspire the Cypriote Turks to rise,[2] and
planned to release the Turkish prisoners-of-war in Famagusta.
Intelligence of this reached Stevenson, who promptly interned
them. Yet in the same year, out of twenty-six officers and 763
N.C.O.s and men in the Cyprus police force, 420 were Turks.

The excuse of Ottoman sovereignty had now gone, but the

---

[1] The Turks claim that they constituted 67 per cent of the population in
western Thrace (124,000 persons), whereas the Greeks were only 17 per
cent.
[2] The arrangement of 'provocations' is a speciality of Middle Eastern
politicians.

British still had the interests of the Turkish minority as a reason and excuse for not granting too much autonomy. A parallel is to be found in Palestine, where they also deferred self-government in order to protect the interests of a minority,[1] though after the First War that minority constituted only 8 per cent and even that was largely foreign-born. In Cyprus, the *Enosis* memorial of December 1925 prompted protests not only from the Turks but also from the Armenians, the Latins, and the Maronites. It was not only the Turks who helped to frustrate the majority, and Greek animus was not only directed against them.

Kemalism grew slowly in the relatively conservative Moslem community of Cyprus, and the flutes and drums of the whirling Mevlevi Dervishes were occasionally heard after Atatürk suppressed the monastic orders in 1925. Even opposition to the Greeks was still expressed in mainly religious terms. The Archbishop was absent with a diplomatic cold from Storrs's swearing-in by the Chief Justice in 1926, the reason being that the traditional precedence of the Mufti was maintained. Kemalism was fostered above all by the Turkish Consul Asaf Bey, who was recalled after Storrs had protested about his activities to the British government. Asaf Bey followed the Atatürk line of cooperation with the Greeks where Turkish interests were not involved. He procured the election of a Turkish member, who in April 1931 voted with the Greeks against an import duty, so that it had to be imposed by Order in Council. Other Turks, such as the popular Munir Bey, C.B.E., managed to reconcile their Kemalist tendencies with friendship for the British, just as Atatürk himself did.

Kemalism was emancipatory in many respects, but not in all. History in Turkish schools tended to become the story of the 'Turks' from the Sumerians onwards, all awkward questions being glossed over.[2] Thus the glories of Gallipoli are known to every Turk, but most have never heard of Allenby's victories in Palestine and Syria.[3] In 1930, a British assistant master at the Turkish lycée in Nicosia was stoned by his pupils, and the Turks objected strongly to Palmer's impartial restrictions on the teaching of Turkish as well as Greek history.

[1] Cf. Robert Stephens, *Cyprus, a Place of Arms* (London: Pall Mall, 1966), p. 110.
[2] The Sumerians were counted as Turks because they spoke an agglutinative language, and the Scots and the Irish were accounted superior to the English on the simple and sufficient ground that the Galatians were also Celts and occupied a part of what is now Turkey (*ergo* they were Turks). Still, even odder theories are entertained by other ethnic groups.
[3] It must be admitted that for the uninstructed in Britain 'Lawrence of Arabia' stills looms larger than Allenby.

The late 1930s brought an example of Turkish irredentism which may be set against the Greek example of Crete. Despite her declaration at the Treaty of Lausanne that she had no territorial claims, Turkey took advantage of France's need for allies to put pressure on her over the Sanjak of Alexandretta, known in Turkish as Hatay. As in the case of Crete, the take-over was piecemeal.

Statistics vary, but the Turks certainly constituted the largest ethnic group in the Sanjak (over 40 per cent). However, the rest, mainly Arabs and Armenians, formed an overall majority. France had invaded Cilicia at the end of the war, and vacated it in 1921, all except the Sanjak in question. Turkey now claimed it, and in 1937, despite Syrian protests, it became autonomous under League of Nations auspices. The League commissioners who were sent to supervise elections produced registers showing the local Turks to be in an overall minority, whereat the latter demonstrated, and Turkey ostentatiously moved troops up to her frontier (a gambit which was to be successful *vis-à-vis* Cyprus in 1967). In July 1938, Turkish troops were allowed in to police the area jointly with the French. Non-Turkish minorities now began trekking out of it, and the Turks were soon an overall majority. At the elections in August 1939 they won twenty-two out of forty seats in the local assembly, and on 29 June 1939 proclaimed union (i.e. what the Greeks call *Enosis*) with Turkey. In this way, Aleppo, the second city of Syria, was cut off from its natural outlet. The main reason why Atatürk wanted the Hatay was that southern Turkey is as poor in natural harbours as Cyprus, and Alexandretta has a fine one.

During the Second World War the Cypriote Turks formed a National Party and showed some signs of favouring Germany, since they feared that a British victory would lead to *Enosis,* while the Germans would have considered their own and Italian interests, and would have wished to placate Turkey.

The religious separation of Greeks and Turks in Cyprus was not the work of the British. As we have seen, it has its roots deep in history. In essence, it expresses the need felt by ethnic groups to differentiate themselves culturally. In 1914, a government report makes reference to separate schools, 'all religious difficulties being thereby eliminated'. It has been said that the British deliberately fostered the Turkish language, but the fact that most Cypriote Turks knew Greek should not necessarily be regarded as significant. One thinks of many educated Dutchmen and Portuguese, all of whom understand German and Spanish respectively, but who pretend not to. The debates of the Cyprus Legislative Council were trilingual from the beginning.

By the time of the Emergency the close proximity of Greeks and

Turks over nearly four centuries had produced friendships which were outweighed by animosities, animosities for which one might coin the term 'postjudices', since they were based upon close observation and not ignorant preconceptions. Of course, there was 'integration' of a kind. Unified municipalities had been in existence since 1882, though the Turks frequently complained of unfairness in the allocation of funds. Some coffee-shops were shared, though in general the poorer Turks went to the ones in their own quarters. Trades unions were in common until 1943, and even after that most Turkish workers belonged to Greek ones and participated in their athletic events. Regular soccer matches took place between Greek and Turkish teams, though integrated teams at adult level were very rare. Until 1960, the Teachers' Training College, the Scout Movement, cinemas, and many cooperative societies were in common. However, there were few mixed marriages and no mixed social institutes.

Among the merchant and professional classes there was naturally more mixing. Better-off Turks lived in Greek areas, Chamber of Commerce membership was in common, the Rotary Club of Nicosia had Turkish presidents, and a few enterprises had promoters from both communities. Rauf Denktaş and the Turkish Chief Justice Zekya belonged to the local Masonic lodge, and the Marine Club at Kyrenia included among its members Mr Örek, Dr Manyera, and Mr Ali Dana. What is significant is not that present Turkish separatist leaders were once members of integrated organisations, but rather that they were once members of integrated organisations and later became separatist leaders. When communities so different are left to work out their destinies, former political, social, and commercial links count for little where the communities as wholes are concerned.

The State of British Morale

The Parkinsonian law that 'success leads to expansion, and expansion leads to decay' holds true for all empires, but Great Britain's rule in Cyprus lasted no longer than that of Venice, and the Venetian empire was of much longer duration. The Ottoman empire also flourished much longer than the British, and retreated over a period of two centuries, not over a matter of twenty years. However, this is not the place to give reasons for the rapid dissolution of the British empire or to discuss the extent to which that dissolution was voluntary or otherwise. It will be sufficient to emphasise those two concomitants to Great Britain's withdrawal from power which are relevant in the case of Cyprus: loss of faith in the imperial system and weakness resulting from participation in the Second World War.

During the 1930s, Great Britain lost the loyalty of a substantial part of the bourgeois intelligentsia, who sought emotionalist solutions rather than those of the intellect. Those in question advocated socialism, but showed few signs of willingness to forego their social and economic advantages. They found natural allies among those representing the forces of inertia, whose philosophy is so beautifully expressed in Lord Halifax's oft-quoted dictum: 'I distrust anyone who foresees consequences and advocates remedies to avert them'. The Janus of internationalism spoke with one face of freedom to invest, and with the other exhorted the world's intellectuals to unite in the name of the world's workers. Thus the greed of speculators and the treachery of the clerks, sometimes combined in the same persons, made for a creeping paralysis of the will.

The withdrawal from India in 1947 made the intermediate colonies on the Suez route redundant, but British policies were now mostly responses to events, and the government made no move to liquidate hopeless assets in agreed stages while a peaceful atmosphere still prevailed. Cypriotes who saw how Great Britain was forced out of Palestine, and then witnessed the transfer of the R.A.F. Middle East Command H.Q. to Cyprus in October 1948, may be pardoned for supposing that she was in retreat. The withdrawal from Libya in 1951 strengthened that supposition (besides causing resentment among the Cypriotes who were more advanced, because they had not been accorded independence first), and the announcement of withdrawal from Suez in July 1954 made the supposition a certainty. Great Britain's expressed reasons for remaining in Cyprus : to support the Baghdad Pact (later CENTO), the Anglo-Jordanian Treaty, and the Tripartite Agreement over Israel, had nothing to do with her main interest in the Middle East, which was to keep the oil flowing. Other European nations, with no bases there, paid no more for their oil than she did.

In Cyprus, the British government, a Conservative one this time, achieved the remarkable feat of alienating the parties to the dispute while putting the interests of its own people last. The main complicating factor during the Emergency was the primarily ethnic character of the struggle for *Enosis*. It naturally reminded British politicians of the struggle of many Austrians (including Adolf Hitler) for *Anschluss* with Germany, and there was therefore a feeling that there could be no compromise. In the press all the usual methods were employed against EOKA : the lurid, carefully selected details, the wildly exaggerated adjectives, the propaganda statements in the form of questions, the sentimental human-interest items, the moral disquisitions, the catchy remarks allegedly made by (unidentified) local persons. Certainly, EOKA was responsible for many crimes, some of them despicable, but to treat these as though they equalled the unprintable atrocities of the Mau Mau showed an unbalanced judgement or a deliberate desire to distort the truth. Yet the newspapers which inveighed most shrilly against EOKA had few practical suggestions for dealing with the problem.

On the Left, the main concern was to decolonise quickly, regardless of British interests in the colony concerned. To begin with, there was the Labour M.P. who declared, for the benefit of the Cypriotes, that 'Britain never gave Freedom to its colonial people until blood was shed'. This attitude was faithfully reflected in the left-wing press. For instance, on 8 March 1957, at the height of the Emergency, a poem in praise of an EOKA-member killed in a clash with security forces was printed in *Tribune*.[1] The man in question, Afxentiou, died well, and in former days it was the custom for Englishmen (e.g. Kipling) to write poems in praise of dead enemies. The difference in this case was one of attitude. The British Left actively desired the defeat of the British security forces.

In Cyprus itself, the anti-government activities of Percy Arnold, as editor of the *Cyprus Post* between 1943 and 1945,[2] were carried on during the Emergency by Charles Foley, as editor of the *Times of Cyprus* and a Greek fortnightly. Foley propagandised against the authorities and expressed selective indignation over British army reactions against the Greeks. Nicos Georghiades, alias Sampson, worked as a correspondent for the *Times of Cyprus*, which gives a good idea of its political bent. He was sentenced to death for murdering 'a single British policeman',[3] and when this sentence was quashed on the grounds of ill-treatment having been used to extort his confession, he was again sentenced to death, for carrying a firearm.[4] Foley agitated in his favour, and persuaded the 'Cyprus Conciliation Committee' in the Houses of Parliament to exert political pressure on his behalf. The Committee numbered among

---

[1] The editor, Michael Foot, was a brother of Sir Hugh's. Pallekarides also had poems written about him in the British press (Xydis, op. cit., p. 394).

[2] Originally founded as *Embros* after the Great War, this newspaper was bought by the British Council, which renamed it and appointed Arnold editor.

[3] Charles Foley, *Legacy of Strife: Cyprus from rebellion to civil war* (Penguin, 1964 edition), p. 95.

[4] Grivas, who is in a position to know, records that Sampson and his 'execution group' were 'responsible for more than twenty killings in their area between the months of August 1956 and January 1957' (*The Memoirs of General Grivas*, ed. Charles Foley, London: Longmans, 1964, pp. 102–3). So Sampson's murders were perpetrated before he was captured and sentenced.

its members Lord Attlee, Mrs Lena Jeger, Sir Robert (later Lord) Boothby, and Francis Noel-Baker (with his large interests in Greece); and its influence, coupled with the approach of a United Nations debate, secured Sampson's reprieve. The author is not aware of any attempt by these influential persons to secure adequate compensation for the families of murdered policemen and civilians.

By the 1950s, the British people had been half-convinced that their living-standards could be maintained indefinitely without any control over the raw materials which they processed; but there was already a deep spiritual malaise, to which inefficiency was the psychological response. Grivas writes of British soldiers (many of them National Service men) making searches perfunctorily and lazily, of how they skipped attics and the dark parts of forests, and of their bad discipline in leaving food and empty cigarette packets about. On more than one occasion too many pulls at a 'fag' or a prolonged gossip enabled EOKA-men to escape. Grivas records one case in which three British deserters actually bartered their stens with EOKA in return for a motor-boat. Brought up on countless films in which Resistance heroes knifed sentries in the back or derailed troop-trains, the average British soldier was not mentally prepared to maintain order when similar tactics were used against himself. Above all, he was the guileless dupe of the smile and the proferred drink, as exemplified by an occasion at Spilia where a girl used those weapons with effect against troops who were supposed to be searching a house in which Grivas was then hiding. Similarly, schoolboys during demonstrations would push girls to the front, knowing that this would embarrass the troops and that any roughness in removing them would be well publicised. Again, women assaulting British troops would often compel the release of prisoners. One has only to imagine the same tactics being used in East Germany in 1953 or in Hungary in 1956 to realise how handicapped the British were in Cyprus. At no stage did the authorities really crack down, and their half-measures merely helped to polarise the population against them.

With the passage of time, the morale of the troops worsened, owing to conditions in the disgracefully inadequate camps outside the towns to which they were so often confined, and even more owing to the number of EOKA killings. As Grivas says, they offered mass targets to gunmen, who might spring up from anywhere. But there was another element in the British soldier's resentment, to which attention has not been drawn, and which was very evident by the time the author visited Cyprus at the beginning of 1959. It seemed to him unfair that an EOKA supporter should be allowed to enter England with full privileges and perhaps become better-off than many of the natives. Besides, he had good reason to believe that few of the EOKA terrorists would be condignly punished even if caught. The secret 'Cromwell' society which emerged among British troops in the summer of 1958 was a token of the resentment which might have spread to England if the Cyprus Emergency had lasted longer. 'Cromwell' put out leaflets threatening indiscriminate reprisals against the Greek population, but the organisation did not get as far as actually killing anyone.[1]

The inefficiency and resentment to be found among British troops in Cyprus reflected the failure of their political and military leaders. In some cases this was a failure to grasp the nature of what they were up against, in others a failure to confront it. On the administrative side the deficiencies were particularly glaring, as though the colonial authorities could not be brought to realise that Enotist words were being translated into action, and that the nationalism of Europe had moved into a wider world. Dudley Barker tells us that the authorities were aware in 1955 that arms were being smuggled through the mails; yet smuggling was going strong in January 1956, when a message was intercepted from an arms factory in Brescia, thanking its business friends in Cyprus for their support over the previous year. There was no adequate organisation for examining parcels until the last part of the Emergency, by which time the civil service was so thoroughly infiltrated by EOKA that rubber stamps, whether forged or not, could be used to continue the smuggling. Athens Radio was allowed to disseminate the most virulent propaganda over its 'Voice of the Fatherland' programme until March 1956, when it was belatedly jammed.[2] A hundred schoolmasters from Greece were only retired half way through the Emergency, though all were propagandists for *Enosis*, many helped to organise demonstrations, one had mined a bridge in company with his pupils, and another had been caught instructing his pupils in the use of arms. The army made frequent and quite unavailing complaints to the civil authorities about the free sale of chemicals which they knew, from captured mines and bombs, to be used by EOKA for manufacturing explosives; but, as Grivas says, 'for some curious reason no attempt was made to prohibit their sale until the struggle was virtually over, by which time we had sufficient reserve to sabotage for over two years'.[3]

[1] Other similar abortive organisations were the 'British Resistance Party' and 'Akoe' (EOKA spelt backwards).

[2] Athens Radio deprecated the first EOKA bomb-attacks, but it soon changed its tone and began yelling for blood.

[3] Grivas, *Memoirs*, p. 166.

An added danger to British morale in Cyprus was a split, mainly along class lines, in attitudes towards Greeks and Turks. The average British soldier liked the reticent Turk, with whom he had a great deal psychologically in common. Greeks have pointed to the number of Britons killed by the Turks at Gallipoli, far surpassing the number of Britons killed by the Greeks, but that is to miss the point. In any case, guerrilla warfare generates more abiding dislike than the open variety.

On the other hand, a number of officers and officials preferred the Greeks, partly owing to a confusion in their minds of the Byzantine tradition with the Hellas about which they had learned at school, partly because they enjoyed the Greeks' vivacity and conversational ability. That is not to say, by any means, that among such people the liberal Philhellenes outnumbered the conservative element, whose respect for the Turks was rooted almost as deeply in the nineteenth century as their own real, if ironical, passion for the Greeks.[1] But the Philhellenes were more articulate and influential.

Among the officials in Cyprus were a number of able professional men, who naturally felt out of place in post-war Britain, but who were nevertheless affected by the slow crumbling of British morale. Most did their duty, whatever their preferences, but they can hardly be blamed for not showing the same kind of spirit as their EOKA adversaries when they knew that their political masters would not back them if they did.

Archbishop Makarios III

The Greek protagonists of the Cyprus struggle were Archbishop Makarios III and Colonel George Grivas, and it is fitting that a few words should be said about their background and previous experience.

Makarios has been described as like Rasputin[2] and also as a 'bloody-hearted hairy monk'.[3] Other critics have berated him for conduct unbefitting a clergyman, though he has plenty of precedents in church history. But the truth about him is much less sinister, if no less interesting, than the legend.

Makarios was born Michael Christodoulos Mouskos in the village of Pano Panayia, in the Paphos district, near the monastery of

---

[1] An extreme example of the philo-Turk was, curiously enough, a Frenchman, Pierre Loti. When the Turks killed some secessionist Armenians, he described their reaction as 'un peu vif'.

[2] See W. Byford-Jones, *Grivas and the Story of EOKA* (London: Robert Hale, 1959), p. 145.

[3] *Daily Sketch*, 10 August 1964.

Chrysorroyiatissa. The date of his birth was 13 August 1913 and, while disclaiming any tendency towards superstition, he has always regarded thirteen as his lucky number.[1] His father was a shepherd, and he spent much of his time as a boy living in a small hut beside a sheepfold among the trees. However, it was a homogeneous society he grew up in, not a fragmented cosmopolis. So, although his family was poor, he had many friends and could enjoy the village weddings and feasts with the other children. His attention was drawn to religion by a remarkable sermon he heard, in which the preacher impressed him deeply with the clarity and directness of his diction. On finishing elementary school in 1926, he entered Kykko Monastery as a novice. He was then thirteen, and Kykko was the largest and most famous monastery in the island. As an ordinand he took the name Kykkotis, thus recalling Dionysios Kykkotis, who led the Nicosia riot in 1931. Another person he admired was Nicodemus Mylonas, Bishop of Citium, and he was in time to become a successor to Mylonas. He stayed at Kykko for twelve years, and meanwhile also attended the three top classes of the Pancyprian Gymnasium, so that he had reason to be grateful to the Church for the best education Cyprus could afford. It is indicative of his poverty that he was almost eighteen before he saw the sea for the first time, and not until his enforced visit to the Seychelles (on 13 January 1957) did he have the opportunity to venture into it.

In view of the attention which has been drawn to Makarios's beard, it is of interest that he refused to grow one for some time, and was almost expelled on that account by his Abbot. In 1938, he was ordained deacon and sent to the University of Athens on a scholarship. There he was cut off by the German occupation. In 1942, he graduated from the Faculty of Theology, thus following in the footsteps of Sophronios II. He had also studied some law and came to know Athens very well. His next task was to serve at the Church of St Irene in the same city, and he was still there at the time of his ordination as priest, on 13 January 1946. Some months later, he obtained one of ten scholarships offered by the World Council of Churches, and in September departed in discomfort on a cargo-boat for the Methodist Theological College at the University of Boston. A rich American Greek was among those with whom he became acquainted on board, and had him transferred from his bed near the constant noise and overpowering fumes of the engine-room to a passenger's cabin.

Makarios was out of Cyprus for most of the time between the

[1] E.g. he suggested thirteen emendations to the 1960 constitution and the same thirteen points reappeared in 1963 (see below, p. 320).

ages of twenty-five and thirty-five, and his stay in America was the turning-point in his long period of withdrawal. America bewildered him at first, but he learnt a lot there about modern life, and this stood him in good stead when he had to deal with sophisticated persons later on. His theological studies over many years seem to have been thorough, and he even came to hold one view which in past ages would have been regarded as heretical, namely the opinion of Origen that the damned would not burn eternally. Over the years he also studied oratory and developed the precious ability to say exactly what he intended to say, no more, no less.

Makarios has told the author that while still a student of the Boston college he spent a month in Cyprus, made a number of speeches and sermons, and came in contact with some persons who had influence in the Church. Evidently he impressed them, because a few months before his final examinations he was elected Bishop of Citium. The people of his district had voted for him, partly because local loyalties are strong in the island, partly because they held him in high esteem. At first he refused the bishopric, for he had set his heart on becoming a professor at the University of Athens, but he was told that it was his duty to accept. As a student abroad he had been beardless, and he now had to grow an apology for a beard as soon as possible. Later, his beard and priestly hat were to become as much a gift to the caricaturist as the height, nose, and gestures of General de Gaulle, and as much a symbol for his own people. On 13 June 1948, he was consecrated Bishop, though he had never visited his diocese.

Makarios's qualities of leadership and his zeal for *Enosis* soon became even more widely recognised, so that on 18 October 1950 he was elected Archbishop by the representatives of 97 per cent of the Cypriote Greeks. The method of election, through intermediaries, casts doubt on the size of the percentage in his favour, but after all a similar system is in use for the election of Presidential candidates in the United States, and there can be no doubt that a large majority supported him. At the age of thirty-seven he was now the spiritual and ethnic leader of his people. The son of a shepherd was now Archbishop Makarios III, heir to the privileges granted by the Emperor Zeno.

Makarios was active from the beginning in promoting the Enotist cause. Unlike some of his forerunners, he did not neglect to engage the sympathies of the Left, and he saw that anti-colonial feeling among the newly-independent states could be turned to advantage. An unofficial Greek-Cypriote delegation had already gone to the United Nations in order to publicise the result of the January *Enosis* plebiscite, and Makarios made his first appeal to that organisation early in 1951. In July of that year he met Grivas in Cyprus and discussed with him how best to promote the cause. In November came a fateful meeting between Evangelos Averoff-Tossizza, Foreign Minister of Greece, and Anthony Eden, Foreign Secretary in the recently elected Churchill government. In return for *Enosis,* Averoff offered the British not only what bases they needed in Cyprus, but also four more bases in Greece itself, including Cephallonia (in the Ionian islands) and Suda Bay (in Crete). Eden, a sick man with a bad temper, replied that the British empire was not for sale and that the Cyprus question did not exist. He could not see that the Second War, together with the withdrawal from India and Palestine, had greatly diminished the importance of Cyprus as an imperial link. If bases were needed for cooperation in American 'policing' activities, or for defence of the Middle East against the Soviet Union, Averoff's offer would have more than filled the bill.

In 1952, Makarios became chairman of the revolutionary committee set up by Grivas and his associates in Athens, and visited Egypt, Syria, and the Lebanon. Having been unsuccessful in the previous year when he asked Greece to sponsor the Cyprus cause at the United Nations, Makarios now threatened that he would ask Syria to do so. That would have been a mistake, for during the debates on the Cyprus issue at the U.N. the Syrian representative was to state that 'Cyprus had always been a part of Syria'.[1] From October 1952 to March 1953 Makarios visited the United States, France, and Germany, and continued to promote the Enotist cause.

As head of the Panhellenic Committee for the Cyprus Struggle, Archbishop Spyridon of Athens ably seconded the efforts of Makarios, to the point of embarrassing Field-Marshal Papagos (Prime Minister of Greece since November 1952). However, Eden continued obdurate on the subject of Cyprus, and in February 1954, when Makarios visited Athens, Papagos was willing to meet him. From that time forward Greek politics were dominated by the Cyprus question. Papagos's final decision to put it before the United Nations was taken in April. On 3 May, Papagos publicly declared his intention to do so, unless the British were prepared for bilateral negotiations. On the 14th, the British government restated its previous views, and on 28 July came a turning-point, when H. L. d'A. Hopkinson, Minister of State for the Colonies, stated in the House of Commons, with reference to Cyprus : 'There

---

[1] Xydis, op. cit., p. 420. The Syrian National Party, founded in 1932 by Antūn Sa'ādih, seems to have been the first to put forward this claim to Cyprus.

are certain territories in the Commonwealth which, owing to their particular circumstances, can never expect to be fully independent'. This was an unprepared remark in answer to an Opposition questioner, and Hopkinson added that he was not going as far as that with regard to Cyprus, but the damage had been done.[1] On 29 August, Greece appealed to the U.N. A postage-stamp was produced in Athens showing a large ink-blot on the page from Hansard containing Hopkinson's statement.

In Cyprus on 2 August the Attorney-General warned of penalties of up to five years' imprisonment for advocacy of *Enosis,* and several newspapers ceased publication in protest, but on the 15th, when Makarios defied the law at Trooditissa Monastery, it was left in abeyance.

It was on 19 October 1954 that Great Britain signed an agreement with Egypt for the complete withdrawal of British troops within twenty months. In fact, the decision to transfer the main Middle Eastern garrison to Cyprus had been made in principle as early as 1952. It was now implemented, so that Cyprus became more vital as a base for support of stated British policies than it had been before.

The first Greek U.N. appeal on the subject of Cyprus was frustrated through the adroit diplomacy of Sir Leslie Munro, the New Zealand representative, and on 15 December 1954 the General Assembly decided not to consider the Cyprus question further for the time being. At once, there was a general strike in Cyprus, and demonstrations by schoolchildren leading to the worst riots since 1931. Fortunately, casualties were few. A couple of students were injured in a demonstration on the 18th at Limassol, of whom one was treated in Great Britain. Makarios was not in Cyprus at the time. He returned from the United Nations on 10 January 1955. But we may be sure he was not unaware of the preparations for the riots.

During the Emergency it became an article of faith among British liberals that Makarios's organisation of EOKA was a lie concocted by conservatives. This view persisted even after the authorities published incontestable proof in 1956 that Makarios was in fact the chief organising hand behind EOKA. Not that he arranged its actual structure or directed it in action. He did not himself plan the killings, and he was absent during the worst of the Emergency, but he was fully privy to the initial campaign of sabotage, the idea being that thereafter the organisation should 'respond to events'. Makarios is being over-modest when he says he has no knowledge of military matters, though he certainly

[1] See Xydis, op. cit., p. 10.

cannot compete with Grivas on that score. Nevertheless, he was responsible for the financial and political preparations for the campaign, and has indeed chided Grivas for taking all the credit. When in Nicosia on 1 April 1967, the author saw posters saying: 'ΖΗΤΟ Ο ΜΑΚΑΡΙΟΣ Ο ΕΜΠΝΕΥΣΤΗΣ ΤΗΣ 1ΗΣ ΑΠΡΙΛΙΟΥ', 'Long live Makarios, the inspirer of the first of April' (the date on which the Emergency began).

In 1952, Makarios had founded PEON (the Pancyprian Youth Organisation) which, with its special initiation ceremonies, became a recruiting centre for EOKA. Stavros Poskottis was appointed to head the organisation, and the stout and jolly Papastavros Agathangelou, Chief Priest of the Phaneromeni Church (like Kykkotis in 1931), was appointed leader of a similar body called OHEN (Organisation of Orthodox Christian Youth). Both were concerned with storing smuggled arms as well as finding suitable young men for Grivas. Owing to its part in the 1952 riots in Paphos on the occasion of Queen Elizabeth's coronation, PEON was made illegal; but OHEN continued to function. Having seen to this, Makarios, in the autumn of 1954, set about organising the P.E.K., or Farmers' Union, the Secretary of which was the same Socrates Loizides who had been deported in 1931. The P.E.K. was particularly active in procuring arms and explosives in preparation for the struggle, so that Makarios was well aware of the arrangements for killing even if there is no evidence to connect him directly with any specific case of killing. He also paid attention to the S.E.K. (or Free Trades Union body), thus covering the towns as well. Another useful organisation was EMAK (the National Front for the Liberation of Cyprus).

Makarios made his preparations under a code name. He was the chief political organiser in Cyprus, while Grivas attended to the military side and the Greek government carried on its campaign at the United Nations. The Greek Foreign Minister, Stephanopoulos, has also been accused of complicity in the financing of EOKA.

In time, all was ready, but the Archbishop passed some worrying moments before the outbreak of hostilities. On the night of 31 March to 1 April 1955, '... the Ethnarch, from a balcony of the Archiepiscopal Palace, was anxiously watching to see the spurts of flame from the first explosions in Nicosia and to hear their dull boom'.[1]

The Church was not only active in preparing for the campaign. Those joining EOKA had the binding oath administered to them by priests, and it was taken in the name of the Holy Trinity.

[1] Xydis, op. cit., p. 71.

Monasteries and churches were used as supply-centres for EOKA throughout the Emergency. At Kykko, for instance, fifty-three sticks of dynamite were found by security forces. In view of the number of theological students and priests who were active in EOKA, it is extraordinary that Grivas and others should complain of occasional disrespect shown by British soldiers towards the priestly garb. Not only did the troops know of the clergy's EOKA activities, but during demonstrations and riots they saw priests urging on schoolchildren from the pavement. The latter, of course, were delighted to miss lessons, to throw stones, and to make use of catapults. Before the Emergency began they were already using blue paint for bloodthirsty slogans on the walls.

Grivas

George Grivas has been described as a 'fanged dynamo' (Byford-Jones) and as 'the little man who looks like a cross between Groucho Marx and Adolf Hitler' (Lord Caradon). As in the case of Makarios, such descriptions hide the reality. They hardly fit the man who continued to collect postage-stamps while directing the activities of EOKA. Ruthless he certainly is, though he does not order killing without an end in view; but he is not a comedian, nor, curiously enough, is he gifted with outstanding political acumen.

He was born on 23 May 1898 in the village of Trikomo, set in good farmland north of Cyprian Salamis. His father was a prosperous grain-merchant, and had the finest house in the village. He was pro-British, like George himself for most of his life. At that time it was possible to combine such an attitude with Enotism because Great Britain might always hand over the island to Greece. George was one of six children, and his only brother, Michael, became a doctor.

Grivas went to the Pancyprian Gymnasium (subsidised by the British), just as Makarios was to do. He seems to have been a bright pupil, and in his final year won the 100, 200, and 400 metre races, as well as the high jump. At home and at school he heard the glorious commonplaces about Marathon, Thermopylae, and Attic Salamis, as also the tales of Dighenis, and he ranged widely over the island, thus unwittingly storing up practical experience.

Towards the end of 1916, Grivas went to Athens, and before the end of the war enrolled at the Greek Military Academy there, graduating in time to take part in the ill-fated Anatolian expedition. On one occasion, he was fascinated by the way in which some Turkish irregulars, armed only with rifles, held up his division for a whole day. Later, he retreated with his comrades by way of

Bursa. Thus he had gained some early experience of war, besides a wound and a decoration for bravery. Afterwards, he studied at various French war schools, the first time in 1925, the second in 1932/3. So, like Dr Küçük, he speaks French more readily than English. Between times, in 1929, he revisited Cyprus on leave. In Athens he lectured at the Military Academy on tactics, his particular forte.

When the Italians invaded Greece in 1940, the Greeks reacted bravely under General Metaxas, and Grivas became Chief of Staff to the 2nd Athens Division. He was promoted to Lieutenant-Colonel for his services on the Albanian front. There the outnumbered Greek forces, under the command of General Papagos, backed by a small contingent of the R.A.F. and by the Fleet Air Arm, inflicted a remarkable, if costly, defeat on the Italians. Then came the German occupation, and in 1943 Grivas organised the *Khi* (X)[1] resistance movement against the Axis. Times were bad, and both he and his mainland wife, Vassiliki (Kiki), suffered privations.

Khi had some success against the occupiers, and managed to make contact with the Greek army in Egypt, but its chance to shine did not come until towards the end of the war. By that time Grivas had organised it in groups about twenty strong in each of the fifteen districts of Athens, and had devised counter-assassination techniques against the Communists. By 1943, the Communists had set up a front organisation called EAM and organised a strong force, armed by the British, which they called ELAS (National Popular Liberation Army). In December 1944, ELAS, backed by terrible execution squads (called, with grim humour, OPLA), made an attempt to seize power. Political enemies were liquidated whenever possible; 8,752 hostages were executed by the Communists in Athens and the Peloponnese alone. Grivas and his three hundred men, armed with revolvers, a few machine-guns, and some grenades, managed to hold out for a time, against a vastly superior force, in the Theseion quarter of the city. But eventually they had to be evacuated by the British.

In 1945, Grivas retired on his pension, but the civil war of 1947/9 naturally prompted him to support Papagos. The cost of the fighting was terrible: 75,000 killed and 700,000 rendered homeless, while 25,000 children were abducted into Communist countries. Nevertheless, with aid supplied under the Truman doctrine, the struggle was won.

Despite civil war, Grivas's thoughts were turning more and more to Cyprus. From 1948 onwards he held discussions with Greeks of

[1] This letter in Greek represents the unknown.

his way of thinking, including Cypriotes like Christodoulos Papa-dopoulos and Achilles Kyrou (brother of Alexis, who had been Consul in Cyprus in 1931). In 1951, having failed twice to be elected as leader of his own political organisation (founded upon 'X'), Grivas stood for Parliament as a Populist Party candidate, but failed again.

Also in 1951, Grivas went to Cyprus with his wife, and stayed with her for a few weeks at Kalopanayiotis in the Marathassa valley, famous for its sulphur springs. He got to know the area well. It was mountainous and conveniently near Kykko Monastery. At that time, Makarios seems to have been a little sceptical of the whole idea of guerrilla war, but on 2 July he presided over the first organisers' meeting, in Athens. Archbishop Spyridon of Athens was delighted when he heard what was afoot, and declared : 'Freedom is never won without bloodshed'.[1]

Grivas was back in Cyprus in October 1952. There he met Andreas Azinas, a young protégé of the Archbishop's, educated at Reading University and now Secretary-General of the P.E.K. For five months they were able to travel about the island together more or less openly, making contacts and undertaking a thorough reconnaissance. On his return to Greece, in February 1953, Grivas wrote his general plan of operations, from which he was not to depart between 1953 and 1959. On 7 March 1953 came a fateful meeting in Athens of the political and military leaders of the Cyprus struggle. Makarios, who had just returned from New York, presided, and all present took an oath of secrecy and dedicated themselves to the cause.

By now the British authorities were becoming suspicious of visitors from Greece, and Grivas was denied a further visa, so his final mode of entry had to be illicit. However, the authorities obviously had no inkling of what was to come. In 1954 Richard Crossman visited Cyprus and was told by British officers that if the Cypriotes wanted *Enosis* they would have to fight for it. It is a military mistake not to take a potential threat seriously. In March 1954, the first caïque (light sailing vessel) came from Greece with arms and ammunition, and it was followed by another in October. Makarios, well supplied with money by rich American Greeks, was in a position to pay.

On 26 October 1954, Grivas left his house in Athens without giving any indication as to his destination, though two days later a friend told his wife a little of what was going on. Grivas travelled via Rhodes, which he left on 8 November with Socrates Loizides, younger brother of Savvas, who had been deported from Cyprus

[1] Grivas, *Memoirs*, p. 18.

by the British, not only in 1931 but also four years earlier. After a sea-sick journey in a small craft, they landed at Khlorakas, a village north of Ktima, at 8 p.m. on 10 November. Khlorakas was the home of Azinas, who had arranged Grivas's reception, and who was to head the *Enosis* liaison committee in Athens.

At the end of November 1954 Grivas moved to Nicosia. Before the outbreak of hostilities he rented a bungalow in a residential area outside the walls which was largely occupied by British families. In it he and his men constructed a tiny, cement-lined hide.

On 11 January 1955, Grivas met Makarios in the Bishop's house at Larnaca. Makarios told him that Papagos was now in full sympathy with their aims and that permanent liaison had been established with the Greek government. It was then that they decided to call their organisation EOKA and discussed when the first blow should be struck. Grivas declared that he would not lay down his arms until Makarios told him to.

The first set-back to Grivas's plans occurred on 26 January 1955, when Socrates Loizides went to meet the caïque *Ayios Georghios* at Khlorakas. A British destroyer intercepted it, while a shore party closed in, catching Loizides and eleven other men. He was sentenced to twelve years, remaining in a British prison until 1959. Meanwhile his wife left him. One of the biggest psychological problems that revolutionaries have to face is that many women are unhappy in revolutionary situations, and a prison term for their menfolk puts an extra strain on them, for obvious reasons. The other men received terms of from two to five years, and the haul included the explosives on which Grivas was counting: 10,000 sticks of dynamite, 2,200 detonators, 2,200 metres of fuse, and grenades, besides boxes of pistols, automatic weapons, and ammunition. However, his lieutenant Gregoris Afxentiou improvised by drawing on a source of supply known to be used by Famagusta fishermen when dynamiting for fish, namely British surplus shells which had been dumped into the sea, and which contained T.N.T. This was usable, if dangerous to handle. With it they could fill pipe-joints with screw caps, through which passed fuse wire. At this early stage, crude bombs were also made which consisted of petrol-filled whisky-bottles to which dynamite sticks (stolen from the Amiandos mines in workers' lunch-baskets) were attached with adhesive tape.

On 29 March 1955, Makarios gave Grivas his blessing. The bomb attacks on the night of 31 March/1 April took place on an island-wide basis, hitting government buildings and the houses of officials. The radio transmitter in Nicosia was blown up (by a four-man group under Marcos Drakos) and the unguarded Secretariat was damaged, as well as the wireless installations at the Wolseley Barracks. At Limassol several men were arrested after bombing the two main police stations and the Episkopi power plant, and at Larnaca those captured after bombing the law-courts, the Police H.Q., and the D.C.'s office included the district leader, Poskottis. In Famagusta the bombs failed to explode, and Afxentiou was on the run, with a reward offered for his capture. It was there that one EOKA-man, Modestos Pantelis, was killed. He threw a damp rope over some high-tension wires. His brother Christophis, when sentenced for his participation in the sabotage, declared his adherence to EOKA in court. Damage at the main radio station alone was estimated at £60,000, and responsibility for the explosions was claimed in mimeographed leaflets signed 'Dighenis' and apparently bearing the Byzantine double-headed eagle.[1]

The dawn of All Fools Day brought embarrassment to the British authorities. It has been said that they had a good idea of what was going on but, if so, they did nothing much about it. Of course, there is always a temptation for those doing intelligence work not to stamp out a revolutionary organisation, for in that case it will probably spring up in a new form, and have to be located and penetrated again. But on 20 June 1955 Police Commissioner Robins admitted to journalists that he was in the dark about EOKA. By November there were correct rumours as to the identity of 'Dighenis', yet Percy Arnold, whose *Cyprus Challenge* was published in 1956, makes no mention of either Grivas or Makarios in connexion with the continuing sabotage. Even Harding, after his term as Governor, had to admit, in the *Daily Telegraph,* that almost nothing was known about EOKA. All this secrecy was maintained in an island where gossip is known within a very short time from one end to the other. Warnings by EOKA to café-chatterers proved effective.

Harding himself described 'Dighenis' as 'a highly skilful organizer . . . an expert guerrilla leader' and 'a man of great personal courage and endurance, a stern disciplinarian and austere in his habits . . . unsparing with his subordinates as with himself'[2]—all of which is true. Grivas claims to have taken part personally in attacks by all his groups.

His discipline was sometimes savage, as when he had a youth shot for seducing a girl, but at least no incident occurred such as that in October 1964, when Nicos P. Agouros, a young Greek of Yalova, became a Moslem and gave the Turks a signed statement

---

[1] This is said to have been the Carbonari device also. It was used on EOKA berets.
[2] *Daily Telegraph,* 3 January 1958.

to the effect that Greek irregulars were indecently assaulting Greek women and had put pressure on his own wife. In some other cases, Grivas's morality was both simple and justifiable, as when he turned out EOKA-men for defaulting on payments to grocers.

His asceticism is reminiscent of the early Christians who withdrew into the desert. He trained himself to live on two dozen oranges a day. This kept him reasonably healthy, though he lost a stone in weight by 1959, and three of his teeth were rotted by the citric acid. (On one occasion he had to escape from a house which was surrounded when he was having a filling done.) Other food, such as cold meat, he partook of very sparingly. Indeed, temperance in diet, not a very common Cypriote characteristic, is one of the few things in which he resembles Makarios.

To a hunted man, Grivas's height (five foot three) was a great advantage, and he is said to have adopted such devices as padded shoulders to make himself look shorter, besides a number of disguises, widely rumoured at the time to include that of an old woman.[1] For some time the British had only a fourteen-year-old photograph of him, with a military cap concealing his thinning hair. When he reappeared in 1959 several people remembered having seen him, but had not recognised him owing to the change in his appearance. One or two did recognise him, but kept it to themselves.

This then is the man who speaks of all his decisions during the Cyprus struggle as 'consistently right', and ascribes his rightness to divine providence.[2]

EOKA

The initials EOKA stand for *Ethniki Organosis Kyprion Agoniston,* National Organisation of Cypriote fighters. It did not achieve its political objective, but militarily it was a success. The reasons for that success are of more than purely Cypriote interest because, as Grivas says, there will be more guerrilla activity in the future. Nuclear weapons have created a stalemate situation in which the guerrilla has come into his own, and even if they were used it would be necessary for fighters to disperse and fight in small groups. Any large force would present a target for nuclear rockets and shells.

By now it is widely accepted as a truism that guerrilla activity must provoke the authorities into taking indiscriminate action

---

[1] Grivas's reappearance with a moustache at the end of the Emergency renders this disguise highly unlikely.
[2] Grivas, *Memoirs,* p. 113.

against the civilian population, so that polarisation is achieved.
That happened in Cyprus, as the British were goaded into making
too many arrests and mass searches. However, mere provocation
would not have been enough without the ruthless killing of those
who collaborated with the authorities. In purely realistic terms,
killing one's own people is more important to guerrilla warfare
than killing the enemy, and therein lay the key to Grivas's success.
Of course, the notion of liquidating 'collaborators' was borrowed
from the Communists, and corresponds to the gangster's need to
'bump off stool-pigeons'; but there was a significant difference in
the case of Cyprus. Whereas Communists (and indeed all Marxists)
see history in terms of class struggle, there is always a substantial
section of the working class which is not prepared to replace its
actual rulers with persons who have co-opted one another into the
party; and even the intellectuals cannot always be relied upon to
subvert existing institutions in the interests of cosmopolitanism.
Therefore, class struggle is always confused, and it is necessary to
kill large numbers of 'collaborators', thus risking a reaction. Grivas,
however, was concerned only with ethnic realities, and so could
be more selective. It may not be obvious from a man's social group
on which side he stands, but when under pressure ethnic groups
may be expected to cohere, and those who collaborate become
relatively easy to isolate. Thus, the killing of some collaborators
helps to create a situation in which the remaining ones are
increasingly isolated and many former collaborators begin to work
for the guerrillas. These considerations apply even when a minority
is asserting itself, as in north Africa, where the Communist *colons*
mostly displayed ethnic rather than class solidarity; but Grivas
rightly regards the O.A.S. as having made a great mistake in not
carrying the battle on a bigger scale to Metropolitan France. In
Algeria, polarisation, short of Territorial separation, could
only favour the F.L.N. Fortunately, Makarios, in March 1957
(after his release from the Seychelles), turned down Grivas's plan
to explode bombs in England. So he was prevented from making
the same mistake as the I.R.A., who inflamed public opinion
against them by doing just that.[1]

To offset the disadvantage (for a guerrilla) of good roads, Grivas
had the asset of a large rural population, which provided the
'water' in which his revolutionary fish could swim outside the
towns.[2] (Significantly, the British succeeded in suppressing an uprising in Malaya because the Communist guerrillas, being Chinese,

[1] The position of the I.R.A. in England was obviously comparable to that
of the F.L.N. in France, not to that of the O.A.S. in France.
[2] In 1960, the rural population numbered 367,583, the urban 205,983.

were not accepted by the Malays, who were a majority in the countryside.)

Grivas planned his campaign in four stages, each supplementing the other. The first involved children's riots, the spreading of leaflets, and bomb-sabotage. (The headmaster of the Pancyprian Gymnasium was beaten by his own pupils for opposing the riots, and subsequently acquiesced in whatever was done.) The second stage, once a suitable atmosphere had been created, was to send out young gunmen to kill not only collaborators (such as over-zealous Greek police) but even those Greeks who openly disapproved of EOKA. The third stage involved the killing of British troops and Turkish police, who had been powerless to prevent the former killings. Interrogators in particular were struck down, and British civilians also became targets, the first one being murdered exactly one year after the beginning of the Emergency. The fourth stage was less successful than the others because it was more political than 'military'. This involved passive resistance, which went fairly well, and economic boycott, which did not.

As the struggle progressed, the vague Enotism of most Cypriote Greeks expressed itself in fearful admiration of EOKA's exploits. This hardened into conviction as they realised that it was far more dangerous to cooperate with the authorities than with EOKA. There was much truth in the statement of Dr Dervis, then Mayor of Nicosia : 'We all belong to EOKA'.

Grivas had difficulty at first in recruiting suitable men for EOKA. Cyprus is not rich in adventurous, aggressive types, and the Cypriotes are far less warlike than, for example, the Cretans, though they did well, mainly in a subsidiary capacity, during two world wars.[1] However, the sabotage campaign stimulated recruiting, and Grivas showed how much could be gleaned, even from an unwarlike population, by means of selection. On anniversary parades, EOKA-men stand out as far tougher-looking than the average. This is not to imply that they had not men among them like Phidian Symeonides, who impressed the author with the apparent gentleness of his disposition and his unsuspicious friendliness. A few criminals were also included (no doubt on the Nietzschean principle that a criminal may only be a strong man sick), but once in the organisation they had to conform to the rules.

The exploits (and crimes) of individual EOKA-men will be recounted in the following pages. Most of them justified Grivas's confidence, though there were inevitably some rotten apples, looking at the matter from Grivas's viewpoint. For instance, there was Andreas

[1] Cypriote Turks also joined up in the Second War.

Lazarou, who had been forced into EOKA on account of his British army experience. He wrote a letter to Grivas asking to be permitted to find work in London, where he could free himself of debt and support his wife, who was suffering from inoperable cancer. He was shot dead in his watchmaker's shop by way of reply.[1] Even if we accept Foley's explanation that Lazarou was an informer,[2] Grivas's reaction seems to have been rather strict under the circumstances.

Then there was Michael Ashiotis, who gave himself up to the British in October 1957.[3] Two other EOKA-members were found dead in the hide he had been using. He handed over some documents, as well as arms and ammunition.

Elias Samaras, the traitor of Liopetri, was the brother of Xanthos, who remained loyal to Grivas. Elias was flown to England, but remorse and the fear of EOKA reached him there, so that he returned to Cyprus, where he was tried in a secret EOKA court and executed by order of Grivas. Grivas tells of another informer who went mad when put in Coventry by the whole village of Akanthou. With those who gave way under interrogation and revealed secrets he was quite ruthless, though he did not mind if prisoners gave away details of no consequence in spinning a yarn to the interrogators. As he says, the Cypriotes are 'inventive and imaginative'.

Grivas concentrated upon the young, for their inexperience makes them less concerned for their own safety. That is why an attacking army needs a high proportion of young men. Indeed, teenagers have shown themselves to be as good, if not better, than veterans, provided they do not have to fight and endure for any length of time. A.N.E. (the EOKA Young Stalwarts) supplied Grivas with many killers and spies, and there were even bomb-throwing girls, such as Pitsa Constantinou and Rita Anthoulis. One woman, Elenitsa Seraphim, became district leader in Larnaca. Captured in December 1956, she was released a year later and regrouped her sabotage and 'execution' squads. Young girls, grown women. small boys, and old men shadowed targets and carried the weapons before and after each killing. Yet the searching of women could lead to allegations against individual British soldiers which might be taken at their face value. Therefore, women were mostly searched by trained women, of whom there were never enough.

---

[1] Dudley Barker, *Grivas: portrait of a terrorist* (London: Cresset, 1959), pp. 141–2.

[2] See Foley, *Legacy of Strife*, p. 73.

[3] He had intercepted a message ordering his own execution. Among the documents he surrendered was a death-list of 200 people, some of whom were killed anyway (see Byford-Jones, op. cit., pp. 137–8).

Grivas records that none of his 'executioners' was ever caught at work.

Grivas's killers were given all-round training, but specialised in sabotage, ambushing, or execution work. Later, there were special anti-Turkish groups also. At the start, there was a group of eight to ten men in the Pentadactylos range (Kalogrea-Ayios Amvrosios). At Pitsilia, in the Troödos range, there were eight to ten men under the command of Gregorios Afxentiou, Grivas's second-in-command. He was a lorry driver from Lysi who had been a Lieutenant in the Greek army from 1948 to 1952, a good teacher and leader. In the Kykko area were four groups of five to six men each. Some areas had to be avoided, like the treeless eastern Mesaoria and the clusters of Turkish villages south of the northern range. Ten sabotage groups were based on the towns, and in the villages were O.K.T., or shotgun, groups, which attacked mostly on their own initiative. Each member of the shock-troops was under Grivas's direct command, though minor matters were delegated to section leaders, who took over when communications were broken. The men each carried up to eight days' rations, and the hides contained up to a month's supplies (tinned food, dried fruit, and biscuit). More supplies were available at monasteries. First Aid was provided, but no medical services as such.

The hides were carefully prepared, usually in houses (like priest-holes in Elizabethan England) or in rocky ground, where footprints would not show. The outside ones were provided with hard tops, over which the British sometimes walked. In particular, there was a chain of such hides from Kykko to Limassol, one of which was found in a British intelligence officer's quarters, while others were located in monasteries or outside. EOKA standing orders were to attack at a distance from the hides, and to escape from them if attacked in turn. Seldom has so much ingenuity gone into the construction and location of places of concealment, yet only towards the end of the Emergency were the British sappers provided with cavity-detecting equipment.

To begin with, there were no more than eighty members of EOKA, and the number in the organisation proper never rose beyond three hundred, of whom not all were constantly engaged in guerrilla activities.[1] In February 1956, there were 273 members of EOKA and 750 in the O.K.T. shotgun-troops. They were hunted by 4,500 police and 20,000 troops, the total in the security forces rising at one time to about 37,000. These forces were commanded

---

[1] Grivas points out that saturation point is soon reached in a given area when guerrillas are armed. The more make an attack, the more have to escape afterwards.

at various times by a field-marshal and three generals. The question naturally arises as to how EOKA managed to hold its own in an area as small as Cyprus. The smallness is not so great as might be supposed, for surface area is larger in mountainous country, but the main reason for EOKA's success in this field lay in the tactics adopted by Grivas. He did not make the same mistake as the Communists in Greece, who had tried to hold territory. In any case, open confrontation in a small country with such good roads would have been suicidal under the circumstances. Therefore, he presented the enemy with no firm front and no fixed targets, keeping himself, his own men, and the British constantly on the move. So the enormous British advantage in war material was largely nullified. In such circumstances, superiority of fire-power cannot be used without hitting the population indiscriminately (which the Americans have discovered in Vietnam). As Grivas says, one cannot chase monkeys with elephants. The British in their armoured cars, keeping to the roads and avoiding night-moves, might just as well have been hunting field-mice. Mountain and forest sweeps were conducted like manoeuvres, and the large numbers of troops were slow to move and react.

Many EOKA weapons were smuggled in, either directly, through the post, or masquerading as something else, like the comic cats which turned out to be solid T.N.T. enamelled over. A priest might conceal a pistol inside his hat, or a schoolboy in his satchel. There must also be a suspicion that diplomatic bags were used. A radar watch checked smuggling by boat, so that individual parts of larger weapons had to be taken in separately and reassembled. The Deacon Anthimos Kyriakides cooperated with the businessman Socrates Eliades in organising an arms-smuggling network which was never discovered. World War II mines, stolen from open dumps (such as those once so common in Britain), now reappeared. Explosives were stolen from the chrome and asbestos mines, and fertiliser was also used in their manufacture. Indeed, most of the EOKA explosives were home-made, by a team headed by Christos Papachrysostomou, Deputy Headmaster of the Pancyprian Gymnasium and the chemist Nicos Servos. A favourite mixture was 78 parts potassium chlorate, 12 parts potassium nitrate, six parts sulphur, four parts carbon, and 20 parts urotropine (hexamine).[1] A useful incendiary was 75 parts potassium chlorate, 25 parts sugar, a higher proportion of sugar providing more fire, and more potassium chlorate a bigger explosion. The Afxentiou cocktail-bomb consisted of a small flask filled with the latter mixture, in which was placed a test-tube filled with sulphuric acid which in turn had

[1] Grivas's measurement in 'parts' is no doubt for convenience.

been attached with sticking-plaster or Spitfix to the underside of a cork which had been soaked in paraffin. A cast-iron rod passed through the cork and into the test-tube, with a lead weight on the outer end. When thrown, the lead naturally landed first, and the rod broke the test-tube, causing an explosion on the same principle as the Mills bomb. A crude timing device consisted of a cork stopper in an upside-down test-tube of sulphuric acid in a container full of the same incendiary mixture. Corrosion of the stopper led to explosion. A variant was also developed with an electric detonator.[1] Mines set off by pressure completing an electric circuit could be disconnected by a switch system when local people were using the road. Another ploy was to place a smaller, explosive-filled tin inside a larger one, with shrapnel between the two casings. Pipe-bombs were also made, with ordinary plumbing equipment, but these were detectable when used as mines, so that bakelite and wooden ones replaced them. Wooden mines even blew up a tank. Particularly ingenious was a small cannon used against convoys. It consisted of a strong metal tube of any size, closed at one end and filled with explosive (e.g. gunpowder) and fragments of iron plugged in with wadding. When firmly fixed to a tree or buried in a bank, and electrically detonated, it could destroy a lorry. Booby-traps were also used. Douglas Williamson, a civil servant at Platres, was killed by a letter-explosive, and a British N.C.O. was killed opening a receptable containing EOKA arms. However, the manufacture of arms was likewise dangerous. On 21 June 1955, an EOKA-man blew himself up, the first of several killed or injured. (Similarly, on 1 September 1957, four members of a Turkish team blew themselves up.) EOKA also manufactured a small automatic weapon, using 9 mm. ammunition.

Grivas's success depended upon surprise, alertness, flexibility, secrecy, and speed. Surprise was immensely facilitated by the network of EOKA agents, especially in the police force. One Special Branch member, George Lagoudontis, tape-recorded top-level British conferences at Police H.Q. Also, the Greek army is largely modelled on the British. (Indeed, a platoon of Greek troops gives very much the impression of a British one, except that the men are generally shorter and thicker-set.) So Greek officers like Grivas and Afxentiou had a very good idea what a British regular was likely to do. Nor was their task rendered more difficult by the blowing of bugles and other loud noises in British camps, preparatory to big sweeps. As Grivas points out, to defeat EOKA the British needed specially-trained groups. These could have been

---

[1] See George Grivas-Dighenis, *Guerrilla Warfare and EOKA's Struggle.* Tr. by A. A. Pallis (London: Longmans, 1964), pp. 101 et seq.

moved very rapidly by helicopter, but helicopters were only used from July 1957, and nearly always for reconnaissance purposes.

Other British deficiencies also helped Grivas: the poor equipment of the police; the confining of curfews to those under twenty-seven years of age, so that he made use of those above that age; the inadequate cloaking of informers during searches; the failure to check sufficiently on those women who provided services for the troops; the failure to block off the Carpass peninsula, which would have prevented EOKA activity there. Some fairly effective methods were employed, however. Tracker-dogs were used, and Grivas had to have his clothes burnt on that account, but they were countered with garlic and pepper. Tear gas, truncheons, shields, and body-protectors were used in dealing with riots, and troops stood on rooftops during searches. In the course of time, the instinct of self-preservation made them more alert, so that many casualties were thereby prevented. British Intelligence made use of interrogation, as well as a reward system, for securing information. Turks, Communists, and Cypriotes from Great Britain (some of them criminals) were sent among the Greek population as agents, but they had a tendency to invent details in order to justify their pay. From the end of 1956 there were also 'Q' patrols of British and Turkish police, which proved a reasonably effective deterrent. In dealing with the population at large, collection fines were imposed over a six-month period in 1956, culminating in a fine of £40,000 in Famagusta and another of £35,000 in Limassol. However, the intelligent suggestion made by a D.C. to Sir Robert Armitage (Governor since 1954), in July 1955 that such fines should be automatic wherever sabotage or killing took place was unfortunately not adopted. On occasion, buildings found to contain EOKA arms were destroyed, though there was no destruction of houses which had merely sheltered terrorists. It is probable that trade sanctions would have been very effective, although measures adopted unhesitatingly by a later British government against its own kin in Rhodesia were never even considered in the case of Cyprus.

Of course, British Intelligence agents, however well they spoke Greek, could seldom infiltrate the local population because they were mostly markedly different in physical type; whereas a refusal to face ethnic realities led the government to rely on a largely Greek civil service, which was soon riddled with EOKA informants. On one occasion racial criteria misled EOKA, when the U.S. Vice-Consul, William Boteler, was killed in mistake for an Englishman and other American citizens were injured.[1] Grivas put out a leaflet

---

[1] Averoff tried to throw the blame for this on the British (Grivas, *Memoirs*, p. 210).

saying that a mistake had been made and pointing out that 'it is not always possible to distinguish them' (viz Americans) from Britons.

The main credit for the maintenance of EOKA security must go to Grivas himself. He has not chosen to give many details of his intelligence network, though it is clear that he used a number of different code-names for the same people and that his whereabouts were never known to more than one or two people at a time; and only he knew the whereabouts of each EOKA group and what it was doing. Thus, when individual EOKA-men defected, relatively little information could be gleaned from them. Also, the authorities were very slow to act on what information they did procure. Grivas kept the direction of affairs entirely in his own hands, and his messages were taken by hand 'through road-block, curfew and search'.[1]

The strength of such a system is also its weakness. Grivas is speaking nothing but the simple truth when he says that had he been eliminated the whole struggle would have collapsed because no one could have taken his place.

Mindful of conflict in Greece, Grivas regarded a Right-Left split as a danger more serious than a Greco-Turkish one. He suppressed his detestation and allowed left-wingers (though not Communists) to join EOKA. Among these was Kyriakos Matsis, reputedly fond of discussing Kropotkin, Mill, Rousseau, and *New Fabian Essays*. He was killed three months before the London Conference of 1959. Most prominent of the left-wingers was Dr Vassos Lyssarides, alias Spartacus. The left-wing E.A.E.M. (United Unbroken National Front), an organisation founded at the beginning of the passive resistance campaign, included AKEL supporters who were used against the Turks. (EDON, the United Democratic Youth Organisation, also inclined to the Left.) However, EOKA help from members of the Pancyprian Federation of Labour should not be assumed to be left-wing, for one-third of them were of the Centre and Right. The Communist leadership was another matter, and Zachariades, head of the Communist Party of Greece, was well enough informed to reveal the identity of Dighenis in a denunciation of EOKA on Radio Moscow during the first months of the campaign. At that time the British would not believe him. Later, Grivas charged that the Communists were in league with the British, and there seems to have been some substance to his claim. His relations with AKEL deteriorated at the beginning of 1958, when two left-wing trades unionists were killed and three wounded by EOKA. The Left demonstrated against Grivas, and

[1] Grivas, *Memoirs,* p. 28.

Makarios annoyed him by receiving a left-wing deputation in Athens. A particularly unpleasant incident occurred at Lefkonico, where the left-winger Savvas Menacas was tied to a tree and beaten to death over a full hour before his wife and a large crowd of people. Such behaviour is counter-productive, for it tends to arouse resentments which overcome fear. Swift elimination is far more effective than the indulgence of sadism.

The Toll of the Emergency

Estimates vary as to the number of casualties over the four years of the Emergency. Doros Alastos says that 'it cost nearly 650 lives —half of them Greek Cypriots, the rest English and Turkish Cypriots'.[1] Dudley Barker says some 600 were killed and 1,260 wounded;[2] while Byford-Jones says that there were 1,768 casualties, mostly the work of EOKA, 508 of which were fatal.[3] Thus, the two British writers agree pretty closely as regards the number of wounded.

Only Byford-Jones provides detailed statistical tables of the casualties.[4] The breakdown of the figures for those killed comes out as follows: in 1955, 24 (12 Greeks, 12 British); in 1956, 214 (115 Greeks, 81 British, 14 Turks, 4 others); in 1957, 34 (21 Greeks, 10 British, 3 Turks); in 1958, 236 (130 Greeks, 39 British, 67 Turks). Of the 278 Greeks killed, 60 died at the hands of the Turks (56 of them in the riots of the summer of 1958). As regards the remainder, Dr Hans E. Tütsch states that 106 were killed by the security forces, including the nine who were hanged under Harding.[5] That leaves 112 Greeks killed by EOKA, which is much too low. Those who estimate the total number of deaths during the Emergency at over 600 tend to estimate the number of Greeks killed by EOKA at some two hundred.

Of the 142 Britons killed, 104, according to Byford-Jones, were in the services, 12 were in the police, and 26 were civilians. When one adds to these the 84 Turks (including 22 police) killed by the Greeks and those Greeks and others killed by EOKA, one arrives at a figure of 342 for those killed by the insurgents, as against 166 Greeks killed by the security forces and the Turks. When one takes into account Grivas's claim that the number of Britons killed

---

[1] *Cyprus Guerrilla: Grivas, Makarios and the British* (London: Heinemann, 1960), p. 7.

[2] Barker, op. cit., p. 8.

[3] Byford-Jones, *Grivas and the Story of EOKA* (London: Hale, 1959), p. 178.

[4] Ibid., pp. 185–6.

[5] *From Ankara to Marrakesh: Turks and Arabs in a changing world* (London: Allen & Unwin, 1964), p. 51.

was much greater than officially announced, the disproportion is even greater. Such relative proportions are not paralleled in any similar situation, and indicate very clearly both the restraint of the British security forces and the willingness of the British government to sacrifice the lives of its own people in what was, after all, a mere holding-operation. Conversely, the Greeks can claim that the overall casualties, proportional to population, were lower than in any similar situation. Deaths have never been estimated at more than 650, the kind of toll to be expected after a single day's (under-reported) communal rioting in an Indian city with the population of Cyprus. The smallness of the death toll in Cyprus (even relative to population) is to a limited degree owing to the restraining hand of Makarios before his deportation,[1] but mainly owing to the efficiency of the British security clamp during 1957 under Harding. Casualty figures rose again steeply during the following year.

Some of the EOKA killings were of a particularly unpleasant nature. Thus a Greek woman, presumably an informer, was shot early in 1956 and then shot again while in hospital. Assistant-Superintendent Aristotelou was killed while visiting his wife in a Nicosia clinic. Nor were prominent persons safe. The Abbot of Chrysorroyiatissa was shot dead for allegedly betraying two EOKA-men. (Makarios made no complaint.) Nor was a church considered to be a sanctuary: Manolis Pierides was killed in his pew during a service at Kythrea. Dudley Barker tells us that in May 1959 an informer called Zacharias Karaphotias, of Ayios Amvrosios, was burned to death with petrol before his wife's eyes. In this case, EOKA disclaimed responsibility, and its was suggested that the victim 'had enemies'. The British had little success in making propaganda out of the EOKA killings, relying on expressions of moral outrage when action was more obviously indicated. However, some impression was made when a Maltese shopkeeper, Mompalda, was shot down just before meeting his fiancée. Dudley Barker tells us that she was flown to England, where she made an impassioned broadcast in denunciation of EOKA. Another such broadcast was given by a bereaved 'Greek Cypriot mother'.

Grivas justifies the shooting of British servicemen in the back on the grounds that the enemy was so much superior in numbers, and the Greeks regard the British authorities' concern over this issue rather as some people regard objections to shooting a sitting bird. However, some of the killings, especially those of civilians, may be considered as dastardly, and the same holds true for several of the attempted killings. Dr Charles Bevan, a specialist in preventive

[1] E.g. Makarios vetoed Grivas's plan to kill General Keightley, C-in-C Middle East Land Forces, at the end of June 1955.

medicine, was shot in the back by one man while the killer's accomplice was asking him for medical attention. On 16 May 1956, Corporal T. J. Hale was on duty at a hut on the edge of Nicosia airport, and was shot while getting water for three Cypriotes. Two of the three were later hanged. On 3 June that year, Roy Garrett, aged eighteen, was shot in a country place with his hands tied behind his back. Four Cypriotes walked by as he lay gravely wounded and pleading for help, but none stopped. Indeed, the deliberate ignoring of the wounded became the rule among the Cypriote Greeks, and some could not conceal their delight at the victims' predicament.

Then, on 8 July 1956, there was the case of Mr George Kaberry, a customs official, who was beaten up in front of his pregnant wife and then killed with a shotgun blast in the stomach.[1] In 1958, there was another big spate of murders. Lieutenant-Colonel F. L. Collier, for instance, was killed in Limassol while watering his garden.

Age and long residence in Cyprus did not always give protection, any more than did feminine sex. In Larnaca, a schoolboy tossed a bomb into a room containing Mrs Smith, the wife of a British sergeant, and two children. She threw herself across the children and had her foot blown off. If more were not killed, it was certainly not for want of trying. For instance, on 4 March 1956 a bomb was placed by order of Grivas in a Hermes aircraft which was about to carry R.A.F. families. Fortunately it exploded wrecking the plane, before sixty-eight people boarded it, mainly women and children.

Not that Grivas was quite undiscriminating in his choice of targets and methods. He turned down suggestions for the shaving of British women's heads (an idea inspired by the widespread practice of the French Resistance in 1944). There was also the case of seventy-eight-year-old Jack Cremer, who was gagged, bound, and abducted after giving an English lesson to some girls in the Turkish village of Temblos. He was held as a hostage for three EOKA-men, Zakos, Michael, and Iakovos Patatsos, who were in prison waiting to be hanged. They commendably asked for his release, and the Church was said to be somewhat uneasy about it. Grivas ordered that he be let go, and five days later the three convicted men were hanged, to the accompaniment of explosions at the military bases. Still, Grivas chose most of the targets himself, especially among his fellow-countrymen, and should be judged accordingly. He would doubtless argue that those who are horrified by slaughterhouses have no right to eat meat, but his record hardly

---

[1] Dudley Barker, op. cit., pp. 131–2.

justifies his penchant for delivering sermons on morality to little girls.

Until 1958, and even then as a rule, British troops displayed almost preternatural restraint in the face of constant provocation. The break-down of Byford-Jones's statistics for the wounded shows this clearly. Of 1,260 wounded, 601 were British servicemen, and 187 were policemen (of whom 43 were Turks, 34 were Britons, and two were of other non-Cypriote origins), while 472 were civilians (including 150 Turks, 49 Britons, and 21 other non-Cypriotes). Of the 252 Greeks wounded, 98 were casualties of inter-communal clashes (as against 86 Turks). Thus the insurgent population suffered an even smaller proportion of wounded than of killed. When active resentment was aroused among the Highland Light Infantry by a bomb exploded among them after a football match,[1] killing two and wounding five, Harding told the Greeks that they ought to be grateful they had the British to deal with. That is true enough, but Byford-Jones's statistics do not reflect the roughness with which the troops began to treat the civilian population as they slowly became exasperated. A blow on the face, for instance, cannot count as a 'wound', but to a Middle Easterner it constitutes a terrible blow to his pride. There is no tradition of unarmed, cathartic conflict, with the participants bearing no grudges. Certainly, Dudley Barker's statistics for those convicted of assault on the Greeks do not reflect the true position. He tells us that only six cases were brought against the police. Three of the accused policemen were acquitted, two were convicted of minor assault, and one was sentenced to three years for wounding two Greeks with a gun. Also, two British officers, O'Driscoll and Lindsay, were court-martialled and dismissed the service for having maltreated a prisoner, A. Koronides, in April 1956. It is of interest that the extension to Cyprus, on 23 October 1953, of the European Convention for the Protection of Human Rights and Fundamental Freedoms seems to have made no appreciable difference once passions were aroused, either before or after independence. Yet the Greeks later expected the Turks to accept such rights as a guarantee.

The British had interrogation centres at Lefka, Ktima, Platres, Ayios Memnon, and Nicosia, plus detention camps scattered about the island in which up to 2,000 suspects were detained. Foley alleges that 'no more than six' people died under interrogation, though he offers no evidence in those cases, and it is said that as many as 150 youths under eighteen were whipped. Yet not until the end of 1958 did Grivas express the fear that 'all our secrets

---

[1] The British Left was appalled at the troops' reaction, but not by the deaths.

19—C

will be gradually betrayed' if the interrogation brutality continued. The only conclusion we can draw is that the army's exasperation in that year had a serious effect on EOKA.

Certainly there was ill-treatment, though the reaction of the Greek propagandists was grossly disproportionate. As Storrs puts it : 'The Balkans and the Levant are past-masters in the craft of manufacturing atrocities'. For instance, there was the case of Loulla Kokkinou, described by Makarios as having 'lost her front teeth after a rough blow by a sadist tormentor'. Selwyn Lloyd revealed that she still had her front teeth, only one of which was false. Her dental records showed the original tooth to have been lost before 24 June 1955, whereas she was arrested for the first time on 23 May 1956. Another Greek-Cypriote ploy was to put on bandages for the benefit of reporters. When the bandages were removed no injuries were to be seen. More care should have been taken by the authorities to ensure that people had the injuries of which they complained.

Grivas's own contribution to the horror stories is one of how, after one Tassos Elia had his fingers blown off while planting a home-made bomb, a soldier put his severed fingers in a cigarette packet and handed them round as a joke. For what it is worth, Ashiotis, after his surrender, said that Grivas had sent out an order to fabricate atrocity stories. In fact, the worst atrocities, as might be expected, seem to have taken place in the Greco-Turkish riots during the summer of 1958, but they are not well documented.

When Caraolis and Demetriou were hanged in May 1956, a pamphlet was issued in Athens by the Committee for the Self-determination of Cyprus, entitled *Un des plus grands crimes de notre siècle*. The front cover has a picture of two gallows-trees situated on an imaginary hill, with a large union-jack in the background and an unexplained stream of bright red blood flowing from the foot of each gallows.

In March 1957, the Deacon Anthimos, on behalf of Grivas, put out a rumour that Grivas was hiding at the village of Milikouri near Kykko. As a result, a 54-day curfew was imposed on Milikouri and nearby Kaminaria, and there were horrifying allegations in Athens which were not borne out by the villagers. Two British doctors attended on them throughout, and they received free food to the value of £1,000, besides mail and other services. In May and June of the following year Mathykoloni was searched for forty-five days, also without giving cause for the allegations made (except where damage to buildings was concerned). Still, the impassioned Greek denunciations, including a reference by the Archbishop of Athens to 'the barbarity of the Tory cannibals', are almost endearing in an age when the most vicious hatreds are expressed in the language of conciliation and understanding.

The EOKA killing which made the greatest impression on the British army was that of Mrs Cutliffe, wife of Sergeant D. J. Cutliffe, while she was shopping in Varosha (the Greek area of Famagusta) on 3 October 1958. The Greeks are prone to stress the background to the murder, notably the incidents at Geunyeli and at Avgorou (not far from Famagusta). There had been others as well. On the previous 14 April, when the police officer William Dear was killed, together with Lance-Corporals B. F. Turvey and W. N. Cameron, 712 Greeks had been rounded up, of whom fifty-one later complained of ill-treatment. The emergency regulations had been brought back after two military policemen had been killed in the streets of Famagusta on 4 May. On 12 June, thirty-five Greeks were arrested by a British police-sergeant near the mixed villages of Skylloura and Ayios Vassilios.[1] They were armed with clubs and stones, and were on their way to fight local Turks. With the help of an escort of the Royal Horse Guards, the sergeant was taking the prisoners to be charged in Nicosia when he heard there was a demonstration outside the Central Police Station there. In circumstances which are obscure, the prisoners were taken back beyond the Turkish village of Geunyeli and told to walk home.[2] Turks waiting in ambush (armed with cleavers and other weapons, some of them on motor-cycles) went after them killing four of them, mortally wounding another four, and severely wounding five more. It is said that a Grenadier Guards armoured car prevented more Turks from leaving Geunyeli. The subsequent Commission of Inquiry established no blame where the security forces were concerned, but Greek suspicions were naturally aroused.

On 5 July, armoured cars of the Horse Guards were attacked by the people of Avgorou with sticks, stones, and bottles. Eventually, after twenty-three soldiers had been injured with bricks, bottles, and other missiles,[3] they opened fire. A man and a woman were killed. Three days later, a cornet and a trooper, both of that regiment, were shot dead in Famagusta. On 30 July, two Greeks were killed when they attacked troops at Akhyritou, nearer Famagusta than Avgorou, and in reprisal a sergeant and an officer were killed. The kind of murder which aroused the troops' anger was that of Sergeant Reginald Hammond, who was shot down in the street while holding the hand of his two-year-old son.

---

[1] Later to be the scene of a much worse atrocity than that of Geunyeli (see below, p. 327).
[2] See Foot, op. cit. p. 172; Barker, op. cit., p. 177.
[3] Some fifty villagers were also injured, according to Grivas and Foley.

Mr Glafcos Clerides has given the author a Greek version of the events leading up to the killing of Mrs Cutliffe. It seems that after Avgorou Grivas rescinded his previous orders against indiscriminate attacks on British civilians. The EOKA group in Famagusta assumed that women were no longer excepted and did not deem it necessary to query the order. Grivas subsequently issued a leaflet disclaiming responsibility for what took place.

There can be no doubt that the murder of Mrs Cutliffe was premeditated in that British women were the intended targets. On 1 and 2 October, prams were set on fire in Varosha and British women were insulted. On the 3rd, no Greek women were shopping at the time the attack took place. Mrs Cutliffe was shot five times in the back and her companion, Mrs Robinson, another sergeant's wife, was also shot several times, two different weapons being used. Mr George Cavounides, spokesman of the Greek Foreign Ministry, gallantly alleged that Mrs Cutliffe had been shot by a rejected lover,[1] but he did not explain why two weapons were used nor why Mrs Robinson was also shot.

The husband of the murdered woman, Sergeant D. J. Cutliffe, was in the Royal Artillery, and many members of his regiment, together with others from the Royal Ulster Rifles, broke discipline and went on the rampage.[2] Hundreds of Greeks were rounded up and the majority were beaten. Three of them died, including a thirteen-year-old girl, and a British soldier was accidentally shot dead. The young girl, according to Grivas, died of shock and heart failure after seeing the violence. A forty-eight-hour curfew had to be imposed on the entire island. The British left-wing press execrated the behaviour of the troops without showing equal concern over the killing of Mrs Cutliffe, and the right-wing press showed a natural horror at the Cutliffe murder, while failing to emphasise the Greek girl's death. Editorial policy had long been more important than the impartiality which had been so highly regarded among journalists in the nineteenth century.

Some of the Greeks saw that the Cutliffe murder could not be regarded in quite the same light as the death of the Greek girl, and Dr Dervis made the gesture of offering a reward of £5,000 for information leading to the apprehension of those responsible. The forces' reaction to the murder seems to have convinced both Makarios and the British government that if there was no lessening of tension the situation would degenerate.

[1] Grivas more tentatively mentions the possibility, but he emphasises the casualties among Greek women (not differentiating between the dead and injured) and does not rule out the chance of 'some misunderstanding' (*Memoirs*, p. 169).
[2] According to a British Information Officer.

The Emergency

As a background to the Emergency, the Greeks struggled with some success to influence other governments in their favour. In April 1955, Makarios went as an observer to the Afro-Asian Conference at Bandung, where he was promised a great deal of support. It was the turning-point in his political career, after which he became a world-figure. On 23 September, the second Greek recourse to UNO over Cyprus led to a decision not to include the question on the General Assembly's agenda. At that time, the composition of the United Nations favoured the West, and within NATO only Iceland (which had a fishing dispute with Great Britain) could be counted on to support the Greek cause. The situation changed radically towards the end of the year, when many more of the states represented at the Bandung Conference were admitted to the organisation. The third Greek recourse over Cyprus resulted, on 26 February 1957, in Resolution 1013 (XI) which favoured an outcome in accordance with the U.N. Charter. However, opinion gradually began to swing against *Enosis,* while remaining in favour of independence. In particular, Krishna Menon of India saw a strong resemblance between the *Enosis* movement and the movement in favour of uniting largely Moslem Kashmir with Pakistan; and satisfaction of the natural aspirations towards unity of ethnically similar groups would have played havoc with the artificial frontiers of many other newly-independent states. Besides, the United States was fearful of alienating Turkey if she supported *Enosis.* At her fourth attempt, in December 1957, Greece had her draft resolution accepted in committee, but it failed to gain the required two-thirds' majority in the Assembly. Eventually, Greece herself reluctantly proposed independence rather than *Enosis* for Cyprus, and on 5 December 1958 the Assembly, in effect, repeated its Resolution 1013 (XI). The airing of the Cyprus case before the United Nations was one of the chief aims of Makarios and Grivas, but not too much importance should be attached to the results. There had been much lobbying behind the scenes and less than subtle pressures had been exercised, as on 11 December 1957, when Averoff had reminded Henry Cabot Lodge of the tens of thousands of American citizens of Greek origin in his native Massachusetts.[1] On the other hand, the Greek government was concerned not to antagonise the British more than absolutely necessary. For instance, in March 1956 a British plane carrying arms for use in Cyprus was allowed to land at Athens airport.

*

[1] See Xydis, op. cit., p. 417.

In April 1955, the efforts of the British to deal with the bomb-throwing in Cyprus were unsuccessful, largely because they were working in the dark. On Empire Day (24 May) some seven hundred schoolboys drove off police with stones, and a time-bomb went off at the Pallas Cinema five minutes after the Governor (Armitage) and his party had left it. Marcos Drakos, an energetic member of EOKA, had arranged for a coca-cola bottle, filled with explosive and equipped with a time-pencil, to be placed near the Governor's seat. Fortunately, the film ended five minutes before the scheduled time. In June, Grivas began a terror campaign directed primarily against the Greeks in the police force. On the 6th, he met Makarios in an annexe to Kykko Monastery to coordinate plans, so presumably the latter was privy to his intentions. The campaign did not go very well to begin with. Michael Caraolis, who had killed P.C. Michael Poullis within full view of hundreds of people attending a Communist meeting in Nicosia, was captured.[1] Bomb-injuries to two Turkish policemen at the Nicosia Central Police Station brought a warning from Dr Küçük. On 23 June, Grivas wrote to Makarios, warning him that the Turks were planning to assassinate him.

The *Kıbrıs Türktür,* or 'Cyprus is Turkish' organisation, had been in existence since 1954, and its president, Hikmet Bil, claimed that it had 100,000 members (in Turkey, Cyprus, and Great Britain). The Cypriote Turks had become extremely concerned over the trend of events since the British had begun to propose limited autonomy in Cyprus, and had gone back to insisting, despite the Treaty of Lausanne, that if Cyprus were ceded to any other nation, it should be Turkey. In answer to the Lausanne Treaty objection, they claimed that that treaty envisaged the British as staying in Cyprus. When, on 30 June 1955, Eden asked Greece and Turkey to send representatives to discuss Cyprus and other problems in London, he reintroduced Turkey into the dispute as an interested party, thus arousing the indignation of the Greeks. The argument that the British government had an obligation to consider the interests of the Cypriote-Turkish minority may sound plausible, but no such concern was demonstrated by British post-war governments where the interests of British minorities were concerned. As Peregrine Worsthorne was to remark in the *Sunday Times* (12 July 1964): 'If the Cyprus minority were British rather than Turkish it would, on African precedents, have been abandoned years ago'. It is arguable that insistence upon no more than paper guarantees for the Cypriote Turks would have been more in the British interest than the assumption of responsibilities she was unable to fulfil in the

---

[1] It is of interest that Caraolis was a model pupil of the Nicosia English School.

long term. Turkey could have been relied upon to look after the interests of the Cypriote Turks, as in fact she did after December 1963. There seems little point in playing off one side against the other if one has not the will to remain more than a few years.

On 6 July 1955, Grivas moved into the Troödos area, first to Kakopetria, later to the Marathassa valley, with which he was already so familiar. His chief activity was planning ambushes and instructing his followers in military techniques. Meanwhile, the anti-police campaign was gathering momentum, and resignations were beginning to come from frightened policemen. It was in July that Makarios congratulated Grivas on what he had achieved so far. Thus, it is hardly surprising that when Lennox-Boyd flew in to see Makarios on 9 July his visit was not a success.

The Tripartite Conference was convened in London on 29 August, and lasted until 7 September. Fatin Rüştü Zorlu, the Turkish Foreign Minister, was a tough nut to crack, or typically overbearing, depending on the point of view.[1] On the day that Harold Macmillan, as British Foreign Secretary, put forward a plan for self-government in Cyprus under a tripartite commission, sovereignty being retained by Great Britain, riots broke out in Turkey. Adnan Menderes, the Turkish Premier, seems to have decided to bring pressure to bear upon the Greeks in that country. A Turk made a dynamite attack on the Turkish consulate in Salonica and on the nearby house in which Atatürk was born. Accepting this as a Greek outrage, mobs ran wild on 6 September in Istanbul and Izmir. Their excesses went far beyond what Menderes had planned. Hundreds of Greek shops and other premises were destroyed, as well as a score of churches. Greek tales of rape and massacre seem to have been exaggerated, and Selim Sarper, the Turkish representative at the United Nations, was to deny two years later that there had been any loss of life.[2] Foley's statement that 'Armenians and Jews as well as Greeks were dragged from their beds and murdered'[3] is unaccompanied by supporting evidence, though one or two lives may have been lost. In any case, the Greek government had good cause to protest, and the NATO partnership was for a time in danger. However, in early 1956 the Turkish government agreed to pay the sum of 40 million liras in compensation (at least £3 million). No Turks were killed in Cyprus during 1955.

The Tripartite Conference broke up indecisively on 7 September,

[1] Averoff admits that Zorlu had qualities of a statesman (Xydis, op. cit., p. 563), and even Foot speaks of his 'ability' and 'patriotism' (*A Start in Freedom*, p. 150).
[2] Xydis, op. cit., p. 345.
[3] Charles Foley, *Legacy of Strife*, p. 36.

and EOKA continued its activities as a way of influencing the coming U.N. debates. On 17 September, the library at the British Institute, the finest British library in the Middle East, was burnt down by schoolboys using petrol (a practice reminiscent of the 1931 riots). During the same month, Marcos Drakos and fifteen others, who had been confined for EOKA activities in Kyrenia Castle, escaped through the arrow-slits and got clean away; £5,000 was placed on Drakos's head. It was he, with his *Astrapi* (Lightning) squad, that had dynamited the Wolseley Barracks. After this, EOKA prisoners and suspects were put in Camp K, near Nicosia. On 28 October, Caraolis was sentenced to death. Island-wide riots took place and there were many arrests.

Armitage had been a suitable Governor in time of peace, but a man who compared the Cypriote devotion to Hellenism to the Welsh attachment to their language was ill-equipped to deal with the situation which had arisen. The man appointed to replace him, Field-Marshal Sir John Harding, former Chief of the Imperial General Staff, was a brave and efficient soldier, the sort of man who does well in war, but not necessarily in guerrilla operations. Makarios respected him, and Grivas regarded him as his most dangerous adversary, besides liking his frank outspokenness. However, Grivas also saw him as obstinate and without political acumen. Obstinacy may be no bad quality, and Grivas himself is not especially known for his political acumen, but his judgement of Harding is borne out by the latter's expression of the opinion that only 5 per cent of the population supported EOKA. Evidently, Harding was judging by what Cypriotes said, and did not consider the likelihoods arising out of the 1950 referendum. Not until a time-bomb was placed in his bed did he find it necessary to dismiss his Greek servants. In the field of propaganda, Harding did not apparently realise that his own heartfelt revulsion at the idea of shooting a man in the back was not shared by the population at large. As Grivas puts it, Harding 'could not understand that by reviling EOKA as cowards and murderers, he was insulting the whole Cypriot people'.[1] At the same time, one should remember Grivas's admission that Harding was not given a free hand in the political field.[2]

Harding was appointed on 25 September 1955, and 300 police

[1] Grivas, *Memoirs*, p. 90. Greek propagandists have made much of the fact that British commandos are taught to knife their enemies in the back, but the analogy is not close because commandos presumably wear uniform of some kind. The author finds widespread disagreement as to the morality or otherwise of civilians using such weapons against an occupying force, but those who adopt them can scarcely complain if the same methods are used against themselves.
[2] Ibid., p. 126.

were sent out from the United Kingdom, an attempt being made to weed the Cyprus police of EOKA agents. He arrived as Governor on 3 October, and the next day began talks with Makarios which dragged on until 3 March 1956. Meanwhile Makarios abetted EOKA so as to improve his own bargaining position and Harding did his best to suppress it. AKEL was banned, and eighty-five of its members detained, only to be released in January 1956. Grivas alleges that this was a device to promote popular sympathy for AKEL, and points to the fact that no member of the party's polit-buro was arrested. The AKEL newspaper was banned as well, but reappeared with the same staff under another title. It was also in October that General Papagos was replaced as Greek Prime Minis-ter by Mr Karamanlis, but that involved no change in policy on Cyprus.

Up to the time of Armitage's departure only five people had been killed, all of them Greeks; but now Grivas became more eclectic in his choice of targets. Twelve Britons and seven Greeks were to die by the end of the year. The day after Harding's arrival, Afxentiou led the Kyrenia group in a successful raid on the police armoury at Lefkonico. A big haul of explosives was made at the Mitsero mines, and another on warehouses at Famagusta produced twenty-two bren-guns, besides mortars and rocket-launchers. The first killing of a Briton came at the end of October. Lance-corporal A. R. L. Milne died when a bomb was thrown at his vehicle. Ambushes of British troops took place in November, and on the 26th a state of Emergency was declared. By the end of the year there were nine British battalions on the island, which, together with auxiliaries, brought the security forces up to about 15,000 men. The sum of £10,000 was placed on Grivas's head after the attempt on Harding's life, and curfews became the rule when EOKA attacks took place. By that time over 1,000 buildings had been damaged by EOKA, besides the killings and woundings, and it is extraordinary that the British Left should have protested with such an appearance of righteousness against the Cyprus government's Detention of Persons Law.

On 11 December, a clash with EOKA occurred at Spilia, but the first genuine gun-battle between EOKA and the security forces took place on the 15th, when Major Brian Coombe and his driver were ambushed by four EOKA-men near Soli, on the road to Polis. The driver was killed, and Coombe grabbed the wheel, driving the land-rover into a ditch. He fired back from the nearby hillside against a barrage of bullets and a couple of grenades, before running out of ammunition and going back, still under fire, for his driver's sten-gun. His attackers tried the trick of giving themselves up while leaving one of their number behind a rock with a machine-gun to shoot down Coombe when he came into the open. However, Coombe had served in Greece in 1941 and 1945, and knew what he was about. He spotted the machine-gun, and fired a burst, killing the machine-gunner, who was Charalambous Mouskos, a cousin of the Archbishop. He also wounded Andreas Zakos, whom he captured, together with Charilaos Michael. The fourth man, Marcos Drakos himself, escaped with a head-wound. This exploit earned Major Coombe the George Cross, but the Greeks celebrated the clash as 'the famous battle of Soli' and venerated the memory of Mouskos. Makarios conducted the funeral service, and a British tear-gas bomb hit the hearse during a demonstration as it passed down the street.

Harding had brought with him as an inducement a £38 million development plan, the implementation of which was conditional on the acceptance of limited self-government with the possibility of self-determination in the future. The Greek government regarded the proposals as constructive, but Makarios refused to be drawn, perhaps partly because of extremist demands within Cyprus itself. Dr Dervis, writing in *Ethniki* ten years later, was to refer to Makarios's rejection of Harding's proposals as 'a great mistake'; Radcliffe was to offer less. Meanwhile, the killings, strikes, and demonstrations continued, and the Pancyprian Gymnasium had to be closed down for a time. On 22 January, EOKA made raids throughout Cyprus, taking shotguns which had been collected at the police stations. About 800 were secured, with which Grivas was able to arm his O.K.T. groups. Using heavy lead pellets, these shotguns had a range of 80 yards (100 yards downhill).

On 15 February, Grivas suspended operations for a time, but struck again on the 29th, when Lennox-Boyd flew in on another visit to Makarios. That evening nineteen bombs went off in Nicosia.

Lennox-Boyd made no headway with Makarios, so the British tried another expedient. On 9 March, Makarios was arrested on the plane in which he was about to fly to Athens, and deported to the Seychelles, where he was to stay thirteen months.[1] With him were sent Bishop Kyprianos of Kyrenia, who had incited the people to violence and bloodshed, the Papastavros Agathangelou, organiser for EOKA, and Polycarpos Ioannides, the hater of all things British.[2] A one-week general strike followed in Cyprus, in which Petrakis Yiallouros, standard-bearer in a procession, was killed.

[1] It is wrongly stated in *Cyprus: the problem in perspective* (P.I.O. Nicosia, April 1967), p. 2, that 'negotiations were initiated between ... Makarios ... and ... Harding' in 'April, 1956 ...'. By that time Makarios was in the Seychelles.
[2] He had praised the killing of P.C. Poullis.

Harding sent a telegram of condolences to Yiallouros's brother in London. On 14 March, Eden referred to the need for Cyprus as a base and to British obligations under the Treaty of Lausanne.

After the deportation, a pamphlet was produced in Athens, entitled *Ein Erzbischoff hinter Stacheldraht,* the cover of which showed Makarios standing behind some (wholly imaginary) barbed wire. As a matter of fact, the four deportees were lodged comfortably at Sans Souci, the summer residence of the Governor of the Seychelles. Their stay is described in a good-humoured and informative book called *Makarios in Exile,* by Captain P. S. Le Geyt (the Controller of the Household) and his wife Margaret. Bishop Kyprianos was uncooperative.[1] His assistant-organiser, Ioannides, remained morose and refused to speak English (which he understood perfectly well), but indulged his love of gardening. On the other hand, Papagathangelou was as cheerful as ever, bursting frequently into song; while Makarios took the opportunity to learn English better and to explore Mahé, noting particularly the brilliant colours of the tropical sea. The whole story is a credit to Makarios, Papagathangelou and, above all, the Le Geyts, who seem to have shown unflagging patience and done their best to make the deportees' life as pleasant as possible. Nowadays Makarios refers to his exile as 'a great experience and an unforgettable event'. Some 250 children in the Seychelles have been given the name Makarios.

Shortly after His Beatitude had been temporarily translated to a different sphere, a bomb was placed in Harding's bed by Neophytos Sophocleus, an EOKA agent working at Government House as a servant. Fortunately, Harding followed the healthy habit of sleeping with his window open, so that the temperature of the room fell and the time-pencil did not work on time.

Now that Makarios was out of the way, Grivas was in sole command, making the political, as well as the military, decisions. He did not err on the side of moderation. There were 246 EOKA attacks in the last three weeks of March, and nearly as many in April. Yet in March Harding felt confident enough to reduce the rewards offered for capture of Grivas and his followers. It was in April that Harding undertook large-scale operations against EOKA in the Troödos.

Michael Caraolis and Andreas Demetriou were hanged on 10 May, the latter for wounding a British intelligence agent. Lance-corporal Gordon Hill and Private Ronnie Shilton, who had been held for some months as hostages, were then executed by EOKA as a reprisal. Their bodies were found in October 1956 and

[1] His younger brother, Renos Kyriakides, was leader of EOKA in the Pitsilia area.

February 1957 respectively. In Athens, seven people were killed and 200 injured when the authorities took action to control the disturbances resulting from the hangings, and the Mayor of Athens solemnly smashed to pieces a marble plaque dedicated to the Queen of England and her consort.

In May, Harding turned his attention specifically to the Kykko area. Grivas, of course, received warning of what was to come from his agents in the police, and retired with some of his men into an area of the Paphos Forest called Mavron Kremas (Black Chasms). On the 17th, the big sweep began. By the 20th two group-leaders were captured, and seventeen others. Among the prizes were a bren-gun and 3,000 rounds. Guided by Antonis Georghides, whose native village was Milikouri, Grivas made a dangerous night-march to a mountain in the Dipli area. Then he gave orders for diversionary attacks in other parts of Cyprus, which he thinks had the effect of drawing off some of the troops hunting him. Bombs were thrown from roof-tops in Nicosia, and one in Famagusta landed in a lorry carrying soldiers, causing deaths. In Limassol, the local EOKA-group killed two soldiers in the 'King's Arms', a local tavern.[1] Grivas and his little party were kept constantly on the move. At three in the afternoon on 9 June, they were surprised and fired on by a British patrol when about to fill their water-bottles from a stream. They managed to escape, and eventually reached another stream near Kaminaria, after being without food for thirty hours and without water for eighteen. Then they made their way via the monasteries of Troöditissa and Mesopotamos to a place in the hills a mile from Saittas, which they reached on the night of the 15th. There, says Grivas, they rested until the evening of the 17th. The point is of importance, for it was on the 16th that a fire began in the forest twelve miles to the east of Saittas. Nineteen British soldiers were burned to death and eighteen suffered bad burns. It was the worst single disaster of the Emergency. Grivas has been accused of starting the fire, and has replied that it was begun by the troops hunting him.[2] Whatever the truth of the matter, it must be conceded that a man on the run, with every likelihood of being shot or hanged when captured, might understandably light a fire to cover his retreat. Grivas now made Limassol his centre for the rest of the Emergency, using hides in two houses there.

[1] The 'Jolly Roger' in Nicosia was attacked so often that it had to close down.

[2] During the Emergency nearly thirty square miles of forest were burnt down, with a loss of 6,038,000 cubic feet of standing timber. EOKA cut the telephone lines during the Paphos area fires, so that fire-fighters were late in arriving, and EOKA was also responsible for burning down forest stations in the northern range.

On 8 August, when Zakos, Michael, and Iakovos Patatsos were hanged in the Central Prison, there were extraordinary scenes in Nicosia. Patatsos, an extremely religious youth, paid the penalty for shooting at a Turkish policeman. Mr Justice Shaw, while sentencing Zakos, had described him as a youth 'of excellent character'. All three seem to have died well, as did Caraolis and Demetriou before them and others after them.

Despite the hangings, Grivas declared a truce on 16 August, one of several during the Emergency. The object of the truces seems to have been tactical, to gain himself a breathing-space during a regroupment period (making a virtue of necessity), to demonstrate his control over his men, or to make himself appear as a moderate to the world at large. On the 22nd, he refused Harding's offer of a free passage to Greece for all members of EOKA. On the 26th, the British were able to publish excerpts from part of Grivas's diary, which had been betrayed to them by a man called Pascalis in Lysi. The revelations were damaging, so Grivas decided to pretend that they were forgeries. (As he reveals this fact in his *Memoirs*, it is permissible to wonder how much else he has misrepresented for his own reasons.) On 28 August, he resumed hostilities. A plea was made by the Greek Consul, Vlachos, for another cease-fire, but Grivas turned it down on 1 September. The Bishop of Citium and Nicos Kranidiotis, Secretary-General of the Ethnarchy, who had been mentioned in the diary, were now under house arrest.

During late August and September, 1,500 paratroops were being flown out to Cyprus, to be used in hunting EOKA and in the Suez adventure. Grivas kept up the pressure, and was ably supported by his lieutenants. One such was Polycarpos Georghadjis, who had already escaped from Camp K with Antonis Georghiades and others in January of the same year. Now he pretended to be ill, so that he was taken to the General Hospital in Nicosia for an X-ray. Four EOKA-men then burst in to free him. They shot a soldier who had a Sterling sub-machine-gun, but he fired a burst as he fell, killing two of them and a male nurse. A week later, two Famagusta leaders escaped from the detention camp at Pyla. On 8 September, a raid was made on the armoury of the Kyrenia police station. However, a successful ambush of two army lorries led to a sweep in the Kyrenia range which resulted in the capture of its perpetrator, Tassos Sophocleus, and five of his men. On the 21st, Michael Koutsoftas and Andreas Panayides were hanged for killing British airmen, and Stelios Mavrommatis for firing on some.

There is no doubt that the British presence in Cyprus greatly facilitated the attack on Suez. When the French troops poured in,

Grivas befriended them, as might be expected of one who owed the French army so much. However, a German journalist who went about with a placard on his back reading 'Don't shoot, I am German' was advised to remove it. EOKA might be sensitive about the implication that its victims were usually shot in the back.

Towards the British Grivas behaved differently, despite the anxiety of the Greek government not to embarrass them too much at that juncture. The main runway at Akrotiri was blown up a few days before Suez, and could not be repaired in time. During 'Black November' there were 416 acts of violence and thirty-four people died, more than in any previous month of the Emergency. After the collapse of the Suez operation, Harding had more troops available, and in December he began to strike some telling blows at EOKA.

Mr Duncan Sandys, as Minister of Defence, had now visited Cyprus and advised the British government that the whole of the island was no longer needed (though it is hard to see in what way the Middle Eastern situation had changed in Britain's favour since Eden had insisted that all of it was needed). Now Lord Radcliffe, the eminent jurist, arrived to suggest a solution to the problem. On 19 December, he put forward his proposals. He had decided that none of the prerequisites existed for federation or partition in Cyprus, as desired by the Turks. The island was too small, for one thing, and the minority was not concentrated in one particular area.[1] He therefore suggested that there should be a unitary state governed by a legislative body consisting of twenty-four Greek elected members, six members elected by the Turks, and six more appointed by the Governor to represent the other minorities. The Cypriotes were to govern themselves in all save foreign affairs, defence, and internal security. There were to be safeguards for the Turks, and a promise to review the possibility of self-determination in the future, but the Cypriote Greeks were warned of the possibility of partition in that case. The Radcliffe proposals envisaged the release of Makarios if he denounced EOKA, but he refused to discuss them while in the Seychelles. In addition, he had reservations over the proposed extent of British internal control. For instance, would the proposed British control over the police be temporary or permanent? At that time Greece felt that independence under majority rule was the least she could expect to gain for Cyprus. Therefore, she rejected the Radcliffe proposals before they had been proposed to the

---

[1] The different Ottoman *millets* had administered their own affairs in the same areas, but the system fell apart when the ruling people lost control.

Greek-Cypriote people.[1] In May 1968, *Kypros* was to refer to the Harding and Radcliffe proposals as examples of opportunities lost when people were afraid to speak out.

To begin with, Turkey was favourably disposed towards the Radcliffe proposals, but she later reverted to a policy of federation or partition for Cyprus. The *Kıbrıs Türktür* organisation (now run by Necati Sağer), which had never seriously expected to gain the reversion of the whole of Cyprus to Turkey, was very much encouraged when Lennox-Boyd, in explaining the Radcliffe proposals to the House of Commons, first mentioned the possibility of partition if they were not accepted. Tension had already risen between the two communities in Cyprus over the killing of Turks by EOKA, and now it rose again. After eight killings of Turks in April, May, and June 1956, the number of Turks killed in the rest of the year was only three. The reason seems to be that the Turks had begun to riot indiscriminately whenever one of their number was killed. In May, they killed two Greeks. Prompt riot-reaction acted as a deterrent, for otherwise Grivas would have been tempted to take more action against those who provided the British with so many active police. Grivas's initial determination to leave the Turks alone, provided they did not intervene on the side of the British, does not explain his forbearance in this matter. Violent riots after two killings in January and February 1957 brought the Turks immunity until the next November, when another Turk was killed.

In fact, so Mr Foley informs us, 'although Eoka had orders not to attack Turks, it was difficult to distinguish between an armed British policeman and a Turk wearing identical dark-blue uniform; by night it was impossible'.[2] One can only conclude that regrettable mistakes might have been avoided if the authorities had been considerate enough to put luminous distinguishing-marks on the backs of the British police.

According to Byford-Jones, 214 people were killed in 1956, the overwhelming majority by EOKA. One young journalist, whose identity was strongly suspected at the time, had murdered his victims, thrown his gun to a girl accompanying him, and then photographed them for the press.[3] A total of 11,816 persons had been dealt with by military courts, including 357 juveniles. These measures helped to damp down terrorism, though they also helped to polarise the population against the British. Curfews, however, were of little use, for bombs continued to be thrown at patrolling

---

[1] The Turkish government's unilateral rejection of Makarios's thirteen points in 1963, before they had been proposed to the Turkish community as a whole, offers a parallel.
[2] Foley, *Legacy of Strife*, p. 89.
[3] See Dudley Barker, op. cit., p. 145.

troops within the areas under curfew. From December 1956 onwards, British Intelligence improved radically, as information began
to come in from the interrogation centres. The EOKA town gangs
were mostly cleaned up, and so were many villages ones. In fact,
the whole organisation was dealt a blow which temporarily crippled
it. On 25 February 1957, Harding had thousands of leaflets scattered abroad which stated that the days of EOKA were numbered.[1]
By April, sixty EOKA-men were facing capital charges and sixteen
had been killed, including one who was executed.

The new General Officer Commanding was Major-General D. A.
Kendrew, whose success at mountain sweeps was such that Grivas
was to criticise the military mistake of replacing him with less able
men.

In January 1957, Marcos Drakos was shot in the heart by the
Suffolk Regiment in the Troödos. Polycarpos Georghadjis and
Argyros Karademas, a handler of explosives, were caught in the
house of a village policeman at Omodhos when a fire was lit in the
hearth above their hide. Lack of oxygen forced them out. Later,
Georghadjis escaped yet again, earning himself the journalistic
nickname of 'Houdini'. In February came the turn of Nicos
Sampson, who was caught in hiding near Dhali with a sten-gun
and ammunition. On the 17th, Stylianos Lenas, whose skill in
manufacturing bombs had earned him the nickname 'Krupp', was
badly wounded in a clash with troops at Pelendri. He died in hospital six weeks later.

On 3 March came the turn of Afxentiou, then aged twenty-eight,
with £5,000 on his head. On the last day of 1956 his group had
been surprised and one of his men killed. After being harried for
weeks in conditions of extreme cold, he took refuge in a hide near
the Monastery of Machaeras with four of his followers, Avgustis
Efstathiou, Phidian Symeonides, Andreas Stylianou, and Antonis
Papadopoulos. They were provided with food by the Abbot, Irineos,
who also lent them books. Hitherto, EOKA had usually given up
in circumstances where escape was impossible—but Afxentiou did
not. He ordered his men to surrender and stayed to fight it out
alone, even though he was wounded by a grenade. Efstathiou was
sent back to his leader with a message telling him to surrender,
but stayed to fight beside him. They continued the fight for at
least eight hours, from dawn to 2 p.m. A soldier, Corporal Brown
of Leeds, had been killed on approaching the hide, and the British
commander was probably right not to risk his men unnecessarily.
However, tear-gas and shooting would have been preferable to the

---

[1] Harding had made the same claim on 1 January 1956 (Grivas, *Memoirs,*
p. 60).

method finally adopted. Petrol was poured down on the hide,[1] and Efstathiou was forced out. Afxentiou tried to get out himself, and then, very understandably, shot himself. It was a question of choosing the preferable death. Altogether, it was a fine example of sustained courage, witnessed by a number of reporters, and for the Greeks the effect was enhanced by the evidence of Afxentiou's character. He had been solicitous in promoting the education of his men, and on one occasion had even pardoned an informer, which Grivas would never have done. Antonis Georghiades,[2] the theologian, now became second-in-command to Grivas, in succession to Afxentiou.

On 14 March, Evagoras Pallekarides, aged eighteen, was hanged for having a gun (Grivas says guns) on a donkey. He was certainly a member of EOKA, and the authorities stated, though they did not prove, that he had killed someone. However, the gun was heavily greased and, in the opinion of a British expert, unfit to fire. It is sad that the prerogative of mercy was not exercised in this case. But the case should be seen in perspective. Killings had been taking place within sight of scores of persons who refused to identify the culprits.

The measures taken by Harding and Kendrew were highly effective. In the third year of the Emergency, beginning on 1 April 1957, it appears from Byford-Jones's tables that no Britons were killed, and only one Turk and nine Greeks. However, a nucleus of EOKA had been left in existence, and Grivas was able to rebuild the organisation.

Other factors also contributed, though less importantly, to Grivas's announcement, on the day of Pallekarides's hanging, that he would suspend operations if Makarios was released. On the home front, the army was becoming exasperated and might well terrorise the civilian population enough to offset the fear of EOKA. On the international front, he had succeeded in bringing the Cyprus problem to the attention of the world, and the U.N. resolution of 26 February was there to prove it. John Clerides, the last remaining member of the Cyprus Governor's Executive Council, had resigned long before, so that there was no vestige of representation left in the Colony. In default of a united Europe, Suez had shown that Britain could not function as a power without American help, and the commonest attitude of those American politicians who were under pressure from Greek constituents was exemplified in a

---

[1] Thus Byford-Jones (op. cit., p. 112), Grivas (*Memoirs*, p. 112), and the author's Greek informants. Dudley Barker (op. cit., p. 151) and Foley (*Legacy of Strife*, p. 92) speak of explosive charges being used.
[2] He later became Minister of Public Works.

20—C

statement by the Mayor of New York : 'Our hearts go out to those Greeks in Cyprus who are fighting for what we fought for in this country'. Also, Britain was under pressure from her multi-racial Commonwealth to placate majority opinion at the United Nations. Macmillan, who had replaced Eden as Prime Minister after the Suez débâcle, therefore took the decision to release the four deportees, though he did not for the present allow them to return to Cyprus. On 29 March, Lord Salisbury resigned from the government in protest against the release.

Makarios and his companions flew into Athens on 17 April and received a heroes' welcome. He immediately contacted Azinas, and in the following month asked for bilateral negotiations on the basis of U.N. Resolution 1013 (XI). But the British government was in no mood to treat with him alone. The Greek government behaved in a moderate fashion, despite irritation over the discovery of wiretapping activities which had been carried on by members of the British Embassy staff for two years past, and over the attempt by Britain at the United Nations to pillory Greece for aiding and abetting terrorism in Cyprus.

Meanwhile, Grivas was facing great difficulties. On 6 June, he was very nearly caught, when soldiers opened the door of the sink cupboard leading to his hide. (They were distracted by the offer of a drink.) Also, the Greek government was putting pressure on him to make the cease-fire permanent.

The preliminary debates for a further review of the Cyprus question began at the United Nations in the autumn of 1957, and Makarios flew to New York in order to exercise his influence. Grivas meanwhile brought the pot to the boil again by having six Greeks struck down, and promised to leave Cyprus when *Enosis* was attained.

In November, Harding retired on completion of the two-year tour of service previously agreed upon. He had relaxed the Emergency regulations, but without any response from Grivas. When asked to call for a cessation of EOKA violence, Makarios had characteristically responded by deploring all violence, including the British.

After Harding's departure EOKA managed to hole a merchant-ship, the *African Prince,* below the water-line. At Akrotiri, an EOKA-agent with a job on the base planted two bombs which destroyed five jet planes, worth £4.5 million. The perpetrator went on working at the base for another two months afterwards.

Harding's successor was Sir Hugh Foot, previously Governor of Jamaica and Colonial Secretary for Cyprus from 1943 to 1945,[1]

[1] See above, p. 226.

who arrived on 3 December. His appointment was a clear indication that the British government wished to withdraw from most of Cyprus; for then, as now, he was 'antagonistic to the concept of British rule'.[1] His aim was to relax tensions in Cyprus by creating for himself a publicity 'image' of bonhomie. To this end, he lighted a candle for peace in a Greek-Orthodox church, went out to the villages on horseback, and argued in the coffee-shops. Foley tells us that he was wont 'to confide in Greek Cypriots with a jolly laugh : "If I were not a British Governor, I would probably be an EOKA leader" '.[2] For some reason, such an attitude failed to inspire confidence in most of those serving under him, but they nevertheless did their best to carry out his orders.

Foot appealed to Grivas for 'a credit of time', and at Christmas 1957 released one hundred detainees, including eleven women. But, in common with the Turks (and many of the British) Grivas disliked and distrusted Foot, far preferring Harding. In 1958, he again went onto the offensive. After the surrender of Ashiotis the authorities had some idea of what was coming.

Grivas's idea was to extend his passive resistance measures to include a boycott of British goods, and accompany them with widespread sabotage. The notion of a boycott was no doubt encouraged by the success of such limited measures as the boycott of newspapers lukewarm to *Enosis* and that of British examinations. In 1956, there had been 352 examinees at the British School in Nicosia, in 1957 sixty-one, and in 1958 a mere sixteen. But Grivas also wished to stimulate the local production of replacements for British goods. In a country with large natural resources a boycott either way may actually be stimulative in effect, but a country like Cyprus needs a long time and a certain amount of help in order to become self-supporting.

In the summer of 1956, Grivas had created PEKA (the Political Committee of the Cyprus Struggle), which had since organised demonstrations, arranged hiding-places for EOKA, and prepared for acts of violence by collecting information and shadowing government agents. Now it became particularly active, as did the A.E.A.M. There was also a youth movement known as A.N.E., which threw stones through the windows of boycott-breaking shopkeepers and published an underground magazine called *Reveille*.

Sabotage began on 4 March 1958, and the boycott on the 6th. Grivas has made exaggerated claims for the latter, but it had a strong puritan element which was not an asset to the revolutionary cause. Such measures as tearing British-made dresses from the backs

---

[1] Lord Caradon (formerly Sir Hugh Foot), *Irish Times*, 22 January, 1968.
[2] *Legacy of Strife*, p. 113.

of Cypriote women aroused resentment, and although Grivas managed to stop the government lottery by forbidding the buying of its tickets and blowing up its machines, he was unable to prevent many of his countrymen from participating in the British football-pools. Most important, businessmen who feared that Britain might take economic reprisal measures appealed to Makarios, who arranged a compromise whereby existing stocks of British goods might be sold. In fact, the businessmen need not have worried. The Conservative administration refused to take the obvious (and probably highly effective) step of a counter-boycott.

By now AKEL had come out openly in favour of the independence line, and Grivas's pamphlet 'The Communist Leadership against the Cyprus Struggle' helped to widen their breach with the Enotists, as did Grivas's killing of prominent left-wingers.

The truth is that the tide was now beginning to turn against Grivas, mainly for economic reasons. During 1958 more and more Cypriotes were becoming tired of the whole business. The G.N.P. declined from £86.6 million in 1957 to £84 million in 1958, and by 1960 had fallen to £78.4 million. Revenue from agriculture, mining, and manufacturing had fallen, and by 1960/61 trade and services (mostly to British troops) had risen to 35 per cent of the GNP, with trade declining by 3.2 per cent per annum at constant 1950 prices, but between 1958 and 1960 *per capita* income fell, in real terms, by 13.8 per cent.

Foot obtained a temporary respite from EOKA sabotage attacks when he wrote to Grivas in April 1958 asking for them to cease and offering to meet him alone at a place of his choosing. Grivas stopped the sabotage for a short time, but regarded the offer of a meeting as a trick. Over subsequent months casualties again climbed steeply as Grivas reverted to his former full-scale terror. In May, 'Operation Kingfisher' was launched in the southern Troödos, and Grivas was said to have escaped by moving with a flock of sheep and goats. In fact, he seems to have remained in Limassol. Searchers often walked over the roof of his hide, but he was never found.

The Turks Intervene

It was in 1958 that the Turks intervened decisively in the Cyprus struggle, replacing Britain as one of the two main participants. On the international front, Turkish politicians were pressing for partition. Averoff admits that in September 1956, when talking to the Turkish Ambassador İksel about the Turkish demand for partition of Cyprus on a fifty-fifty basis, he may have given the impression that, although such a solution was unacceptable, the Greeks might consider a more favourable ratio.[1] In February 1957, Averoff put forward a plan for a customs union linking Turkey, Greece, and Cyprus in the event of *Enosis*. The Cypriote Turks were to have dual nationality and exemption from conscription. The Turks did not accept the plan, and their distrust of Greek motives was heightened in March 1957, when Averoff spoke to the Greek Parliament of the 'manoeuvre of a temporary independence' for Cyprus.[2] On the 30th of the same month, Makarios made the first of many statements underlining the need to grant the Turkish community special minority rights. In December 1957, Selim Sarper, Turkish representative at the United Nations, referred to the precedent of the Aland islands, which had been awarded to Finland by the League of Nations after the Great War on geopolitical grounds (despite the fact that their 21,000 Swedish inhabitants had voted overwhelmingly in favour of joining Sweden). His object was to show that a case existed for perpetrating a similar injustice where Cyprus was concerned. As an alternative, he pointed to the partition of the Trieste area between Italy and Yugoslavia.[3] An attempt by Eisenhower to patch up the Menderes-Karamanlis quarrel was of no avail.

The Cypriote Turks were angry over Harding's replacement by Foot, whose views were soon known. There was rioting and arson in Nicosia on 9 December 1957. On 26 January 1958, Foot and Selwyn Lloyd went to Ankara for a four-day conference, ostensibly in connexion with the Baghdad Pact. Meanwhile, the pro-partitionist Cypriote Turks rioted again, and seven of them were killed by the security forces in Nicosia and Famagusta. The British never took such a terrible toll of the demonstrators in any Greek riot over the four years of the Emergency, and Zorlu's anger with Foot is therefore understandable. On his return, Foot confided to Foley that he had 'looked . . . into the pit of hell'.[4]

As the Turkish political campaign gathered strength, Makarios, who was still not allowed to return to Cyprus, grew perturbed. On 3 March 1958, he wrote to Grivas suggesting that 'we should throw a grenade or two from some balcony and give them [viz the Turks] a sharp lesson, so that they will not dare to gather in mobs in future'. On 18 April, he repeated the suggestion. Grivas was irritated at this interference, and when the Archbishop again

[1] See Stephens, op. cit., p. 149.
[2] See Xydis, op. cit., p. 53.
[3] Ibid., p. 334.
[4] Foley, *Legacy of Strife*, p. 112.

repeated his suggestion, he broke off contact with him for some time.[1]

The Turkish government now decided to lean heavily on the Greeks, and a Cypriote-Turkish underground organisation called *Volkan* (Volcano), modelled on EOKA, was ready to do its bidding. It was led by Rauf Denktaş, an admirer of Menderes. *Volkan* was to be officially proscribed in November 1957, but survived into the independence period. The fighting arm of *Volkan* was called the *Türk Müdafaa*[2] *Teşkilatı* (Turkish Defence Organisation), known as the T.M.T. for short.

At the Yassıada trial of the Menderes government in 1960, Aydın Konuralp, of the Turkish-Cypriote weekly *Nacak,* was to testify that news of a coming massacre by the Greeks was fabricated in the summer of 1958 in order to incite the Cypriote Turks into action. This is borne out by the evidence of Emin Dirvana, who was Turkish Ambassador to Cyprus after independence. He states that on 7 June 1958 Turkish terrorists planted a bomb outside Turkey's information office in Nicosia. This was the signal for hundreds of Turks to go on the rampage shouting 'Partition or Death'. On the following day their numbers grew, and the Olympiakos Club, among other places, was burnt down. This time the authorities seem to have gone to the other extreme, and initially let the Turks have too much of their own way. Troops were soon working round the clock to protect both sides but, even so, when the riots subsided two months later, fifty-six Greeks and fifty-three Turks had died. Greeks were driven from the largely Turkish suburb of Omorphita, just as Turks were to be over five years later. Most Greek dwellings in Lefka were burnt down, and some in Paphos. Dr İhsan Ali states that Turkish irregulars forced Turkish villagers to leave their homes in the Paphos district in preparation for partition, but if that is the case, it is hard to explain why Turks who left (or rather were driven out of) mixed villages in different parts of Cyprus could not return to seventeen of them even after independence.

On 19 June came Macmillan's response to the situation. He proposed an 'adventure in partnership' based on proposals he had worked out with Foot. It involved deferring a solution to the Cyprus problem for seven years. Cypriote Greeks and Turks were meanwhile to administer the separate municipalities which now existed *de facto,* with a separate House of Representatives for

[1] Grivas, *Memoirs,* pp. 135–6. One wonders what His Beatitude's reaction would have been if the British or the Turks had adopted his novel method of crowd-control.
[2] Sometimes the M is said to stand for *Mukavemet,* 'Resistance'.

each community. The governing council was to consist of the British Governor (who would retain control over external affairs, defence, and internal security), four Greek and two Turkish representatives, and a representative each of the mainland Greek and Turkish governments. Cypriote Greeks and Turks were to have Greek and Turkish nationality respectively as well as British. The Greek government rejected the plan, as did Makarios, and Turkey, while willing to support the British initiative, still preferred the idea of partition.[1]

In July, Grivas struck back against the Turks without relaxing pressure on the British, and Foot's detention of some 2,000 Greek suspects had next to no effect.[2] On 4 August, in response to appeals from the Prime Ministers of Greece, Turkey, and Britain, Grivas declared a cease-fire. The T.M.T. followed suit two days later. Meanwhile, the United States, the International Monetary Fund, and the O.E.E.C. arranged a massive aid programme to help Turkey out of financial difficulties caused by overspending on the part of the Menderes régime.

The August cease-fire soon broke down, for the authorities continued to hunt Grivas's men, killing at least four of them and suffering losses themselves. Grivas ordered his 'execution' squads back to work, and resentment in the British army increased once more. At Liopetri on 2 September four EOKA-fighters, Xanthos Samaras, Andreas Karios, Elias Papakyriakos, and Photis Pittas, made a stand reminiscent of that by Afxentiou and Efstathiou. Cornered in a solidly-built barn, they fought for three hours against great odds. Finally, the place was set on fire with petrol and they were killed as they came out. Such deaths recall that of Nicocreon in the fourth century B.C.

Foley records an instance of British army exasperation at Kathykas. After one of their number had been killed and another wounded in an ambush, some Argyll and Sutherland Highlanders made a search in which a man was shot dead (he had knifed two of them when they burst into his house) and other villagers were injured. The mayor alleged that a woman had been raped.[3] Mrs Barbara Castle, Vice-Chairman of the Labour Party, flew in from Athens four days later, and visited Kathykas among other places. She rightly expressed her shock at the injuries sustained by the villagers, but failed to show an equivalent concern for the troops. She had visited Makarios in Athens and went back to see him after leaving Cyprus. On 17 September, Makarios informed the

[1] See Xydis, op. cit., pp. 668–9.
[2] Only 60 Turks were detained.
[3] *Legacy of Strife*, pp. 136–7.

Greek government that he would accept independence for Cyprus after a period of self-government under United Nations auspices, in other words, the plan mooted by Krishna Menon eighteen months before. On the 22nd, he authorised Mrs Castle to give the news to the press. Then he wrote a letter to Grivas explaining the reasons for his decision : the need to scotch the Macmillan plan, the state of British public opinion, American support for Britain, and the refusal of the U.N. to consider any solution but independence. In reply, Grivas stated his opposition to the idea, and Bishop Kyprianos was understandably irritated by Makarios's change of line. On 14 October, Averoff wrote to Grivas complaining obliquely about the murder of Mrs Cutliffe, which had increased coolness in the Labour Party. (As Foley explains in connexion with Gaitskell's disowning of Mrs Castle over her remarks at Kathykas, a General Election was in the offing.)

In September and October the EOKA campaign was intensified. On 26 September came an attempt on the life of General Kendrew. A mine was exploded a second or two after Kendrew's car had gone over it. The escorting landrover received the main effect of the explosion, and one soldier was killed, two injured. On 11 October, Kendrew was replaced as G.O.C. by Major-General Kenneth Darling. Darling had some good notions, dressing troops in gym-shoes and jerseys, and providing them with torches. Sometimes he had soldiers playing dead to act as decoys. He offered British civilians arms with which to defend themselves, and many accepted them. Some tactical successes were registered during his time in Cyprus. For example, on 19 November Kyriakos Matsis was cornered in a hide at Dhikomo. (He ordered his two companions to surrender, and warned the troops that he would come out firing. He was blown up with a grenade.) Unfortunately, Darling claimed to have nearly broken the back of EOKA, but the large quantities of arms turned in by EOKA at the end of the Emergency made the claim look rather previous.[1]

Two police superintendents, known to the press as the 'Heavenly Twins', were sent out from Scotland Yard to overhaul intelligence, but they left, apparently dissatisfied, after a few weeks.

After a bomb had killed two airmen in a NAAFI canteen, Foot at long last dismissed over 5,000 Greeks employed in British camps and bases. Many of their places were taken by girls recruited in England or from service families. Grivas characterises this move as

---

[1] On one day alone, 13 March 1959, EOKA turned in over 600 guns, 2,230 bombs, 2,230 pounds of explosives, thousands of rounds of ammunition, 22 sten-guns, and a mortar (Byford-Jones, op. cit., p. 160). Many other weapons also came to light.

'heartless', yet he records many acts of sabotage carried out by just those employees. For instance, shortly before, on 20 October, a Canberra worth £800,000 had been destroyed by one such person. Besides, Grivas mentions having British girls dismissed from their employment with Cypriote firms as one of the successes of his passive resistance campaign.

Although there was plenty of fight left in EOKA, the independence compromise was being more and more widely canvassed at the United Nations, and Grivas was under pressure from Averoff and Makarios to declare a truce. After Foot, at the request of Zorlu and Averoff, had reprieved two EOKA killers on the point of execution, Grivas ceased fire on Christmas Eve. The Turkish and Greek Foreign Ministers met in Paris between 17 and 22 January 1959, and on 5 February they met again, this time in Zurich, in attendance on their respective Prime Ministers. The agreements they arrived at will be discussed *in extenso* in the next chapter. By that time, Britain had abdicated her position as one of the major parties to the dispute and was content to let others work out a compromise, provided she could keep bases in Cyprus. Grivas was now politically outmanoeuvred, and under pressure to maintain the cease-fire he had declared. To his chagrin, EOKA was not properly represented among those who went to advise Makarios at the Lancaster House Conference and voted 27 to 8 that the terms should be accepted. Tassos Papadopoulos, the young Nicosia leader of PEKA, was present, but on his own initiative. Afterwards, Makarios wrote Grivas a conciliatory letter, informing him, apparently in misleading terms, of what had been agreed, and mentioning nothing about the bases granted to the British. The Bishop of Citium, in putting the case to Grivas, gave it as his 'personal opinion' that Britain would soon vacate the bases 'and even suggested that under international law Cyprus might be able to denounce the very treaty which made her independent and thus get the British out!'[1] Averoff also failed to send data on the base areas when he wrote Grivas his letter of explanation. Makarios returned to Cyprus on 1 March, unwelcomed by EOKA.

Although most of the Cypriotes were by now heartily sick of the struggle, a large minority, who joined the short-lived EDMA (United Democratic Renascence Front), was still willing to fight for *Enosis*. The Bishop of Kyrenia returned on 15 February, and the author well remembers the enthusiasm generated by his Enotist speech to a crowd of several thousand in Kyrenia itself. A Greek shepherd whom the author met while climbing in the nearby mountains

[1] Grivas, *Memoirs*, p. 190.

informed him that 8 million Greeks would have no difficulty in defeating 30 million Turks.[1] Back in Kyrenia, he saw a teen-age soldier lean out of a British army lorry and pull down a string of small Greek flags. In a flash, the lorry and its sheepish-looking occupants were surrounded by a gesticulating crowd. Usually, however, it was Greeks who provoked the British, spitting, barring their way, tripping them up, and following them down the street with jeers and insults.

For a time Grivas considered defying the Greek government and fighting a civil war if need be within Cyprus itself (the classic situation in which the revolutionary has to fight his more moderate allies who are tired of the struggle), but the difficulty he would then have in obtaining continued arms supplies decided him regretfully against it. After some bargaining, he got a total amnesty for his followers on 8 March, and moved up from Limassol to Nicosia on the following day. It was also on 9 March that he explained in a leaflet to the people why he had decided against continuation of the struggle, because of his fear of the evils resulting from 'national divisions'. One passage omitted at the request of Makarios reads as follows : '. . . it would be difficult for me to achieve any more alone, faced with an all-powerful Empire'. Foot had just made a speech, in a voice trembling with emotion, which certainly did not strike the author as coming from the representative of an 'all-powerful' institution. He was proud of the settlement and professed to be hopeful for the future.

On the evening of 9 March, Grivas met some fifty members of EOKA, many of whom he had never known before save as code-names. Not until the 17th, the day of his departure from Cyprus (one of the conditions agreed upon by Ankara and Athens) did he appear in public. He was slightly emaciated, yellowed from his time in the darkness, but otherwise well. The Greek government had sent him an escort of four officers who had served under him in Greece, and British officers were among those who went to see him off at the airfield. An escort of R.A.F. Javelins was provided, and he flew into Athens for a hero's welcome. He was made a Lieutenant-General and granted full pay for life at that rank. Henceforth he was to be known as one who had added a new dimension to guerrilla warfare. His career was by no means over, and George Papandreou was to express a view not uncommon in Greece when he said of Grivas that he 'became glorious by hiding and infamous by appearing in public'. Many will dissent from the first half of this epigram but, moral questions apart, they can

---

[1] In an Ankara night-club during the same month a Turk in his cups told me that now was the time to cut the throats of the Greeks (cf. above, pp. 244–5).

hardly deny his extraordinary toughness, singlemindedness, and organising ability.

The island was finding a new status, not in the security of union with Greece, but in the unstable compromise of a negotiated independence. No words seem more appropriate than those of a French reference to Cyprus adapted by Durrell: 'vaisseau qui a rompu ses amarres et s'en va à la dérive sur les mélancoliques couloirs de l'histoire du Moyen-Orient, balotté par les vents hasardeux de la passion et des préjugés'.[1]

[1] Cf. Lawrence Durrell, *Bitter Lemons* (London: Faber, 1967 edn), p. 204; Georges Ténékidès, 'Chypre', *Cyprus Today,* vol. IV, nos 1–4 (Jan.–July 1966), p. 20.

Chapter 7

Cyprus since Independence

The Community Problem

POLITICAL ATTITUDES EVOLVE with events, and sometimes very rapidly, but the essential, genetically-determined characteristics of each ethnic group change much more slowly, and in turn determine the nature of its political evolution. Because the groups are complexes of interbred individuals, each group differing in history and composition, it follows that their political attitudes will also tend to differ. Since the events of December 1963, the Greek and Turkish communities of Cyprus have been polarised in open enmity. As we have seen, this enmity is nothing new, and has its roots deep in the past. Of course, during the British period, and to a lesser extent during the Turkish, the two communities frequently cooperated, and one has tried to show the nature and extent of that cooperation. But the removal of British power allowed the basic differences between them to come more and more into the open. What is fundamentally the same phenomenon has also been observed in other ex-colonial countries, though the argument that the imperial powers themselves created the present tensions will not hold water. At most, they exacerbated tensions already in existence, as when the British made use of a disproportionate number of reliable Turkish police during the Cyprus Emergency. The fact is that when imperial order breaks down, each ethnic group tries to improve its own position, inevitably at the expense of others and, in the absence of a powerful arbiter, their aspirations are very difficult to reconcile.

Official Greek propaganda looks back to a mythical golden age when Greeks and Turks lived together in complete amity and brotherly love, and implies that as soon as a handful of Turkish terrorists are removed the two communities will fall in happily and march off in quick time for the Enotist millennium. The chief spokesman for this view is himself a Turk, Dr Ihsan Ali of Paphos. He may be visited in company with the local Greek District Officer, and his pleasant house in the suburbs is permanently guarded by efficient-looking Greek police armed with automatic weapons. He argues that relations between the two communities were good during and after the First World War, despite the fact that Greece and Turkey were on different sides, and also during the Second, although Greece was a combatant and Turkey was not. He contends that all the differences between the communities stem from the British policy of divide-and-rule during the Emergency, and conveniently ignores the consistent opposition of most Turks to *Enosis* throughout the British period. It is true that the British, for tactical reasons, permitted the separation of municipalities during the Emergency, but the Turks had always complained that the Greek municipal majorities regarded the development of the Turkish quarters as of secondary importance. At that time, Dr Ali was himself a municipal councillor in his native city and, together with other Turks, protested against the separation.[1] Despite earlier inter-communal clashes, he claims to have retained some influence over his fellow-countrymen until the troubles of June 1958 and the killings at Geunyeli, and states that these (undoubtedly hostile) Turkish acts killed the possibility of a compromise. However, this is to forget the grounds of enmity which already existed, owing to the steadfast Turkish opposition to *Enosis* and the killing by EOKA of Turkish police. Dr Ali's interpretation of the events of 1963 to 1964 has been denied by his own daughter, and his claim that eighty per cent of the Turkish community are now privately supporters of his views may be dismissed as disingenuous nonsense. The author was privileged to meet three such persons, ostensibly chosen at random, in the presence of the District Officer in Paphos-Ktima, and the identities of two of them had been accurately predicted by the leadership in the Turkish quarter. There is, one believes, another in Limassol, who may be visited on application to the local D.C. The few exceptions have been spotlighted to confuse the issue, but their main significance is that they run counter to the norm. Whatever the propagandists may say, the average Cypriote Greek knows very well that a large majority of the Turkish community have a long-standing determination to thwart his Enotist aspirations, and when he reads in *Makhi* of the 'poisonous Turkish viper in our bosom'[2] the message finds a ready echo.

The Constitution of 1960

The main bones of contention between the Greeks and Turks of Cyprus are the Zurich and London Agreements of 1959, which

[1] Turkish officials deny that Dr Ali acted officially.
[2] *Makhi,* 2 November 1966.

brought the Emergency to an end, and the resultant constitution, with its accompanying treaties of Alliance and Guarantee. The members of the 'Alliance' were Greece, Turkey, and the Republic of Cyprus, while the guarantors were Greece, Turkey, and the United Kingdom. Under the constitution, both *Enosis* and partition were specifically excluded, on the principle that fundamental issues, once taken out of party politics, cease to be fundamental. It was the decision of President Makarios to alter or set aside certain key provisions of the constitution that precipitated the events of December 1963.

Talks between the Prime Ministers and Foreign Ministers of Greece and Turkey took place in Zurich, and agreement was reached on 11 February 1959. There followed a conference at Lancaster House in London which began on 17 February. It was attended by the representatives of Greece, Turkey, and the United Kingdom, and also by Archbishop Makarios and Dr Küçük. Guidelines had already been laid down at Zurich, so Makarios was presented with very much of a *fait accompli*. The London Agreement was signed on 19 February. In December of the same year there was a presidential election in Cyprus. Makarios became President-elect with 144,501 votes, as against 71,753 cast for his rival, John Clerides, Q.C. This 73-year-old man, the father and opponent of Glafcos, represented the 'Democratic Union', an alliance of the Left with some right-wing elements. Dr Küçük, on a separate Turkish vote, became Vice-President-elect unopposed. However, there were further difficulties, and the constitution arising out of the Agreements did not come into effect until 16 August 1960.

At Zurich and London, the respective strategic importance of Greece and Turkey had been weighed in the balance and, Turkey proving the weightier as corner-stone of the NATO alliance, the Cypriote Turks acquired powers out of proportion to their numbers. Although less than 19 per cent of the population, they obtained a legal right to 30 per cent of all posts in the public service (as far as possible at all grades of the hierarchy), 30 per cent of all jobs in the security forces (40 per cent for the time being, in order not to discharge any of those serving in the full-time police during the Emergency), and 40 per cent of those in the projected 2,000-man army. The support given to these inequitable ratios by the Greek Foreign Minister, Evangelos Averoff-Tossizza, at the London Conference on 18 February 1959 does not affect the matter. The more inequitable advantages and safeguards a minority obtains in a democratic society, the greater is its danger, owing to the resentment of the majority.

As regards the public service, the Turks point out that the proportion of Turkish employees had considerably declined since Great Britain annexed the island in 1914, and claim that this was because of persistent discrimination on the part of the Greeks, who came to control most of the selection boards.[1] They say that many promising young Turks therefore had to find employment abroad, because the Turkish community boasted a higher proportion of university degrees than the Greek. However, according to figures for July 1960 supplied by the Turks themselves,[2] they were represented in the large departments of Medicine, Lands and Surveys, and Agriculture, in the proportions of 1 :4.5, 1 :3, and 1 :3 respectively, though mostly, it is claimed, in the lower grades. In other departments the proportion of Turks fell below their population ratio, thus : Forestry, 1 : 10 (most of the woods being in the Greek areas), Public Works, 1 : 10, Administration, 1 : 7.6, Antiquities, 1 : 7.5, and Water Development, 1 : 23. The overall proportion of Turkish civil servants, according to one's personal estimate, was 1 : 5.2. While this was under the 1 : 4.2 ratio one would expect from the population figures alone, and probably insufficient to provide all the separate communal services, the rise to a permanent Turkish 3 : 7 ratio was altogether excessive. Cypriote Greeks have pointed out that the quota system puts a premium on a candidate's race rather than his abilities, and they are quite right. It is a built-in disadvantage of egalitarian multi-ethnic societies. But such an objection comes ill from people whose own Foreign Minister strongly supports those who wish to discriminate in favour of the Negro minority in the United States. The Greeks have a stronger case when they point out that the Turks in Turkey would never consider according separate status to their 1,847,674 Kurds (officially designated as 'Mountain-Turks') or their 364,000 Arabs.[3] Nor are the languages of these minorities accorded any official status.

Strangely enough, the Turks' insistence on a yet higher ratio in the proposed army was more understandable, for they had good reason to fear the Greek armed bands. It was their new official powers which were excessive for a minority group on which the prosperity of all did not depend, and the Greeks particularly resented their power to block legislation. The Vice-President,

[1] The Greek reply to this is that the Colonial government actually made the appointments.
[2] The Turkish Case, 70:30, and the Greek Tactics (Nicosia : Press Liaison Office of the Turkish Communal Chamber, 1963), p. 4.
[3] Figures according to the Turkish 'mother-tongue' census of 1960. Many observers believe that in reality the number of Kurdish-speakers is nearly double that given.

elected separately by the Turkish-Cypriote community and empowered to nominate the Turkish Ministers, was not only accorded the same functions as the President himself, promulgating laws and appointing high officials jointly with him, but even possessed the right to veto finally and absolutely any laws or decisions of the whole House of Representatives or Council of Ministers which related to foreign affairs, security, or defence. Furthermore, any modification of the articles of the constitution which were open to emendation required separate two-thirds majorities from the representatives of each community, and any modification of the Electoral Law (enacted before independence by the British Governor) and the adoption of any law relating to the separate municipalities or imposing duties or taxes required a separate simple majority vote. So, in theory, eight Turkish representatives (or even two, if only three were present) could defeat a law desired by thirty-five Greek and seven Turkish Representatives (or, in the latter case, of thirty-five Greeks and one Turk). In practice, the Turkish vote was never split on any matter touching the interests of the Turkish community; but it is easy to see why the Greeks objected to the Turkish 'separate majority right'. Of course, the Turks argue that such powers were necessary to prevent the Greeks from amending the constitution or denying them their rights, but that argument hardly covers the provision concerning duties and taxes, which was to cause trouble later on. The Turks' distrust of the Greeks is understandable, in view of General Grivas's stated intention to annihilate them. All the same, a constitution the basic provisions of which had been drawn up by third parties, and were incapable of being amended, could hardly be regarded by the Greeks as the charter of their liberties. After all, the American forerunner of present-day constitutions has been amended many times (though not necessarily for the better).

The constitutional rights of the Turks have by no means been exhausted. The Council of Ministers was to consist of seven Greeks and three Turks, one of the key Ministries (those of Foreign Affairs, Defence, or Finance) being held by a Turk as of right. With regard to several of the high offices of state, if the holder belonged to one community his deputy was to come from the other. The two separate communal chambers were to have legislative and executive competence in matters of religion, education, cultural affairs, personal status, and even personal taxation where members of the respective community were concerned (all the other Christians opting to be considered as Greeks). The High Court of Justice, having power to nullify laws and decisions of the legislature and of the executive, was to consist of two Greek judges and one Turkish one, with a neutral president having two votes. By a provision reminiscent of the capitulations system of Ottoman days, no court could try a Greek or a Turk unless it consisted of members of his own community.[1] Yet, while under British protection, Greek and Turkish judges had dealt with cases irrespective of the community of the litigant, and without giving rise to complaints. The Turks had reason to distrust the Greeks, whose Enotist aspirations they had often helped to thwart, but it is easy to see why the Greeks considered themselves bound hand and foot by the constitution of 1960. The subsequent history of Cyprus provides a good example of the unworkability of 'functional federalism'.

It will readily be imagined that Archbishop Makarios did not agree to the constitution without misgivings. He certainly voiced his doubts at the Lancaster House Conference in 1959, and although *Patris*, in an article of 6 April 1966, alleges that Makarios has admitted not being forced to sign, there can be no doubt that considerable pressure was brought to bear upon him by Selwyn Lloyd, by the Turkish Foreign Minister, Fatin Rüştü Zorlu, and by the Greek Prime Minister, Constantinos Karamanlis.[2] At the Cairo Conference of Non-Aligned Countries held in October 1964 the Archbishop declared that under the circumstances prevailing at the time he had had no real alternative but to sign the London Agreement: 'Rejection of the Agreements would have meant denial of independence and increased bloodshed'. Certainly, the Turks had already made it clear that the alternative was partition. Another influential factor seems to have been the belief in both Athens and Nicosia that if agreement were not forthcoming the British might tire of being shot at by EOKA, and withdraw their forces, thus leaving chaos, as in the cases of India and Palestine. Alternatively, they might impose partition themselves, to the disadvantage of the Greeks. Besides, the EOKA boycott campaign against British goods had backfired badly, and the British counterterrorist measures were beginning to tell on the Cypriote Greeks, who were growing tired of dismissals from British employment, curfews, and mass detentions. Then there was the danger to the prosperous Greek colony in Istanbul should intercommunal fighting break out in Cyprus. Menderes had already shown himself capable of giving the Istanbul mob a free hand (whereas in December 1963 it could be assumed that Turkey under İnönü would never resort

[1] For this summary of the facts I am partially indebted to Criton G. Tornaritis, *The Legal Aspects of the Question of Cyprus* (Nicosia: Public Information Office, n.d.).

[2] All the Greek-Cypriote mayors and all but two left-wingers among those who went to advise Makarios in London, seem to have been against the terms agreed, though they finally voted in favour (cf. above, p 297).

to such methods). Further, there was the unlikelihood that the government of Greece would be willing to wage an all-out war against an interventionist Turkey while the Communists were poised ready to infiltrate her northern frontiers and revenge themselves for their defeat in the Greek civil war. Finally, the Cyprus case was not going well at the United Nations.

When every allowance is made for the fact that Makarios signed the London Agreement under pressure, the fact remains that he did sign, and that the Greek Foreign Minister Averoff stated: 'I think we have arrived at a solution, an agreement in which the principles of democracy and of modern humanity are upheld and also the fundamental principles of everyone'. Averoff went on to say that he had signed only after Makarios had said he was 'in agreement with the agreements', and indeed Makarios himself described the outcome as 'satisfactory'. George B. Zotiades has argued against the validity of Makarios's signature on the grounds that *'res inter alios acta aliis neque nocere neque prodesse protest'*,[1] but it does not follow that *'nomen subscriptum non valet'*, as he seems in this case to imply. Makarios's own explanation is that he overcame his many reservations about the agreements in a spirit of trust and goodwill towards the Turkish community. However, according to a secret document published in *Patris* on 4 April 1966, he decided not to hold a referendum on the Agreements because the Cypriote public in the mood of the time would undoubtedly have approved them. One should therefore regard the claim that the constitution was invalid because it was not ratified by the Cyprus House of Representatives with some degree of cynicism. On 1 April 1960, the anniversary of EOKA's first attacks, Makarios was to state publicly that the Agreements were merely 'a bastion and starting-point for peaceful campaigns', and he repeated the essence of this on 5 January 1962. In other words, four and a half months before the constitution was promulgated, he showed that he had every intention of amending it. The Turks had reason to feel forebodings about the future, and not long afterwards Mr Osman Örek felt called upon to tell them that 'Makarios will be at the steering wheel, but we are to control the gears and the brakes'. The mention of brakes was also ominous.

The reader may take it that, having signed the London Agreement, Makarios had no intention of allowing the resultant constitution to stand. Nevertheless, he also signed the Treaty of the Establishment of the Republic of Cyprus and its concomitant treaties of Alliance and Guarantee, and the Turks have a strong

[1] 'The Treaty of Guarantee and the Principle of Non-Intervention', *Cyprus Today*, vol. III (1965), no. 2 (Mar.–Apr.), p. 3.

legal case when they argue that a treaty is sacred and cannot be unilaterally abrogated. The author will not try to show that Makarios entered into these undertakings in a spirit of sincerity, because he does not think that can be done. However, the Turks are not on such good ground when they argue that the Archbishop had an excellent opportunity to voice his reservations at the second London Conference, of January 1960, which was convened to review certain difficulties in the working-out of the original settlement. Having signed the London Agreement, he was in no position to return to fundamentals.

One does not by any means regard counter-accusation as in itself a sufficient kind of argument, but it can be a great help in clearing the air of cant. None of the other signatories of the 1960 treaties is in a position to cast the first stone at the Cypriote Greeks for having broken them. In 1915, Greece herself refused to honour her treaty obligation by going to war on the side of Serbia. In the Second War, Turkey, under similar circumstances, refused to honour her obligations to Great Britain and France. And at Yalta in 1945 Great Britain abandoned Poland to the mercy of Russia, although she had gone to war under treaty and ostensibly on Poland's behalf. One's own view is that Makarios's insincere signature of the treaties cannot be condoned, although it is understandable in view of the circumstances. At the same time, one regards the Cypriote Greeks as justified in reacting against certain provisions of the constitution once it was in existence. Conversely, the Greek-Cypriote claim that Turkey had no right to intervene in the Cyprus dispute because under the Lausanne Treaty of 1923 she had divested herself 'of the exercise of any power or jurisdiction in political, legislative, or administrative matters over the nationals of Cyprus' carries little weight in view of the Greek-Cypriote attitude towards the 1960 treaties.

The Cypriote Greeks base their main arguments against the constitution on the premise that it contravenes the Charter of the United Nations in certain important respects. In the first place, it is stated not to be in keeping with the principle of equal rights and self-determination of peoples. Whether or not the Cypriote Greeks, in their weariness of the struggle, would have accepted the constitution in a referendum, there is no doubt that if they had been free to choose for themselves, they would have chosen *Enosis*. Of course, the Cypriote Turks argue that they are a separate people, and therefore entitled to separate consideration, but the United Nations, which is largely an association of states rather than nations, is not disposed to consider the claims of minorities on the wrong sides of borders, let alone those of a minority which is not on any border.

Secondly, the independence and sovereignty of the Cyprus Republic were clearly impaired by Article 182.1 of the 1960 constitution, according to which the constitutional order and structure created thereby were declared to be immutable for ever. Further, that same independence and sovereignty, both of which are guaranteed by the United Nations Charter, were impaired by the Treaty of Guarantee, whereby the guarantors reserved the right to take action in order to restore the *status quo ante* if any of the basic articles of the constitution were altered. However, the U.N. has paid no heed to the principle of non-intervention where southern African countries are concerned. The Cyprus constitution and Treaty of Guarantee are also held by Greek-Cypriote lawyers to conflict in the above and other respects with the 'peremptory norms' of international law, but the theory of *jus cogens* is too vague, and can be regarded as justifying the abrogation of almost any treaty. Nor does one think that the Greeks have a good legal case when they argue against the *sui generis* provisions of the constitution. The United States constitution also contains *sui generis* provisions (though not necessarily good ones).

The Turks insisted upon safeguards built into the constitution because they had reason to fear that the usual minority rights would be inadequate to protect them against those whose unitary aspirations they had thwarted. Yet the author believes that the strongest case to be made against the constitution concerns the disproportionate powers accorded to the minority group. Despite ill-advised remarks made by Zenon Rossides and various Cypriote journalists, the Turks of Cyprus bear little resemblance to the coloured minorities in the United States or Great Britain, but the principle is the same. How large must an ethnic minority be before it can claim special treatment? And how content would Americans or Britons be to allow the constitutional rights of the Cypriote Turks to an ethnic minority on which the prosperity of all does not depend? Such rights are inevitably regarded by the majority in the same light as unjust laws, to change which it is the right of free citizens to agitate; and the failure of the Cyprus experiment should provide a bitter and salutary object-lesson.

The 1960 Constitution in Practice

The breakdown of the Cyprus constitution in practice can only be fully understood if Greek and Turkish weaknesses are first revealed. Both peoples have the defects of their virtues. We are frequently told by environmentalists that there is no such thing as national character (except, inconsistently enough, where the innate wickedness of one particular nation is concerned!), and it is of course true that we shall find a wide variety of persons in every country. However, no well-travelled observer can fail to have noticed that the proportion of those having particular qualities, physical or mental, differs from place to place, and from group to group. Thus, experience teaches that it is very much safer on average to lend money to an acquaintance of one ethnic group than another, more likely that one ethnic group will produce better singers than another, and so on. I will not go quite so far as Sir Hugh Foot in his strictures on 'the heat and hatred' of Greek political behaviour,[1] but the Cypriote Greeks, with all their attractive vivacity, have among them a significant proportion who take pleasure in actively humiliating their enemies. Personal observations of the way in which Britons were treated at the end of the Emergency convinces one that such is the case, and this experience is borne out by a number of photographs taken in 1964, admittedly mostly by British journalists. Now, while the tendency to humiliate under provocation is a quality preferable to cruelty, it paradoxically arouses animosity quite as great. The Turks, on the other hand, with all their quiet friendliness, include a disproportionate number of persons who are ferociously obstinate. Forty-two hours of negotiation, spread over three months, with the Turkish (it would be more accurate to say Ottoman) customs service in Ankara have helped to convince the author of this, and two years of otherwise enjoyable work in Turkey have afforded a number of other examples. Sir Hugh Foot's description of Zorlu as 'the most ruthless' participant in the Cyprus drama and 'the rudest man I ever met'[2] is an instance of the way in which a certain type of Turk will strike a foreigner, albeit an over-sensitive one, under certain circumstances. I would go so far as to say that the Turk who feels himself injured often becomes his own worst enemy.

The reader will easily appreciate that the debit sides of the Greek and Turkish characters are least profitably juxtaposed in a situation inevitably giving rise to suspicion and enmity. It is not at an official level that inter-communal friction is best studied, but in the day-to-day contacts of the less privileged members of the communities concerned. No reasonable person in possession of the facts can deny that the Cypriote Greeks conducted a systematic campaign against those aspects of the constitution which prevented them from becoming masters in their own house. It is inevitable

[1] Sir Hugh Foot, *A Start in Freedom* (London: Hodder and Stoughton, 1964), p. 147. James H. Huizinga (a pro-Greek propagandist) gives a typical example of exaggerated Greek political behaviour in a social context (*A Dutchman Looks at Cyprus,* London: Greek Information Office, 1956, p. 3).
[2] Foot, op. cit., p. 150.

that a people retaining any sense of cohesion should react against the maintenance in its midst of a state within a state. To draw up laws giving special rights to minorities is one thing, but it is quite another to implement them. As for the Cypriote Turks, their primary concern was not just to prevent the Greek community from uniting with those who resemble them most, but rather to prevent a process of erosion which might leave the Turkish community with no protective rights of any kind. Conflict in such a situation was inevitable, though it was embittered by the desire of some Greeks to humiliate and the refusal of most Turks to compromise.

During the period between signature of the Agreements and promulgation of the constitution, Archbishop Makarios and Dr Küçük met under the chairmanship of the Governor in order to draft the constitution, come to terms on its implementation, and set up the necessary governmental machinery. Sir Hugh Foot himself has said that at this period Makarios appeared to have rejected *Enosis* in favour of independence. Apparent agreement was reached on a number of issues, but several important matters were left outstanding, and the Turks charge that this was owing to Foot's desire to please Makarios. The proportion of Turks in the security forces was speedily reduced towards three-sevenths by the discharge of hundreds of Turkish auxiliary police (on the ground that they had only been employed as a temporary measure during the Emergency), but the Greeks made objections to the ratio being enforced immediately in the civil service. Finally, Dr Küçük informed the Archbishop that he would not sign the draft constitution which they had completed by 6 April 1960 unless the Turks obtained their civil service ratio within a reasonable time. If the constitution were not signed, Makarios might not be able to control future events. Accordingly, on 4 July 1960, he compromised by agreeing that the Turks should obtain their full ratio within five months of the declaration of independence. The civil service, with its thirty salary scales, was bracketed into six grades, in each of which the ratio was to apply. The Joint Consultative Committee, which had been directed to deal with the matter, drew up a detailed plan for implementation of the ratio, and agreed that supernumerary posts should be created to maintain the ratio in cases where existing civil servants would otherwise lose their jobs. The plan, in the form of a report, was accepted by Makarios, Küçük, and the Council of Ministers, and passed on to the Public Service Commission for its guidance. Once independence had safely been declared, the Greek-controlled Commission discarded the report, and the ratio was not implemented by 16 January 1961, or indeed ever.

Concurrently, negotiations were proceeding to determine the size of the British Sovereign Base areas. This time Makarios and Küçük were more in accord. They tried to cut down the square-mileage conceded as much as possible, which is ironic in the light of subsequent history, for the bases turned out to be an economic godsend. Eventually, Mr Julian Amery, Under-Secretary for the Colonies, obtained 99 square miles, and conceded £12 million in financial aid, plus £1.5 million specifically for the Turkish community. Over the first five years of its existence, the Republic was to receive grants, loans, and technical aid totalling £30 million, most of it from Great Britain.

Once these matters were out of the way, a general election was held. Polling day was 31 July 1960, and the Archbishop was again elected, ostensibly as a supporter of the Zurich and London Agreements. Thirty of the Greek seats went to his Patriotic Front (including one to a Maronite), and the other five (unopposed by agreement) to AKEL. The fifteen Turkish seats all went to the Turkish National Party under Dr Küçük. Independence was granted on 16 August by Act of the British Parliament. The Archbishop's subsequent statement that he had signed the Agreements under pressure, and that the national aims (i.e. *Enosis*) remained unchanged, caused the Turkish representatives to refuse him congratulations on his accession to the Presidency. The Cypriote Greeks even decided not to celebrate 16 August as the day of their independence. Nevertheless, the Cypriote Turks were later to agree wholeheartedly with Makarios's realistic statement that the constitution had brought into being a state but not a nation. However, Makarios has never been so foolish as to reject *in toto* the document on which Cypriote independence is based. There now began a largely unrecorded struggle for control, the Greeks agitating continually for amendments to the constitution and the Turks resisting fiercely.

For the next four years, Makarios was to retain the initiative. When, on 24 August, Cabot Lodge, the U.S. permanent representative at the U.N., welcomed the emergence of Cyprus as a new nation, cables of protest were sent by Enotist Cypriotes, but Cyprus still became a full member of the United Nations on 20 September 1960, supported by Greece, Turkey, and Great Britain. The independence, sovereignty, and majority rule guaranteed by the U.N. Charter were henceforth to be valuable bargaining counters in the hands of Makarios. On 16 February 1961, the House of Representatives decided by 41 votes to 9 (six of the Turks voting with the Greeks) to apply for membership of the Commonwealth, and Cyprus was admitted on the following 13 March. In the

Commonwealth also, Makarios could rely on the support of the non-aligned nations.

The struggle in Cyprus was not clear-cut and, as we should expect in an ethnic conflict situation, the divisions were most apparent in the majority community. Makarios and Grivas had patched up their differences over the Agreements at a meeting held on Rhodes in October 1959, but Grivas soon began again to attack Makarios for his part in the settlement, and in his *Memoirs,* published in 1961, gave the Archbishop little credit for his part in the EOKA struggle. His suspicions were deepened by Makarios's decision to appeal to his diplomatic supporters by stressing independence rather than *Enosis*. The editor of the Sunday newspaper *Ethniki,* Antonis Pharmakides, was kidnapped for his anti-Makarios diatribes and forced into an abject recantation. On the other side was N. C. Lanites, one of the richest businessmen in the island. Writing in the *Cyprus Mail,* he derided *Enosis* as a 'policy dictated by sentiment', suggested that the national occasions of Greece and Turkey should no longer be celebrated, and was in favour of fulfilling the Zurich and London Agreements, except in their 'divisive' aspects, such as the separate communal chambers and municipalities. His proposals had no influence on the course of events.

Turkish divisions did not come into the open, partly owing to greater Turkish reticence, but mostly because the community was in a weaker position. Emin Dirvana, Turkish Ambassador to Nicosia between August 1960 and October 1962, was appointed by the republican government, and was opposed to Denktaş, who had supported the reactionary policies of the Menderes régime. Dirvana was against the 'From Turk to Turk' economic policy, which turned out to be a failure anyway, and the secret organisation *Volkan* was abolished by his order. (It must be admitted that this last measure may have been in part responsible for relative Turkish unpreparedness in December 1963.) When Denktaş, as President of the Turkish Communal Chamber, wished to celebrate 7 June 1958, the date when *Volkan* planted a bomb outside Turkey's own information office in Nicosia as a signal to attack the Greeks, Dirvana opposed the idea, and was supported by Küçük.

The 'peaceful' post-independence struggle between Greeks and Turks was conducted on several different fronts at the same time. Under the constitution, the existing tax and duty laws, which largely unified finances, were to remain in force until 31 December 1960, to allow time for new laws to be prepared which would benefit the Turkish community. The Greeks, after independence, brought in a bill for continuation of the existing laws, and the Turks compromised by allowing this until 31 March 1961. Thereafter the Turks would only agree to a further extension of two months before the constitutional provisions were implemented, which was unacceptable to the Greeks. However, the Greeks themselves then voted for a three-month extension, and were opposed by eleven of the thirteen Turkish representatives present, the other two abstaining. Therefore, the existing laws technically expired. During the following months of deadlock the Turks changed their minds and said they would agree to a further extension, but were rebuffed in their turn. Meanwhile, in May 1961, an Estate Duty bill was introduced to the House, but the Turks would not pass it until 20 October 1962, by which time members of their community had failed to pay £14,000 in taxes. Nor was the money ever collected.

On 18 December 1961, the Turkish representatives voted against a new income-tax bill, in spite of the fact that the bill had previously been agreed to by the Council of Ministers, including the Turkish ones and Dr Küçük himself.[1] According to the latter, the Turks exercised their separate majority right of veto 'in the belief that their last chance to remind their Greek brethren of their constitutional obligations towards Turks would be lost to them for ever'. In other words, the veto really had to do with the municipalities question, which will be dealt with later on. Makarios seized his chance, and on 20 December issued a statement in which he blamed the Turkish representatives (or at least a 'majority' of them) for their irresponsibility, and declared that 'taking into consideration the general interest of the people of Cyprus' he would 'disregard any Constitutional provision which, if abused, might obstruct the regular functioning of the state'. He further charged that the Turks paid only one-sixteenth of the income tax paid by the Greek community, and enjoyed more benefits than were justified by their proportion of the population. In his reply the next day Dr Küçük made the unconvincing point that the racial composition of the market from which the Greek merchant derived his profits should also be taken into account, but rightly argued that indirect taxation paid by the Turkish community should be included in the reckoning. He also protested that the President's stated intention to delay the implementation of the 3:7 ratio and the formation of the Cyprus army was unjustified in view of a mere shortfall of £1.4 million, as against a revenue of about £19 million. Notwithstanding these objections, Makarios directed that the new bill be regarded as law. The Turks refused to do so, and the country has been without any unitary tax legislation since 1 January 1962. On 8

[1] The Turks expressed reservations about the bill, but nevertheless agreed to its introduction.

February 1963, the Supreme Constitutional Court decided that in view of the Turkish vetoes, the government had no right to collect customs dues or income tax. The decision was ignored.

The above manoeuvres can only be understood in the context of the larger struggle. In the first place, the Greeks wished to share out the development aid proportionately to population, and accordingly allocated 20 per cent of it to the Turks. The latter, however, argued that they were the poorer community, and so needed more aid to enable them to compete with the Greeks. Makarios himself raised their proportion to 28.5 per cent, but this they still deemed insufficient. Significantly enough, the Turks would now be content with a share of aid proportionate to their numbers, if they could get it. Another difficulty, this time on both sides, was that the leaders of each community, having taxed their constituents once already to meet communal needs, were unwilling to impose central government taxation on them as well in order to provide the necessary supplementary grants for education, etc. In practice, this meant that the Turks, who had to provide educational facilities for a much smaller community scattered throughout the island, were much the worse off. Besides, they claim that the supplementary grant which they were to receive was only 12.5 per cent of the total.

By 12 September 1961, Dr Küçük was complaining in a letter to the President of such matters as the blocking by Greek subordinates of projects benefiting the Turks and of a strong impression that the Greek majority on the Council of Ministers decided in previous meetings what line they would take when their Turkish colleagues were present.[1] Other complaints concerned foreign affairs, in that he had not been kept informed. Policy statements were made of which he knew nothing, and with which he strongly disagreed; yet these were technically subject to his veto. He had not been consulted regarding the two Greek emissaries sent to the Belgrade Conference, and an agreement regarding participation by Turkish officials in the Cypriote embassy in Washington and the Cypriote delegation to the United Nations had not been fulfilled. Later, Küçük had cause to make other complaints. For instance, the appointment of Rossides as Cypriote delegate to the U.N. expired at the end of 1962, but Makarios arbitrarily extended his term of office. Then again, senior Turkish officials were kept in the dark by Greek subordinates who acted on their own initiative. All this might be justified on the grounds that it fulfilled the will of the majority, but in other cases Greek behaviour can only be characterised as petty. Thus, in 1962 the Greek majority in the House of Representatives turned down a mainly Turkish amendment to the

[1] Cf. above, p. 221.

Dentists' Registration Law which would have forbidden unqualified persons from practising dentistry. The same kind of spirit was manifested in the case of a Turkish businessman who applied for a loan to establish a biscuit factory. Consideration of the application was delayed until a Greek showed himself willing to undertake the project, whereupon the Turk's application was rejected.

As a background to the other communal disputes, there were the interminable wrangles of the Public Service Commission. Robert Stephens states that no fewer than 2,000 civil service appointments were contested on communal grounds and brought before the Constitutional Court.[1] The basic difficulty was that, despite the Turkish claim to a higher proportion of persons with university degrees there were not enough trained Turks to fill the posts reserved for them in the higher grades, and the Greeks did not intend to pass over their own candidates while Dr Küçük got around to sending a hundred young men to be trained in Ankara. On the Greek side the number of trained men was larger, though not by any means large enough, as is shown not only by the number of posts left vacant before 1963 but also by the decision, not entirely determined by financial considerations, to keep down the number of civil servants since that time. The Turks claim that they never suggested the appointment or promotion of any person who did not possess the qualification laid down in the schemes of service, and give instances of posts being filled over the heads of such persons by unqualified Greeks, in particular ex-EOKA men. One is in no position to comment on all the many cases in which bias is alleged. A separate study of the matter would make an excellent M.A. thesis subject, but would be complicated by the destruction of records in Dr Küçük's office by Greek irregulars early in the troubles. One certainty is that the supernumerary posts promised to the Turks, which would have cost some £50,000, were not created. Again, those Turkish candidates whose appeals were successful before the Constitutional Court had their success nullified in certain cases by such ploys as alteration of the terms of service which happened to debar Greek applicants. Some of the bias, then, is tangible, and might under other circumstances have been offset, but only a servile system could have eliminated the grounds for complaints such as those made on both sides that senior officials favoured men of their own community in writing the reports on which promotion was largely based. The same pattern was observable in appointments to the Security Forces. Not only was the ratio not maintained, but auxiliary Greek police were created far in

---

[1] Robert Stephens, *Cyprus: a place of arms* (London: Pall Mall, 1966), p. 175.

excess of the 2,000 total for the Security Services which were permitted by the constitution. Many of the extra appointments here also went to ex-EOKA men, and both in the police and the gendarmerie many of those promoted had previously belonged to that organisation. It was such auxiliaries who in late 1963 were engaged in searching the houses and persons of Turkish suspects.

The issue which more than any other led to the outbreak of hostilities was that of the municipalities, the 'battle of the five towns'. Robert Stephens says that Averoff told him that it was the Cypriote Greeks who originally pressed for their creation[1] (probably because they did not wish to be obliged to make large grants to the poorer Turks), but now they had come to regard them as the first step towards partition. They alleged that it was impossible to fulfil the constitutional provision for a law separating the municipalities (which was supposed to have gone into effect within six months of independence) because the communities were to some extent intermingled. They were unwilling for Greeks to be included within the Turkish areas and pointed out that the constitution permitted unification of the municipalities by agreement. Meanwhile, the *de facto* boundaries already in existence were renewed annually on a *pro tem.* basis. Probably it was the Turkish refusal to give way on the municipalities issue as much as the preparations of the T.M.T. that goaded Makarios to say on 4 September 1962 in his native village of Panayia : 'Unless this small Turkish community, forming a part of the Turkish race which has been the terrible enemy of Hellenism is expelled, the duty of the heroes of EOKA can never be considered as terminated'.[2] Two months later, Makarios made an official visit to Turkey. In December, when the law regarding the *de facto* municipal boundaries was about to expire, Makarios indicated that the Greeks would refuse to extend it. On Christmas Eve of that year the Greek and Turkish leaders met, and a communiqué was issued suggesting that they had come to an agreement to unite the municipalities. However, within twenty-four hours Dr Küçük stated that no such agreement had been made. The small but significant lapse of time between issue of the communiqué and its rejection lends weight to the Greek suggestion that the Turks either had second thoughts or else received orders from Ankara. When the Greeks, on 2 January 1963, set up 'Development Boards' to run the cities, the Turks refused to surrender their municipalities, and appealed to the Constitutional Court. While the case was pending, in February 1963, Archbishop Makarios stated that, should the Court declare the Development Boards unconstitutional, he would not

---

[1] Ibid., p. 176.
[2] Quotation from a Turkish source, but thought to be accurate.

respect the decision. The neutral president of the Court, Dr Ernst Forsthoff, a distinguished German jurist, had already given judgment in favour of the Turks on the taxation issue, and on 25 April he cast his deciding vote in favour of a judgment that both the Development Boards and the Turkish unilateral 'legalisation' of separate municipalities were invalid.

Whatever one may think of Dr Forsthoff's agreeing to uphold the Cyprus constitution, and one certainly questions his wisdom in doing so, once he had accepted his post he was duty-bound to administer that constitution, and performed that task conscientiously. In return, he was subjected to a campaign of abusive rumour, in which expressions like 'minor Nazi official' and 'second-rate professor of the University of Heidelberg' became common currency, on the liberal principle that any stick is good enough to beat a German with. It seems to be true that Forsthoff taught for a year at the University of Ankara, but if that is supposed to have made him blindly pro-Turkish then there is little hope for the present writer, who taught for two years at the Middle East Technical University in the same city and regularly read the news in English on the Turkish national radio. On 21 May 1963, Dr Forsthoff resigned his post as president of the Constitutional Court, and his decision to do so concerned the treatment of his assistant, Regierungsrat Dr Christian Heinze. Heinze had unwisely become friendly with Mr Denktaş, a fellow lawyer, and as a result had been threatened with death, shadowed by detectives, and accused of living luxuriously on Turkish bribery-money. In a letter to Makarios dated 7 August, Heinze complained of attempts by the Greek Registrar of the Constitutional Court to prevent publication of his translation of a book by Dr Forsthoff on administrative law, of insults by Mr Justice Triantaphyllides, the Greek judge of the Court, and of malicious fabrications previously referred to by Forsthoff. Far from making frequent visits to Turkey, as alleged, Heinze had been there only for a few hours as a transit-passenger, and had met no politically-engaged persons while he was there. His appeal for an investigation was turned down by Attorney-General Tornaritis, who decided that it was not a case of exceptional public importance, and made a quotation from *Henry IV, Part II*, concerning the unreliability of rumour. Dr Heinze then resigned in his turn. Unfortunately, he rather injured his reputation for impartiality when he told a U.P.A. correspondent after the fighting had broken out that 'from the moment Makarios started openly to deprive Turkish Cypriots of their rights the present events were inevitable.' In an interview with an Associated Press correspondent in January 1964 Forsthoff was to go further.

He denounced Makarios's illegal actions in similar terms, and went so far as to deny that Cyprus was an independent country, capable of ruling itself. Also, he was to deny the *de jure* existence of the Makarios government. Some criticism of the constitution itself would have been more in order, but lawyers as a class are more prone to accept than criticise the laws by which they live. The author's own view is that the law may turn out to be an ass, and therefore ought to be capable of emendation.

With regard to the proposed Cyprus army, it is impossible to believe that the two sides were ever willing to trust each other. Arms not handed over by EOKA in 1959 are said by Charles Foley to have included one hundred new American machine-guns recently smuggled in.[1] Before independence, a Turkish caïque, the *Deniz,* was caught by the British minesweeper, H.M.S. *Burmaston,* smuggling in a cargo including rifle ammunition, and Makarios claims that before that another caïque, also from Izmir, was intercepted after dumping its cargo. The new state had no naval forces at first, so smuggling by small fast boats was difficult to check.

The Greek Ministers had no intention of creating a unified army in which the Turks would constitute 40 per cent, especially with a Turkish Minister of Defence. They therefore insisted that units should be integrated at all levels, rejecting even the proposal of the Greek Commander, Major-General Pantelides, that there should be separation at platoon level. Owing to Moslem religious taboos, this would have meant separate kitchen facilities even for platoons, as well as the rejection of the Turkish language for most practical purposes. Certainly, one cannot imagine a platoon commander issuing orders in two languages before going into the attack. For these reasons, and owing to the constitutional requirement that troops of one community should not be stationed in an area inhabited by the other, Dr Küçük insisted that integration should not be below company level, and in October 1961 exercised his personal right of veto for the first and only time. The President responded by saying that the formation of an army should not be proceeded with, and maintained, as he had for some time, that the cost of it would be too great in a small country like Cyprus. Already in the previous month, the Minister of Finance had complained of a shortfall in revenue and recommended that expenditure on the army should not exceed half a million pounds in the ensuing five years, an amount sufficient for a force of 700 men at most. And the Greeks wished to pay the soldiers less than the police or gendarmes. Meanwhile, large sums were secretly set aside for the building-up

---

[1] Charles Foley, *Legacy of Strife: Cyprus from rebellion to Civil War* (Penguin Books, 1964), p. 161.

of Greek irregular forces, and Mr Örek has told the author that their training began in late 1961 or early 1962. In response, ex-members of *Volkan* revived the T.M.T., among them being some Turkish members of the police force. By January 1963, Greek Intelligence claimed to have discovered that the Cypriote Turks already had 2,500 men partially armed and trained with the connivance of the military contingent from Turkey. Only officer-cadets had so far been enlisted in the Cyprus army and, after the deadlock, these also became available for training the forces of their respective communities. The Greek irregulars were all ex-EOKA men, except for the officers from the Greek contingent. Their organisation was left to the President of the House of Representatives, Glafcos Clerides, and the Ministers Tassos Papadopoulos and Polycarpos Georghadjis. In May 1963, close on a hundred officers took part in secret war-games, and large-scale recruiting then began, arms being borrowed for training purposes from government stocks. Within a short time, the Turkish irregulars, with limited training areas at their disposal and insufficient help from Ankara, were outnumbered and outgunned. The Greek training-programme was in full swing by July, and by December there were 5,000 fully-trained Greek irregulars and a further 5,000 partially trained. Of course, the cost of all these preparations did not appear in any official estimates.

The Greek-Cypriote press, seconded by the Cyprus Broadcasting Corporation, meanwhile kept up a propaganda barrage in favour of *Enosis* and against the Zurich and London Agreements. Turkish statements were either quietly suppressed or given limited and unfavourable coverage, in a fashion reminiscent of the B.B.C. in dealing with statements contrary to its policy. However, the C.B.C. was less well practised at conveying a bogus impression of impartiality than the older organisation. Programmes recalling past Turkish atrocities, real or alleged, kept the pot boiling, and on one occasion it seemed that the Turks had cooperated by lending them colour. On 24 April 1962, two Turkish journalists, Ayhan Mustafa Hikmet and Ahmet Müzafer Gürkan, joint editors of *Cumhuriyet*, which had a policy of accommodation with the Greeks, were murdered, apparently by Turkish extremists. Unfortunately, in August 1967 Dr Dervis, leader of the Greek-Cypriote Democratic Union Party, stated that the double murder had been engineered by Georghadjis, and he has yet to be prosecuted for saying so. At the time, good use was made of the incident as illustrating the well-known intransigence of the Turks, but as a propaganda stunt it hardly compares with the triumphs of more practised hands. At other times the Greek mass media overdid it, as when *Eleftheria* referred to the Turks as pigs, and warned them that if the constitution were not revised 'the result would be very regrettable for all concerned, especially for the Turks'. The Turks also injured their cause through too much honesty when they allowed their press to speculate too openly about the preferability of partition. As for the bombs which damaged a Greek statue and a Turkish mosque, they may have been the work of enemies in each case, but one is more inclined to believe that they were put-up jobs which served to focus dislike on the other side.

On 30 November 1963, President Makarios made thirteen proposals to Dr Küçük for revision of 'at least some' of the *sui generis* provisions of the constitution which impeded 'the smooth functioning and development' of the state. In this connexion, it is worth noting that some international lawyers are of opinion that an unworkable constitution should be subject to extra-constitutional remedies. However, Tornaritis's appeal to the 'law of necessity' may be passed over as an aberration. Necessity knows no law; though legality and equity are not necessarily the same thing.

Makarios's proposals, which were 'not for discussion', demand to be examined in detail if we are to understand what was at issue. The first was to abolish the right of veto of both President and Vice-President, so that the latter would no longer have the power to block legislation. The second made the unimportant suggestion that in the absence of the President the Vice-President should deputise for him, and not the president of the House of Representatives, as heretofore. The third was that both the Greek President and Turkish Vice-President should be elected by the House of Representatives as a whole, thus ensuring that the latter should be a creature of the Greek majority. The fourth suggested that the Turkish vice-president of the House should deputise in the absence of its president, another sop to the Turks. The fifth was to abolish separate majority voting, the point being made that any citizen who felt himself aggrieved had the constitutional right to challenge any discriminatory law; but the experience of the Constitutional Court was hardly likely to give the Turks much confidence in that provision. The sixth was to abolish separate municipalities, Greek and Turkish councillors being elected in proportion to the number of their own people in each town (though still elected separately), while proportional sums were to be set aside for both Greeks and Turks after common services had been paid for. The seventh was to abolish the separate administration of justice, the point being made that the unified system had not given rise to complaint even during the Emergency. The eighth was to abolish the distinction between police and gendarmerie. The ninth was that the numerical strength of the security and defence forces should be determined by law (i.e. by the majority in the House of Representatives). The tenth was that the ratios in the public services and forces of the Republic should be modified to accord with the population ratio, the new balance being achieved gradually in cases where present employees would otherwise suffer. The eleventh was that the number of members of the Public Service Commission should be reduced from ten to five, the implication being that the Turkish proportion should drop from three in ten to one in five. The twelfth was that all decisions of the Commission should be taken by a simple majority. And the thirteenth was to abolish the Greek Communal Chamber, its place being taken by 'appropriate authorities and institutions'. The stated objective was to bring the education at least of the majority within the sphere of government social and economic policies. The Turks, on the other hand, might keep their Communal Chamber if they wished.

Küçük is said by Makarios to have been prepared to study the proposals and give his comments at the end of December, though this may have been a device to gain time. However, on 16 December, the Turkish government, which had been provided, like the British, with a copy of the memorandum 'as a matter of courtesy', categorically rejected all the proposals, and insisted upon the inviolability of the constitution. The stage was now set for conflict.

Contingency Plans

There can be no doubt that both sides had contingency plans ready in the event of a deterioration in relations. They would have been foolish not to. On 2 March 1964, the Greeks published in the *Cyprus Bulletin* a document dated 14 September 1963, and allegedly bearing the signatures of both Küçük and Denktaş, which had been 'found in the office of a Turkish Minister'. It provides for partition in the event of a unilateral Greek abrogation of the constitution, on the principle that 'when the obstacle is removed one reverts to the forbidden'. To this end, Turkey was to intervene and the Turkish-Cypriote community was to be forcibly concentrated in a single area. All this sounds plausible enough, until one reflects that Turkey did not intervene until seven and a half months after fighting had broken out. Nor was there any mass movement of Turks from outlying areas until the fighting had begun in earnest, when they had good reason to feel threatened. In the event, the T.M.T. was not taken by surprise when well-armed Greek irregulars emerged from all sides, because Turkish fortified positions were already in existence, but these would probably have been captured had it not been for the extremely strong resistance

22—C

of ordinary Turks, often armed only with shotguns, who played a decisive part in preventing their sectors from being overrun and pacified.

A good deal more is known about the Greek contingency plan because parts of the top-secret document which contained it were published by the pro-Grivas newspaper *Patris* on 21 April 1967, the object being to reveal its organisers, 'Akritas' (Georghadjis), Clerides, and Papadopoulos, as bumbling incompetents. Like the alleged Turkish document, this has not been made available for impartial study but, unlike the Turkish one, it has been published by members of the alleged authors' own community; also, there would seem to be good reason for parts of it not being divulged as they would be if the document as a whole became public property. Again, it seems to have been approved by Makarios, and has not been disowned by him. Finally, it fits in with the four stages of Makarios's plan, as revealed by the Greek Lieutenant-General Karayiannis in a statement to the newspaper *Ethnikos Kiryx* on 15 June 1965.

1. To amend the negative parts of the constitution.
2. To abrogate the international agreements.
3. To advocate anew the case for self-determination.
4. To materialise *Enosis* by means of a plebiscite.

One passage in particular of the Greek-Cypriote contingency plan should be given *in extenso*, first because it reveals the basic principle underlying the plan, second because it shows a highly intelligent, if somewhat Machiavellian, mind at work (not, one thinks, Georghadjis's), and third because it shows how significant has been the double standard applied by 'world public opinion' (viz the international press) to Zionist expansion in Palestine.

Having stated that 'the only danger that can be described as insurmountable' is the military intervention of Turkey, the document continues :

'The history of many similar incidents in recent times shows us that in no case of intervention, even if legally inexcusable, has the attacker been removed by either the United Nations or the other powers without significant concessions to the detriment of the attacked party. Even in the case of the attack on Suez by Israel, which was condemned by almost all members of the United Nations and for which Russia threatened intervention, the Israelis were removed but, as a concession, they continued to keep the port of Eilat on the Red Sea'. It should be explained that Israel had seized Eilath in 1949, in defiance of the U.N. resolution of 14 October 1948 and in violation of a solemn undertaking not to advance beyond the cease-fire line. (June 1967 provided another prime example of the same kind of thing, skilful use being made of the time-lag before, and after, the U.N. cease-fire came into effect.)

The Greek-Cypriote secret document goes on to state that it was planned to amend the constitution rather than declare *Enosis*, which would give Turkey a good excuse to intervene. (In an interview with Radio Luxembourg on 13 May 1965, Makarios was to say that he was obliged to accept a transitional stage towards *Enosis* on the advice of the Greek government.) The document then states that the Turkish community may be counted upon to stage incidents and clashes when the constitution is amended, that they may try to panic the Greeks and take over 'vast areas', and that therefore the government's 'counter-attack' must be immediate and forceful : 'if we manage to become masters of the situation within a day or two, outside intervention would not be possible, probable or justifiable'. Another point made runs as follows : 'We do not intend to engage, without provocation, in massacre or attack against the Turks' because no excuse should be given for intervention. The provocation referred to was evidently refusal by the Turks of Makarios's proposals, for General Karayiannis, who later was officially in command of the Cyprus National Guard, has written that 'when the Turks objected to the amendment of the Constitution Archbishop Makarios put his plan into effect and the Greek attack began in December 1963'. The Greeks were prepared to overrun the Turks in case of trouble, and attempted to do so, but the atrocities which took place seem not to have been part of the actual plan.

The Outbreak of Hostilities

There is no doubt that the Cypriote Greeks were fully prepared for any Turkish reaction to the thirteen proposals. Elias Kyrou, correspondent for the Salonica newspaper *Ellinikos Vorras*, was visiting Cyprus at the time and was warned of a coming all-out attack on the Turks. Turkish houses and business premises were being searched, and Greek Embassy families were being sent home. A week before the outbreak Georghadjis spoke to ex-EOKA Special Branch officers, telling them of the 'tough and merciless attitude' they must adopt. Sampson has also boasted of his forces being in readiness before the outbreak, armed with government weapons. He certainly had plenty of money for his purposes, as emerged at the Aspida trials.

In the small hours of 21 December 1963, Georghadjis's police stopped a Turkish couple in Hermes Street, a part of the red-light district of Nicosia. In an interview with the representative of the Canadian *Daily Colonist* on 4 June of the following year Makarios was to state that the first clash arose out of this incident. The Greeks claim that the police merely wished to check identity cards, and that the Turkish woman was a prostitute, while the Turks insist that the woman refused to be body-searched by men. As it was on the edge of the Turkish quarter, a hostile crowd soon gathered. The police grew jittery, and there was firing (the Greeks say an exchange of fire) in which a Turkish man and woman were killed (apparently those who were stopped in the first place). Either then or later, several other Turks were wounded and also a policeman (who was, according to one Greek source, the first casualty of all). An hour later, Greek irregulars fired on Turkish public buildings. After daylight, Turkish crowds began to gather in Nicosia and in villages on the Kyrenia road. Geunyeli, in particular, had good reason to fear a reprisal attack. Passing Greek vehicles were stoned or shot at when news of the deaths spread northwards. That very day Makarios broadcast that he considered the Treaty of Guarantee void, and the Turks brought out their first *Special News Bulletin* broadsheet. The Greek police were issued with arms, though the Turks were not, and a patrol of the former fired on pupils of the Turkish Lycée, wounding two. The Greeks maintain that the pupils were throwing stones, but even so their reaction seems to have been excessive. Turkish leaders protested to the President, and at the crowded funeral of the two Turks killed, which took place on the next day, it was arranged that Greek police should stay away. There were no incidents. It was on the 22nd that Dr Küçük appealed for calm, though the C.B.C. did not broadcast his statement. The Turks' decision that all their public servants should return to work was, however, broadcast. Owing to the subsequent worsening of the situation, few of the Turkish public servants ever saw their offices again, and effective government of most of the island has been in Greek-Cypriote hands ever since.

Just who began the firing on the night of the 22nd is hotly disputed. Foley says that Turkish snipers were already active, and there was certainly more trouble on the Kyrenia road. The Greeks maintain that the Paphos Gate police station in Nicosia was attacked, and that may well be so. The Turks are not the kind of people to take two killings lying down. Where independent witnesses agree is that in the middle of the night the Greeks began heavy firing into the Turkish quarter with automatic weapons from high buildings, such as the Cornaro and Ledra Palace Hotels, the General Hospital, the Cyprus Telecommunications Building, and the Severis Flour Mill, as well as the Cold Storage Building and the Nicosia (English) Club, which dominate roads to Kyrenia. Of these, the Severis Flour Mill and the Cold Storage Building were to be taken later by Turkish irregulars. In an adroit move, all Turkish telephone and telegraphic communications were cut off, and also such water pipes as did not serve Greeks as well. All these services were subsequently to be turned on and off again, which shows that they were not destroyed. Nicosia airfield and all ports throughout the island were taken over by Greek forces. Stephens states that the firing in Nicosia stopped at 3 a.m. and that Makarios made a broadcast at 7 claiming that the government was in control and that civil servants should go to work as usual that day.

At this stage, one believes, the Turks realised that if they returned to work as if nothing had happened, and allowed the Greeks to retain control, revision of the constitution would become a *fait accompli*. They therefore decided to act. Turkish police and gendarmerie, including T.M.T. members, began to leave their posts, sometimes bringing their weapons with them. At Kyrenia, the Turkish police commander and his Turkish personnel were held as hostages. The Nicosia gendarmerie centre was seized by Turkish irregulars, and they are said to have fired with bren-guns on flats housing the families of members of the Greek security forces in a mixed suburb, presumably Omorphita. Ahmet Niyazi, a Turk, was to remain as Commander of Gendarmerie until January, when he was ordered to leave his post by Dr Küçük.

On 23 December, Makarios and Küçük met at the Paphos Gate Police Station and by noon had agreed to a truce. Both were to broadcast an appeal for a cease-fire, and the C.B.C. duly broadcast their appeals half-hourly, interspersed with anti-Turkish propaganda.[1] Fighting continued throughout the day and spread that night to Larnaca. There the Turks claim to have defended themselves with shotguns, a rifle, and a couple of pistols. Greek irregulars now began to take more Turkish hostages. The next day, the 24th, the Turks put up the first sandbagged road-blocks in Nicosia, and set up bren-guns on their two city minarets. The latter action was in response to Greek fire from other high buildings, but the Turks should not claim, as they do, that for the Greeks to shoot at the minarets was sacrilege. The author has since established, in conversation with young and politically guileless Turks in other Cypriote cities, that other minarets were later put to the same use. At the same time, the C.B.C. and Greek-Cypriote newspapers were misleading, to say the least, when they referred to firing from

---

[1] The Turks make much of the circumstance that Küçük's appeal was broadcast in his own voice, not so Makarios's.

mosques in Ayios Kassianos and Ayios Andronikos, villages where no mosques exist.

Later on the 24th, another cease-fire was arranged, in the presence of the American Ambassador and the British Deputy High Commissioner, who were concerned at the turn events had taken. Makarios suggested mixed police patrols to ensure observance of the cease-fire, whereupon the Turkish leaders insisted that Turkish members of the patrols should have the same weapons as the Greeks. The Greek Commander of Police, Hassapis, was called in soon afterwards, and said that he had already issued all the available arms to Greek police and 'auxiliaries'. His leaders did not press him further, so no mixed patrols were formed.

At 8 p.m. Greek irregulars launched an all-out assault on the Omorphita-Kumsal area, ostensibly, and partly, to release Greeks, some of whom are said to have been killed. The hero of the day was Nicos Sampson, who commanded the irregulars and had the clever idea of sending a bulldozer forward with raised excavator to lead them in the attack.

Atrocities

Omorphita was overrun and the Turkish inhabitants, who constituted a majority in the area, were driven out. Scores of them were killed on the spot and some 700 taken hostage, of whom a number were murdered at a later stage. The Greeks themselves were to state four days later that they had 'evacuated' 500 Turkish women and children from the danger areas. In Kumsal, the wife and three small children of Major Nihat İhan, a doctor with the Turkish army contingent, were murdered in the bathroom at the back of their house, number 2, İrfan Bey Street, where they had taken refuge. Visitors with them in the bathroom were badly wounded, and the wife of one of these was shot down and killed in the lavatory next to them. Two R.A.F. officers resident in Kumsal witnessed the assault on the suburb. The Turks left the dead where they lay, and called in foreign reporters when it was possible to do so, five days later. A photograph of the dead woman and her three dead children in the bath was published in the *Daily Express* and also in *Time* and *Quick* magazines. Other journals went to absurd lengths in playing down the affair, perhaps in the name of responsibility. On 9 January 1964, *The Times* published an article on its leader-page referring to the İlhan killing in the following misleading terms : 'Turkish losses were higher than Greek. Among them were two babies shot, according to the best available evidence, by a spray of Sten gun fire through a darkened doorway...' The

Turks, who have strong stomachs, have left the dried blood and patches of brain sticking to the ceiling of the bathroom just as they were, and have turned the house into a 'Museum of Barbarism'.

Fighting quickly spread throughout most of the island, and a still worse massacre took place at the village of Ayios Vassilios, north-west of Nicosia. There twenty-one Turkish bodies were discovered on 13 January 1964, all buried in the earth. Some had been bound in uncomfortable positions before death, including one who had been blown open by a bomb placed in his lap. The discovery of fourteen of the bodies was made in the presence of the British army and Miss Irene Checkley of the St John's Ambulance Association. The other bodies came to light soon afterwards. At least twenty foreign journalists were on hand to film and otherwise record the facts. Among the dead was a small girl of ten who was said by her father to have been shot before his eyes, together with his two teen-age sons. Another bad incident occurred in Famagusta during May 1964. Costas, son of the local Greek-Cypriote police commander Pantelides, and two officers from Greece were killed after entering the Turkish sector. In reprisal, at least thirty-two Turkish hostages were taken at random, including the Assistant-Director of Barclay's Bank. Of these, none reappeared. Those released at Nicosia airport as a result of representations by UNFICYP were quite unconnected with this incident. Of the various individual cases, that of the small Turkish boy killed 'accidentally' on 23 April 1964 is worth mentioning because it exemplifies the uncooperative and even jeering attitude adopted on several occasions by the Greek police towards those who suggested action towards apprehension of the culprits. Another instance of official callousness occurred in April 1964 when the killing of four Turks outside Nicosia was described by a government spokesman as 'an abominable crime', yet when the bullet-riddled bodies of two of the victims were returned to their relatives death was certified as owing to 'natural causes'. The official Greek attitude towards crimes which could not be concealed had been expressed by Lellos Demetriades, representative on the Political Liaison Committee in January 1964. He argued (a) that not all Greeks were responsible, (b) that he was extremely sorry for what had happened and no repetition would be allowed. However, only one Greek has been sentenced for killing a Turk since the British period, a fact which speaks for itself.[1] An impartial view of the treatment of Turks by Greeks is afforded by the testimony of the Austrian police-inspector Grosa, as reported

[1] The man in question shot a Turk in the back on 23 July 1967. He was sentenced to four years for manslaughter on 17 January 1968, and released under a general amnesty a month or so later.

in *Neues Österreich* for 5 May 1964. He came out to Cyprus as a member of UNCIVPOL and resigned in protest against maltreatment of the Turks which he could not prevent.

In March 1967, at the Turkish Missing Persons Bureau in Nicosia, the author examined samples chosen by himself at random from the records of 225 Turks killed and 203 missing, at least 90 per cent of them having died or disappeared during the period December 1963 to December 1964. Hundreds more were wounded, and the death toll would undoubtedly have been very much higher had it not been for the British. On 18 February 1964, for instance, British troops evacuated the Turks from Vitsadha village after repeated Greek attacks. By June 1967, according to U.N. figures, investigations had reduced the number of missing Turks to 198. One or two more have reappeared since, but it is inconceivable that many more should do so. There are too many disused mineshafts in the island. Besides, on a few occasions foreigners actually witnessed the shooting of hostages by Cypriote Greeks. Of course, many of the Turks killed were combatants. Greek propagandists have claimed that others were moderates murdered by extremists on their own side, but the *Cyprus Bulletin* (for 4 March 1967) did not claim that more than forty met their deaths in this way, and no evidence was offered in any case. It is true, on the other hand, that the Turks are ill-cast as Quakers. Among them even old men will fight. However, this should not be taken to justify the close-range killing of the old İmam of Omorphita, any more than his crippled son, who was killed with him, can be considered as a possible combatant.

By September 1964 only thirty-eight Cypriote Greeks were listed as missing (plus four British nationals and one German). Official U.N. estimates list fifty-three of them as killed, including twenty-eight civilians, and 125 wounded, including fifty-six civilians. There are grounds for believing that quite considerable losses were sustained by mainland Greeks during the Kokkina fighting which were not reported for political reasons, but at all events it is clear that Turkish civilian losses were very much higher than Greek. There can be no doubt that the Turks were mostly on the receiving end. Another good indication of this is that U Thant's Report of 10 September 1964 mentions 527 houses destroyed during the troubles and some 2,000 others damaged or looted, most of which belonged to Turks. The systematic destruction of Turkish villages or, more significantly, of the Turkish quarters of mixed villages, together with the destruction of Turkish gardens and orchards, is shown in a number of air photographs, and nobody has yet suggested that the Turks destroyed their own property. Still, all this does not amount to the systematic genocide of which the Turkish propaganda machine has so frequently accused the Greeks. The total of Turks certainly dead includes only five women and the five children mentioned above, while the total of missing Turks includes only sixteen women and seven children. In all conscience that is bad enough, but the killing of 400 Turks in Cyprus should be compared with the real genocide of the Tutsi people of Rwanda which was taking place, almost unrecorded, at the same time. More recently, hundreds of thousands have been massacred in Indonesia without an outcry being raised in any way commensurate with that over the Cyprus killings. The international press was clearly applying a double standard. Above all, the subhuman element of torture (as opposed to beatings and harassment) seems to have been rather rare during the troubles. True, we do not know how the missing persons died, but most of them are rumoured to have been shot, and as for the 110-year-old Turkish woman found dead at Khoulou on 23 February 1964 the Turks will have to provide more than their own unsupported assertion to convince one that her nails had been pulled off.[1]

Nor is it just to shift all the blame for the ugly aspects of the fighting on to the shoulders of Makarios. Even the Turks admit that he personally prevented a massacre at the General Hospital (although two Turks were nevertheless murdered there). He condemned the destruction of the Bayraktar Mosque (an obvious target for the Greeks because it commemorated the conquest of Cyprus) and also the taking of hostages, which he characterised as a revolting practice. One of the main reasons for the excesses was that lorry-loads of arms were distributed indiscriminately to the Greeks at an early stage in the fighting, so that practically anonymous persons could pay off old personal scores or indulge in the realisation of destructive fantasies. Only the right circumstances were required for the latent mutual hatreds of the two communal groups to be translated into action. It is less easy for the Greek leaders to disclaim responsibility for the behaviour of trained irregulars like those of Nicos Sampson. They cannot have been unmindful of the Palestinian precedent for the efficacy of terror in driving people off their land.

The Turks, for their part, were by no means blameless. The author has been informed by a Greek Public Information officer that a Greek girl was killed by the Turks at Christmas 1963. Another Greek woman was killed in the Neapolis quarter of Nicosia on New Year's Day 1964, and on the same date it was announced

---

[1] More verisimilar is the story of maltreatment, including torture, told by Yüksel Rifat, a young Turk captured the month before.

that two monks and a novice had been killed at the monastery of Galaktoforousa. The latter murders were ascribed to Turks from nearby Kophinou. A fifteen-year-old Greek boy was shot at point-blank range in Trypimeni, and a schoolgirl of the same age, together with a woman of fifty, was killed at Ktima in March when Turks opened fire indiscriminately on a market crowd. In the same month, Panicos Hadjiloizou, one of four Greek policemen captured by the Turks, was released through Red Cross intercession after all his teeth were said to have been pulled out. The trouble with all these Greek allegations is that they are unaccompanied by the chapter and verse or the checkable references to foreign evidence which the Turks often provided.

In August 1964, when Turkish jets intervened in the Tylliria area, they dropped napalm on Greek villages, destroying a hospital and an ambulance at Pachyammos. It was then that the Greeks suffered many of their civilian casualties, including a few children. Bombing is of necessity somewhat indiscriminate, and people in Britain and America have long been accustomed to taking the larger moral view with regard to the pilot who drops phosphorus bombs on (German) civilians. Napalm is now a commonly used weapon but, given the inescapable choice between being napalmed or shot, the author, for one, would unhesitatingly elect to be shot. Armenians suffered the biggest losses of property to the Turks because they tended to live in the Turkish quarter of Nicosia. In January 1964, many fled from the Victoria Street area after being accused of spotting for the Greeks. They had constructed a secret exit from their church which connected with Greek positions. However, that does not explain the ultimatum delivered to the remaining Armenians by the Turks on 3 March 1964. They were told that their safety would not be guaranteed if they did not evacuate their houses. Turkish refugees were then moved in. Perhaps the biggest Armenian business now in Turkish hands (though not operated by them) is the Alfa shoe factory.

History does not show that if dissimilar peoples live in close proximity for centuries they will necessarily come to love each other. In fact, massacres are usually of internal minorities, such as the Armenians in Turkey, the Jews in Russia or Germany, the Chinese in Indonesia, or the Ibos in Nigeria. In particular, both Greeks and Turks had made efforts to bell the enemy's cat with some part of the German experience, thus appealing to international liberal sentiment. The Cypriote Turks do not resemble the German minority in Czechoslovakia, as Greeks have claimed, because the Germans of Bohemia were concentrated in areas contiguous to Germany, while the Turks are scattered throughout Cyprus. On the other hand, they do not resemble the German Jews, for they are the poorer community, and are not disproportionately represented in business and the press. The same goes for any comparison of the Cypriote Turks with the Armenians in Ottoman Turkey, though they are similar to those Armenians in that they represent a threat to the territorial integrity of the country. Again, the Cypriote Turks bear little resemblance to the Negro community in the United States. Unlike the Negroes, the Turks are well represented in the professions and have big landholdings.

Relations between Cypriote Greeks and Turks were not uniformly bad even during the troubles. Some Greek cooperatives showed honesty in paying for Turkish carobs which had been collected before the fighting began, and at Ayios Theodoros, on 25 April 1964, a Greek police-inspector, Philios Tsigarides, is said to have been shot dead by Turks while appealing to his own people to cease fire. The Turks, on their side, showed enlightened restraint when they forbore to destroy Greek houses within the areas under their control. There have also been cases of both Greeks and Turks 'taking out insurance' by performing services for influential persons of the other community. Such exceptions, however pleasant or interesting in themselves, merely serve to emphasise the rule, which is hostility and suspicion. For the present, the two communities are co-existing, however tense their relations may be. That is because they are to some extent answerable to powers greater than themselves. Communal conflict is endemic. Any illusions a visitor may have on that score are rapidly dispelled if he responds to casual Cypriote friendliness towards foreigners and converses at length with chance acquaintances. One can think of a Greek policeman in civilian clothes whom one met in a restaurant in 1967. He was in his cups, and looked forward to killing 'all the Turks' in revenge for a friend who had been killed by them. Similarly, a Turk one met in a barber's shop looked forward to returning with interest the killings perpetrated by the Greeks at Christmas 1963. Many others on both sides expressed a lesser but nevertheless dangerous degree of antagonism.

The Progress of the Fighting

Events between December 1963 and August 1964 are crucial to the modern history of Cyprus, and therefore demand to be examined in some detail. Thereafter, indication and analysis of the main developments should be sufficient.

Severance of communications with the Turkish quarter of Nicosia meant that not until the morning of 25 December did Turkey have enough information to act, and by that time the great powers had become involved. For three days, her Supersabre jets made warning flights over Nicosia, but her forces were not ready, and even if they had been, she lacked the necessary assault craft, so that any landing would have involved serious casualties. Under the circumstances, her announcement of intended invasion was a cardinal error. It turned out to be bluff, and the bluff was called. On the very next day, Rossides protested to the Security Council, appearing as the injured party.

At this low ebb in Turkish fortunes, the 650-man Turkish army contingent, established in Cyprus under the Treaty of Alliance, took decisive (and almost certainly pre-planned) action. Without referring to the tripartite H.Q., as it should have done under the treaty, it marched out of its camp north of Nicosia on the 25th, and took up positions at Orta Keuy (Minzelli) and Geunyeli on either side of the Nicosia–Kyrenia road, the historic jugular vein of the island. A justification at the time was that the Turkish Embassy had been fired on, but on 31 March 1964 İnönü, the Turkish Prime Minister, was to explain that the contingent had merely been seeking its own safety! The Cypriote Greeks did not have enough weapons to prevent the move, and Clerides has told the author that they had received an assurance from the Athens government that in the event of any action by the Turkish contingent the Greek contingent would neutralise it. In the event, the contingent of the Royal Greek Army did not block the move, for its involvement in the fighting would have meant war with Turkey. To this day the Turkish contingent forms the power nucleus of the main Turkish enclave.

Meanwhile, cease-fire talks were taking place at the call of the three guaranteeing powers. They were held at the house of the British High Commissioner, Sir Arthur Clark, who had allegedly endeared himself to the Cypriotes by such antics as crawling under the table at an independence day luncheon. Accounts as to when and how agreement was reached differ markedly. Stephens says that Makarios agreed on the 25th that the British should supervise the cease-fire,[1] and acceded to the suggestion of Major-General Peter Young, the British commander, that a buffer zone manned by British troops should be created between the Greek and Turkish quarters of Nicosia; but that Makarios did not realise that the Greeks would subsequently be denied access to the Turkish areas. Formal agreement was then reached on the next day. Foley, however, gives a highly-coloured account of Makarios, on the night of

---

[1] This accords with the Turkish statement that Makarios and Küçük met for the last time at the Police H.Q. on that day.

the 25th to 26th, being induced to agree to British intervention by a suspect story that the R.A.F. had sighted the Turkish invasion fleet. Stephens is the more worthy of credit. It is worth adding that some Turks have suspected that the British intervened to forestall the projected Turkish invasion.

The agreement of 26 December, resulting from Makarios's formal request for assistance, was only an outline one. Two days later, Duncan Sandys, British Secretary for Commonwealth Relations, flew to Cyprus and drew up a detailed agreement regarding a buffer zone separating the Turkish quarter of Nicosia. The meeting was attended by representatives of either side, including Clerides and Halit Ali Riza, as well as Sandys himself. A chinagraph pencil which happened to be at hand was used to mark the 'Green Line' of division on the map.

On 30 December, British troops moved in from the Sovereign Base areas and interposed themselves between the two communities. Their stated mission was to assist in the restoration of peace and the maintenance of law and order. Accusations of bias in their fulfilment of this function were almost inevitably made by the Cypriote Greeks. It was alleged that they had permitted five Greek postal employees, whom they were escorting to the Central Post Office in the Turkish quarter, to be lynched by a Turkish mob. Certainly, the Turks were not disposed to permit the freedom of movement to which they had agreed. Mr Sandys made good use of his forceful personality when he managed to effect an exchange of hostages (for the Turks, on 27 December, had also begun to take them) : 545 Turks were exchanged for twenty-six Greeks, a number of them having been badly beaten, and there is no doubt that many of these people owe him their lives. On 1 January, he protested strongly to Georghadjis about the burning of Turkish houses since the cease-fire. Unfortunately, the Turks took eleven more hostages the next day, and more again on 3 February.

With the ring held by the British, Makarios could take the initiative. On 1 January, it was announced that he had unilaterally abrogated the treaties of Alliance and Guarantee. However, Sandys insisted that a mere statement of intention should be substituted. The extraordinary nature of Cypriote politics was then emphasised by the holding of a secret dinner-party at which Clerides and Denktaş as well as the British representatives were present. Makarios, like the British Labour Party, wished to take the problem straight to the United Nations, but before flying home the next day Sandys had induced all the principals on both sides to attend a conference in London. Makarios was persuaded to go, under pressure from the Amassador of Greece. He came round to the point of view that it was better to let the conference fail slowly rather than refuse to attend. Besides, under Article 33 of the U.N. Charter it was desirable to exhaust all possible alternative solutions before having direct recourse to the Security Council.

The arrival of British troops on the scene cut down the number of killings, though it did not increase British popularity on the Turkish side either. Just as the Greeks were angry at not being able to prevent the Turks from consolidating their positions, and protested at the failure of the British to provide escorts home for those Christians who had houses in the Turkish quarter, so the Turks were none too pleased to be deprived of an excuse for immediate intervention by the mainland Turkish army. Incidents and killings did not cease, but there were no more major assaults in Nicosia, and the Turks made good use of their breathing space. They were especially active on the propaganda front. Their broadsheet had been coming out since the very first day of the troubles, and on 27 December, the day before Sandys flew out to Nicosia, they had staged a protest march in Whitehall. The next day, Radio Bayrak broke the silence imposed on the Turkish leadership by the C.B.C., and on 7 January Radio Sancak came into being. At this stage, Turkish broadcasts were not only anti-Greek, as is understandable, but also strongly anti-infidel. It was on 28 December that Denktaş gave it as his opinion that the Republic was dead. Already the Turks were operating the nucleus of a separate administration. Two days later, Dr Küçük told reporters that the communities could no longer live together, which was a reasonable enough attitude to take, but he also said that the constitution was dead, and this was a mistake in view of his many subsequent appeals to that constitution. Besides, it struck a heavy blow at the Turkish case that the Makarios government was now merely *de facto* and therefore illegal. On the same day, Makarios answered accusations of illegality by saying that the government remained in being and that Küçük was still Vice-President, but he qualified this the day after by saying that Turks who had shown themselves antagonistic towards the state should be replaced by other Turks. On 10 January 1964, in an interview with the representative of *Le Monde*, Dr Küçük was to say that the Makarios government no longer existed as far as the Turks were concerned. Since he had also said that he had not resigned as Vice-President, Makarios was able to point out the anomaly of his position. How was it possible to be Vice-President of a non-existent government? During the same interview Dr Küçük was unwise enough to state that he lacked confidence in the United Nations, thus further strengthening Makarios's support in that organisation. By 5 January, Küçük had announced that he favoured partition (which was contrary to the constitution), and that Turkish-Cypriote employees would not return to work for the Makarios administration. This last decision was perhaps also a mistake, for it prejudiced the claims of Turkish civil servants to be paid by that administration; but in any case the Greeks did not allow them to resume their employment. On 10 January, Küçük suggested the 35th parallel as the ideal dividing line between the communities, which would have meant that the Turks, with less than a fifth of the population, would have obtained half the island, including Nicosia itself! This was manoeuvring in a vacuum. The Cypriote Greeks were in an excellent position to prevent partition, and having called the Turkish bluff once, would not hesitate to do so again. A cleverer course for the Turks would have been technically to uphold the constitution in every detail, explaining the enclaves as necessary for self-defence. As it was, Makarios could now insist that Küçük should clarify his attitude before he might return to his official duties. In June 1964, Makarios made an attempt to withdraw recognition of Küçük, but was opposed in this by UNFICYP. Otherwise, the Greeks might well have put forward Dr İhsan Ali as their candidate for the Vice-Presidency.

The vast majority of Turks had undoubtedly fled to safer areas because of the treatment they had received from the Greek irregulars since the beginning.[1] For those who returned to their homes there was little encouragement. They found their houses looted or destroyed, their fruit trees felled, or their livestock stolen. In Lakatamia and Dheftera they found their wells filled in, and bombs were thrown at the houses of returned refugees in Ayios Theodhoros. However, in January, particularly in the Famagusta area, there were already a few cases of Turks loath to leave their homes being forced to do so by their own irregulars. Kemal Çoşkun, an organiser from the Turkish mainland, had set up 'Internal Movement Committees' and was accused by the Greeks of bullying the families of those who refused to move. Of the 25,000 Turkish refugees assessed by UNFICYP (27,000 according to the Turks) some 10,000 were in the south (eighteen villages were deserted in the Paphos area alone) and 15,000 in the north, including 7-8,000 in Nicosia. Those in Nicosia were overcrowded, but they soon had their own hospitals and food distribution system. In remoter areas they were badly off both for food and medical attention.

---

[1] U Thant's Report of 8 December 1967 accepts that the Turks 'fled from their land', 'fled from their homes' (pp. 48, 52). Mr M. Christodoulou, Director of the Greek-Cypriote Public Information Office, has put it to me that they expected the Turkish air force to bomb the Greeks, and therefore separated themselves, but this consideration cannot be regarded as a primary one.

The Greek irregulars were too preoccupied with teaching the Turks a good lesson to bother much about strategic considerations. They had neglected to occupy the heights over the Kyrenia Pass in sufficient strength. Had they done so, they could largely have neutralised the advantage gained by the Turkish army contingent when it established itself on the road to the south of it. Such an oversight fully justifies Grivas's accusations of incompetence. By 17 January Turkish irregulars had taken St Hilarion and dominated the pass.

In the international arena, Makarios for a long time proved far superior to the Turks as a negotiator. To begin with, *Enosis* was played down for U.N. consumption. On 11 January 1964, Makarios said : 'If Turkey and the Turkish Cypriots fear that Cyprus will be united with Greece, let them express those fears to the Greek government and ask for guarantees that *Enosis* will not materialise'. Kyprianou was to go farther when he said : 'we are realistic and we realise that *Enosis* is not achievable'. One can well imagine the suspicions awakened in the breast of Grivas and others. Grivas's own plan was to invoke the aid of the Soviet Union as a counterweight to the Western powers, with their need to placate Turkey. Makarios had become nettled at the large number of Cypriote Greeks visiting Grivas in Athens, and on 21 January accused him of acting as Turkey's ally in that he was splitting the Cypriote ranks. Nevertheless, he approached the Russians himself, and on 27 January received their promise of help in the event of the threatened Turkish invasion.

On 14 January, Zenon Rossides had urged U Thant to send an observer to the London talks, and the three guaranteeing powers had done the same. The observer appointed, Mr José Rolz-Bennett, of Guatemala, flew to London on 17 January, and on the same day Lieutenant-General Gyani of India arrived in Cyprus as U Thant's special observer there. On the 22nd, he was witnessing the serious straits to which the Turks had been reduced.

The London Conference had begun on 15 January. The Cypriote Greeks demanded abolition of the treaties of Guarantee and Alliance, as well as the preservation and strengthening of the unitary state. To the Turkish community they were willing to accord minority safeguards, with autonomy in matters of religion, culture, and education. Rauf Denktaş (whose return to Cyprus was forbidden by the Makarios government), insisted on complete separation of the peoples, while Turkey, now under İnönü again, was prepared to modify the demand for outright partition into one of a federal state, so that the economy might not be disrupted. However, Ankara still demanded that the Cypriote Turks be concentrated in a single area for reasons of security. The geopolitical importance of Cyprus to Turkey was also emphasised. Pressure was brought to bear upon Dr. Küçük, and on 11 February he was reported as being in favour of a federal solution himself, with Greeks remaining in the proposed Turkish area, and self-determination for either area should it prove necessary to exercise it. Such a 'compromise' would merely have created another minority situation. Partition was not excluded by the Turks as an alternative, but from that time forward federation was to be their official first choice, and they claimed for the Turkish community 38 per cent of the total area of the Republic. On 17 February, Küçük wrote Makarios an open letter of accusation, ending with insistence upon separate areas.

Ankara's reaction to the plight of the Cypriote Turks was to put pressure on the Greek community in Turkey. In March, the Atatürk–Venizelos Convention of 1930, dealing among other things with commerce and navigation, was denounced; 354 Greek nationals were deprived of their work permits and forty were deported by 29 April. In addition, one hundred businesses were closed down. On the islands of Imbros and Tenedos (Bozcaada), which are 80 per cent Greek, the teaching of Greek in the schools was forbidden, and the Patriarchate of Constantinople also came under pressure. On 11 July 1964, the *Observer* reported that the property of up to 8,000 Greek nationals in Istanbul, amounting in all to about £80 million, had been confiscated, and 1,000 Greeks had been expelled. Since the Greeks of Istanbul had virtual control of the import-export trade, as well as the chocolate and tanning industries, the monetary figure is probably not exaggerated.

As a background to the London talks, Cypriote Greeks demonstrated in Whitehall on 17 January, and Greek-American organisations appealed to President Johnson six days later. The British were coming under increasing pressure in Cyprus, and on 25 January the British Ambassador in Washington called on the acting Secretary of State, George Ball, and informed him that Great Britain was no longer prepared to act as sole peace-keeper in the island. It was suggested that other NATO countries should also send contingents, and Ball then flew off to try to actualise the idea. Greece and Turkey, both heavily dependent on American aid, made no objection. Meanwhile, Makarios had made it known through Rossides at the U.N. that he would accept an international force provided it was under Security Council control. A demonstration against NATO in Nicosia on 3 February was paralleled by one in London by the 'Movement for Colonial Freedom', which was allegedly made by both Greeks and Turks, though no Turk was to be seen in it. On the same day, President Johnson appealed to Makarios to accept the plan, but Makarios, while deploring 'almost daily incidents' which had resulted in American families being flown out of Cyprus, gained time by having 'reservations' and seeking 'clarification'. Ball soon flew to Nicosia, where he had two meetings with Makarios on 12 February. In the first, Makarios merely listened while Ball urged restraint. In the second, he told Ball that the issue of an international force could be left until later. His own suggestion was that the matter should be put in the hands of the Security Council, together with an appeal for endorsement of the political independence and territorial integrity of Cyprus. He had understood that in view of the climate of *détente* between Russia and the United States and her own domestic difficulties, Turkey's strategic position and twenty-two divisions no longer counted for so much. Russia, for obvious reasons, would be against any NATO intervention, so would France; and the Germans, well knowing they would be accused of militarism if they participated, were scarcely enthusiastic. He could confidently expect the support of the uncommitted nations in the period of their greatest influence, not to speak of 500,000 Greek-American votes. Ball's reaction was to emphasise the Turkish threat and to 'tell off' Makarios 'in a fashion remote from diplomatic exchanges'. But a 'bawling-out' by the representative of the world's most powerful nation left Makarios, by Ball's own admission, outwardly unperturbed. Ball now had to fly back and urge moderation in Ankara and Athens. In Ankara, anti-American feeling was to grow in the following months. In Athens also, where he was supported by telephone calls he had arranged to have made by prominent Greek-Americans, Ball was regarded with some suspicion.

It can hardly be said that the Greek-Cypriote leadership was losing its nerve. While Ball was flying to Nicosia, a full-scale assault had been mounted on the Turks of Limassol. The Greeks used bulldozers and an old tank, which had been sold to them as scrap-metal some time before. This last the Turks destroyed with plastic T.N.T., and the Greek advantage of firing down from such buildings as the Keo factory was offset by the existence of carefully hidden fortified houses in the Turkish quarter. Hitherto there had been little trouble in Limassol. The 120 Turkish police and gendarmerie had continued to work for the Greeks until expelled at gunpoint on 1 January as a potential threat. Both sides then prepared.

The British force at Polemidhia (a camp established by Kitchener in 1895), situated two miles from Limassol, failed to intervene for some time, but on the 12th General Young arranged a cease-fire, Georghadjis giving his personal assurance that there would be no attack. On the following day, the Greeks attacked with mortars and rocket-launchers and two old Turks were killed, one of them a man of eighty. As in Nicosia, the Greek leaders could plead that their irregulars were not always under control. Sixteen Turks and one Greek had been killed when the fighting ceased.

The British were now reproached by the Turks for not affording them more protection, and the Greek leadership was obviously intent on the 'salami' tactics indicated by the situation, concentrating forces on one pocket of resistance after another. The Greek over-reaction to the alleged firing on a Greek car at Ayios Sozomenos on 6 February had been a previous example of the same thing. The next day, after the British had arranged a cease-fire, Makarios had stated that their contribution to the restoration of peace was 'considerable'. Certainly, the British were showing very considerable self-restraint. Monsieur Albert de Cocatrix, representative of the Red Cross in Cyprus, referred to their behaviour as 'marvellous'. But the existence of a peace-force which arranged cease-fires after Turkish positions were overrun was thoroughly in the Greek interest. Arms were pouring in for the Greeks, and on 15 February a crate, supposed to be carrying printing machinery, which was being unloaded at Famagusta from the Greek ship *Demetrios*, fell through an accident (perhaps engineered by Turkish dock workers). It burst open, revealing arms and ammunition. Coupled with the Limassol incidents, this proved the last straw for the British, and on the same day they took the whole Cyprus question before the Security Council, beating the Cypriote Greeks to the post by an hour or two (to their extreme annoyance). So ended a typically neo-Conservative episode, the British government hanging on until the situation grew intolerable and then retreating in confusion, with only a diplomatic manoeuvre by way of success.

As tension lessened in Limassol, it grew in the mixed town of Polis (in the north-west), where five hundred Turks of all ages were besieged in a school, surrounded by weapons, searchlights, threats, and taunts. Public opinion in Turkey was at white heat, and an attempt was made to assassinate the moderate Mr İnönü from a range of ten feet. Lieutenant-General Prem Singh Gyani, who had arrived in Cyprus on 17 January as U Thant's special observer, managed to arrange a truce at Polis, though the Turks remained confined to the school. Himself a product of the Imperial Defence College, he was full of praise for the tact of British officers in dealing with such situations, but the Greek-Cypriote government view of the British contribution had changed. It was imperative to overrun as many Turkish positions as possible before the likely arrival of contingents from countries in better favour at the United Nations. Since the British presence was no longer a deterrent to Turkish invasion, it came to be seen only as a continuing factor making for stalemate and the consolidation of the Turkish positions. On 21 February, Makarios demanded a cut in the numbers of the British force, which had now grown to 7,000 men, and constituted a serious hindrance to the pacification activities of the Greek irregulars. On the 25th he told the Cypriotes of his intention to 'disarm all those carrying weapons' and set up a force of 5,000 'special police'. Smuggling of arms was now proceeding apace, and on the next day training of the force began in earnest. At the same time Makarios appealed indirectly to a sympathetic de Gaulle, and the arrival on 29 February of an Ilyushin airliner, on a proving flight for a proposed Moscow-Nicosia air service, tangibly demonstrated the support of the Soviet Union.

Immediately after the British recourse to the Security Council, U Thant appealed for restraint by all parties, but on 25 February had to admit failure in bringing them together. On 4 March, the Security Council adopted a resolution which was a triumph for Makarios. It referred to the sovereign Republic of Cyprus as responsible for the maintenance of law and order, and called upon all nations to refrain from the threat or use of force against its territorial integrity. A peace force of 7,000 men was provided for, and also a mediator to promote an agreed settlement to the problem. General Gyani was appointed commander of the peace force, and Great Britain offered 2,400 men (later rising to 2,700) as a nucleus round which to build. At first the other nations approached dragged their feet. Canada, for instance, with bitter memories of the way in which her troops had been left unsupported when the Japanese attacked Hong Kong in 1941, had no wish to participate alone with a mother-country whose governments could no longer be relied upon. But Canada and several other northern nations agreed to send contingents when the gravity of the situation was brought home to them.

Between 4 and 27 March, isolated engagements took place at Mallia (in the southern foothills of the Troödos), Kazaphani (near the Kyrenia Pass), Ghaziveran and Lefka (in the Morphou area), and in the mixed Tylliria district of the north-west. But the next big clash was at Paphos-Ktima. Tension there had been rising for some time, and fighting began on 7 March. It was the day after the death of King Paul of the Hellenes, who had been a staunch supporter of *Enosis*. Schools had closed and many Greeks had come in from the surrounding villages. Mr Aziz Altay, the leader of the

Turks in Ktima, has told the author that many of the Greeks were irregulars and that trouble began when a Turkish shopkeeper, Ahmet Vreçali, was fatally wounded in the market-place between the two quarters. However, he admits that the Turks retaliated by taking hostages into their area (only fifty according to a Turkish source, though the British procured the release of 228 by the following midday!). Dr Ihsan Ali, who was also a witness, has also told the author that firing first began at noon, from bren-gun positions on the Turkish minarets, and Foley says that the Turks used an armoured bulldozer. Six Greeks were killed (including a fifteen-year-old girl and a woman of fifty) and thirty-eight wounded. There seems no doubt that the Turks in this case were the first to undertake action on any scale, but the Greeks were certainly ready for it. They collected Turkish hostages from nearby villages and, disregarding the cease-fire arranged by General Gyani with Georghadjis, attacked with mortars and rocket-launchers. The nearby mosque was badly damaged, and later the Greeks were to destroy it and asphalt the site. By the time the fighting was brought to an end, the Turks occupied an area only three to four hundred yards wide, an indication that they could not have held out but for General Gyani's intervention. On 11 March, an agreement was reached whereby all Turkish fortifications in Ktima were to be destroyed and the Turkish quarter was to be patrolled jointly by Greek-Cypriote security forces and British soldiers. However, most of the quarter gradually slid back under Turkish control, and Greeks are no longer allowed into it. Fourteen Turks and eleven Greeks were killed in Ktima, which hardly justifies Turkish descriptions of it as 'another Budapest'.

Meanwhile, at Mallia, another situation similar to that in Polis had developed. On 10 March, after the first main onslaught by the Greeks, the British prevailed upon the Turks to surrender their arms. The Greeks then broke their promise not to attack again, and five Turks were killed, including a woman. Whatever the merits and demerits of the Turkish case, the British were, of course, bound in honour to prevent such an occurrence, but did not do so. The incident is remembered with understandable bitterness by the Turks.

Stephens wrongly states that eight days passed 'without a shot being fired'[1] before Turkey, on 13 March, threatened intervention within thirty-six hours if demands for release of Turkish-Cypriote hostages and restoration of freedom of movement (to Turks in areas held by the Greeks) were not met. In Athens, where Makarios had gone for the funeral of King Paul, it was announced that

[1] Stephens, op. cit., p. 190. The mistake seems to arise from his impression that the Ktima fighting took place on 4 and 5 March.

Greece would resist any such invasion, and the Greek navy held counter-exercises to those of the Turkish. Greek-Cypriote emissaries then in the Crimea were assured by Mr Khrushchev of Soviet support. On the same day the Security Council, in emergency session, reaffirmed the sovereignty of Cyprus and also its call to all states to show restraint. The next day, 14 March, two Soviet warships passed through the Turkish straits, and Khrushchev warned İnönü of the danger of a third world war. Turkey withheld her hand, while retaining the right to intervene. As a reward, Great Britain promised to increase her contribution to CENTO from £850,000 to £1 million, and the United States approved long-term loans amounting to £6.5 million to complete the Turkey–Iran rail link by 1968. It should not be thought that pressure and indirect subvention would have been enough to deter most Turks from taking the decision to invade. Fortunately, İnönü faithfully held to Atatürk's policy of moderation in the international sphere, and the Turks had to content themselves for the moment with bringing pressure to bear on their Greek minority.

Also on 14 March, the Canadian advance guard flew in to Nicosia, soon to be followed by other contingents, though the U.N. force did not officially take over its duties until the 27th. The Mediator, Mr Sakari Tuomioja, who had been Finland's Minister of Finance in 1944, was appointed on the 25th. He was acceptable to the Turks, partly on the grounds of distant kinship with the Finns; whereas Rolz-Bennett, who had been involved in the Congo affair, was unacceptable to them. The Mediator's rôle was to 'promote' an 'agreed solution' in accordance with the United Nations Charter.

In the event, the U.N. force in Cyprus (UNFICYP) proved as much a disappointment to the Cypriote Greeks as the British alone had been. They considered that its mandate 'to use its best efforts to prevent a recurrence of fighting and, as necessary, to contribute to the maintenance and restoration of law and order and a return to normal conditions' implied that it should help the majority government to disarm the Turks and search for hidden arms. The new Greek-Cypriote police force even appeared for a time in helmets of U.N. blue, until this was officially described as 'not helpful'. The Turks, on the other hand, assumed that 'normal conditions' meant the *status quo ante,* and that UNFICYP should prevent both the importation of arms and the measures taken against the minority. The balance of opinion in the United Nations was favourable to Greek claims. Nevertheless, Dr Küçük was accepted as Vice-President, and he and the three Turkish Ministers were escorted wherever they wished to go.

The arrival of UNFICYP did little to change the situation. Incidents continued as before, and the Greeks continued to import arms in quantity. The British were subjected to the same insults and indignities whether wearing United Nations insignia or not. But humiliation is inevitable for peoples that lose their grip.

On 29 March, Makarios sent a letter to İnönü demanding that the Turkish contingent in Cyprus should return to its camp by 1 April. According to the Treaty of Alliance the Turkish and Greek contingents had to be garrisoned within five miles of Nicosia. Previously it had been stated that the move to the position astride the Kyrenia road had been taken under orders from General Young, and this had not been denied by the British. Now, however, İnönü made use of the rather thin argument that it had moved for its own security. Makarios declared that Turkey had broken the treaty by moving the contingent without the consent of the tripartite H.Q. and without consulting the authorities of the Republic. Also, he argued that Turkey was encouraging subversive activities in breach of the treaty, and that it was therefore void. On 8 April, the Turks appealed to Great Britain. Mr R. A. Butler, the British Foreign Minister, characteristically upheld the treaty in a technical sense, but urged reliance on the United Nations. The United States was likewise viewed with suspicion in Turkey, especially after the American Information Centre in Ankara had allowed a statement to be circulated in which the Cypriote Turks were referred to as 'rebels'. A visit to Ankara by Dr Stikker, Secretary-General of NATO, failed to yield positive results, and on 16 April even İnönü felt constrained to threaten a breach with the West over Cyprus.

April 1964 saw a determined attempt by the Cypriote Greeks to gain control over the Turkish enclaves. The first of the month was the ninth anniversary of the EOKA campaign, and the President took the salute in Metaxas Square at a parade of ex-EOKA-men and the new 'National Guard', whose arms included rocket-launchers and armoured cars. Later in the month, command of the new force was taken over by a General from mainland Greece, Karayiannis, while recruiting and training proceeded at breakneck speed. On 4 April, a determined attack was made on the north-western coastal villages of Kokkina and Mansoura, where the Turks had established a bridgehead for the import of arms and the landing of a few irregulars from Turkey. Another dangerous situation arose on the Kyrenia road, where the mainland Turkish contingent blocked the passage of one of the eight armoured bulldozers now used by the National Guard. As a result, the contingent's supplies were cut off for a time.

The U.N. force had freedom of movement, but its exact rôle and powers still remained unclarified. British troops in the north-west had been fired on by the Greeks and returned the fire. Later, French-Canadian troops in the Kyrenia area returned the fire of some Turks. On 15 April, while Makarios was visiting Grivas in Athens with a view to arranging his return, Cypriote Greeks entered the Ledra Palace Hotel, where the Mediator and U.N. Commander had their quarters, and fortified it with sandbags. During the resulting arguments a British soldier clubbed a Cypriote who was trying to seize his rifle. Relations of the Greek irregulars with the British continued bad, as was shown also at Kato Pyrgos in the north-west, where seven other British U.N. soldiers were disarmed.

Makarios returned on the 16th, and on the 19th agreed under pressure to demolish the gun-posts round the Ledra Palace. It is characteristic of him that he tried at the same time to negotiate a package deal whereby all strong-points in the Nicosia and Kyrenia areas should be dismantled and the Turkish contingent should replace the British in Nicosia (thus relinquishing its strategic position). Then he announced a plan for a general amnesty, the dismantling of road-blocks and other military positions throughout the island, and the resettlement of Turkish refugees (for whom, on 23 March, he had already shown the most tender solicitude). Since this would have left the Turkish community at the mercy of the Greeks, the offer was not treated seriously by Dr Küçük, but it made a good impression among the Afro-Asians. Not until 1 June were the last posts at the Ledra Palace dismantled.

On 13 April, the Turkish irregulars sprang a surprise on the Greeks by seizing a small hill overlooking the Greek villages of Pano and Kato (Upper and Lower) Dhikomo, south of the Kyrenia range. They also fired on Karmi, north of the range. The Greeks made their preparations, and on 24/25 April launched a full-scale assault on the Turkish hill positions. Under the personal supervision of Georghadjis, who seems to have been effective on this occasion, they captured most of the heights held by the Turks, except immediately around St Hilarion itself. However, according to Foley, the main credit must go to the commando force enrolled at the clinic of Dr Vassos Lyssarides, who had been one of the few left-wing members of EOKA. Reuter reported the wearing of U.N. helmets by some of the attackers.

The Greeks now threatened the Turkish air-strip which had been laid out at Krini, and which might greatly have facilitated an invasion. Not until the 29th was a cease-fire ordered, the day after General Gyani had delivered a warning to Makarios and asked U Thant to reconsider the rôle of UNFICYP. He complained that the Greek assault had taken place despite the absence of trouble in the area over the previous three or four days.

The attitude of the French-Canadian troops throughout the fighting was markedly different from that of the British in their zones. Major Tremblay, French-Canadian officer commanding in the area, said that no action had been taken to stop the fighting because 'we have no orders to interfere. It is felt that as there are no women and children about we can leave them to their little battle.' This was U.N. policy. U Thant had declared that he 'refused to kill Greek and Turkish Cypriots to stop them killing each other' (although he had displayed no such inhibition over the Congo). All the same, one wonders whether it was wise, in that case, to expose non-combatant troops to spectator-risks. In general, the French-Canadians got on much better with the Greeks than the British did, perhaps on account of their common attitudes towards the Anglo-Saxons.

Anglo-Saxon attitudes towards the fighting varied. Mr Harold Wilson went so far as to describe the Greek assault as 'supervised genocide', but Foley rightly points out that official U.N. casualty figures for the first month of UNFICYP's mandate were only seven dead and thirteen wounded on the Greek side, fourteen dead and fifteen wounded on the Turkish. By the end of April, UNFICYP numbered over 6,000 men, and the figures for 8 June were 6,238 soldiers and 173 in the UNCIVPOL. Not until the accidental killing of a Finnish member of the force by Turkish villagers on 21 May did the UNFICYP suffer any casualties. As time passed, and the U.N. soldiers became more and more familiar with the Cypriote (especially Greek) convention that if a spokesman says a thing was not done on purpose then it has not happened, many of them began to revise their previous opinion that their task was merely to clear up the mess left by the British, and to realise that trouble was inherent in the situation itself. This alteration in thinking found no expression in official U.N. documents.

May was a relatively quiet month. Apart from a skirmish at Louroujina on 8 May and the killings and large-scale reprisal at Famagusta, no inter-communal actions of special note occurred, though individual killings and abductions characterised the entire period. On 13 May, Makarios put forward thirteen points to establish the complete independence of Cyprus and termination of the treaties of Guarantee and Alliance. Little notice was taken. On the 26th, Cypriote Turks and Canadian troops again exchanged shots. The next day saw the capture of Senior Aircraftsman Keith Marley who, using his wife and child as a cover, was engaged in running mortars and other arms to the Turks for financial gain. On 6 July, he was sentenced to fifteen years' imprisonment, though he was released by the end of the year. Meanwhile, Greek emissaries were purchasing heavy weapons, motor-boats, and helicopters from Czechoslovakia.

As the flow of arms continued without abatement and the U.N. took no steps to prevent it, the Turkish government, on 25 May, called for action to prevent 'annihilation' of the Turkish community in Cyprus. At a meeting of the NATO permanent Council on the 30th, Mr İnönü expressed pessimism regarding the future and disappointment over lack of support from Turkey's allies. We now know that on 1 June the Turkish Security Council decided to invade Cyprus with forces in readiness at Iskenderun (Alexandretta), the object being to establish a beachhead and then bring about a negotiated separation of the two communities. In Cyprus, it had been arranged that Dr Küçük should demand a meeting of the entire cabinet, as constituted in 1960. When Makarios refused, as it was rightly assumed he would, the invasion would be on. For the time being, Turkish Staff officers turned up as usual at diplomatic functions, and the British Embassy, for one, was deceived.[1] The American Ambassador, however, was informed of the decision to intervene on 2 June. Under the Treaty of Guarantee, 'each of the guaranteeing powers reserved the right to take action with the sole aim of re-establishing the state of affairs created by the present treaty', so Turkey was within her rights to intervene, but only in order to preserve the unitary state, not in order to partition it.

The United States could not afford to allow a struggle to develop between two NATO partners. Accordingly, on 5 June, President Johnson sent İnönü a letter drafted by Rusk, in which there was a good deal of flattery and concern, but in which it was made plain that if Turkey attacked she could not rely upon American help in the event of Soviet intervention. Furthermore, the United States could not agree to American-supplied military equipment being used in any such attack. To add point to the letter, the Sixth Fleet was discreetly placed between Turkey and Cyprus. The Turks, who had helped to pull the American chestnuts out of the fire under cover of the U.N. flag in Korea, resented this letter very much, but desisted from their enterprise all the same. The letter was to be published in full as a calculated indiscretion by the Istanbul newspaper *Hürriyet* on 13 January 1965.

Another American fear was that Cyprus might become 'another Cuba'. They did not like Makarios's dealings with Moscow. Now

---

[1] This is not surprising. The British Embassy in Ankara was also caught off balance by the Turkish *coup* of 1960.

an attempt was made to decide matters without his participation. Both İnönü and the Greek premier Papandreou were invited to Washington for talks, and the former, on 23 June, was associated with Johnson in a communiqué referring to 'the binding effects of existing treaties'. When Papandreou arrived two days later he objected strongly to this clause, and insisted on conducting negotiations with Turkey through the U.N. Mediator. U Thant's deprecation, on 15 June, of Turkey's recurrent invasion threats had led him to expect sympathy at the United Nations. At the same time, Greece's tourist trade was suffering badly on account of demonstrations over the Cyprus problem, and there was also the heavy cost of men and weapons being sent to Cyprus, so the Greek government was anxious to find some solution. The competent politician Acheson was suggested as a person who might help towards such a solution. The two Prime Ministers now flew on to hold more separate talks in London and Paris. Eventually it was agreed that negotiations should be held at Geneva. On his return to Ankara, İnönü set about building the CENTO alliance into a more independent and powerful organisation. Turkish support over Kashmir was traded for Pakistani support over Cyprus.

The most important events of the month of June in Cyprus itself were the disappearance of Major Edward Macey and the return of General Grivas. On 1 June, Major-General Bishop, British High Commissioner in Cyprus, protested at searches by Cypriote Greeks of British nurses and an eighty-year-old woman of the same nationality at road-blocks. On account of the degrading and indecent manner in which such searches were carried out (by the Greek partisans of human dignity and the United Nations Charter) tension rose between the Greeks and British troops, and on 5 June the latter, together with their wives and families, were confined to their camps and homes. On 8 June, it was reported in Nicosia that Major Edward Macey and his driver Leonard Platt had disappeared. As Macey spoke fluent Turkish, was senior liaison officer to Dr Küçük, and had for some time been the target of a Greek press campaign there can be no doubt that Greek irregulars were responsible. The Greek-Cypriote police now went through the usual charade of 'searching' for the two soldiers, but since neither they nor the jeep were ever found it is permissible to record the persistent rumour that they were walled up alive and left to starve. Both men were members of UNFICYP, and on 17 June the United Nations even went so far as to rebuke the Cypriote Greeks over their disappearance. Great Britain, of course, agreed to continue her military and financial contributions to UNFICYP, though on a reduced scale.

In all probability the disappearance of Macey was the factor that decided the Athens government to permit the return of General Grivas. With Georghadjis in control there would never be discipline among the irregulars. When Grivas arrived in Cyprus he made statements protesting his friendship for the Turks, opposing by implication the killing of hostages, and insisting on a referendum to determine the will of the majority. During secret meetings held in July and August he suggested *Enosis* as a solution, with compensation for those Turks wishing to emigrate, and a Turkish base to be established on the site of a British one. He is too realistic a man to ignore Turkey's power and security needs. There seems no doubt that his plan also provided for the ousting of Makarios. Not until 15 August did he take over supreme command of the National Guard from General Karayiannis.

Grivas was not the only soldier to arrive from Greece. Five thousand others came too, together with 3,000 tons of freight. UNFICYP observers and Turkish dock-workers were kept away from the Limassol docks when they landed, and buses and lorries transported them inland by night. The Americans did not oppose the move, and the desire to see Makarios under the control of Athens, coupled with the willingness of Grivas to put forward the Turkish base solution (as Acheson did later), probably accounts for this.

Conscription was introduced by the Greek-Cypriote government at the end of May, and in July the National Guard, with the newly arrived officers and soldiers from mainland Greece, was estimated by UNFICYP to number some 24,000 men, while the armed police force remained at 5,000. Later estimates for the National Guard rise as high as 40,000, which explains its importance as a solution to the unemployment and security problems. Arms also came in via Egypt.

The Turks were estimated to have built up to about 10,000 men, excluding 1,700 police. In early July, according to UNFICYP, some 300 soldiers from Turkey landed in the Kokkina/Mansoura area to supplement 300 or so who had infiltrated elsewhere. On 11 July, Turkey admitted landing troops secretly in Cyprus, only to deny it a day later. The T.M.T. seems to have become something of a law unto itself, though never so ill-disciplined as some of the Greek irregulars. Greek newspapers continued to circulate stories of anonymous Turks terrorised by the T.M.T. The mainland Turkish contingent remained astride the Kyrenia road, ignoring U Thant's statement in mid-June that it would be 'helpful' if they returned to camp. In mid-July, Dr Küçük was to complain that the Greek army contingent had moved west to Yerolakkos village, more than five miles from Nicosia.

After an engagement at Ayios Theodhoros (in the north-west) on 16 June there was a long lull before the storm; though stray bullets from either side kept the pot on the boil. Great Britain, Canada, Sweden, Denmark, and U Thant all protested about the continued arms build-up. President Makarios and Dr Küçük expressed their concern in reply, and the arms came in as before. Lieutenant-General Gyani resigned on 9 July, probably on account of dissatisfaction with the terms under which UNFICYP was forced to operate, and was replaced by General K. S. Thimayya, also of India.

The pump supplying the Dhekelia base with water was blown up for a second time on 3 June, and provocation of British troops continued, though not always on the part of the Greeks. On 28 April, Dr Küçük himself had said in an interview with the *Irish Times* that the proportion of British troops was too high, and on 15 and 16 July a British liaison officer, Major Phillips, was brutally treated by irregulars in the Turkish quarter of Nicosia for expressing allegedly pro-Greek sentiments. In view of these circumstances, and the vote by the Greek-Cypriote House of Representatives in favour of ending the allegedly biased British participation in UNFICYP, the obvious course for the British government to take was to give notice that at the end of the current three-month period British troops would be withdrawn to their sovereign bases. No such decision was taken. American interests demanded that the British should remain, and politicians in Britain still professed to believe that the multi-racial Commonwealth was a going concern. At the July Commonwealth Conference, the case presented by Mr Kyprianou was supported by rulers of countries like Nigeria and Ceylon which had every reason to fear for their own ethnic cohesion. In a common communiqué, the Conference stated that the Cyprus problem should be solved within the framework of the United Nations Charter. Cypriote emissaries were also active in other countries of the underdeveloped world, and a 'Coordinating Committee of Cypriot Self-Determination' was working effectively in New York.

In Cyprus itself the lawyers were hard at work. A new Administration of Justice Law in June was followed on 9 July by the union of the Constitutional Court and the High Court in one Supreme Court. The High Court President, Mr Justice Wilson, had resigned on 31 May, and the Greeks now scored a propaganda victory by appointing the Turk Mehmet Zekya as President of the combined Court. He and two other Turkish judges were given a

U.N. escort to and from the Turkish sector. The tax system set up in 1960 was amended, also without Turkish consent, and on 23 July came a new Electoral Law, despite Turkish protests.

In Geneva, the representatives of Greece and Turkey met Tuomioja separately, the Cyprus government having decided not to send any representative. Together with Lord Hood of the British Foreign Office Mr Acheson acted as honest broker and tried to reconcile Greek and Turkish demands. He had the intelligence to see that other outstanding differences between the two countries might be solved at the same time. His suggestion of *Enosis*, with compensation for those Turks wishing to emigrate, was sensible; and so was his suggestion that Castellorizon, the remote Greek island off the southern Turkish port of Kaş, should be ceded to Turkey. However, his suggested creation of one or two Turkish cantons in Cyprus, as well as a Turkish base, was rejected out of hand by Makarios, and later by Papandreou. İnönü, for his part, pressed for a larger, more viable Turkish area in Cyprus, and threatened that if the territorial balance in the eastern Mediterranean were disturbed the Treaty of Lausanne might have to be reviewed. Still, the Turks showed they were willing, in principle, to discuss revision of the Zurich and London Agreements.

The Tylliria Fighting

By mid-July 1964, tension had grown at Temblos on the Kyrenia coast. The Turks had infiltrated some eighty fighters and the Greeks moved up some newly-acquired twenty-five-pounders. There was renewed firing at Ayios Theodhoros, and since late June the Greek-Cypriote newspapers had underlined the necessity of mounting an assault on the Mansoura-Kokkina beachhead nearby. On the domestic front a ban was placed on the import of all building materials, car-parts, or fuel over a certain quantity into the Turkish enclaves. Even some Red Crescent supplies were banned, while other Red Crescent supplies, on this and other occasions, were sent back to Turkey because the Turks refused to pay tax on them.[1] As a result, the T.M.T. had to exert pressure on a few Turks to prevent them giving in. The increased restrictions were very much resented in Turkey, and General Gürsel remarked ominously that a landing in Cyprus would be unnecessary because 'Turkish bombs could settle this affair'.

---

[1] I am reminded of an incident in the late 1950s when a large gift-shipment of American medical supplies was allowed to deteriorate on the dock at Istanbul because the Turkish customs insisted on payment of unwarranted import duties.

In August 1964, the struggle reached its crisis. The usual shooting incidents continued, which UNFICYP was powerless to stop. The principal complaint of the Force Commander was that his men did not have freedom of movement over much of the island. Occasional Turkish obstruction was dealt with by negotiation, but the Greeks were less amenable. On 6 August, in response to a request from U Thant dated 22 July, Makarios guaranteed the Force 'complete freedom of movement', although no fewer than fifty-seven areas held by the Greeks were to be visited only by senior U.N. officers, after due warning, at predetermined times. The government forces were particularly touchy about possible photography from U.N. helicopters, and they had reason to be. Not only British but also Swedish and Austrian members of UNFICYP had shown themselves to be sympathetic towards the Turks. In the following September, two Swedish officers were to be caught smuggling arms between Kokkina and Lefka. Their sentence of two years was commuted to eight months and they were cashiered. One of them married a Turkish-Cypriote woman, who was arrested in 1967 by the Turks for revealing that she had worked as a spy in the Greek quarter of Nicosia and had persuaded her future husband to provide information.

In late July, the Greeks began to concentrate around the Mansoura-Kokkina beachhead in the Tylliria area. On 3 and 4 August, their motor-torpedo-boats fired light anti-aircraft guns at the Turks on the shore, and all Turkish supplies there were cut off. It was on the 4th that Makarios gave the U.N. Commander a solemn and renewed assurance that the Greeks would not attack. It seems to have been the order to break that undertaking which decided General Karayiannis to resign later in the month as Commander of the National Guard and return to Greece. Even the Turks admitted that he was a good and honourable soldier.

On 6 August, using as an excuse the Turkish occupation of a nearby height almost a month previously, the Greeks mounted a full-scale attack, using 25-pounders, rocket-launchers, mortars, armoured cars, and four 20mm. Oerlikon machine-guns. The 1,500 men of the National Guard taking part in the attack rose to 2,000 by the next day, while the Turks had 500 men with some mortars and rocket-launchers, a number more or less proportionate to the Turkish minority in the population as a whole. The assault continued throughout the following day, and, as the Turks were being forced back, four Turkish air force jets appeared and fired warning shots out to sea off Polis. Turkey made an appeal to the Security Council, which did not meet promptly. By the early hours of 8 August, the Turks had been pushed out of Mansoura and

Ayios Theodhoros and retreated into Kokkina. Meanwhile, diversionary firing across the Green Line was taking place in Nicosia.

The only two remaining Turkish footholds on the north-west coast were plainly doomed to be overrun when, on the afternoon of the 8th, thirty Turkish jets appeared and attacked their Greek assailants. On the next day, sixty-four Turkish jets not only attacked military targets, but switched their activities to the surrounding Greek villages, machine-gunning and dropping incendiaries which destroyed many houses and a hospital at Pachyammos. A government patrol-boat, the *Phaethon*, was burnt out, with a loss of five killed and thirteen wounded, while a Turkish pilot who baled out when his aircraft blew up over Xeros later died as a prisoner. For some time UNFICYP could not find the Greek leaders, who had gone to ground so that they could not be pressured into stopping the attack on the beachhead. Ironically enough, this meant that the Turkish raids continued.

During the fighting the Swedish unit which had been stationed in the zone behaved well, evacuating Turkish women and children to Lefka. At an early stage the Swedes came under fire themselves, but both the local National Guard commander and President Makarios refused to stop the assault.

On 9 August, at 1350 hours, Makarios publicly threatened to attack every Turkish village in the island unless the air attacks stopped within two hours. However, he failed to get the hoped-for support from Greece and Russia, so the deadline was extended indefinitely. Greece had massed forces on her Thracian frontier with Turkey, and had sent two jets on a warning flight over the Turks of Nicosia, but was in no hurry to pit her army of 120,000 men against Turkey's 400,000. Russia had been made aware that her physical intervention would bring in the American Sixth Fleet. The Security Council called for a cease-fire by all concerned on the night of 9/10 August, which was agreed to by Makarios. More Turkish planes came over on the following day, but Turkey complied with a further U.N. resolution of the 11th, calling upon 'all nations' to desist from overflying Cyprus in violation of its sovereignty. The Turkish bombing conflicted with Article 2, paragraph 3, of the U.N. Charter, whereby all members are required to settle their disputes by peaceful means, but it was not officially condemned because it was directed towards restoration of the *status quo*, in accordance with the Treaty of Guarantee. Harassment and occasional killings have continued in Cyprus from that time to this, but no serious assault was launched on the Turkish enclaves until November 1967; so it can be said that the Turkish air attacks were decisive in creating the stalemate which UNFICYP maintained.

One interesting result of the August fighting, albeit a short-lived one, was that individuals (mostly Greek) seem to have renewed acquaintance with persons of the opposing ethnic group after a lapse of some years, but this was more in the nature of insurance than any sudden recollection of past amity.

Meanwhile, the Cypriote Greeks intensified their blockade, in the belief that the Turks would swiftly be reduced to obedience. The water supply of the Turks of Ktima was cut off on 5 August, and their food supply on the 8th. Conditions were especially bad in the two small remaining beachheads at Kokkina and Limnitis, where people were reduced to living in caves. Yet the Turks of Kokkina later refused nine tons of food sent to them by the hated Greek authorities. Some 56,000 people were dependent on relief supplies from Turkey. However, the general strategic position of the Cypriote Turks was not a bad one. There were enclaves in all the major cities except Kyrenia. In the Lefka area were some 8,000 Turks, including 750 to 900 members of the T.M.T., in a good position to link up with any landing near Xeros. The big enclave north of Nicosia almost reached the sea at Temblos, and the one at Ktima, while weak on one side, overlooked the coast from an excellent raised defensive position. The Larnaca enclave, less defensible, included a stretch of coast with shallow waters suitable for light landing-craft. Inland, at Louroujina, near Idalium, and at Kophinou, were other enclaves, the latter in a good position to dominate the main road from Limassol to Nicosia or Larnaca; and every Turkish village was a potential trouble centre.

In Geneva on 16 August, Tuomioja fell ill, dying in Helsinki on 9 September. A modified version of Acheson's plan, involving the lease by the Turks of a base in Cyprus for twenty-five years, alienated the Turks and was unacceptable to Makarios.

The struggle now shifted back to the United Nations, where Makarios was in his element, and he soon set about preparing the ground. On 28 August he flew to Egypt, where Nasser deplored the Turkish air attacks and promised help in the event of any recurrence.

After the Tylliria fighting, the Greek and Turkish national contingents returned to their previous positions from the ones they had taken up some way west. Towards the end of the month, Makarios announced that he would not allow rotation of the Turkish contingent, over half of which was due for relief, and the Turks postponed it at U Thant's request. One way out of the impasse, already suggested by U Thant, was to place both contingents under the UNFICYP Commander, but the Turks insisted on retaining an unacceptable degree of control and on keeping their contingent on the Kyrenia road. Makarios eventually gave way, but in October an agreement was worked out whereby the road was opened to Greek vehicles at stated times, under U.N. supervision.

Incidents continued, though the results should not be exaggerated. An official U.N. estimate of the number killed between 9 June and 8 September, exclusive of the costly Tylliria fighting, was twenty-three, of whom four Greeks and two Turks had been killed in the 259 shooting incidents, while four Greeks and thirteen Turks had been murdered. In addition, twenty Greeks and thirteen Turks had been wounded.

On 10 September, the Secretary-General in his report, based largely upon the Ortega report of the previous summer, described the privations imposed on the Cypriote Turks to force a solution, the plight of the refugees, the defects in the administration of justice where they were concerned, the looting and destruction of their property, and their humiliations at road-blocks. He added the heartening news that 'the beating, shooting and kidnapping of civilians had been greatly reduced'. Makarios responded on the 15th by removing all restrictions on the supply of food to the Turks, though building materials were still forbidden, and offered to remove all armed posts if the Turks would do the same. He also offered a general amnesty 'except in respect of criminal offences' and assistance to those refugees wishing to return to their homes. The offer was taken up by a few, but the effect was largely nullified by the hostility of ordinary Greeks. At the same time, Makarios resisted UNFICYP demands for unrestricted freedom of movement and the proposed right of the Force Commander to create buffer zones. In view of the plan for the Force to become non-operational in the event of a Turkish invasion, this resistance was strategically justified.

When the UNFICYP mandate was extended for a further three-month period to 26 December the British government contributed a disproportionate $1 million towards upkeep of the Force, in addition to the $2.5 million she had already contributed. In the following month, she was to grant £1 million to Greece. In Cyprus three British vehicles were stolen and the insults continued. Nevertheless, the disproportionate British contributions also continued.

On 16 September the Turco–Greek trade, residence, and maritime agreements expired, and 6,000 more Greek nationals were expelled from Turkey in retaliation for the blockade of the Turks in Cyprus. By the time others had been expelled in 1965, few remained of the 12,000 Greek nationals who had been safeguarded by the 1930 Convention.

Diplomatic Manoeuvring and the Plaza Report

On 28 September 1964, Señor Galo Plaza Lasso, ex-President of Ecuador, filled the post of Mediator in succession to Tuomioja. He had already been in Cyprus as U Thant's personal representative the previous May. The Turks had not been antagonistic towards Tuomioja personally, but they had reason to fear his replacement by a South American Roman Catholic, both because Catholics in this oecumenical age tend to have a special sympathy for the Eastern Orthodox Church, and because a majority of the South American nations were specifically sympathetic towards the Cypriote Greeks. Ecuador, with its intractable ethnic problems, could be expected to have a special sympathy for them. Such considerations are apt to be subconscious, but they are none the less important. Besides, Galo Plaza had shown a certain bias before he took up the post. For example, he made statements minimising the effect of the blockade at Kokkina, though General Thimayya, who visited the village, described the conditions as 'scandalous' and 'degrading'. Again, the Secretary-General's report of 10 September 1964 stated that 'the economic restrictions being imposed against the Turkish communities in Cyprus, which in some instances have been so severe as to amount to a veritable siege, indicate that the Government of Cyprus seeks to force a potential solution by economic pressure as a substitute for military action'. But Galo Plaza was to state that the Cypriote Turks 'purported to regard themselves' as being under actual siege. He also said, quite truly though rather foolishly, that this was not the first time the United Nations had recognised an unconstitutional government.

So successful had Makarios been in projecting himself as a supporter of continued independence rather than *Enosis* that he gained the tangible support of the Soviet Union, which feared the extension of NATO power. On 30 September, a secret agreement was signed between Cyprus and the Soviet Union, which later turned out to be a commercial and arms deal and not in any way political. In fact, Makarios was turning to Russia as an alternative source of arms supply, just as Nasser had done in 1955.

The arms deal acted as a warning to Greece, which had given Makarios little support over the rotation issue. It also sparked off newspaper recriminations in Cyprus. Sampson urged Grivas to abandon his hostility towards the Eastern bloc, and Dr Dervis replied by condemning the secrecy of the agreement. A 'Press Counsellor' was sent out from Greece whose task it was to counter anti-Enotist propaganda. He was not made welcome. The Cypriotes of the National Guard clashed in argument with their comrades from mainland Greece, and there were also disputes among the Cypriotes themselves. Sometimes (as on one occasion in the Miami Cabaret in Nicosia) abuse led to physical clashes, and a number of people received gunshot wounds. On 11 October, Sampson and Papaioannou, Secretary-General of AKEL, organised a demonstration against the British bases, apparently unmindful of the number of Cypriotes employed there. *Eleftheria* put out such statements as 'If there is to be a world war over Cyprus, let it be now', so that Western opinion naturally began to swing in favour of *Enosis*, or at least 'double *Enosis*'. The situation seemed to be getting out of hand.

Makarios's chief success during the month of October 1964 was at the Cairo Conference of non-aligned countries, which brought together forty-seven heads of state. In a speech on 9 October he pleased all those present with an attack on the British S.B.A.s, well knowing that they were essential to the economy, and having no intention of liquidating them as yet. The common declaration included two paragraphs calling upon 'all states in conformity with their obligations under the Charter of the United Nations ... to respect the sovereignty, unity, independence and territorial integrity of Cyprus and refrain from any threat or use of force or intervention directed against Cyprus and from any efforts to impose upon Cyprus unjust solutions unacceptable to the people of Cyprus'. There followed the statement that 'Cyprus, as an equal member of the United Nations, is entitled to and should enjoy unrestricted and unfettered sovereignty and independence, allowing its people to determine freely, without any foreign intervention or interference, the political future of the country, in accordance with the Charter of the United Nations'. President Tito called in at Cyprus on his way home, and received a hero's welcome. Cypriote emissaries were later sent out to visit various non-aligned countries in preparation for the forthcoming campaign at the United Nations.

In view of these developments, Turkey had good reason to fear diplomatic encirclement and political isolation, and so began making frantic efforts to mend her fences. Closer trade links were sought with Bulgaria, Romania, and Yugoslavia, while goodwill missions were sent out on the heels of the Cypriotes to Afro-Asian and Latin American countries, as also Spain, which was once more becoming a diplomatic factor in world affairs. On 6 November, the Turkish Foreign Minister, Cemal Erkin, managed to elicit from the Russians a statement accepting the legal rights of the Turkish-Cypriote community and implying opposition to *Enosis*. Trade and cultural agreements were signed, and there was talk of re-establishing the good relations of Atatürk's time. Obviously, Russia was only interested in keeping the pot boiling and seizing whatever advantage she could. In Palestine also she had supported both sides.

News of the Moscow talks brought Signor Manlio Brosio, NATO Secretary-General, post-haste to Ankara, fearful that the eastern flank of the alliance was being eroded. He was reassured that Turkey intended abrogating none of her treaties. The United States was also becoming worried, and seems to have promised support to the deputy chairman of the Justice Party, the successor to the Democratic Party, which was in opposition to İnönü and after wards came to power. The Cyprus problem had been well publicised by Greek organisations in North America, and no fewer than thirty-seven senators, thirty-six congressmen, and four State Governors, together (inevitably) with the Mayor of New York, had made statements in favour of *Enosis*.

As November drew on, the leaders of either side in Cyprus made proposals which they knew would not be accepted. Dr Küçük again asked the President to convene the 1960 Council of Ministers, while the President offered to help the refugees to return to their homes provided all property taken over by the Turks was restored. The Turks were then (metaphorically) up in arms over the vote for abolition of the municipalities by the Greek-Cypriote House of Representatives.

Makarios pleased the non-aligned countries and embarrassed the Greek government by appearing to make *Enosis* conditional on complete demilitarisation of the island. After a visit by Galo Plaza towards the end of the month the British government unofficially let it be known that its base areas in Cyprus were dispensable in the age of the Polaris submarine, but later officially denied any intention of giving them up. But his liking for the idea of demilitarisation did not mean that Makarios was prepared to allow Communists to increase their power, and on 2 December his insistence on the disbanding of private armies and an end to their propaganda activities seems to have been directed mainly against AKEL. In mid-December Soviet military aid began to arrive, including tanks said to be of Second World War vintage. However, Makarios was not content to strengthen the island militarily, and an agreement in principle was signed with Shell-Mobil for the building of an oil refinery at an estimated cost of £3 million. Playing off the East against the West meant, for the time being, getting the best of both worlds.

The situation one year after the outbreak of hostilities was one of wait-and-see, with the Greeks waiting in some comfort and many of the Turks living in tents, or even caves, in the worst rains for thirty years. The extent of inter-communal animosity could be gauged from such pointers as the Greek-Cypriote campaign (in line with mainland Greece) against reference to certain commodities as Turkish; so that 'Greek coffee' (as well, presumably, as 'Greek delight') were supposed to become standard usage. Cypriotes tend not to meet your eye when they refer to the coffee in this fashion.

In his report to the Security Council of 14 December 1964, U Thant was able to point to a relaxation of tension, giving due credit to UNFICYP and his special representative in Cyprus, Senhor Carlos Alfredo Bernardes of Brazil. However, looting, deliberate humiliation, and wilful destruction of Turkish property at road-blocks, together with the ban on factory machinery and road-mending or building materials for the Turks, continued as before. So did the occasional killings. The Greek-Cypriote campaign to 'pacify' the Turks had limited success with a few small groups, but the enclaves remained completely outside Greek-Cypriote jurisdiction, and the Turkish villages outside them gave the Greeks grudging cooperation at best.

The year 1965 was one of intense diplomatic activity over Cyprus. In January there was renewed support for Makarios at the Conference of Commonwealth Prime Ministers at Lagos, and a statement from the Russians that federation was a 'possible solution' in Cyprus. In the island itself the only incidents giving rise to increased tension were the blockade of the Turks at Ambelikou in March, the raid on the Turks of Kato Polemidhia in September, and the fighting at Famagusta in early November. In the first case UNFICYP was successful in getting food and supplies through to the Turks. In the third, the Turks fired on Greeks who were encroaching on their positions, and the Greeks mounted an assault with rocket-launchers which had some limited success in cutting off the Turkish suburbs outside the walled city; but UNFICYP was permitted to establish a buffer zone after Turkey had appealed to the Security Council, and the Famagusta defortification agreement followed.

In a period of 'phoney war' morale difficulties inevitably arise, and the Greeks had their full share of them. Greece, having lost an estimated £8 million in tourist revenue over 1964 owing to the left-wing demonstrations, and destined to have spent some £110 million on the defence of Cyprus by August 1965, was disposed to be more placatory than the Cypriote Greeks liked. In Cyprus, there were explosions at storage tanks near Limassol and Larnaca in March, April, and October. Fortunately, fire-fighters arrived swiftly from the British bases and earned high praise for their prompt action. In May 1966 one Henri Weiss was to be sentenced for bombing the Shell installations at Larnaca, with confederates paid by the Cypriote Turks. Weiss was released on suspended sentence after only one year. Communists were also antagonistic towards the Western oil consortia, but on 30 July the House of Representatives approved plans for a big refinery at Larnaca, costing £3,650,000. However, no action was taken towards constructing it for at least eighteen months. The whole story of oil installations in Cyprus is a murky and confusing one.

Political arguments between mainland Greek soldiers and active Enotists on the one hand and AKEL supporters on the other remained quite frequent. On 28 May, there was an AKEL demonstration in left-wing Limassol against conscription and the Greek army. In September, at Ktima, Grivas was actually abused to his face. Small-scale desertion by Cypriotes and the almost inevitable differences over local girls played their part in exacerbating petty tensions. Makarios acted as arbiter, and strengthened his hand against his opponents both of the Left and the Right. Soviet arms and lorries were being stockpiled in Egypt and ferried over, but the United States, mindful of the Cuban precedent, would not allow in large missiles. A few Cypriotes, under an officer from Greece, went to Egypt to learn how to use the missiles, but returned to Cyprus after about three weeks on orders from Grivas. Good relations, involving trade agreements, continued between Cyprus and Egypt.

The Plaza Report, following on three rounds of talks with all the interested parties, was formally submitted to U Thant on 26 March 1965, and proved to be a bombshell for the Turks. The document itself is lengthy, repetitive, and discursive, and is written in often deliberately vague United Nations English. It includes a background description of the Cyprus problem and of the Mediator's activities, together with a summary of the positions of the parties to the dispute, and a number of suggestions disguised as 'observations'.

Much of the summary is reasonably accurate and some of it is genuinely informative, but certain remarks, and particularly the suggestions, show a lack of logic. Thus, Galo Plaza regrets that 'little was done under any of the previous régimes, ancient [sic] or recent, to bridge the separateness of the Greek-Cypriote and Turkish-Cypriote communities'. But the only two régimes concerned were those of the Turks and the British. The former were rulers and not differentiated from the bulk of the Moslem settlers in Cyprus, while the latter were technically lease-holders for the first forty-four years of their rule. In view of the strong cultural links between the communities and their respective motherlands, what were the British to do—subordinate Turkish culture to Greek and so break their agreement with Turkey, or impose British culture on both parties (as was done, with singular lack of success, in India)? After the First or Second War the British could have handed over the island to Greece, and might have been wise to do so, but it can hardly be said that such an action would have bridged the separateness of the two communities. We can conclude that the Mediator is trying to blame the colonial administration for difficulties it did not create and which it could do little to reconcile even by the imposition of its own culture.

In describing the respective positions of the interested parties Galo Plaza gives due credit to both the Greek and Turkish governments for exercising a moderating influence over the previous months. Indeed, those governments have always had reason to be more moderate than the respective parties to the dispute in Cyprus itself.

Galo Plaza records the Greek case, which is that the Cypriote Turks with their 'lesser ownership of land and contribution to public expenditure' could not justifiably be put on the same level as the Greek majority 'with regard to the exercise of political powers in the State', and should therefore be regarded as a minority. In this connexion, Galo Plaza's statement elsewhere that the Turkish-Cypriote minority 'obtained from the Zurich and London Agreements a series of rights greatly superior to those which can be realistically contemplated for the future' is (barring a Turkish invasion) quite justified.

In summarising the Turkish demands, the Mediator says that their original insistence on outright partition has been modified to physical separation under a federal government. More specifically, the Turks demanded an area of 1,084 square miles,[1] north of a line running from the village of Yialia (west of the Tylliria zone, in Chrysochou Bay) through Nicosia and Famagusta, so that the Turkish quarters of those cities were included, and the exchange of some 10,000 'families' on either side in order to give the Turks a majority in the area. The Mediator does not say so, but the line running from Yialia is defensively speaking absurd, since it would be dominated by the foothills of the Troödos. Interestingly enough, Galo Plaza tells us that at one stage of the negotiations the Turks were prepared to agree to an area of only 750 square miles (comprising some 20 per cent of the total area of the Republic). However, the Mediator tells us that the proposed line of separation for

---

[1] Dr Plaza (no doubt with the help of United Nations mathematicians) assesses this as 'about 38 per cent of the total area of the Republic'. Since the area of the Republic is the total area of the island (3,572 sq. m.) minus the British bases (99 sq. m.), I assess 1,084 square miles as 31.2 per cent of the area of the Republic.

the latter area would start from 'a point on the north coast to the west of Kyrenia, from which it would run southwest to take in the Turkish sector of Nicosia...', which is a geographical impossibility. Kyrenia itself stands somewhat west of north from Nicosia. At all events, it is clear that the modified Turkish demand would include the north-east of the island, with the same line as formerly proposed running from Nicosia to Famagusta. So the Mesaoria would still be divided into two. The Turks proposed that a federal government would control matters of island-wide concern, but the areas would have cultural and economic relations with Greece and Turkey directly, as the case might be. Despite strong Turkish denials and their proposal that union with mother countries should be ruled out and that the treaties of Alliance and Guarantee should remain in being, we must agree with Galo Plaza that such an arrangement would 'inevitably lead to partition'. Galo Plaza objects that the proposed line of separation would cut through 'interdependent parts of homogeneous areas', be 'a constant source of friction between two mutually suspicious populations', and be 'economically and socially disruptive'. On all points save the social one, this is sound, but Galo Plaza's main objection to the Turkish plan is that it would entail a compulsory transfer of population 'contrary to all the enlightened principles of the present time, including those set forth in the Universal Declaration of Human Rights', and he describes it elsewhere as 'a desperate step in the wrong direction'. The truth is that the hardship and human misery occasioned by the mixing on a basis of equality of incompatible peoples is much greater than that which need be occasioned by their separation, as the experience of western Anatolia shows. A much more reasonable objection would be that the Turkish plan did not envisage a full-scale separation of the peoples, but rather a transfer taking place over five or ten years, and not even then complete. Thus two minority situations would be created instead of one.

Galo Plaza's passionate objection to the separation of peoples colours his view of the situation in Cyprus and influences his suggestions for resolution of the problem. He speaks of the Turks' 'purported dread of Greek rule' as if it had no basis in reality, and of the claims of the Turkish-Cypriote leadership regarding the 'impossibility' (inverted commas Galo Plaza's) of the two communities living together in peace. He himself claims that 'in those parts of the country where movement controls have been relaxed and tensions reduced' the two communities 'are already proving otherwise'. At the same time, he admits that 'there are personal hatreds which will last beyond any political settlement', and that 'not all of the too many weapons which are in too many hands are likely to be surrendered readily'. His solution is that there should be 'safeguards of an exceptional kind' for the Cypriote Turks, and he speaks with approval of Makarios's willingness to incorporate in an agreed constitution 'human rights and fundamental freedoms conforming with those set forth in the Universal Declaration of Human Rights adopted by the United Nations; judicial procedures for their application; and vigilance to ensure equal treatment in appointments and promotions in the public services'. In addition, the Turks would have 'a continuation of their previous autonomy in certain fields of religion, education and personal status', together with 'representation . . . in the governmental institutions' over 'a transitional period' and a 'general amnesty'. We are back to square one. All this is strikingly reminiscent of the constitution of 1960, the entire second part of which consists of 'Fundamental Rights and Liberties' of the most far-reaching kind, closely following those set forth in the European Convention for the Protection of Human Rights and Fundamental Freedoms and the U.N. Universal Declaration of Human Rights. Galo Plaza has foreseen the necessity 'to abrogate or at least modify' the treaties of 1960, and has stated the truth accepted by both sides that 'the problem of Cyprus cannot be resolved by attempting to restore the situation which existed before December 1963'. Yet, in effect, what he is proposing is a return to a similar situation, with the difference that the Turks would now have fewer rights and guarantees than before.

The guarantees Galo Plaza himself proposes are derisory. They are that the United Nations should act as guarantor, that 'any complaint of violation or difficulty in implementation' should be brought immediately before it, and that a U.N. 'commissioner' should be appointed 'whose very existence would', he believes, 'engender confidence in all Cypriots'. Indeed, his very existence would have to be sufficient for the purpose because Galo Plaza does not envisage 'any treaty arrangements which would affect the internal affairs of the Republic', and by present rules no United Nations force may enter a country without the consent of its government. No wonder the Turks regard such 'guarantees' as inadequate.

Yet despite such attempts to patch up a *modus vivendi* between the two communities, Dr Plaza does not entirely disapprove of population movement, any more than Makarios does. He believes that there should be 'adequate compensation and help in starting a new life' in Turkey for those wishing to do so. He also speaks elsewhere of 'provision for the resettlement of Turkish-Cypriots who wished to leave the island and for the rehabilitation of those who would remain' and of 'appropriate assistance . . . to rehabilitate all those whose property has been destroyed or seriously damaged as a result of the disorders'. But rehabilitation is by no means necessarily the same thing as compensation for losses suffered.

Dr Plaza's Report not only fails to reassure the minority, it guarantees frustration for the majority. He agrees with Tuomioja 'that there could be no concealing the fact that the formal "prohibition" of the *Enosis* idea did not suppress it in Cyprus', and admits that if Cyprus were 'fully independent' (his own inverted commas) it would have the right to choose *Enosis*; but he adds that a state's right of self-determination 'is governed by its obligations' under the U.N. Charter to promote 'the well-being of all its citizens' as also 'international peace and security'. Accordingly, he suggests that as long as the risks of conflict persist, the government of Cyprus should 'refrain . . . from placing before the population the opportunity to opt for *Enosis*'. In support of this suggestion he puts forward arguments already hoary in the British period, namely that Cyprus and Greece have different systems of law, that *Enosis* 'does not enjoy unqualified support among the Greek Cypriots as a whole', and that the Cypriotes rely for their higher standard of living on the system of Commonwealth preference; whereas the experience of history is that ethnic similarities can override all environmental differences and all considerations of short-term comfort.

Galo Plaza is right when he indicates that many Cypriote Greeks have a vague idea of *Enosis* and do not necessarily mean by it 'the complete absorption of Cyprus into Greece'. Nevertheless, link-ups between several organisations in Cyprus and their counterparts in Greece had already taken place, and it is significant that the only part of the Report about which Makarios had 'reservations' was precisely the self-imposed restraint in the matter of *Enosis*. On 2 February 1966, Makarios and the Greek government in a joint communiqué said that 'any solution ruling out *Enosis* would not be acceptable'.

Finally, having made clear that any settlement should, in his view, be based upon 'continued independence', Galo Plaza suggests that the people of Cyprus 'should be asked to accept or reject' the basic settlement 'as a single package', thus laying himself wide open to the favourite liberal charge against all those who rule by referendum, that of promoting a package deal, parts of which would be unacceptable by themselves.

The Turkish government reacted harshly to the Plaza Report, stated that he had exceeded his terms of reference in that he had made recommendations and suggestions as to substance, and considered that his functions as a Mediator were terminated. U Thant refused to regard the Mediator's mission as having come to an end, but on 17 December 1965 Turkey stated that her decision was irrevocable. On 22 December, Galo Plaza resigned. His Report was 'noted' by the Political Committee of the General Assembly in the same month, and so can be said to have been approved to that extent by the United Nations.

Turkish-Cypriote Morale and Greek-Cypriote Success at the United Nations

The Turkish government was angered by the attitude of the Western powers over the Plaza Report, and particularly by the fence-sitting attitude of Great Britain, which was, after all, a partner to the London Agreement.

The effect on Turkish-Cypriote morale was initially profound, and the leadership had to act quickly to restore it. Protest meetings against the blockade had proved reasonably successful, so others were occasionally held during 1965 (e.g. on 19 April). More important was the emphasis on military parades in Turkish Nicosia. Instead of concealing their arms as heretofore, the Turks now flaunted them as openly as the Greeks. The parades took place on such dates as 23 April (Turkish National Sovereignty and Children's Day), when weapons on display included a modern cannon, 19 May (Turkish National Youth and Sports Day), 30 August (Turkish Victory Day, celebrating the driving of the Greeks into the sea at Smyrna), 29 October (Turkish Republic Day), and 10 November (Atatürk Remembrance Day). Weekly parades were also instituted, and continue to this day, while a special cemetery was constructed in the middle of the city for those killed by the Greeks.

There is no doubt that the Turks now had more arms than in the previous year, more than they could have obtained either from the beachheads or through the rotation of the Turkish contingent. Presumably some of the arms came from non-Turkish sources. To judge by the evidence of Mrs Theresa Osman, the British wife of a Famagusta Turk, life was hard in the enclaves, especially for those who contravened the orders of the leadership. On 11 April, two trade unionists, Derviş Kavazoğlu (a left-wing Turk who had gone over to the Greeks in 1957) and Costas Misiaoulis (a Greek) were ambushed and shot dead on the Nicosia-Larnaca road, near the Turkish township of Louroujina. Probably the T.M.T. wanted them out of the way, but in view of the revelations of Dr Dervis concerning the 1961 murder of Hikmet and Gürkan, one cannot be certain that the Turks were responsible. In October 1965, there was a diphtheria outbreak among the crowded Turkish refugees.

At least sixteen fell ill, of whom at least one died before it was brought under control.

The Cypriote Greeks had some limited success with an effort to offset the effect on foreign opinion of the privations suffered by the Turks by drawing attention to the past sufferings of the Armenians at Turkish hands. On 24 April, Greek officialdom was present (for the first time ever) at ceremonies marking Armenian Independence Day. As a propaganda gambit this was reasonably fair. The Turks had exploited deprecation by the Armenian Bishop Gregor Tokatlian of Diyarbakir and others of the killings of Turks by Cypriote Greeks at Christmas 1964 (although the Armenian hierarchy outside Turkey had not shown any concern). Still, it is worth recording that, according to Turkish sources, 60,000 Armenians in Turkey boast four lycées, eleven secondary schools, two daily newspapers, two weeklies, three monthlies, and one annual, and are much better off than the Turks in Greece, who have only one lycée, one newspaper, and a much lower standard of living.

The terms of office of all those elected in 1960 officially expired in August 1965, and no serious exception was taken when each side unilaterally extended their own, as they have done at yearly intervals ever since. After all, the same thing had been done in France and Britain in time of war, and also in the neutral Irish Free State. However, the decision by the Greek-Cypriote House of Representatives to change the electoral law and introduce a common roll of voters angered the Turks and was frowned on by the Security Council. A public service law providing for a commission to be appointed by the President of the Republic likewise drew Turkish protests. But there was little the Turks could do about it. Greek prosperity continued to increase, and more foreign aid was now forthcoming, very little of which benefited the Turks.

In the second half of 1965 Greek-Cypriote activities at the United Nations were in top gear. As an exercise in persuasion before the General Assembly vote requested by the Cypriote Greeks, Makarios, on 4 October, sent U Thant a Declaration of Minority Rights along the lines suggested in the Plaza Report and a Memorandum listing 'Fundamental Rights and Freedoms' which differed in no essential respect from those already guaranteed in theory under the 1960 constitution, but incorporated Galo Plaza's suggestion that a U.N. Commissioner be appointed as a safeguard, together with an 'adequate staff of observers and advisers'. By this time, the Cypriote Greeks had adopted a position 'in basic agreement with the considerations and guidelines of the U.N. Mediator's report', and disagreement with Galo Plaza's suggested exclusion of

Enosis for the foreseeable future was treated as a matter of detail. The Turks, for their part, had fallen back on the constitution of 1960, which they had already admitted to be unworkable. Such is the hypocrisy demanded on both sides in a dispute under consideration by the United Nations.

After a good deal of speech-making by Mr Kyprianou in tune with the aspirations of the non-aligned, the General Assembly voted on 18 December that 'the Republic of Cyprus, as an equal Member of the United Nations, is, in accordance with the Charter, entitled to, and should enjoy, full sovereignty and complete independence without any foreign intervention or interference'. The vote was the climax of all the efforts of Makarios to win over the non-aligned nations, from the Bandung Conference onwards. The General Assembly resolution specifically recalled the Cairo Declaration of 10 October 1964 in its references to Cyprus.

In Turkey the resolution was taken as the most serious foreign policy reverse suffered in years. There even appeared a newspaper headline : 'We have lost Cyprus'. The Turkish government went so far as to make it clear that it did not regard the resolution as binding. However, an analysis of the vote shows that a reverse swing of the pendulum was already under way. The forty-seven countries voting for the resolution were mostly Afro-Asian and Latin-American, while the fifty-four abstaining included a number of Arab states to which the Turks had appealed as fellow-Moslems. The abstention of Great Britain was regarded by Turkey in a different light because of her technical adherence to the London Agreement. The five voting against included the United States, which was anxious not to alienate Turkey but not so anxious as to manipulate the Latin-American votes, as had been done on many other occasions where Middle Eastern affairs were at issue. The other four voting against were Persia, Pakistan, and Turkey, all of which belonged to the same regional treaty organisation, and Albania, presumably because of her Moslem background and her extreme hostility towards Greece. Pakistan had a further reason for voting with Turkey in that she counted on Turkish support over Kashmir on a *quid pro quo* basis. At the Commonwealth Conference in September 1966 Pakistan was to be the sole dissentient to the view that the Cyprus problem should be settled 'within the framework of the United Nations'.

Erosion of the Greek-Cypriote Diplomatic Position

In 1966, the diplomatic situation of the Greeks deteriorated considerably. After the resignation of Galo Plaza under Turkish pressure, Makarios refused to allow the creation of any further Mediator, even when it was suggested that U Thant himself should try his hand. However, pressure for the achievement of a solution continued strong, and on 2 March U Thant was able to direct his Special Representative, Senhor Bernardes, to promote discussion among the interested parties, or at least between Turkey and Greece. The government of Greece acquiesced in this move, but promised the protesting Cypriotes that any solution reached would have to be approved by them. From 5 to 11 May the Foreign Ministers of Greece and Turkey held informal talks during the NATO ministerial council meeting in London. On 15 June, Kyprianou declared that no solution arrived at by other parties would be binding on Cyprus, but Turco-Greek talks continued nevertheless, as they have done on and off ever since.

Meanwhile, the Turks were active in awakening the fears of the non-aligned nations as regards the possibility of *Enosis* and the consequent extension of NATO power. They no longer gave un-critical support to Israel, but stressed their Moslem background for the benefit of the Arab nations. In this they were enormously helped by the obtuseness of the Greek-Cypriote authorities. At the end of 1965, the National Guard had taken over the shrine of Hala Sultan *Tekke*, a place of small strategic importance. From May 1966 they prevented all Moslem access to it, so that Mehmet Dana, Mufti of Cyprus, could exploit the misuse of one of the holiest places in the world of Islam. The description by a British journalist of the behaviour of the soldiers at the shrine, the minor damage caused and the rubbish left lying about, was to spark off strong reactions.

By June 1966 no fewer than seven of those states which had voted for the Cyprus resolution the previous December (Nepal, Uruguay, the Lebanon, Syria, Gabon, Ethiopia, Ghana) made declarations against interpretation of their vote as favouring *Enosis*, and there were to be joint declarations to the same effect by Turkey and Iraq as well as by Turkey and Afghanistan; so that by October the situation for the Greeks had deteriorated consider-ably. The Soviet Union, having allowed the Greek Cypriotes to run up a bill for a sum still unspecified (and only partially offset by Cypriote agricultural exports to Russia), repeated its previous declaration that federalism was a possible solution for Cyprus, and omitted the usual mention of Cyprus among the Soviet May Day slogans. At the same time, Moscow insisted that Cyprus was a problem for the Cypriotes alone. As in the case of Palestine, the Soviets were chiefly interested in keeping the problem simmering and deriving what advantage they could.

In January 1966, UNFICYP was reduced by 750 men (350, 200, and 200 from Sweden, Finland, and Denmark respectively), and the Irish were also showing signs of becoming restive over un-recouped costs. General Thimayya had died on 18 December 1965, and the British Brigadier A. J. Wilson then acted as interim Commander. The British contingent continued to be by far the largest, but a permanent British Commander would have been unacceptable both to the Cypriote Greeks and to the General Assembly. Therefore, on 17 May Lieutenant-General A. E. Martola of Finland took over command. In March, four British members of the Force were convicted of running arms to the Turks. On the whole, it was a quiet year for UNFICYP, though not without its difficulties and incidents. For instance, the Turks near Mora began to construct fortifications with a view to controlling the Nicosia–Famagusta road, just as they had done near the Nicosia–Kythrea–Lefkonico road farther north, but UNFICYP arranged a with-drawal. And for those who have not had to deal with the Turks in an intransigent mood the detailed account in U Thant's Report of 21 July 1966 of recent trouble over a road between the villages of Trypimeni and Vitsadha will make instructive reading. The year 1966 was also one in which General Carl von Horn's book came out, describing the espionage and corruption at the United Nations. But UNFICYP, being almost entirely north European in composition, was free from the worst excesses, and the soldiers came more and more to resemble tourists, as indeed Makarios had described them. UNFICYP successes in arranging the transfer of records from the lands and surveys office in the Turkish sector and (with considerably more difficulty) in having limited postal services restored to Nicosia and Lefka have already been referred to.

For the Turks the blockade continued, and Georghadjis publicly warned businessmen against dealing with them. However, in the more relaxed atmosphere the Turkish leadership could turn its thoughts to tourism. The parades continued as before, but there was much more emphasis on folk-dancing and other cultural displays. On Turkish National Sovereignty and Children's Day, the children now provided the main attraction. On Turkish Youth and Sports Day, Greek-Cypriote reporters were allowed in for the first time, and duly noted that the Turks were better armed and in better heart than had been thought. Photographs of manoeuvres by Turkish-Cypriote fighters, similar to those of the National Guard, helped to enhance that impression. Some disciplinary action seems to have been taken by the leadership against those who fraternised with the Greeks, but in general the blockade of strategic materials, the deprivation on occasion of such essentials as water and paraffin, and the constant humiliation at road-blocks were more than enough to offset the effect of such doubtless sincere gestures as Makarios's New Year message of friendship. That summer the Greeks tried to impose a tax of 30 per cent on the grain sold by the Turks through the Grain Commission, in addition to the 20 per cent tax already in force, as compensation for Greek land under Turkish cultivation. The Turks, very much more of whose land was under Greek cultivation, then ceased to deal with the Grain Commission. From March onwards more aid was forthcoming from Turkey, so that Turkish-Cypriote living standards rose a little. The only event of political importance which took place among the Cypriote Turks during the year was on 29 December, when Dr Küçük made use of his newspaper *Halkın Sesi* to attack those who were trying to discredit him as a leader.

On the Greek side only a common determination not to let the Turks exploit the situation prevented more outright clashes between Right and Left, such as the one at Kholetria in the Paphos district. Mysterious bombs went off at more frequent intervals, and Georghadjis advanced the theory, denied in *Patris*, that they were all the work of O.A.S. saboteurs employed by the Turks; but the explosions continued after the capture of Weiss, and though the Turks themselves may well have been responsible for some of the subsequent explosions, these often took place where there were no Turks, as for instance at the quarters of officers sent over from Greece. In such cases AKEL supporters were the most likely culprits. In March, an attempt by Georghadjis to lay the blame for an explosion on two Finnish members of UNFICYP, with no more supporting evidence than their being seen in the area, met with disapproval from U Thant, and Makarios had to eat humble pie. Still, it is true to say that the Finnish national character does not suit well with the Greek, and petty friction between Cypriote Greeks and Finnish troops was becoming more common.

Georghadjis also tried to bring the war into the enemy camp, but the Turks had little trouble in maintaining security in their crowded sectors. On 12 March, two saboteurs were caught in Turkish Nicosia who confessed to having been sent by Georghadjis to plant bombs, one of them having been previously employed to spy on officers of the Greek army. On 16 June, the Greek-Cypriote deputy Costas Christodoulides, an ex-member of EOKA and supporter of Grivas, accused Georghadjis of political murders, and courageously stated the obvious truth that there had been a far greater sense of security in the days of the British administration. He was expelled from the Patriotic Front, but his outburst is a sign of how much some Greeks value freedom of expression.

25—C

June was a bad month for Georghadjis, for he unwisely decided to punish the Turks for the continuing explosions by twice sealing off their quarter of Nicosia. On the first occasion the outright blockade lasted only three days, but it provided the Turkish judges with a reason for not attending their courts in future, having previously only been absent for a short period after December 1963. This was a big setback for Makarios's campaign to get the Turks to work with the Greeks, and the latter now had to make do with an acting President of the Supreme Court (made permanent in the following January) and other replacements. In September three Turkish judges in Limassol likewise ceased to attend their courts. The second blockade of Turkish Nicosia was lifted on the intervention of U Thant.

By contrast, the Turkish propaganda mistakes, such as the issue in Turkey of a travel brochure map laying claim to Cyprus, were small indeed. In September, when fires, started in all probability by saboteurs from nearby Turkish villages, burned down 7,786 donums[1] of good timber in the Paphos Forest, the world at large was less disposed to sympathise than it might formerly have been.

In 1966, left-wing agitation in Cyprus against conscription remained strong. Newspapers such as *Teleftea Ora* and the Communist *Haravghi* carried articles criticising Greece. Differences of attitude could also be gauged from small details, as when *Agon* referred to Greece as 'a brother nation' rather than the 'Motherland' beloved of Enotists. A new party came into being to counteract anti-Enotist tendencies. It was called EPEKA, the Party of the National Patriotic Greek Struggle. An attempt to put the National Guard under the control of Georghadjis aroused the suspicions of the Athens government, and had to be dropped. In April Grivas stated : 'There is only one army in Cyprus—the Greek army'.

The Makarios régime tried to adopt the same tactics as in dealing with the army before 1963. The allocation for the National Guard was cut down and on 24 February 1966 the order was given to set about increasing the size of the police force. Clerides arranged for a consignment of 1,000 rifles, 1,000 sub-machine guns, twenty rocket-launchers, twenty mortars, and twenty armoured cars to be imported from Czechoslovakia. U Thant made no demur when he learnt of their purpose, namely to replace out-of-date weapons and arm 300 (later 500) new members of the police. The small arms duly arrived, but a second consignment, including the armoured cars, was stopped by the Czechs in December, under pressure from Turkey. An additional, though minor, irritation for the Turks occurred when the Cypriote Greeks insisted on payment of dues on

[1] Cf. above, p. 47.

a Red Crescent shipment of second-hand clothes. Greco-Turkish talks remained in abeyance.

The Czech arms deal also aroused strong suspicions in Greece, which had troubles enough of its own. As a result of investigations made by Grivas among Greek army officers in Cyprus, the Aspida conspiracy, headed by Andreas Papandreou, the Prime Minister's son, had been uncovered. George Papandreou's government had fallen, and Grivas was the star witness at the trial of the conspirators.

Makarios, for his part, was perturbed over the revelation of a letter which seemed to show that Grivas was working for his overthrow, but Grivas denounced it as a forgery, said that if he had been planning a *coup* he would not be writing about it, and reminded Makarios of his own intrigues in the past.

On the economic side, Greece seems to have been concerned at the statement of Mr Araouzos that there was no customs union of Cyprus with Greece owing to technical (i.e. Commonwealth preference reasons), and in November he went to Athens in order to promote trade. Cyprus was now breaking all past records for agricultural exports, and so made little protest at the gradual rundown of forces at the S.B.A.s. Conditions were stable enough for Makarios to go on his travels again. In the autumn he visited six Central and South American nations, including Ecuador, where he lunched with Galo Plaza, and in January 1967 he was to proceed to the Lagos Conference on Rhodesia, where he cultivated African favour at the U.N.

Quite a serious situation arose in early 1967 over the import by the Cypriote Greeks of the Czech small arms. On 5 February, Turkey gave warning that unless the arms were surrendered to UNFICYP she would despatch an equal number to the Cypriote Turks (i.e. 1,000 rifles and 1,000 sub-machine guns). An agreement was made whereby the weapons remained in a warehouse, subject to inspection by a UNFICYP officer.

In 1967, the Makarios government, partly because of Turkish diplomatic successes, partly because of the diplomatic isolation of Greece after the April *coup*, adopted more conciliatory attitudes towards the West. Dr Lyssarides and his Nicosia branch of the Afro-Asian People's Solidarity Organisation was strongly anti-NATO, but in an interview with an Arab editor Makarios spoke of Cyprus deciding for herself whether she would join NATO after *Enosis,* and in July he appeared to support *Eleftheria* when it came out openly in favour of a NATO base as part of a compromise solution. Under such circumstances, it is not surprising that the Turkish Foreign Minister was well received in Cairo. On 6 March,

Makarios pointed to the differences among the non-aligned nations, implying their unreliability. Another indication of Cypriote adherence to the Western camp came in the same month, when the uncovering of a Soviet spy ring led to the expulsion of a Russian Embassy attaché, the Aeroflot representative, and an Armenian and a Maronite working for R.A.F. Nicosia and CYTA respectively.

In May and June, Clerides forcibly expressed his opposition to any Turkish military base in Cyprus, and in early July he and Araouzos visited London, ostensibly to inaugurate a new through flight. The suspicions of Athens were also aroused when Makarios opined that the Greco-Turkish dialogue, resumed after the *coup,* would not produce favourable results.

With regard to Israel there was a slight but perceptible shift in Greek-Cypriote policy. On 2 May 1967, Makarios had warned that Cyprus would 'react in many ways' if the British bases were used against the Arabs. On 1 June, *Agon* reported feverish activity at the bases, as in 1956. All leave was suspended and Cypriotes were not allowed near the installations. In the event, the Wilson government did not find it necessary to intervene directly against the Arabs, as would certainly have been the case had the war gone against Israel. On 7 June, during the war, Makarios expressed support for the Arabs, and on the 17th a team with supplies of medical equipment was sent to Egypt. However, Rossides at the U.N. warned the Arabs against ignoring 'the existing realities of international life'. On 21 July, Lanites predictably came out in the pro-Zionist *Cyprus Mail* for a policy either of neutrality or support for Israel, a suggestion he was to repeat in *Eleftheria.* In August fifteen other Cypriote businessmen went on a goodwill tour of Israel. Meanwhile, the government officially supported Israeli withdrawal from the Arab territory most recently occupied, but was concerned over the reduction in the number of Jewish tourists.

That a 'pre-emptive strike' could be carried out with impunity, and the resulting gains retained, showed that the international brakes were fading and that weak countries like Cyprus could not afford to alienate too many powerful ones. Even the structure of UNO was tentatively under review, as shown when U Thant suggested associate membership for micro-states. Cyprus is not a micro-state, but the trend was ominous. By October, definite disagreements over foreign policy were being voiced in Nicosia. On 20 October, the normally pro-government *Eleftheria* deplored Kyprianou's call for the use of force in Rhodesia and drew attention to Greek and Greek-Cypriote interests there. Indeed, as had been pointed out in *The Times* on 2 October, the Greeks control a substantial part of the retail trade in Salisbury and so are anxious to force the Asians out. On 7 December, *Eleftheria* stated that a non-aligned policy of friendship with all had led to friendship with none. The government meanwhile cultivated India as a counter-weight to Pakistan's support for Turkey, and strengthened its connexion with France when it permitted Cypriote art treasures to be shown in the Louvre from November 1967 to January 1968.

As instability in Turkey had lessened, it had increased in Greece, to the point in early April when Clerides had reason to call the Kanellopoulos government incompetent in its handling of the Cyprus question. In the early hours of 21 April 1967 came the military *coup* in Athens, which altered the Cyprus situation in that the international press became more than ever opposed to *Enosis*. In early May, a Greek general and two other officers crossed into Turkey, the first of several, who perhaps provided the Turks with useful information. In September, the Council of Europe was preparing a resolution warning Greece of expulsion if there was no return to a parliamentary régime, and at the meeting of European Education Ministers the Cypriote Turks scored a success when Dr Spyridakis was forced to admit that he did not represent them. By the middle of that month, most Western nations had come round to the view expressed in the *Guardian* that 'continual vigilance and persistent nagging' were the best way to deal with a new régime. In this respect there was a parallel with Rhodesia.

The left-wing element in Cyprus was anti-Enotist in practice, if not in principle. A number of Cypriotes were among those who invaded the Greek Embassy in London by way of protest against the military *coup*. Two of the five sentenced in Athens on 21 October for exploding bombs were Cypriote physics students, the ringleader being one of them, Petros Demetriou. On 19 July, it was announced that an AKEL official in the Paphos district had been detained for aiding a Greek army officer who had deserted, and *Patris* was probably right when it charged that AKEL planned to go underground in the event of *Enosis*. *Haravghi* and *Teleftea Ora,* of course, came out strongly against the *coup,* but newspapers sympathetic to Makarios were also critical, so that on 9 August Colonel Papadopoulos, who was visiting Cyprus, complained of the attitude of the Cypriote press.

For the Enotists the *coup* seemed initially to provide excellent opportunities. In July, a bill was passed by the Greek-Cypriote House of Representatives giving legal status to the Greek army officers in the National Guard. The Greek army oath and insignia were now in use among the Cypriotes also. However, difficulties continued to arise. Thus, General Prokos, National Guard commander under Grivas since 1964, refused to hand over his accommodation to General Moronis, who had arrived to take over the command on 18 September. Also in September, moves were afoot thoroughly to Enotise the sports movement. At the same time, the Enotists showed willingness to make concessions in order to gain the desired end. Dr Dervis, leader of the Democratic Union Party, writing in *Patris* on 5 June, implied that territorial exchanges should be acceptable to Greece in return for *Enosis*. In July, Osorio-Tafall, U Thant's Special Representative, temporarily postponed his visits to Ankara and Athens owing to accusations, notably in *Patris,* that he was planning to undermine the Greco-Turkish dialogue, in favour of an 'independence' (i.e. internationalist) solution. Archbishop Ieronymos of Athens, who arrived with two other bishops to promote the cause at an ecclesiastical level, gave assurances that in the case of *Enosis* Cyprus would never be used as a base against Turkey.

August brought persistent rumours of an Athens-inspired *coup* in Cyprus, and it is said that Rossides woke Makarios in the middle of the night with a telephone call from the United Nations to check on one such report. But Makarios made no demur when General Spandidakis visited Cyprus and said it was part of southern Greece. Indeed, he was outspokenly Enotist himself up until the November crisis, and on 17 September 1967 he was reported in the *Sunday Times* as saying that if he had 'any ambition' it was 'to associate [his] name with the historical event of the union of Cyprus with Greece'.

To begin with, Turkey showed restraint. She might so easily have followed the example of Biafra and tried to force a solution while world attention was distracted by the Middle East crisis. But Turkey had more hopes of the new Greek régime than of her allies. Britain, for example, had technically upheld the validity of the 1960 treaties, but done little else, so that the *Special News Bulletin,* on 27 May 1967, bitterly commented : 'There was a time when Britain honoured her obligations'. Turkey contented herself for the time being with diplomatic moves, such as the Turco-Romanian communiqué in May which recognised the rights of both communities in Cyprus. There was also a natural gas agreement concluded with Iraq, and on 20 October 1967 Mr Demirel himself visited that country. Quite evidently, the two countries had a common interest in containing the Kurdish problem. Turkey was much less equivocal than Cyprus in her condemnation of the Israeli 'pre-emptive strike', and on 29 September joined with Russia in a communiqué calling for Israeli withdrawal. Russia, however, remained opposed to any double *Enosis* solution, which would benefit the Greek régime and perhaps NATO. In November, Turkey and Pakistan issued a joint statement to the effect that the Cyprus and Kashmir problems were 'identical', despite the fact that the Moslems are in a majority in the latter case.

Turkish tempers in 1967 were in no way improved by Kyprianou's reference to the 'so-called suffering' of the Cypriote Turks. Restrictions continued, and in March two Turks were assaulted by Greek-Cypriote police under the eyes of UNFICYP soldiers at the Famagusta Gate. According to U Thant, only one Cypriote Turk defected to the Greeks in 1967, while some who had previously defected as many as four times returned to their community. One good reason for this can be seen in the need for Mr Tassos Papadopoulos, on 16 April, to declare that the exploitation of Turks in Greek areas must stop. Minor pinpricks were the municipal taxes imposed on the Turks of Limassol and Paphos in July, non-payment of which resulted in the water being cut off.

Within the Turkish-Cypriote community itself all was not well. The *Cyprus Bulletin* reported a Turk executed by the leadership in Ktima on 23 January, together with alleged killings of other Turks by Turkish irregulars at Kophinou and Nicosia. On 24 February, Kemal Çoşkun, leader of the T.M.T., left for Turkey. In April, according to the Greeks, he was found to have deposited 1.5 million Turkish liras (*c.* £60,000) in a Swiss bank, and was charged with debiting his government with £50,000 for the blowing up of Shell installations at Larnaca, while paying the French saboteurs only £4,000. On 4 May, 438 Turkish-Cypriote high-school students were flown out to continue their education.

According to UNFICYP, over 600 shooting incidents took place in Cyprus during 1967, one reason for them being that the Greeks, and to a lesser extent the Turks, were constantly extending their fortifications. The National Guard did so all over the island, constructing 'coastal defences' as much as ten or eleven miles from the shore. Greek positions were fortified in the demilitarised zone north of Famagusta which had been established in 1965, on Patsalo Hill overlooking Scala, and around the *Tekke* of Hala Sultan. The Turks did the same in the demilitarised McKenzie Hill area at Larnaca, and also at Sakharya village and astride the Salamis road. The Turkish irregulars now had better personal equipment than hitherto.

In March, elements of the National Guard threatened and manhandled UNFICYP personnel over the demolition of a sandbag wall at the Ledra Palace Hotel, and in April the Greeks fired on a U.N. helicopter. The Turks at Mari were a thorn in the side of the National Guard, and had interfered with the passage of hundreds of French tourists. On 8 April, eleven Turks there were wounded by the National Guard, which withdrew after Turkey had made threats. On 13 May, the Cypriote Greeks produced a master-plan which restricted still more areas from entry by UNFICYP. *Patris,* on 18 April, called upon UNFICYP to withdraw, leaving only observers. In June, U Thant had cause to complain of the National Guard treating UNFICYP officers high-handedly and sending them threatening letters. National Guard manoeuvres that summer caused great alarm, and on 24/25 August a potentially serious incident took place in Limassol, when the National Guard responded massively to stone-throwing by local Turks.

UNFICYP soldiers in general can be said to have become rather pro-Turkish than pro-Greek, largely because of the disabilities suffered by the Turks. For instance, on 20 February two U.N. soldiers were caught smuggling a Turk from Lefka (in the Irish zone) to the Nicosia enclave in the boot of their car. After court-martial, they each received nine months' imprisonment. However, in terms of violence UNFICYP was destined to have as much trouble with the Turks. On 1 March, the U.N. Chief of Staff and the Commander of the Famagusta zone were manhandled when they tried to inspect a Turkish forward position near Ayios Theodhoros and Kophinou. A new and uncompromising fighter leader had come to Kophinou in November 1966, who would not even cooperate with proposed Greek postal arrangements. Greek place-names were painted out (as indeed is the Greek custom with Turkish place-names). On 25 January, a Greek bus had been stopped on the road below, and National Guard armoured cars were sent to the area.

For UNFICYP, trouble centred on the Kophinou police compound. On three occasions before 1967, the Turks had used force to obstruct UNFICYP entry. On 2 March, some Turks forced their way in and were ejected. A Turkish flag was taken down from some outbuildings, and Turkish families who had been allowed to remain in quarters within the compound (an arrangement resulting in a good deal of friction owing to differing social customs) were requested to leave. A campaign against UNFICYP then began in the Turkish press, which again complained of UNFICYP in October, when the Force refused to allow Turkish flags over school buildings in Larnaca.

The culmination of Turco-UNFICYP friction at Kophinou came on 11 March 1967, when about eighty Turks, armed with iron bars, spades, logs of wood and machetes, attacked the occupants of the compound, who consisted of Swedes and members of the Black Watch. Two of the soldiers received nasty head-wounds during a fight of some forty minutes, but the Turks were ejected. The incident did little for Turco-UNFICYP relations, but brought the Scots and Swedes all the closer.

On 26 March, near the village of Kourou Monastir, not far from the Nicosia-Famagusta road, two American marines were wounded by the Turks, for no apparent reason. A typical incident which occurred on 9 April illustrates the chain effect of communal tension. The fight was started by a Turk, whose brother had been shot by the Greeks the previous September, when he saw his uncle fraternising with a Greek. The story also illustrates the greater tolerance of the older generation once polarisation has taken place, and so provides a parallel to the attitude of the older Cypriote Greeks towards the British during the Emergency.

May saw more trouble in the Larnaca district, and from 22 July to 18 August a vicious chain of murders, five of the dead being Greeks, six of them Turkish, with a woman and a child killed on either side, took place in the Paphos district. On 31 July, *Kypros* had reason to complain that murders were attributed to Turks 'no matter what the circumstances'.

Bombing incidents continued as before. On 12 August, at Alaminos, near Ayios Theodhoros in the Larnaca district, five Turks were killed by a booby-trap (a man, two youths, and two children), while a sixth was blinded and badly wounded. A week later, another Turk drove a car over a mine and had his left leg blown off, while his passenger suffered eye injuries. At Apliki, a British officer seconded to UNFICYP had his foot blown off by one booby-trap while trying to defuse another. UNFICYP commented on the sophisticated nature of the devices, which pointed to an organisation behind them. *Patris,* in the same month, accused a section of the government of deliberately fomenting trouble with the Turks, and Dr Dervis, in *Ethniki,* complained of mischief-making and terrorism. In October, an aeroplane, apparently scheduled to carry Grivas, exploded in the air between Athens and Cyprus. Investigations indicated that a bomb had been planted in it,[1] presumably by left-wing elements, but the inconsiderateness of murdering an entire planeload of guiltless people in order to kill one man has its beginning in Grivas's own EOKA period, when a bomb was planted in a plane about to carry R.A.F. families.[2]

---

[1] The crash, on 20 April 1967, of a Swiss Britannia five miles from Nicosia, with 126 killed and four injured, appears to have been a natural disaster.

[2] See above, p. 272.

Bombs were not unknown on the Turkish side, which was badly under strain. In May, three exploded outside the houses of leaders loyal to Dr Küçük, including Dr Manyera's. *Zafer* went so far as to say : 'We have not the slightest confidence in those who consider themselves our leaders'. Later, in the autumn, Dr Küçük wrote self-justificatory articles in his *Halkın Sesi*, referring to 'some upstarts who are trying to set me aside'. He was advised to desist by the Turkish government.

Makarios's frequent proposals for talks among the Cypriotes themselves were having some limited effect, for on 14 July *Akşam* published an article suggesting such talks should take place. On 18 August, Kasım Gülek, the independent deputy for Adana (where there are many Cypriote Turks), had an interview with Makarios. This was balanced to some extent on 13 October, when Küçük granted an interview to Mr Dopoulos of the Greek Associated Press.

A Greek land consolidation bill, published in May 1967, aroused intense opposition among the Turks, who saw that it was aimed at large landholdings, many of which are Turkish. Tornaritis denied that it constituted an 'agricultural reform', needing Turkish consent under the constitution, but said that it came under the heading of 'town and country planning' for the public benefit, which needed no such consent, also that redistributed land would go to members of the same community as the former owners. Land consolidation is a necessity in Cyprus. Indeed, Mr Plümer, as Minister of Agriculture, initiated plans for it before the troubles. But the Turks had bitter memories of land reforms which had operated to their detriment in Greece, and expressed the fear that they would be expropriated like the Palestinians. In the end, no steps were taken to put the bill into effect.

The Greek government was said to be spending as much as £10 million a year to maintain forces in Cyprus, and General Stylianos Patakos, as Minister of the Interior, expressed his desire for a solution. Other spokesmen conceded that *Enosis* without compensation would be unrealistic, and Dr Dervis expressed the view that partition was already a reality, and should be accepted, as it could not be done away with unless Turkey was first defeated.

Partly as a prelude to the Turco-Greek talks, plans were announced on 2 September for normalisation in the Paphos area, free access to Hala Sultan *Tekke,* the removal of check-points from the main roads, and the easing of traffic through the use of more police for the searches at the Famagusta Gate. The talks took place between the Prime Ministers, Constantine Kollias and Süleyman Demirel, at the border-towns of Keshan (on 9 September) and Alexandroupolis (on the 10th). Greece predictably offered Turkey a large military base in Cyprus, but the Turks insisted on an area large enough for most of their Cypriote community. On 11 September, the Prime Ministers issued a joint communiqué expressing 'identity of views . . . in respect of all agreements' between the two countries (an obvious reference to the Zurich and London Agreements), and pledged themselves to work for 'a peaceful and agreed solution'.

Superficially happy as relations might be at the highest level, grass-roots tension remained. On 21 September 1967, troops of the Turkish contingent who were being driven to the docks at Famagusta on rotation, threw stones which smashed the windows of twelve vehicles and two shops. The Greek-Cypriote government kept its temper, and in October Makarios not only promised an amnesty to the Turks, but even claimed that it was a reaffirmation of an amnesty he had been 'disposed' to grant in September 1964. This came as a surprise to the Turks, for as late as the first half of 1967 two of them had been sentenced to two years and nine months respectively for having been seen in their enclaves bearing arms, one of them in April 1964. No wonder *Eleftheria* criticised Makarios for not having made his long-standing amnesty clearer. On the whole, the Makarios government had learned to behave well towards its Greek-Cypriote critics, though on 17 September the publishers of *Patris* were fined £300 for criticising the police and the administration of justice.

The November Crisis and Its Aftermath

In October 1967, tension rose in Turkey over the treatment of the Turks in Thrace. On the 17th, it was claimed that within a month about a thousand of them had taken refuge across the Maritsa (Evros). They had indeed been crossing before the Keshan talks. Turkish community councils in Komotini, Xanthi, and Alexandroupolis itself had now been replaced with old-fashioned government appointees, and western Thrace became a restricted area (rather like the Kurdish areas of Turkey). The Greeks could point to Turkey's uncomplaining reception of 30,000 Turks from Bulgaria, but there is no doubt in the author's mind that the Turkish minority is better off in Bulgaria than in Greece.

On 17 October, the day after President Sunay and Mr Demirel had conferred on the subject of Cyprus, Denktaş, among others, called for drastic measures to halt creeping *Enosis* there. Osman Bölükbaşı, leader of the Turkish Nation Party, made inflammatory statements, and so did Alparslan Türkeş, leader of the Republican

Peasants' Nation Party.[1] By 20 October an organisation called the Youth of 101 Oaths had been set up in London, presumably by Necati Sağer, who went there to set up a Cypriote-Turkish information centre at about that time. Its object was to destroy the Makarios government. A sign of the change of mood was the strong exception taken by the Turkish government to some *Enotist* remarks of Mr Economou-Goras.

On the morning of 31 October, Denktaş and two other Cypriote Turks, Konuk, chairman of the Cyprus Students' Association in Ankara, and İbrahim, were found in the minor state forest of the Ayios Theodhoros which is situated on the south side of the Carpass peninsula.[2] An alert gamekeeper, Antonis Christodoulou, managed to wrest a pistol from one of them,[3] and then informed the local police and National Guard units, who arrested the new arrivals. Denktaş later declared that his original intention had been to land in the shallow waters controlled by the Turks near Scala, but a poor navigator dropped the small boat far to the north, opposite two large Greek villages. His ostensible reason for coming was to discount Greek reports that he had deserted his community.

After two or three days of interrogation, Denktaş requested to be sent back to Turkey, promised not to return by illegal means, and regretted 'causing embarrassment to all concerned'. Both Georghadjis and Clerides visited him in prison, and he testified to his good treatment, but his two companions were to state that they had been beaten twice and threatened with hanging.

The official attitude of the Makarios government, which rather lamely denied having exiled Denktaş, was that he was free to return but would have to face criminal charges. The Turkish government, even more implausibly, denied having sent him. There was much agitation for his release by Turkish-Cypriote representatives, and demonstrations in Nicosia and Polis on 6 and 7 November, together with others in Turkey. On the 12th, after the U.N. had used its good offices and the Turkish government had made representations to the Greek, Denktaş and his two companions were released and flown back to Turkey. The charges against them remained open and their Cyprus passports were cancelled. Over this period, frequent bombs exploded in the Greek sectors and the Right distributed leaflets against Denktas's release.

---

[1] Colonel Türkeş, a highly intelligent person, is a Cypriote by birth. He was one of those who masterminded the 1960 *coup* which overthrew Menderes, but unfortunately anti-reformists in the Turkish junta expelled him in November of that year.

[2] There are several villages of that name in Cyprus.

[3] Denktaş, at least, had a Cyprus government permit to carry arms, which was arguably still valid.

The initiative now passed temporarily to the Greeks, who badly miscalculated the degree of Turkish determination. Tassos Papadopoulos's declaration of an 'armed fist' policy in dealing with recalcitrant Turks did not take enough account of Turkish power outside Cyprus, unless indeed the intention was to bring about the withdrawal of mainland Greek forces, which is highly unlikely. The pressure was predictably exerted in the Larnaca area. Firing incidents had already taken place in Ayios Theodhoros on 8 April and 20 July, and on Tuesday, 14 November, the National Guard surrounded the 500 Turks there with about 3,000 men. Later that day, the National Guard resumed police patrols, which had been suspended after the July incident. This was done despite UNFICYP pleas for delay, and the National Guard passed twice through the village. Grivas, who had been humiliated by the release of Denktaş, was photographed lecturing the Turks, and was reported in the Greek-Cypriote press as having told them that he would have 'drowned them in blood' if they had fired a single shot. The conflict began shortly after 2 p.m. on Wednesday 15th, the National Guard using about forty armoured cars, 2-pounder cannons, machine-guns, and mortars, and the Turks firing down with lighter weapons from the heights commanding the road. U.N. representations to Makarios were of no avail, as the Greeks pressed on to secure their objectives. According to *Agon,* the Athens cabinet met that evening to discuss a Turkish ultimatum to withdraw (failing which, Turkish bombers would unload their cargoes on the Greek assailants) and then ordered Grivas to cease fire. Firing stopped before 9 p.m., and at 9.45 UNFICYP was able to announce the cease-fire. The National Guard retired by 6 a.m. on the 16th, with the loss of one dead, the number of Turkish dead being twenty-six. The Turkish leadership had agreed to resume patrols in company with the Greeks, but nevertheless interfered with a police patrol which came to Ayios Theodhoros that day under UNFICYP escort.

What had definitely been demonstrated was the limited effectiveness of UNFICYP (and indeed of the U.N.) within its terms of reference. The U.N. troops in Kophinou (Royal Green Jackets and Inniskillings) were forcibly disarmed by the National Guard, and their wirelesses disabled. One British soldier was wounded when he refused to hand over his rifle. The British government protested, but predictably took no action. U Thant also protested without taking any action, though he rightly pointed to the speed of the operation as evidence that it had been pre-planned. Clearly, the Turks could hardly feel their own people were safe in the care of UNFICYP. Nor did UNFICYP have troubles only with the Greeks.

On 20 November, three Canadian soldiers in the Kyrenia area were beaten up and disarmed by Turkish irregulars.

The number of Turks killed in the Greek assault scarcely justifies *Halkın Sesi's* reference to it as 'the worst atrocity of the century', but one of the victims was reported to be aged ninety-five, and Mehmet Emin, aged eighty, was wrapped in a petrol-soaked blanket and burned alive. The *Special News Bulletin* also spoke of eyes gouged out, but produced no evidence in that case. Turkish-Cypriote journalists who went to the area were deprived of their notes and film under the eyes of UNFICYP. However, other journalists went there too, and by the next day the Turkish and foreign press carried pictures of a desecrated Turkish flag and a Cypriote Turk who had been bloodily beaten up. The biggest impression on the Turkish public was made by the horrifying close-ups of Mehmet Emin. Nor was this all. A Turkish shepherd had been killed at Ambelikou on 15 November, five days after a shooting incident there, and an eight-year-old Turkish child was killed by a bomb which had been planted in a Nicosia playground. The killing of three or four Greeks, including a woman, since the beginning of November hardly amounted to an equivalent cause for resentment. Another reason for irritation was that some of the Czech small arms had been distributed to the police as a result of Turkish planes overflying Cyprus air space.

In matters involving national honour Turkish governments are very responsive to public opinion. On 17 November, the *Meclis* gave the government special powers to deal with the situation, and at midnight an ultimatum was delivered to the government in Athens. Its five conditions were the removal from Cyprus of Grivas, the removal of all troops from Greece, the payment of an indemnity for the Turks killed, the cessation of pressure on the Turkish-Cypriote community, and the disarming of Greek-Cypriote paramilitary organisations, including the National Guard. Failing compliance, Ankara would send its own troops to defend the Turks of Cyprus. The Turkish air force violated Greek air space from 17 November onwards, and on the 18th Turkish troops were massed on the Thracian border and at Iskenderun.

On 19 November, Grivas was flown to Athens, and resigned his supreme command of the Cyprus forces on the next day. But the Turks were determined to maintain their build-up until their other conditions were also met. In Izmir, 30,000 people demonstrated for war, in Istanbul 80,000. Turkish-made landing-craft, produced under a five-year plan for naval construction costing £21 million, were readied for commandos at Mersin. Turkey had 390,000 troops, as compared with 118,000 in Greece, and correspondingly more weapons and aircraft, though the navies were less unequal. Therefore, she was in a good position to strike, and it was no unreasoning panic which prompted the evacuation from Cyprus of British and American families, and the evacuation of the American monitoring base at Kyrenia.

In this situation, with the U.N. powerless, the United States intervened. President Johnson's special envoy, Cyrus R. Vance, flew in to Ankara on the 23rd. He was prevented from landing at the airport by demonstrators who remembered that the United States had prevented Turkey from using American NATO arms against the Greeks, while the Greeks had used such arms in Cyprus. So Vance had to touch down at a military airfield. On the next day, President Sunay warned world leaders that Turkey intended to solve the Cyprus problem 'once and for all'.

The difficulties which faced Vance were very considerable, owing to the obvious precedent established by the June war. Several press reports remarked on this, notably the *Financial Times* on 28 November : 'There can be little doubt ... that Turkey has been encouraged by the precedent of the June war, which showed that even in the 1960's [sic] it is still possible to grab large areas of foreign territory by force and hold on to them despite widespread world disapproval'. Nevertheless, Vance managed to avert war. After all, the United States had given Turkey $2,100 million in aid since the Second War (in addition to large grants specifically for military purposes), as well as $1,719 million to Greece and $19 million to Cyprus. Besides, as in June 1964, the Sixth Fleet was waiting in the wings. Rolz-Bennett of the U.N. and Manlio Brosio of NATO also flew their rounds, though to less effect.

The Athens junta displayed remarkable restraint, which was not entirely owing to their military inferiority or their diplomatic isolation, of which Turkey was taking advantage. The same or similar men had not been afraid to face superior forces in 1940, and Greek public opinion had long been ready for war with Turkey. For men of that type a stable Turkey is almost as important as a stable Greece for their Turkish equivalents. To make Greece the bastion of Europe and reject Turkey is to pit Greece, with its inadequate resources, against an enormously strengthened East.

On 27 November, Greece agreed to withdraw from Cyprus all forces in excess of her contingent, provided Turkey did the same with her much smaller excess of troops and also stood down her invasion forces, U Thant cooperating in this face-saving operation by calling for the same policy himself. He was also at one with the Turks in wanting relaxation of pressure on the Turkish-Cypriote community and increased powers for UNFICYP (to which Makarios would not agree, because they would have affected the sovereignty of the Republic).

The whole package deal was threatened on 2 December by Makarios, who insisted on 'delaying' disbandment of the National Guard, and who asked for guarantees against a Turkish attack. Vance, who had flown 10,000 miles and spent 100 hours bargaining with leaders since the crisis began, and who had reconciled the Turkish and Greek governments, failed to shake Makarios. It is in situations like these that Makarios shows his political acumen, and he now realised that the danger of invasion had passed, at least for the time being. On the previous day it had been strongly rumoured that the R.A.F. had edged a Turkish plane out of Cyprus air space.

For Cyprus the crisis period, from 19 November to 17 December, was punctuated by a series of thirty-one explosions in the non-Turkish areas. On 8 December, Makarios went to Kantara, where he bade farewell to Greek army troops with the usual heroes-and-martyrs eulogium. They then departed via the east-coast port of Boghaz, which had been developed for their rotation since 1964. Others left via Famagusta.

A crisis soon developed in Greece itself, as King Constantine tried to take advantage of the junta's set-back. On 13 December, he set up a government at Larissa, but within a few hours he and the rest of the royal family had taken refuge in Rome. A royalist general in command of the Evros district crossed into Turkey with some of his officers.

Things in Cyprus seemed to be returning to normal, now that the heat was off. Even the bombs were nothing unusual, and British and American families returned from Beirut. However, friction between Cypriotes and what some of them inevitably regarded as an 'army of occupation' now came into the open. On 16 December, some Finnish officers and men were beaten up by Greeks in Nicosia, and on the following day the Finns smashed some cabarets, including the Copa-Cabana and the Ambassador. Two other UNFICYP soldiers were court-martialled in connexion with a scheme which involved the Turks running arms into their areas in UNFICYP vehicles. Also, off-duty relations with the National Guard were not always good, as might be expected in a situation where a Danish private, for instance, was receiving £150 a month and a Greek-Cypriote one only £4 10s.

In the vacuum created by the withdrawal of most of the Greek army personnel, the Makarios government fell back on the 'independence' solution because, as Kyprianou explained on 4 December, it did not seem that *Enosis* was attainable within the immediate future.

The Cypriote Turks, who were still prevented by the Greeks from sending their representatives to the House, were more active. On 27 December, there arrived Mr Zeki Kuneralp, Secretary-General of the Turkish Foreign Ministry, and Professor Suat Bilge, the Ministry's legal adviser (who had taken part in the pre-independence negotiations). On the 28th, a 'Provisional Cyprus Turkish Administration' was set up, to be valid until such time as the 1960 constitution was fully implemented. The eleven members of the executive council were headed by Dr Küçük, and included the three Turkish-Cypriote Ministers. The U.N. was not informed until the day after, and U Thant expressed his 'misgivings'. On the 30th, Kuneralp was expelled, and the Makarios administration gave warning that accredited representatives of foreign nations should not visit the provisional administration, which it declared to be illegal. Later on, this prohibition was relaxed, but not before Küçük had stressed that the Turkish administration had only undergone a 'functional reorganisation'.

By 16 January 1968, 7,000 Greek troops had withdrawn, as well as some Turks, though many Greek soldiers, and some Turkish remained behind to train the Cypriotes on either side. In Turkey, the invasion forces stood down.

Makarios was now free to carry out his own policies. On 12 January he announced that he was going to hold a new presidential election as a way of testing public faith in his government. It transpired that the election was to be held under the rules obtaining in 1959, although the Greek-Cypriote representatives had unilaterally introduced a common electoral roll in 1965. Inspired reports began to appear in the press of possible concessions to the Turks, provided a unitary state was maintained. On 14 January, all check-points were removed, save round the main enclave and at Kokkina.

Meanwhile, Greek-Cypriote opinion-moulders were in disarray. On the 22nd, *Kypros* went so far as to advise a reversion to the 1960 constitution as the only way to avoid partition, and *Makhi*, of all newspapers, criticised Polycarpos Ioannides for his extreme Enotism before the Emergency. On the 26th, *Eleftheria* blamed Makarios and Grivas for starting the EOKA campaign without sufficient consideration of its consequences, and claimed, perhaps rightly, that *Enosis* would otherwise have been achieved by then.

Küçük's reaction to the election news was to announce that he was going to hold an election for Vice-President on the same day. On 22 January, ex-Chief Justice Zekya announced his candidature.

26—C

but he withdrew it on the 27th to avoid an election campaign which would have been a source of discord.

Those who felt that Makarios was forgetting *Enosis* soon grew alarmed at his new line. At Epiphany the Bishop of Citium, Anthimos, gave a sermon deploring indifference to *Enosis* and slander of the Greek army. On 25 January, he and two other bishops, Kyprianos of Kyrenia and Yennadios of Paphos, met Makarios and told him that he should resign as President if faced with a settlement which was not consistent with *Enosis*. On behalf of the Holy Synod, they insisted that the Church should not be involved in that case. (Clerides was being referred to as his most likely successor.) Makarios had no public comment to make.

Abroad, there was much coming and going among the interested parties, and on 29 January *Alithia* deplored a leak by Panayiotis Pipinelis, the Foreign Minister of Greece, to the Turkish newspaper *Yeni Sabah* that a solution had been found satisfactory to all parties. Pipinelis was holding talks with his Turkish opposite number, İhsan Sabri Cağlayangil, though they agreed to deny the fact. Between March and June, two senior diplomats, Mr Bulak for Turkey and Mr Tzounis for Greece, were to hold talks in Athens, Ankara, and Vienna.

In February, there was a scandal when four Zambians were arrested by the National Guard when training with Cypriotes in the use of machine-guns and dynamite. The matter was hushed up, but it was a sign of what entanglements uncritical cooperation with the 'Third World' might involve. An Immovable Property Law, ostensibly brought in to deal with Turkish *mukhtars* who opposed the execution of judgments ordering the sale of property in cases of debt, was resented by the Turks. There was also a Greek-Cypriote scare that Ankara might be contemplating a direct air link with a landing-ground at Aghirda, in the main enclave, south of the Kyrenia Pass.

Makarios's opponent in the election was Dr Takis Evdokas, a psychiatrist, who represented the newly-formed '*Enosis* Front'. He seems to have been a sincere, if somewhat unrealistic, candidate. The election was marred by interference with one of his meetings, but otherwise passed off well enough. In all 93.45 per cent of the Greek-Cypriote electorate voted. Makarios gained 220,911 votes (95.45 per cent of the total cast) and Evdokas 8,577 (3.71 per cent), which amounted to a massive endorsement of Makarios's policies. Dr Müderrisoğlu, as vice-president of the House of Representatives in the 1960 government, asked Clerides to convene a meeting so that the President and Vice-President could make their affirmations according to Article 42 of the constitution. No notice was taken, any more than it was when Dr Küçük said that he was prepared to nominate three Turkish Ministers.

By the time U Thant made his report of 9 March, the situation was much eased. On that very day Makarios withdrew all road-blocks and defensive positions around the main enclave, including the one at the Famagusta Gate. Only sixty-seven shooting incidents had taken place over the previous three months, as compared with 284 in the period from June to December 1967, 346 from December 1966 to June 1967, and 289 in the six months before that. U Thant makes much of the cases of fraternisation which had occurred between the two communities, but his mention of theft from Turkish orchards, destruction of Turkish crops, and minor assaults, was ominous. By 16 March, thirty people had been arrested for leaving the main enclave without a permit from the Turkish-Cypriote leadership. However, Dr Küçük was trying to drive a hard bargain on behalf of those bereaved at Ayios Theodhoros and Kophinou. The Turks' view was that they were only getting back some of their rights, so long denied, and had no reason to make counter-concessions to the Greeks. On 11 March, *Alithia,* while telling the Turks to abandon extremism, also told the Greeks to stop looking upon the Turks as second-rate citizens.

Clerides now told Sami Kohen, of the Turkish daily *Milliyet,* who is a favourite with the Cypriote Greeks, that direct talks with the Cypriote Turks were contemplated. In due course, Denktaş was allowed to return to Cyprus, and held his first press conference there in over four years. He had already met Tornaritis in London. On 23 May, he and Clerides met at the house of Osorio-Tafall for procedural discussions. On 2 June, they flew to Beirut, where they stayed in the large Phoenicia Hotel, overlooking the sea, and continued their discussions. In all probability, they were discussing the detailed implementation of agreements already reached between the Greek and Turkish governments.

In Cyprus, tensions eased somewhat, though on 15 May a Turkish lorry-driver was caught smuggling five Thompson sub-machine-guns, two Browning machine-guns, and appropriate ammunition, from the main enclave to Limassol and Ktima. On 26 May, Kamil Hasan, a Turkish village constable of Vrecha, in the Paphos district, was shot several times and killed, while allegedly poaching. In Nicosia, the Turks dismantled some of their road-barriers, and Turkish businessmen were beginning to complain that the relaxation of restrictions was having an adverse effect on their trade. Turkish custom was beginning to shift to the better-stocked shops in the Greek quarter.

Internationally, there was a general air of optimism over the

Cyprus problem, and it seemed to be taken for granted that it was well on the way to solution; yet there was no indication as yet that agreement had been reached on fundamentals. On the contrary, these seemed to have been swept under the carpet in favour of some sort of compromise based upon the *status quo*.

Conclusion

Until the power of Turkey was effectively manifested in November 1967 the erosion of the Turkish-Cypriote position was inevitable.[1] The plan at Greek-Cypriote government level had been to prevent survival of the Turkish-Cypriote community as a separate entity by restrictions and harassment, by allowing individuals to leave the island and not to return, and by enlisting UNFICYP support in gaining free access to the enclaves, thus undermining their security. With regard to the Turks, the Greeks thought in terms of the carrot and the stick : the carrot of better living standards for those who accept the Greek terms, and the stick of punitive restrictions for the recalcitrant. The stick was more in evidence than the carrot because most of Makarios's supporters had not realised, as he did, the necessity of providing an alternative. If the safety of cooperating Turks were assured, comparison of their own lot with that of the prospering Greeks must eventually undermine the morale of those in the enclaves, and the Turkish leaders must become more and more like their image in the Greek press, maintainers of draconic discipline over a dwindling community.

Pari passu with the above programme for dealing with the Turkish minority, Greek-Cypriote civil and military organisations were practising 'creeping *Enosis*' by uniting with their counterparts in Greece. Despite the support for AKEL in the cities and the occasional brawls between Cypriote and mainland Greeks, there is no doubt that a majority of Cypriotes would vote for *Enosis* in a referendum. In fact, some influential American politicians have sensibly advocated some kind of *Enosis* because it would drastically lessen the influence of AKEL. In the world at large, however, there is now left-wing antagonism to *Enosis*, which has been encouraged by Turkish references to it as equivalent to an *Anschluss*. Small nations with highly-developed sensitivities do not appreciate one of their number becoming part of a larger entity, more especially if it is then included within the framework of a Western military alliance. Such fusions reduce the number of government jobs for the boys. As for the *Anschluss* charge, there are even more compelling historical, linguistic, economic, and cultural reasons for the

[1] The Turkish bombings of August 1964 only prevented the enclaves from being directly overrun (cf. above, p. 352).

union of Austria with Germany than for that of Cyprus with Greece. In view of Greek-Cypriote objections to the imposition of unequal treaties containing unamendable provisions, it is strange that the Attorney-General of Cyprus should go out of his way to justify the imposition on Austria, by powers in occupation of her territory, of a treaty precluding in perpetuity any sort of union with Germany. To refer to this as a 'reasonable, self-imposed restriction'[1] is to justify the perpetual exclusion of *Enosis* under the Cyprus constitution.

Since the Athens *coup* of April 1967 all the old anti-Enotist arguments have been more frequently repeated. The Turks have charged that in a united Greece Cyprus would be a distant province ruled by a governor from Athens; but Crete had thirty members representing it in the old Parliament, and when the Parliament is revived, Cyprus, as part of Greece, could look forward to having a larger proportion or a similar proportion of a reduced number in the Parliament as a whole. And until that time individual Cypriotes may be expected to have some influence over the ruling junta. The objection that Greece has lower social norms has been urged in the past, but is losing much of its force as the crime figures in Greece drop dramatically, almost to the Cypriote level. Interested parties still urge the economic objection as strongly as ever but, as Makarios has pointed out, in the long run Greece may be more prosperous than Cyprus. Despite official American disapproval, American firms are investing in the new Greece and her economy is stable. Cypriote prosperity has not escaped from heavy dependence upon British expenditure in the island and, in view of the considerable British trade gap, its continuance is not to be counted on. Besides, the government of Greece could offer Cyprus a special economic régime, as was done in the case of Rhodes. It is true that Clerides and others have said that there should be no *Enosis* while the price is too high, but overseas Greeks, like overseas Britons, are not necessarily disloyal because they wish to protect their own interests. Grivas and his supporters accuse members of the Makarios government of being at heart anti-Enotists for fear their own importance might diminish, but only time can tell whether the charge is justified. In any case, one cannot believe that Makarios is an anti-Enotist. His attitudes have been too consistent all along, and even if he stood down as President, as he has repeatedly said that he would do in the event of *Enosis*, he would still retain the position of Ethnarch by virtue of his ecclesiastical office.

While the Turkish problem remains, union of the whole of

[1] Criton G. Tornaritis, *The Legal Aspects of the Question of Cyprus* (Nicosia: P.I.O., n.d.), p. 9 n.

Cyprus with Greece is an impossibility. Dr Küçük has made it plain that in the event of *Enosis* he would immediately declare the annexation of the enclaves to Turkey, which would no doubt intervene to ensure access to them. Of course, the Turks could accept Makarios's charter of minority rights, but any temptation to do so is countered by the simple and sufficient reminder that an equally comprehensive charter of human rights was contained in the constitution which operated up to 1963. Tornaritis has disingenuously argued that those rights are still in existence, and 'cannot be altered except by constitutional amendment',[1] but the constitution has been unilaterally amended so often that it is barely recognisable. Also, Tornaritis admits that the rights may be suspended 'in case of war or public danger threatening the life of the Republic or any part thereof . . .';[2] and they have been suspended in practice without any legal process. The truth is that a charter of minority rights is no substitute for the goodwill of the majority. Even when the judiciary is determined to uphold such a charter, the minority can only protect itself by a process of squalid bargaining which degrades the litigants and irritates the majority. Nor can any charter yet devised protect an unpopular minority from studied coldness or veiled hostility. One has only to question the average Greek about the Turks (or vice versa) to see signs of how deep the hatred goes : the shifting glance, the change of subject, the over-effusive expression of goodwill towards all save 'a few extremists'. In any case, the perpetrators of excesses during the Emergency and the troubles are still walking about as free men. The Cypriote Turks have reason to put any charter of minority rights (unaccompanied by cast-iron guarantees) to the same vulgar but practical use as Gondomar is said to have put Middleton's *Game at Chesse.*[3]

A solution favoured by many 'liberals' is assimilation. They argue that the trend of the age is towards the merging of peoples into larger ethnic units, and so it is—where the peoples are similar enough, and willing enough, to be so merged. Otherwise, the worst kind of contempt is implied by the decision to assimilate a minority. In fact, assimilation of an unwilling or markedly dissimilar minority involves the breakdown of its cultural patterns, and has the just effect of threatening the culture of the assimilating majority. However, a poorer minority provides a fund of cheap labour which can be used to undercut the main labour force, and it is no surprise to find that businessmen are among the main proponents of

---

[1] *Cyprus Today,* vol. IV, nos 5–6 (Aug.–Dec. 1966), p. 15.
[2] Ibid.
[3] Gondomar was Spanish Ambassador at the Court of James I. Middleton's play satirised him unmercifully.

'assimilation'. To this kind of mentality, ethnic and cultural connexions count for little; all that matters is the sacred cash nexus.
The Greeks and Turks of Cyprus have too much self-respect to
permit the cultural loss which large-scale integration would entail.

If Cyprus were not where it is, one would unhesitatingly advocate
immediate union of the entire island with Greece. However, geo-
politics are not to be ignored. It is obvious that Turkey has a
strong security interest in preventing Cyprus from falling completely
into the hands of an unfriendly power. To quote a passage by
Shakespeare of which the Turks are especially fond:

> When we consider
> The importancy of Cyprus to the Turk;
> . . .
> We must not think the Turk is so unskilful
> To leave that latest, which concerns him first.[1]

Unfortunately, Turkish apprehensions that Cyprus might become
a base for future attacks have been justified by the irresponsible
pronouncements of the old school of Greek politicians. In Salonica
on 27 October 1964, George Papandreou, then Prime Minister,
announced that 'Cyprus must become the springboard for the
dreams of Alexander the Great in the Orient'. Taken at its face
value, such a statement is more ludicrous than criminal. One cannot think that it caused much concern in the Hindu Kush or
trembling in the wastes of Bactria. But it was a definite indication
that the *Megalo Idea* might be revived when the circumstances
were favourable. Taking the long view, it is possible that the loss
of Greek territory in Anatolia justifies the complete *Enosis* of
Cyprus with Greece. The author is sure Makarios thinks so, and it
is very natural that he should. Zionist-type claims to all the lands
where Greek was once spoken are another matter altogether. Larger
issues are involved. A Turkey which felt itself rejected by the West,
threatened by a fellow-member of the same alliance, might well
become the leader of a hostile Middle East; or the unrealistic designs
of Papandreou might be matched by the far more dangerous spectre
of pan-Turanism, the dream of a union of all Turks up to the
borders of China which apparently died with Enver at Bokhara.

Another good reason why Turkey should wish to maintain a
military presence in Cyprus is the unequivocal statement of the
official Cypriote Communist newspaper, *Haravghi*, that, whatever
the outcome of a Greco-Turkish war, the Turks of Cyprus would
be annihilated. The Cypriote Turks put their faith in an invasion
which would take place so quickly as to prevent that happening.

[1] *Othello,* I. iii, ll. 19–28.

The first thing to understand in connexion with an agreed solution to the Cyprus problem is that there must be compensation for the Cypriote Turks. In purely financial terms, that should not present insuperable difficulties. After all, UNFICYP is estimated to have cost £85,045,000 by March 1968, and the countries concerned should be glad to pay the much smaller sums needed for compensation, if thereby they are relieved of their burden for good. The Cypriote Greeks should also be prevailed upon to pay a considerable share, for in the long run they would be the main beneficiaries. Individual Cypriote Turks should be fully compensated, not only for loss of money and property, but also for sufferings endured, non-combatant relations killed, and set-backs in careers. Communal compensation would also be necessary, though it should be offset to some extent by the lesser damage suffered by Greeks and Armenians at the hands of the Turks. Such a solution would be immensely facilitated if a large part of the Turkish community were prepared to accept the compensation and retire to Anatolia. Certainly, one finds that most ordinary Cypriote Greeks are sympathetic to the idea of such a mass emigration. Their authorities favour the emigration of Turkish 'extremists', and in March 1964, when Senator Keating suggested mass emigration as the solution, Makarios said that he had no objection, provided that the United States paid the cost. So the principle of Turkish emigration has been accepted by the Greeks. Of course, there is no reason why the American taxpayer should foot the whole bill but, with the Vietnam war costing over £23 million a day, and millions of dollars contributed to the maintenance of UNFICYP already, it should not burden him overmuch to pay a final contribution towards a Cyprus settlement.

For the time being, discussion of a possible solution based upon compensated mass emigration seems academic, for the Cypriote Turks insist upon territorial concessions in Cyprus itself. Such insistence raises the question of how much territory they actually possess. There is little agreement on the answer, whichever side is consulted. The Turks have laid claim to 38 per cent of the island on the basis of owning 38 per cent of the land. This is the figure quoted, for instance, by Stephens. However, in their official pamphlet *Struggling for Existence* the Turks claim only 30-35 per cent of the land area, and 35 per cent is the figure quoted both by their Public Information Officer and in the *Special News Bulletin* for 27 April 1966. In another official Turkish-Cypriote pamphlet, *Turks and Cyprus*, Turkish-owned land is said to be 29 per cent of the country, or 1,051 square miles. On the Greek side there is equal confusion. In the official Greek-Cypriote pamphlet entitled *The Cyprus Question*, which came out on 26 September 1964, it is stated that the Turks own 17.1 per cent of the land by area (i.e. below their numerical proportion), but in the equally official *Cyprus Republic: summary of main statistical data* (December 1964) it is stated that the Turks owned 16.6 per cent of the land area in 1957 and 17.5 per cent in 1964, '*excluding Government lands, roads, forests, etc.*' (p. 3).[1] Obviously, the Turks are including in their higher figures a proportional share of the public lands, whereas the Greeks are not. Nor do the discrepancies stop there. In a secret memorandum addressed by Makarios to the Mediator Tuomioja on 13 May 1964 it is stated that Turkish ownership of land by area is 20.4 per cent. This figure seems to be taken from Table 13 of the *Census of Population and Agriculture*, volume VI, *Agriculture*, issued by the Department of Statistics and Research of the Ministry of Finance in 1960 (as quoted in the *Special News Bulletin* on 9 September 1967), and refers only to the area of farming land under cultivation at that time. Even so, this figure is not accepted by the Turks. In their booklet *Federation and the Cyprus Economy: a report presenting the economic basis of federation* (Nicosia, 6 June 1964) they charge that the figure 20.4 per cent was assessed dishonestly by Greek officials, and should not be less than 30 per cent of the total arable land in Cyprus (pp. 14–15). The charge seems to be borne out by the Greek assessment of total arable land at over 1 million donums less than was actually the case,[2] both by comparison with the official *Statistical Abstract of the Republic*, published in the same year, and with the U.N. report of Dr Thorpe, so that the percentage of agricultural land held by Turks would appear smaller by comparison with the total land area; and there is the further circumstance that 'the Census was taken on the basis, not of ownership of land, but on the race of the then tenant-farmer. As . . . much Turkish-owned land is leased to Greek farmers, this device over-reflected Greek holdings at the expense of the Turkish community'.[3] Such confusion is worse confounded by a statement in *Facts about Cyprus: background notes on the present situation* (Ser. no. 3/64) put out by the Greek-Cypriote P.I.O. : 'There is no way of accurately defining boundaries of property ownership or occupation . . . [in Cyprus]' (p. 9). Finally, the Greek emphasis on holdings of cultivated land may be conditioned by the fact that a higher

[1] See also *The Economics of Federation in Cyprus* (issued by the Greek-Cypriote Ministry of Finance in October 1965), p. 8, where specific figures are given, and it is made plain that built-up areas are included in the assessment.
[2] 1 donum = 0.33 of an acre. 1 sq. mile = 1,936 donums.
[3] *Federation and the Cyprus Economy*, p. 15.

proportion of the Turkish land is used for grazing purposes, as befits an originally semi-nomadic people. The Turks claim 38 per cent of the total sheep population of the island, 25 per cent of the goats, and 24 per cent of the cattle. Pending production of an impartial Ph.D. thesis on the subject, we can only conclude that the Turks of Cyprus own a larger area of Cyprus than one would expect from their numbers. So did the British settlers in Kenya. But Cyprus is not Kenya. The government of Turkey is determined to see that the Cypriote Turks get proper compensation.

In 1956, Lord Radcliffe pointed out that there was no territorial basis for federation, and even now in no single administrative district do the Turks constitute a majority. The Turks point out that the proportion of Moslems in India before partition was 'exactly identical to the present proportion of Turkish Cypriotes in Cyprus', but they omit to mention the appalling slaughter which accompanied partition on the Indian subcontinent and the thousands of refugees who still sleep in misery on the railway-station platforms.

The solution to the Cyprus problem which is still preferred by the Turks is that outlined in the Plaza Report. They estimate that their area would comprise 'about 37 per cent' of Cyprus, while Makarios estimates it as 1,292 square miles, or 36.2 per cent of the island (37.4 per cent of the total area of the Republic).[1] However, in the official pamphlet *The Economics of Federation in Cyprus* the proportion of the Turkish-claimed area to that of the entire island is estimated at 38 per cent and specified as 1,357 square miles. Since the object of the exercise would be to solve the Turkish minority problem, it would obviously be unreasonable to leave a Greek minority in the Turkish area. The above-mentioned pamphlet contains the further claim that, according to the 1960 census figures, 133,468 Christians live in the proposed Turkish area, and only 59,342 Turks, so that a number of Greeks greater than the entire Turkish-Cypriote community would have to make way for the remaining 45,008 members of that community. The Turks write vaguely of 20-25,000 'families' moving from their present places of residence to settle in one area or the other, and when they do give a figure it is 125,000. Allowing for the fact that the Turks are now more concentrated in the north than they used to be, the author thinks that this must be an underestimate. There has been considerable population increase since 1960. The move in itself would be no great hardship because it would not be more than a few miles in any one case, but the Greeks claim that the

---

[1] See Makarios's secret memorandum to Tuomioja of 13 May 1964, p. 11. Dr Galo Plaza, it will be remembered, estimated it as 1,084 square miles.

density of population in the Turkish-claimed area would have to drop to 76.9 per square mile, while that in the Greek area would rise to 202.6 per square mile. The Turks contend that the best land would not be in their area, and that the biggest water resources are in the south and west, including 90 per cent of the biggest perennial rivers. The Greeks answer that the Turks are claiming not only the principal mining area, and many of the best tourist resorts, but also 'the whole of the highly developed Morphou plain, all the perennial springs of the Northern range, three of which are the best in the island [e.g. at Kythrea and Lapithos], most of the fertile plain of the Eastern Messaoria, a large area of citrus groves to the west of the walled town of Famagusta, and Famagusta harbour itself', while the Greek region would contain 'a high proportion of forest and hilly and uncultivable land'.[1] The Greeks claim that the Turkish area would contain 359,500 donums, or 60.4 per cent of the 595,200 donums of irrigated land in Cyprus, leaving only 39.6 per cent for the other four-fifths of the population, so that 103,000 of the displaced Greeks would have no land to go to. Furthermore, they state that an estimate of agricultural production based on a survey of 1963 shows that only 12.57 per cent of the total was contributed by Turks, so that the disparity is even greater. Making due allowance for cooked statistics, it is certain that the Greeks would lose proportionately more of the irrigated land. Indeed, Dr Küçük has said that those Greeks who are thrown out of farming 'can solve their problem by becoming merchants'.

On the other hand, when the Greeks turn to express concern for the plight of the Turks in the proposed area the effect is less convincing. They claim that since 42,000 Turks are urban dwellers, as against 62,350 rural ones, large tracts of land would be left uncultivated. But natural increase has swollen the ranks of the Turkish peasantry since 1960, and the land consolidation which could be effected in the new situation would be an added bonus. Machinery makes possible the cultivation of much larger farms. The Greek objection that it would cost an enormous amount to build up separate services in each of the areas envisaged is offset to some extent by the fact that concentrated populations are cheaper to administer and by the Turkish claim that the regrouping of the communities would 'automatically reduce the running cost of various [communal] services, and of education in particular, because fewer schools and teachers will be required'.[2] Besides, the Turks do not officially envisage any division of public utilities like

1 *The Economics of Federation in Cyprus*, pp. 7–8.
2 *Federation and the Cyprus Economy*, p. 13.

water and electricity supplies. Again, the Greeks state that with
such a very small market at their disposal the Cypriote Turks could
never form a separate economic unit. However, the Turks do not
want a separate economic system. They say they want either a
federal system in Cyprus (which would almost certainly break
down initially in bickering and ill-will) or integration of their area
with Turkey. It is hard to believe that the Turks genuinely want
federation, because the only revenue they envisage the federal
government as having is from the customs dues (i.e. *c.* £8 million
a year).

As an example of the benefits to be derived from a strong connexion with an overseas land of origin, the Turks might point to
Northern Ireland, where 'an artificial frontier line' similarly cuts
through 'interdependent parts of homogeneous areas'.[1] The objection that Turkey is less prosperous than Great Britain would come
oddly from those who have consistently pressed for *Enosis* with
Greece.

At first sight, Northern Ireland offers a hopeful precedent for the
Turkish separatist venture in Cyprus. The minority which created
Northern Ireland is being encouraged to become involved economically with the formerly inimical majority, partly because
economic logic demands it. Of course, the creation of Northern
Ireland meant the creation of a new minority which was no more
happy about the situation than the Northern Irish Protestants
would have been as part of a united Ireland in 1922; but at least
the latter have ensured that they will enter any future partnership
on an equal basis, and not as a suspect group dragged in against
its will. Although the differences between the groups are much
greater in Cyprus than in Ireland, one might take comfort from a
sentence in the Turkish *Special News Bulletin* for 2 May 1965:
'History has shown that disputes, however bitter they may be, do
not form an insuperable barrier to later peaceful and orderly co-
existence of the former enemies'. However, such a happy consum-
mation presupposes large-scale separation to begin with, and those
members of the majority community included against their will in
the minority area are likely to be the main obstacle to reconciliation. The fundamental difference between the Cypriote and Irish
situations is that in Ireland a large part of the minority was heavily
concentrated so as to form a substantial majority in one particular
area. In Cyprus the Turks possess no such viable area, nor can they
expect to do so without military intervention. Furthermore, while
the Irish problem is not soluble to the satisfaction of both parties
if considered in the context of Ireland alone, the unification of

[1] Cf. above, p. 361.

Europe would involve not only an economic union of Ireland, but also an economic union of the whole of Ireland with Britain. Provided the Protestants retained control over areas in which they are in the majority, especially as regards education and local affairs, no serious problem would then remain. However, the associate membership of the Common Market which has been envisaged for Greece and Turkey does not allow for such a solution in the case of Cyprus, even supposing the peoples concerned were more compatible than they are. The present Greek government has shown much goodwill towards the Turks, which has been reciprocated to some extent, but the minority problems remain.

Turkey may well invade Cyprus if all other expedients fail, and she is still strengthening her diplomatic hand. An influential statesman like Acheson now favours partition, and the Cypriote Turks seem wholly in favour of Turkish intervention. Of course, the invasion would be fiercely resisted, and would be stopped by the great powers acting through the United Nations. But by that time Turkey might well hold the 750 square miles mentioned as an alternative in the Plaza Report; and the principle whereby quick gainers are not forced to disgorge has been tacitly accepted at the U.N. since the Palestine crisis at the beginning of its existence.

In October 1967, the pro-government newspapers in Greece quoted apparently inspired reports to the effect that Turkey had made four alternative proposals at the Keshan-Alexandroupolis summit talks :

1. An independent Cyprus on a cantonal basis.
2. The federal solution.
3. A Greco-Turkish condominium, should Greece wish the abolition of Cypriote independence.
4. A return to the Zurich and London Agreements.

The first solution has been suggested often enough by Dr Küçük as a second-best if the federal solution is unacceptable to the Greeks. He gives few details, but the plan seems to amount, in effect, to a recognition and expansion of the existing enclaves, and is presented as part of an independence plan excluding *Enosis* or outright partition. It is quite impossible to believe that the institutionalisation of the enclaves would lead to any lessening in friction between the peoples, and Dr Küçük would find it hard to justify the permanent duplication of municipal services in a town the size of Paphos-Ktima. In fact, the plan is simply an attempt to gain breathing space for the time being. The federal solution is rather more workable, but grave objections to it have already been outlined. The third solution would never be freely accepted by the

Cypriote Greeks because it would mean that Turkey would have partial control over their affairs. As for the fourth suggestion, it is impossible to believe that it was offered as a solution in itself. To reaffirm the validity of the Zurich and London Agreements is one thing, and that was, in effect, done by the new Greek leaders, but it is only a starting-point for further negotiations. The Turks would regard a return to the situation created by those agreements as a desirable solution, any more than the Greeks would.

Obviously, it is in the interests of Greece to placate Turkey before she passes the point of no return, and the present government of Greece shows more signs of recognising the fact than any since the time of Venizelos. It has frequently been suggested (by Greeks) that Turkey would be content with a base in Cyprus, but there is no evidence of this. A base without an adequate hinterland would be costly to run, and amid a hostile population would be more a factor making for strife than stability. Besides, the only place so far suggested as a base area for the Turks is the British S.B.A. of Dhekelia, and that is virtually defenceless against attack with heavy weapons. A NATO base might be established in the event of *Enosis*, and would provide some welcome revenue, but there is no reason why the Turks should be content with such an arrangement. Of course, Cyprus could be demilitarised, as in the case of Rhodes and the Dodecanese, and that would help to solve Turkey's security problem, but it could only happen in the event of *Enosis*, because an independent, demilitarised Cyprus would present a standing temptation to its neighbours. Nor would demilitarisation guarantee protection of the Turkish-Cypriote community.

The most valid objection to the partition of Cyprus is that there is no area of the island except the Carpass peninsula which could be separated without disrupting the economy; and the Carpass is not big enough to contain the Turkish community. Nor does it have a port, though that deficiency might be rectified, as it has been at Mersin on the opposite coast. However, the Carpass might be acceptable to Turkey if the Greeks were willing to make concessions elsewhere. Such a course would provide a golden opportunity to solve all the Greco-Turkish problems still outstanding. As for the consistent Turkish refusal to talk in abstract terms of Greek territorial concessions, it has been explained by Mr Feridun Cemal Erkin, who was Turkish Foreign Minister at the time of the Cyprus troubles : Turkey does not wish to be accused of designs for territorial self-aggrandisement.

The most important Greco-Turkish problem after Cyprus is that of the populations stranded on the wrong side of the present frontiers. It is generally agreed that there are about 100,000 Turks in Thrace and 3,500 in the Dodecanese, including Rhodes. Concerning the number of Greeks in Turkey there is considerable disagreement. The Greeks claim that of the 100,000 originally living in Istanbul and the islands of Imbros and Tenedos only a third now remain; while the Turks put their Greek community at about 60,000. There is no doubt that the stranded communities on both sides are under pressure and dwindling. The press in each country is full of the sufferings of its own people. In fact, it cannot be said in either case that the minorities lead 'lives of hell', but Thracian Turks and Istanbul Greeks to whom the author has spoken often have grievances. The Turks claim that 60,000 of their people have left Thrace since 1912, and that more are still doing so; also that in 1947 there was a Turkish community 22,000-strong in Rhodes.[1] The Greeks can point to the crushing selective tax imposed by the Turks on their minorities during the war, and the Turks can reply that those who fled from Greece to Turkey after the war had their property confiscated. The recent expulsions of Greeks from Istanbul are well known, while the Turks can point to the expropriation of big Turkish landholders in Greece, the derisory compensation being based upon unfair assessments of value. The situation of the Greeks in Turkey is much more prosperous than that of the Turks in Greece. They have six junior high schools, a theological college, and five lycées, though their orphanage on the isle of Prinkipo was closed down in 1964. There was no lycée for the Turks in Greece until 1952, and there is still only one. They have few trained teachers, and the Greek authorities object to the importation of Turkish text-books. The Greeks can answer that they subsidise the Turkish elementary schools and mosques of Thrace, and that the Turks of Greece are mostly peasants, so that their position can hardly be compared with that of the prosperous Greek merchants of Istanbul. The Turkish press claims that the Thracian Turks are deliberately kept backward, and that the Greeks encourage outmoded fashions and reactionary religious leaders. In one's personal experience, however, Turkish villagers outside Turkey, and even inside it to some extent, tend to keep up the old ways where they can. More serious is the Turkish charge in 1967 that the Greeks have done away with the elected councils of the Turkish communal bodies in western Thrace, and replaced them with government nominees. The same has for some time been the case in the Dodecanese, although the Italians did not interfere in Turkish communal affairs.

Even if it is suggested that the greater wealth of the Istanbul Greeks balances the greater numbers of the Turkish community in

[1] See the *Special News Bulletin* for 23 October 1964.

Greece, the Turks of Cyprus could not be included in a simple population exchange without tipping the balance heavily in favour of Greece. Therefore, the Greeks must make other concessions if they want a permanent, agreed settlement. The main trouble is that there can be little question at the moment of territorial concessions in the obvious area—Thrace. Any rectification of frontiers there would mean a revival of Bulgarian demands, backed by Russia. An alternative would be the cession of island territory, including in any case the outpost islet of Castellorizon. However, there is no Greek island of any size along the Turkish coastline which is not a living link with the Greek past, and the thought of any one of them being lost to Greece is bitter and unwelcome. It is just possible that the Turks would agree to accept only the Carpass and Castellorizon in the event of a population exchange, provided there was very considerable financial compensation, and provided that historical anachronism, the Patriarchate of Constantinople, were finally abolished. Turkey has much more territory per head of population than Greece. The author assesses that in 1960 the number of people per square mile in Turkey was 84.5, while in Greece in the following year it was 166 per square mile. Provided her security needs are met, what Turkey needs is not more territory, but more money to develop what she already has.

It requires both courage and imagination to solve ethnic problems before they get out of hand. Neither quality is much in evidence at the United Nations, which is more intent on preserving the integrity of existing states than on encouraging the aspirations of those who wish to join with their kinsfolk in larger unions. Yet nothing conduces to conflict so much as frustration of those aspirations. The Commonwealth is even more impotent, for it lacks any power of concerted action, and several of its member states have unrealistic frontiers. In the United States and Great Britain, influential bodies of opinion are unwilling to support any solution in Cyprus involving the necessary separation of peoples because of the implications nearer home. If the Cypriote Greeks and Turks, who are relatively similar in world terms, are unwilling to live peacefully together on a basis of equality, what expectation is there for the peaceful 'integration' of much more dissimilar peoples? There are American statesmen who favour *Enosis*, either in its single or double form, but they are fearful of any deal involving abolition of the Constantinopolitan Patriarchate because of the increase in the prestige of the Russian Orthodox Church which might result. The hands of Britain are tied by her adherence to the Zurich and London Agreements.

In Cyprus also, the forces of inertia are strong. There are those who favour the stalemate because they are sure of their jobs for the duration. Makarios appears to lend them support when he makes statements to foreigners which apparently discount the possibility of *Enosis*, but his true sentiments are more probably expressed in the speeches he makes to his own people. He works for *Enosis*, which will take time, for he is determined to bring the whole island into union with Greece.

As yet, most Cypriote Turks show no disposition to move from the island. One of them told the author that he felt foreign when he went to visit a small town in Anatolia, and others have said that they will fight to the end in defiance of Turkey should an emigration deal be made. However, in all probability the bulk of the Turkish community would leave Cyprus if the protection of Turkey were withdrawn.[1] The author is not one to deny the strength of the territorial instinct, for which there is growing evidence, but nowadays people move more, and the wrench is likely to be felt less than formerly. Besides, many of the Cypriote Turks are already refugees, and they have embraced the principle of separation, which necessarily involves a further movement of population, even though over a lesser distance. The emigration and subsequent return of many Cypriote Turks in the 1920s should not be taken as a precedent, for at that time Great Britain could guarantee law and order. As for the suggestion that the Turkish minority should now emigrate to Britain, that country is no longer to the same extent a repository for the world's surplus populations, and the Cypriote Turks have too much pride to regard themselves in that light.

At the time of writing, the Greeks and Turks of Cyprus are under pressure from Athens and Ankara to find a *modus vivendi*, and it seems likely that some compromise solution will be arrived at which will leave the situation very much as it was before the troubles began. True, there is a difference in that there is now a United Nations presence in Cyprus, but some of the nations providing UNFICYP contingents are becoming restive over the financial burden of maintaining them. However, Makarios has the answer. He has often urged that UNFICYP should be reduced in numbers. Such a reduction would also reduce the cost to manageable proportions, while a token U.N. presence would be a partial deterrent to invasion by Turkey. Meanwhile, for those in the contingents there is the carrot of a happy touristic existence, and for their governments the stick of moral obloquy should they withdraw altogether and permit the situation to degenerate. As a Turkish propagandist

[1] A small number remaining would present no problem.

27—C

has put it, the Greeks would be silly to 'kill the goose which acts as a watchdog . . . and lays the golden egg' !

Whatever compromise is arrived at, we may be sure that the Greeks of Cyprus will continue to feel as Greeks, and the Turks as Turks. The Turks quote Hilaire Belloc with approval when he says that in a non-homogeneous population 'made up of various races, or fundamentally different religions, a majority means nothing towards making a decision. It is a mere affirmation of discord'.[1] There is a lot in that. The author would like to see a solution based on repatriation and compensation which would leave the Cypriote Turks happier, more prosperous, and above all more secure, than they can ever be while scattered about Cyprus. On the other hand, the full realisation of their partitionist ambitions would divide the island in an unstable fashion and conflict with the aspirations of the Cypriote Greeks, which are not only based upon their claims as a majority, but are rooted deep in the history of the island. However mistaken they may have been to unleash terrorism in the 1950s, however cynical their treatment of the Turks, the Greeks of Cyprus have the stronger claim.

The conclusions of this book may come as a surprise for those who believe that proximity and time are necessarily healing factors in inter-communal relations. Their conviction springs either from that over-emphasis on short-term economic motives which is characteristic of a declining culture, or from a fundamental misunderstanding of the genetically-determined differences between human groups. Ethnic conflict has become more common with the breakdown of empires and the growth of egalitarianism. The close intermingling, on an egalitarian basis, of very different peoples in the same environment merely deepens their enmity, and makes the clash more violent when the opportunity occurs. Potassium chlorate and sugar are both excellent things in their way, but if you mingle them freely in a confined space there will always be the danger of a conflagration.

[1] See, e.g., the *Special News Bulletin,* 23 May 1968, p. 2.

Books on Cyprus

AN ALL-EMBRACING BIBLIOGRAPHY of Cyprus would be altogether too unwieldy in this place, as a glance at the following will confirm : G. H. E. Jeffery and C. D. Cobham, *An Attempt at a Bibliography of Cyprus* (new edn, Nicosia, 1929); and Sir George Hill, *A History of Cyprus* (4 vols, C.U.P., 1940–52) : vol. I (1949 edn), pp. xv–xvi; vol. II (1948 edn), pp. xiii–xl; vol. III (1948 edn), pp. 1143–55; vol. IV, pp. xvii–xxxi. A list of works read or consulted by the author would also be over-long, and would contain many works which touch on Cyprus only peripherally. Points of special importance which might otherwise be difficult to follow up are provided with footnote references.

Unquestionably the most scholarly history of Cyprus is Sir George Hill's, but it is rather long and detailed for the general reader. A number of other works deal with the history of Cyprus as a whole, and of these the one which the author recommends is by Doros Alastos, *Cyprus in History—a Survey of 5,000 Years* (London, 1955). A more orthodox Greek-Cypriote view is provided by Dr C. Spyridakis in his *Brief History of Cyprus* (Nicosia, 1964 edn).

A good picture of early neolithic life in Cyprus is provided by James Mellaart in *The Dawn of Civilization,* ed. Stuart Piggott (London and New York, 1961). The best introduction to the archaeology of the succeeding ages is a visit to the Cyprus Museum, but Stanley Casson's *Ancient Cyprus, Its Art and Archaeology* (London, 1937) still contains much of value. It will be as well to mention that scholars like V. R. d'A. Desborough and H. W. Catling, in light of the evidence available to them, have tended to discount the notion of a large-scale Mycenaean influx at the end of the thirteenth century B.C., but the concrete findings of Dr V. Karageorghis and others have since confirmed the approximate date of that influx. Studies of the Byzantine period in Cyprus deal mainly with art, architecture, or ecclesiastical affairs, no work dealing specifically with its history having appeared in English to the author's knowledge. The Lusignan period is succinctly covered in René Grousset's *L'Empire du Levant* (Paris, 1946). C. D. Cobham's

Excerpta Cypria (1929 edn) contains numerous fascinating travellers' accounts of what life was like in Cyprus during the Venetian and Turkish periods. The latter period is covered in Sir Harry Luke's *Cyprus under the Turks, 1571–1878* (Oxford, 1921). Probably the best piece of writing on Cyprus in the British period is in Sir Ronald Storrs, *Orientations* (London, 1943 edn). The most evocative book on the Emergency is Lawrence Durrell's *Bitter Lemons* (London and New York, 1957, etc.). He is very much of a Philhellene, and in some of his works extremely anti-Turkish, but in this one his Turkish house-agent is sympathetically portrayed, and the account of buying a house at Bellapaïs is one of the funniest things in modern English literature. In the author's opinion, none of the many works dealing with the history of the Emergency can be regarded as unbiased. For the post-independence period, the best book, on balance, is Robert Stephens's *Cyprus, a Place of Arms* (London and New York, 1966). Since then the best work on Cyprus the author has seen is an article by Kenneth Mackenzie (an ex-editor of the *Cyprus Mail*) entitled 'Cyprus— 1968' in the *Geographical Magazine* for February 1968, pp. 895–908.

The British case in Cyprus is well covered in a number of readily available parliamentary papers, of which good use has been made by Hill, and many pamphlets of the British period are offered for sale by the Cyprus Government Printing Office in its Price List of Publications. H.M. Stationery Office has available a publication entitled *Cyprus* which contains the draft treaties of Establishment, Guarantee, and Alliance, as well as the constitution of 1960 (Cmnd. 1093). The author has also made use of a number of Greek and Turkish pamphlets in English, of which a list should be helpful to future investigators :

Greek-Cypriote Pamphlets

Political

The Cyprus Cause (official correspondence with Lloyd George in 1919). London. 1920.

The Greek Students Accuse ... (dealing with the Koronides affair). Athens. n.d.

Chr. Papachrysostomou. *The Imprisoned Graves* (short accounts of EOKA-men who died in the Emergency). Nicosia : National Struggle Museum. 1965.

The quarterly *Cyprus Today*, issued by the Publications Department of the Greek Communal Chamber, provides information on the post-independence troubles among other things, and the following supplements should be mentioned in particular.

Who is Violating Truce. 5 February 1964.
The Abrogation of the Treaty of Alliance. 10 April 1964.
Cyprus—Anatomy of a Crisis. 29 April 1964.
Turkey Spreads Death over Cyprus. 19 August 1964.
Recourse to the United Nations. 20 January 1965.
Zotiades, George B. *The Treaty of Guarantee and the Principle of Non-Intervention.* Repr. from *Cyprus Today,* vol. III, no. 2 (March–April 1965).

Facts about Cyprus: Background notes on Present Situation. Nicosia : P.I.O. Ser. no. 3/64.
Dr. İhsan Ali Addresses Turkish Cypriots. P.I.O. Ser. no. 4/64.
Tornaritis, Criton G. *The Treaty of Alliance* P.I.O. [1964]
—— *Is the Present Government of the Republic of Cyprus DE JURE or DE FACTO.* (Broadsheet.) n.d.
—— *The Legal Aspects of the Question of Cyprus.* P.I.O. n.d.
The Economics of Federation in Cyprus. Preface by Renos Solomides. Nicosia : Ministry of Finance. October 1965.
The Cyprus Problem before the United Nations. P.I.O. October 1965.
Jacovides, Andreas J. *Treaties Conflicting with Peremptory Norms of International Law and the Zurich–London 'Agreements'.* Nicosia. 1966.
Short Biographies of the President of the Republic of Cyprus, the President of the House of Representatives and of the Ministers. Nicosia : P.I.O. September 1966.
The Function of the United Nations Force in Cyprus: an assessment. Nicosia : P.I.O. April 1967.
Cyprus: the Problem in Perspective. P.I.O. April 1967.

Economic
Makarios, President. *Five-year Programme of Economic Development.* Nicosia. 1961.
Sparsis, M. *Four and a Half Years of Independence.* Nicosia : Ministry of Labour and Social Insurance. Labour ser. no. 6. October 1964.
Cyprus Republic: summary of main statistical data. Nicosia : Ministry of Finance. December 1964.
Dams in Cyprus, 1964–1965. Nicosia : P.I.O. for the Ministry of Agriculture and Natural Resources. March 1966.
Polycarpou, A. *Annual Report of the Forest Department for the*

Year 1965. Nicosia : Ministry of Agriculture and Natural Resources. 1966.

Economic Report, 1965. Nicosia : Ministry of Finance. 1966.

Statistical Abstract, 1965. No. 11. Nicosia : Ministry of Finance. 1966.

Solomides, Renos. *Prospects for Balanced Economic Growth in Cyprus: The Second Five-Year Plan.* Nicosia. 1967.

—— *Budget Address, 1967.* Nicosia. 1967.

Cyprus in Brief. Nicosia : P.I.O. March 1968.

Turkish-Cypriote Pamphlets

Political

The Turkish Case, 70:30, and the Greek Tactics. Nicosia : Turkish Communal Chamber. 1963.

Riza, Halit Ali. *The House of Representatives and the Separate Majority Right.* Nicosia : Turkish Communal Chamber. 1963.

Looking Back: an official Briefing. Nicosia : Turkish Communal Chamber. 1963.

The Cypriot Turkish Case and the Greek Atrocities in Cyprus. Nicosia : issued by the Vice-President, etc. January 1964.

Turkish Cypriot Community Struggling for Existence. Nicosia : Turkish Communal Chamber. August 1964.

History Speaks. Nicosia : Turkish Communal Chamber. November 1964.

Who is at Fault? Nicosia : printed by Halkın Sesi Press. n.d.

Federation and the Cyprus Economy. Nicosia : Turkish Communal Chamber. June 1964.

Bedevi, Vergi H. *Cyprus Has Never Been a Greek Island.* Nicosia : Cyprus Turkish Historical Association. 1964.

Turks and Cyprus: introduction to the problem of Cyprus. No place. n.d.

Conspiracy to Destroy the Republic of Cyprus. Nicosia : Turkish Communal Chamber. May 1966.

Cyprus: the problem in the light of the truth. Nicosia : Turkish Information Centre. September 1967.

New Greek Atrocities in Cyprus. Nicosia : Turkish Cypriot Information Office. [1967.]

The author also has in his possession a pamphlet in French, *Chypre Pourquoi? Pourquoi?*, published by the Association Culturelle Cyprio-Turque, Ankara. 1964.

Index

Printed in Great Britain by The Garden City Press Limited
Letchworth, Hertfordshire

THE AUTHOR: H. D. Purcell was born in Singapore in 1932. After receiving his bachelor's degree from Jesus College, Oxford, in 1953, he became a National Service Officer. He traveled in North America and elsewhere, taught for a year at the British Institute of Rome, and spent the years 1958-63 lecturing both at the Middle East Technical University, in Ankara, and at the Pahlavi University of Shiraz, in Iran. In 1963, he returned to England, where he obtained his Ph.D. degree at Trinity College, Cambridge. Since 1966, he has taught English literature at the Queen's University in Belfast. He was first in Cyprus in 1959, and he revisited it in 1967. He lectures on Cypriote affairs and contributes regularly to the periodical *International Affairs.*